PUBLICATIONS OF THE OSGOODE SOCIETY

The Osgoode Society was formed in 1979 to encourage research and writing in the history of Canadian law. Its efforts to stimulate legal history in Canada include the sponsorship of a fellowship, research support programs, and work in the field of oral history. The Society will publish volumes which contribute to legal-historical scholarship in Canada including studies of the courts, the judiciary, and the legal profession, biographies, collections of documents, studies in criminology and penology, great trials, and work in the social and economic history of the law.

This volume, containing ten essays, is the first of two designed to illustrate the wide possibilities for research and writing in Canadian legal history and reflecting the current interests of those working in that area. Topics covered include historical aspects of company law, the law and the economy, legal reform in Ontario, custody law, the law of master and servant, the law of nuisance, origins of the Canadian Criminal Code, and women's rights in Quebec. Professor Flaherty supplies an introduction to the writing of Canadian legal history and, with his contributors, provides an important building block on which a significant tradition of indigenous legal history in Canada may grow and flourish.

Essays in the History of Canadian Law

Edited by

DAVID H. FLAHERTY

VOLUME I

The Osgoode Society

Reprinted in paperback 2017

ISBN 978-0-8020-3382-6 (cloth)
ISBN 978-1-4875-9858-7 (paper)

Canadian Cataloguing in Publication Data

Essays in the history of Canadian law
Includes bibliographical references and index.
ISBN 978-0-8020-3382-6 (bound). ISBN 978-1-4875-9858-7 (pbk.)
1. Law – Canada – History – Addresses, essays, lectures. I. Flaherty, David H.
II. Osgoode Society
KE394.Z85E87 349.71 C81-095131-2

To the Honourable R. Roy McMurtry, QC
founder of The Osgoode Society

Contents

Foreword

THE OSGOODE SOCIETY

The purpose of The Osgoode Society is to encourage research and writing in the history of Canadian law. The Society, which was incorporated in 1979 and is registered as a charity, was founded at the initiative of the Honourable R. Roy McMurtry, Attorney General of Ontario, and officials of The Law Society of Upper Canada. Its efforts to stimulate legal history in Canada include the sponsorship of a fellowship, research support programs, and work in the field of oral history. The Society will publish (at the rate of about one a year) volumes which contribute to legal-historical scholarship in Canada and which are of interest to the Society's members. Included will be studies of the courts, the judiciary, the legal profession, biographies, collections of documents, studies in criminology and penology, great trials, and work in the social and economic history of the law.

Current directors of The Osgoode Society are John D. Bowlby, Archie G. Campbell, Jane Banfield Haynes, John D. Honsberger, Kenneth Jarvis, Allen M. Linden, R. Roy McMurtry, Brendan O'Brien, and Peter Oliver. The Annual Report and information about membership may be obtained by writing The Osgoode Society, Osgoode Hall, 130 Queen Street West, Toronto, Ontario, Canada, M5H 2N6. Members receive the annual volumes published by the Society.

Essays in the History of Canadian Law, Volume I, edited by David H. Flaherty, is the Society's first publication. A second volume of essays is expected to follow shortly. In commissioning an essay collection as its initial effort, the Society intended to involve scholars from several disciplines in writing Canadian legal history and to demonstrate to readers the range of possibilities available for research and writing in the field. David H. Flaherty, a Professor of History and Law at the University of Western Ontario, is a distinguished scholar whose earlier work has been in the field of American legal history. In agreeing to organize and edit this volume, Professor Flaherty undertook a difficult and demanding task; the Society is in his debt for the skill and judgment which he has brought to his editorial duties.

The contributors to the current volume have investigated a wide range of subject matter and collectively their work represents a significant step forward in the evolution of Canadian legal history. Each essay is based on original research, strives for a high level of analysis, and is presented in a manner which it is hoped will satisfy the specialist yet prove attractive to the general reader. Nonetheless, the essays are not of a piece. In his own provocative contribution, Professor Flaherty makes an important distinction between internal and external legal history. The former focuses on areas such as the legal profession, the judiciary, and the analysis of judicial decisions which are unmistakably legal in nature, and analyses them primarily in terms of strictly defined legal processes and concerns. External legal history is far more interested in the broader relationships between law and the larger society, and at times legal history of the external variety shades into more general social or economic history. Although Flaherty's interest lies primarily in the external approach, he makes it clear that the scholar who has chosen to focus on more narrowly legal materials and issues also has an important contribution to make. As these essays demonstrate, the law in Canada has been much more than a merely reactive agency which reflects the general social and economic forces present in society. Notwithstanding the conservatism of the Canadian judicial tradition, which is a leading theme in this volume, the law at certain times and in certain places, while it has embodied larger societal values, has also helped to shape those values.

Undoubtedly readers of these essays will differ as to which of them fall within the tradition of specialized legal-historical scholarship and which adopt the more sweeping law and society approach. Probably the majority might be categorized as external legal history, although Professors Backhouse and Nedelsky, for example, who deal with themes which will be entirely new to many Canadian historians, develop their argument primarily through the analysis of reported cases. Yet they also place their work in a larger context by drawing on a thorough knowledge of the secondary literature in social and economic history, and as a result they successfully demonstrate that internal legal history has much to add to general historical understanding.

Frequently the distinction between internal and external legal history will reflect differences in training and interest between the lawyers who often write the former, and the historians, usually based in university history departments, who almost always take the latter approach. Sometimes the law professor in particular will be critical of the historian's failure to grasp the legal subtleties of the documents; more frequently, the historian will be sceptical of the apparently narrow legalisms and lack of methodological and theoretical sophistication which on occasion seem to characterize the lawyer's attempt to engage in serious historical scholarship. The difficulty of combining work in two demanding and very different disciplines ensures that these differences in interest and approach will not soon disappear. Yet the essays in this volume demonstrate that intellectual interchange between law professors and historians can be fruitful indeed and that the dichotomies described above will yield to the efforts of legal historians using legal and other materials to cast new light on varying aspects of the Canadian past. One of the important features of this volume is the number of contributors with some training in both law and history.

There is as yet no significant tradition of indigenous legal history in Canada. Professor Flaherty and his contributors have provided an important building block on which such a tradition may grow and flourish.

Brendan O'Brien
President

Peter N. Oliver
Editor-in-Chief

Preface

This volume of essays is the first of two designed to illustrate the wide possibilities for research and writing in Canadian legal history. It is a pioneering volume in every sense, and no doubt suffers the same limitations as any other attempt to develop a new field. The contents also reflect the current interests of people working in the history of Canadian law. Although the variety of their concerns reflects the wide-ranging scope of legal history as an intellectual discipline, this volume has a nineteenth-century Ontario focus largely as a result of happenstance rather than editorial design. Invitations to contribute were extended from the Atlantic provinces to British Columbia. My hope is that the second volume of essays in this series will have a broader geographical focus.

I have prepared and edited this volume at the invitation of the Publications Committee of The Osgoode Society, which permitted me complete independence in the selection of contributions. The Society has served in the vital roles of facilitator and promoter of my efforts, including the sponsorship of a conference on Canadian legal history in Toronto in May 1980, attended by most of the contributors to this volume. The editor and authors are most grateful to The Osgoode Society for their generous support.

My own background has of course influenced my approach to Canadian legal history, especially as shown in the introductory essay to this volume. I have been teaching and pursuing research in United States legal history for more than fifteen years, with particular emphasis on the seventeenth and eighteenth centuries and the history of criminal justice. In the last few years I have taught a comparative course on the legal histories of England, the United States, and Canada since approximately 1800. The introduction thus reflects both my basic training in American history and law and my concern for a comparative approach.

My experience has encouraged me to favour an expansive conception of what Canadian legal history should ultimately be about. The main objection to my expansive approach is that it is somewhat elusive. Traditional legal history owes much of its popularity to its narrow focus and its ease of accomplishment. One result has been a relative lack of intellectual development in Canadian legal history.

My greatest debt is to the authors of the individual contributions. I must also acknowledge the help of the historians and lawyers who acted as referees for specific articles. Peter N. Oliver, of York University, the editor-in-chief of The Osgoode Society, has been an invaluable associate in the entire enterprise, including the preparation of detailed comments on each draft contribution. R.C.B. Risk of the University of Toronto has also been a constant source of good advice on all matters relating to this volume; his example has encouraged me in the belief that Canadian legal history will become in the 1980s a creditable field of intellectual inquiry.

Another essential person has been Mary Stokes, a third-year law student at the University of Western Ontario, who has worked intensively as my research and editorial assistant. Her work was funded in part by the generous support of the Faculty of Law. Curtis Cole, a doctoral candidate in history at Western, became our expert in footnoting style and indexing at a critical stage in the proceedings. Finally, the secretaries in the Department of History of the University of Western Ontario have greatly eased the burden of correspondence and mailing. All the essays are published for the first time, except for the contribution by R.C.B. Risk, which is reprinted with permission of the University of Toronto Press.

David H. Flaherty
London, Ontario
1 May 1981

Contributors

CONSTANCE B. BACKHOUSE is Assistant Professor of Law at the University of Western Ontario. A member of the Ontario Bar, she received a Master of Law degree from Harvard Law School in 1979.

MARGARET A. BANKS is Law Librarian and Associate Professor of Law at the University of Western Ontario. She is the author of two books and numerous articles relating to history, law, and parliamentary procedure.

KATHRYN M. BINDON is Assistant Professor of History at Concordia University in Montreal. She received her PH D in history from Queen's University in 1979.

JOHN D. BLACKWELL is a doctoral candidate in history at Queen's University, where he is working on a study of the Blake family in nineteenth-century Ontario.

PAUL CRAVEN is Associate Professor in the Division of Social Science at York University. He is the author of *'An Impartial Umpire': Industrial Relations and the Canadian State, 1900–1911* (Toronto 1980).

DAVID H. FLAHERTY is Professor of History and Law at the University of Western Ontario. He has written extensively on the social and legal history of the United States.

JENNIFER NEDELSKY is Assistant Professor of Politics at Princeton University. She received a PH D from the University of Chicago in 1977 and was a Killam Postdoctoral Fellow in Canadian legal history at Dalhousie Law School.

GRAHAM PARKER is Professor of Law at Osgoode Hall Law School, York University. He has written extensively on Anglo-American legal history.

R.C.B. RISK is Professor of Law in the Faculty of Law at the University of Toronto. He has written extensively on Canadian legal history.

JENNIFER STODDART is a recent graduate in civil law from McGill Law School and a member of the Department of History at the Université du Québec à Montréal. She has written several articles on women's history and is co-author of a book on the history of women in Quebec.

Essays in the History of Canadian Law

1

Writing Canadian Legal History: An Introduction

DAVID H. FLAHERTY

This introductory essay seeks to accomplish several goals in order to promote the development of Canadian legal history both as a vehicle for research and for an improved understanding of the role of law in the Canadian past. My primary concern is that legal historians must keep in mind what they are ultimately attempting to understand and also try to function at as sophisticated a level of analysis as possible. Thus my first argument is for the adoption of a comprehensive perspective on the appropriate scope of legal history and, second, for pursuit of both the broad and narrow dimensions of any research topic so as to illuminate the interaction between law and society. The introduction includes frequent summary references to studies published by leading legal historians of the modern era. In part these are intended to serve as a guide to the secondary literature for interested readers, since self-education is essential in this specialized field. But these references also are intended as a source of positive example and inspiration for persons writing the legal history of Canada after 1800. One result can be Canadian writing that reflects peculiar Canadian problems and issues while remaining comprehensive, comparative, and in touch with the concerns of other historians of the Western legal tradition. The final section of this introduction is a brief excursion into the legal history of Upper Canada.

Only in the last generation have scholars in United States legal history produced a corpus of articles and monographic studies to illuminate the intertwining of law and society in the American past.[1] Modern British legal history has not yet undergone so significant a development, although the process is under way.[2] The study of the legal history of Canada in the nineteenth and twentieth centuries is at an even more fledgling stage of development, but the opportunities are equally great to use the history of law, legal institutions, and legal processes to improve our understanding of the past.

My argument for a multifaceted approach to the writing of Canadian legal history implies that there is no single right way, although in my view there are a number of decidedly wrong ways. Depending on the questions asked, legal history can find itself closely allied with political, social, economic, or intellectual history; this in part attracts historians and lawyers to the subject. The varied contents of this volume further illustrate the range of acceptable approaches. As the merits of comprehensive, comparative, and regional approaches to Canadian legal history are reviewed below, it will become evident that I strongly favour an approach that goes beyond the narrow aspects of legal developments to focus ultimately on general relationships between law and society. In discussing these various avenues of study, I also try to identify some important themes and provocative questions in the legal history of nineteenth-century Canada.

COMPREHENSIVE APPROACHES

Since legal history is first and foremost a branch of history, it is worth remembering that historians should not plunge into the task of explaining past human behaviour without devising a scientific and ordered approach to their subject matter. Legal history no less than other fields requires a systematic (as opposed to impressionistic) and dynamic approach (emphasizing the measurement of change over time). Once a significant problem has been defined, research can proceed on a sound theoretical base derived from existing secondary literature, especially model studies, to test ideas empirically in a systematic way.[3] In this sense legal historians of Canada are fortunate in finding their field relatively undeveloped. There is little conventional wisdom to mislead the novice or inhibit the formulation of new approaches. As part of a research enterprise, work done elsewhere can also be employed to formulate conceptual frameworks or approaches. A meaningful legal history should thus do more than simply illuminate the internal history of a topic. Focusing on the broad interactions between law and society requires the identification of important general questions in advance of detailed empirical research.

Working on a topic simply because it has not been previously studied is a particularly inappropriate rationale, since so little productive research has been carried out on Canadian questions. This approach also means that the choice of research topics has to be justified in terms of a larger picture. One must, then, attempt to formulate hypotheses about the interactions between law and society and move from the general to the specific.

During the last forty years one scholar in particular has exemplified breadth of vision concerning the scope of legal history. J. Willard Hurst is the leading historian of modern American law. A member of the Faculty of Law at the University of Wisconsin since the late 1930s, he has produced a wealth of stimulating publications.[4] Hurst's importance for the legal history of North America lies in the generalizations he has set forth to explain the role of law in the United States since 1800 and in the way he has tested these hypotheses. Hurst has sought to develop a broad, all-encompassing explanation of how the legal process actually functioned in the United States during the nineteenth century. It is Hurst's belief from a methodological perspective that:

> The study of the United States legal history will come of age when its practitioners give as much effort to framing questions as to assembling answers. ... Because the historian's job preoccupies him with concrete particularities, he incurs occupational hazards which may rob his work of meaning. Immersed in detail, he may be diverted into the collector's mania, and wind up an antiquarian. The passing days make him painfully aware how time-costly it is to uncover the full dimension of events. Harassed by the calendar, he begrudges time taken from collecting data in order to shape and test the theoretical framework of his enquiries. So he is tempted into a naive empiricism – using his research simply to document the unexamined assumptions and prejudices of common sense or tradition, or behaving as if he believed that meaning could be squeezed out of data by the sheer weight of their accumulation.[5]

On the other hand and more recently, Hurst has issued a timely warning against the dangers of too much theory:

> We don't know much across the board about how law has really worked in social experience. Trying to find out is costly in time, money, energy, thought, courage, and persistence. In contrast, spinning theory can be more fun, less work, and more quickly satisfying to the ego, which is happiest to see itself reflected promptly in print. Turning out solid monographs does not yield such quick and

easy returns. If a new generation of legal historians is not wary of its capacity for original sin, it might wind up full of talk and short of matter. Theory must go to work on recalcitrant raw materials, if it is to deserve full respect.[6]

These reminders are especially appropriate in the early stages of writing about the role of law in the Canadian past. Theory and practice should be married, not divorced.

Three of Hurst's publications are particularly applicable to forming suitable approaches to the writing of Canadian legal history; like other works mentioned in this introduction, brief references do not do justice to their contents. In *The Growth of American Law: The Law Makers* (1950) Hurst dealt with the growth of the principal agencies of law in the United States between 1790 and 1940. Although presented in an institutional framework with successive sections on the legislature, the courts, the bar, the constitution-makers, and the executive, this volume demonstrated a path-breaking approach to the study of legal history that remains relevant today. For example, the author repeatedly focused on the social functions of the legislature and other legal agencies rather than simply on their formal structure.[7] Hurst asserted that although the law has been a significant force in United States history, 'on the whole its role has been much more to organize, channel, legitimate, and in a substantial measure to redirect the course of changes that started outside the law.'[8] The applicability of such a generalization to Canada, as well as those discussed below, should be tested.

In *Law and the Conditions of Freedom in the Nineteenth Century United States* (1956) Hurst 'sought to define some key values and attitudes out of which men consciously shaped their uses of law in the society.'[9] He argued that the central impulse in nineteenth-century American legal development was the release of human creative energy. To attain this general goal, the law, especially through the medium of the courts, produced two fundamental assumptions, what Hurst calls 'working principles.' The first was that the legal order should 'protect and promote' individual initiatives to the greatest extent compatible with the democratic character of society. Second, the legal system should promote an environment and the use of resources so as to increase the opportunities for persons to act freely.[10] The business community welcomed this dual orientation: 'the substance of what business wanted from law was the provision for ordinary use of an organization through which entrepreneurs could better mobilize and release economic energy. Partly this business demand was to get rid of a limiting governmental policy ... But it is characteristic of the nineteenth century that there was here also a demand for positive help from the law.' This perspective was also shared by the legislators, whom Hurst sees as the prime exponents of a policy of shaping the environment to enlarge men's range of choice.[11]

Hurst's masterwork, *Law and Economic Growth: The Legal History of the Lumber Industry in Wisconsin 1836–1915*, appeared in 1964. In addition to contributing to a general theory of United States legal history, this massive study was an attempt in Hurst's own words to serve four principal ends:

1 It investigates relations between law and the processes of economic growth.
2 The study is concerned with identifying the distinctive impress of law-embodied attitudes and choices, and distinctive roles of the principal agencies of law in defining, determining, and implementing values particularly involved in economic effort.
3 The study pays attention to those aspects of its materials which bear upon the history of ideas (political and social, as well as economic) in the nineteenth-century United States, upon the influence of inertia and drift in social affairs, upon the creative and destructive tensions generated by interplay of general and special interests, and upon the tendency of means to fashion ends...
4 A fourth purpose of the study [is] to seek more meaningful and more useful concepts of the subject matter of legal history ... The particular story of law and lumber in Wisconsin is a matter only of secondary interest in this book; of prime concern is to learn, from trying to tell this particular story, how better to tell the story of the distinctive parts which law has played in the general course of social experience.[12]

This quotation furnishes some sense of the breadth of Hurst's vision of the scope of legal history. In *Law and Economic Growth* as in most of his other books, Hurst has concerned himself both with integrated description and analysis of what actually happened, such as the rise and decline of the lumber industry, and with the history and theory of social processes involving the law. One result is that his findings do not lend themselves to capsule summaries; as with a number of other sophisticated legal historians referred to in this introductory essay, Hurst has to be studied to be fully appreciated.

Legal historians of Canada searching for insightful models should start with Hurst, even if some problems of transfer exist. Hurst and his students, using the experience of the state of Wisconsin for understanding the legal history of the United States, have written about such matters as contracts, railroads, insurance, and mineral wealth.[13] A similar orientation to specific topics and regions can be employed usefully in Canada.

The work of R.C.B. Risk of the University of Toronto Law School already indicates the considerable utility for Canadian legal history of Hurst's approach. Risk is a Hurstian in the best sense of the term. In 1973 he published an expansive prospectus for Canadian legal history outlining his conception of legal history as the study of the history of legal processes in three overlapping elements: the influences of societal values on the law, the effect of law itself on the minds and events of the society, and the structures, procedures, and functions of such institutions as the legislature, the courts, and the legal profession.[14] Risk's prospectus also suggested eight general concerns for Canadian legal history in the post-colonial period: 'They are not proclamations of an exclusive domain for legal history. They are ways of ordering Canadian history that seem to me to be useful for legal history.'[15] The major themes are worth summarizing as an initial agenda for comprehensive approaches to Canadian legal history:

1 The function of law in the creation and expression of a distinctive Canadian identity.
2 The influence of England, the United States, and France on Canadian law.
3 The role of law in the economy, including government regulation and the growth of both public and private power.
4 The role of law in the community, including the introduction of such legal changes as workmen's compensation and unemployment insurance.
5 The impact of law on individuals, including the regulation of economic affairs and changes affecting the family.
6 The role of law in regulating use of the physical environment.
7 The function of law to control anti-social conduct, especially violence.
8 The structures, procedures, and functions of legal institutions, including the constitution, the legislatures, the courts, the administrative agencies, and the legal profession.

Risk's articulation of conceptual themes is a good illustration of a systematic approach to Canadian legal history leading to the building of hypotheses.

Canadian legal historians also have been well served by the four seminal articles Risk published in the *University of Toronto Law Journal,* dealing with the role of law in the mid-nineteenth-century Ontario economy.[16] The series traced the foundations of the business corporation, the law about the market, especially the 'golden age' of contract, and the law of property in the allocation of losses caused by economic activity. The fourth article studied legislation, the courts, and the common law as related to the economy in an overall perspective on institutions and processes. Reading this essay, which is included in this volume, one is struck by Risk's sweeping perspective and the perceptiveness of his judgments on a wide range of legal-economic issues.

As Risk's work shows, legal history can and should contribute to understanding the general history of Canadian society. American legal history has not yet had a significant impact on general interpretations of United States history, except in the writings of Hurst, Daniel J. Boorstin, and a few others, perhaps because too few of its proponents have addressed significant and relevant themes raised in the general historical literature. Canadian legal historians can avoid this pitfall by wide and systematic reading in general historical literature, as well as by formulating working hypotheses and conceptual frameworks to use in approaching a particular research design. In this connection I have in mind, for example, the significance for legal history of the work of H.C. Pentland on the development of a capitalistic labour market in Canada or the writings of Gad Horowitz on conservatism, liberalism, and socialism in Canada.[17]

Canadian legal historians should also concern themselves with the general theses on Canadian development advanced by such leading historians as Harold Innis, Arthur Lower, J.M.S. Careless, Frank Underhill, and Donald Creighton, of an older generation, as well as a number of able younger scholars doing groundbreaking work on social and economic history. The problem with the leading twentieth-century Canadian historians of the 1930 to 1970 era, however, is that the grand hypotheses they advanced to explain the origins of Canada essentially ignore the legal dimension. Certainly this is true of Innis's 'staple theory' explanation for the geographical basis of Canadian development, Creighton's emphasis on the commercial empire of the St Lawrence River created by business élites before Confederation, Underhill's notion that the 'United States was Canada writ large,' and J.M.S. Careless's articulation of the influence of metropolitan centres in Canadian history. Except for the constitutional historians of the early twentieth century, such as Chester Martin or W.P.M. Kennedy, the role of law and the legal system in Canadian development seems either to have been entirely ignored or treated as simply a pale reflection of what the dominant commercial élites wanted. With respect to this latter point, Carl Berger has suggested that Creighton regarded Upper Canadian merchants as 'the creative and progressive group who imparted élan and direction to their society.'[18] It is interesting to note that the newer generation of Canadian historians seems in turn to be paying relatively little attention to our legal traditions. Canadian legal history may have been neglected to date because major interpreters of the Canadian past regard the legal system as secondary and passive rather than an instrumental and dynamic aspect of historical development.[19] This seems unlikely to be an accurate judgment in the Canadian context, given the well-known deference in this country to peace, order, and good government.

The final aspect of a comprehensive approach to Canadian legal history is that it should strive to be comparative at all levels. The argument for writing in a comparative mode is twofold. In the first instance Canadian law and legal institutions have been exposed to significant external influences at various times from Britain, the United States, and France. One of the central questions of Canadian legal history is then to evaluate the respective role of external as opposed to internal and indigenous influences and developments. Mr Justice Brian Dickson of the Canadian Supreme Court has suggested, for example, that the High Court's subordination to the Privy Council until 1949 meant that the Supreme Court only recently has been 'liberated.'[20] All Canadian legal history functions under a heavy weight of external influences, whether *de facto* or *de jure*. Second, the doctrine of *stare decisis*, whereby courts are supposed to abide by, or adhere to, decided cases, meant that nineteenth- and twentieth-century Canadian judges sometimes cloaked their decisions in the mantle of adherence to precedent even when their decisions were innovative. In addition, a number of Ontario high court opinions during the nineteenth century, for example, were not very explicit about the rationale for a decision; hence interpretation of the innovativeness of decisions is a sensitive enterprise.

The answers concerning American and British influences on Canadian legal developments at the national and provincial levels likely will depend very much on the time period and area of law being considered. Risk ventured into the comparative approach in his prospectus of 1973 and in his summary article of 1977. Indeed, his entire work has a comparative inspiration because of the influence of his association with Hurst. In drawing contrasts and comparisons between Ontario and the United

States, Risk observed that 'by the mid-nineteenth century, the organization and structure of law and most of the terms of doctrine were substantially the same in Ontario and the United States, and a lawyer from one jurisdiction would have had little difficulty understanding and coping with the differences.'[21] Of course, Risk also found a number of differences. Another legal historian has shown that nineteenth-century Canada followed the rules about conflict of laws developed by Justice Joseph Story of the US Supreme Court in his landmark treatise on the conflict of laws; Story was similarly influential in England.[22] A comparative approach may also make Canadian legal history more relevant to the general intellectual concerns of scholars in several countries.

The case for the utility of a comparative dimension to Canadian legal history is in large part inspired by the serious neglect of such an approach by legal historians of the United States and the United Kingdom.[23] For instance, Morton Horwitz's theory of the emergence of an instrumental conception of law in the early stages of industrialization in the United States suffers significantly from the lack of such a perspective on what happened at similar stages in Canada or the United Kingdom. Legal historians of Massachusetts or Wisconsin sometimes write as if their chosen territory is self-evidently a microcosm of the legal history of the United States. Even comparisons between states remain an exception, though Michael Hindus's study of criminal justice in Massachusetts and South Carolina before the Civil War is a model effort to remedy this defect.[24]

The need to write comparative history has been a common recommendation during the past generation, but it would be an overstatement to say that such advocacy has led to considerable progress. Successful comparative history is a very difficult enterprise; it requires substantial knowledge of at least two countries or two jurisdictions within a nation for successful execution. Moving beyond superficial generalizations about obvious similarities or contrasts is the ultimate task. Some of the essays in this volume illustrate at least a few steps towards a comparative approach, when the authors ask questions about how a particular problem, such as custody disputes, the reform of equity, or women's rights were handled in other jurisdictions inside and outside of Canada. The comparative approach has special relevance to an evaluation of explanatory models for particular legal developments that are insular or local in character. Someone working on an issue in Canadian legal history should always inquire how England and the United States, to cite the most obvious examples, have handled the same problem. Excellent comparative legal history will ultimately have to depend upon a solid base of careful research.

INTERNAL AND EXTERNAL LEGAL HISTORY

In a perceptive critique of the common law tradition in the writing of American legal history, Robert W. Gordon has distinguished between internal and external legal history:

> The internal legal historian stays as much as possible within the box of distinctive-appearing legal things; his sources are legal, and so are the basic matters he wants to describe or explain, such as changes in pleading rules, in the jurisdiction of a court, the text assigned to beginning law students, or the doctrine of contributory negligence. The external historian writes about the interaction between the boxful of legal things and the wider society of which they are a part, in particular to explore the social context of law and its social effects, and he is usually looking for conclusions about those effects.[25]

Scholars approaching Canadian legal history should keep this fundamental distinction in mind as they shape their research.

The following section will illustrate internal and external approaches to a select series of topics in Canadian legal history with particular reference to Ontario. Unfortunately, most legal historical writing in the English language has fallen solely into the more limited internal or 'in the box' category. This is not to say, however, that internal legal history is to be disregarded. It is necessary to investigate many issues that at one level are internal to the legal development of Canada, such as law reform, legal education, the judiciary, the legal profession, procedure, and substantive law. Nevertheless the best research will also lead to external aspects, whatever interaction of law and society seems appropriate, and this will include informed speculation concerning the relevance for broad hypotheses central to Canadian historiography. No single topic is by itself in or out of the box of legal things; it depends on the perceptions of the observer. Legal history should seek to shed light on the precise role that law and legal institutions have played in the history of a province and of the country as a whole. To this end a critical and objective perspective is also essential: we should, for instance, avoid the temptation of exaggerating the achievements of bench and bar in advance of an examination of the larger evidence.

Several general works will prove useful to Canadian legal historians for comparative purposes, for the formulation of hypotheses to be tested in their specific area of interest, and for developing an external approach. One of the most significant works in modern American legal history is Lawrence M. Friedman's *A History of American Law* (1973). Although Friedman focuses primarily upon the nineteenth century, his is the first treatment of the entire sweep of American legal history. It is in fact an extremely eclectic account, which tells the reader something about almost every aspect of legal developments in the United States and is thus an invaluable source of basic comparative information for the legal historian of Canada. Friedman's central assumptions demonstrate his external approach: 'This is a *social* history of American law ... This book treats American law, then, not as a kingdom unto itself, not as a set of rules and concepts, not as the province of lawyers alone, but as a mirror of society. It takes nothing as historical accident, nothing as autonomous, everything as relative and molded by economy and society.'[26]

Friedman's perspective, heavily influenced by Hurst, has become a magnet for opposing theses. Mark Tushnet of the Wisconsin Law School has argued persuasively that Friedman neglects both the autonomous development and the ideological functions of law. He accuses Friedman of adopting a pluralistic and materialist approach, which ignores the influence of autonomy on the legal order and 'the possibility that some changes in the law may be explicable solely in terms of the autonomous internal dynamics of the legal process and the possibility that the legal order may become an active influence, to some degree, on the social and economic order.' According to Tushnet, the relatively autonomous legal order is 'responsive directly to social or economic needs at some times with respect to some matters, responsive indirectly at other times or on other matters, and not responsive at all in still other instances.'[27] Tushnet is in effect emphasizing the importance of both internal and external legal history.

The most controversial and stimulating study in Anglo-American legal history published in the 1970s was *The Transformation of American Law, 1780–1860* by Morton J. Horwitz of the Harvard Law School. Horwitz describes how in the seventy or eighty years after the American Revolution industrial and mercantile groups associated themselves with judges and courts to transform the system of private law in their own interests.[28] These ideas are worked out in chapters dealing with the internal and external aspects of such substantive areas of law as property, contract, and commercial law. The alliance of commerce and the judiciary overthrew the pre-commercial and anti-developmental legal doctrines and institutions of the eighteenth century. The legal system then became an instrument for the direct promotion of economic growth. The result was that the American legal system underwent a major transformation which was essentially complete by 1850, becoming an instrument in the hands of the newly powerful commercial groups in society. Common-law judges played an essential role in this emergence of a new conception of law in the early nineteenth century. This instrumentalism is perhaps the most central and most crucial aspect of the Horwitz argument. The fruition of an instrumental conception of the common law in promoting economic development was accompanied, especially after 1850, by what Horwitz describes as the rise of legal formalism. After the creation of new common-law rules supportive of economic development, a flexible and instrumental conception of law was no longer needed.[29] The commercial interests and the judiciary then recognized that it had become essential to give common-law rules the appearance of being self-contained, apolitical, and inexorable. Horwitz suggests that the deep pressure towards formalism in nineteenth-century law was ultimately designed to preserve the advantages secured in the initial transformation of the law.

Willard Hurst has sensitized legal historians to the central importance of the legislative process. In the Canadian context this leads to questions about the respective roles of the legislature and the courts in the evolution both of a province's legal system and the structure of society as a whole. What attitudes and approaches did legislators and judges bring to their respective tasks? Although Risk suggests that the legislatures have been the dominant legal institution in Canada, little work has been done on the structure, procedures, personnel, and functions of the legislatures with reference to their law-making functions.[30] In the immediate aftermath of the American Revolution, state legislatures in the United States exercised the preponderance of power under the existing constitutional arrangements. The first state constitutions provided for weak executives and only the limited exercise of judicial review, which did not really become significant until after the middle of the nineteenth century. In Ontario by contrast, until the achievement of responsible government in the late 1840s introduced the principle of self-government, the powers though not the political significance of the legislature were severely restricted. Indeed one needs to emphasize the small size and restricted scope of governmental legislative activities throughout the nineteenth century in comparison to the twentieth.[31]

The question of law reform, one of the central issues in modern legal history, also helps illustrate the internal/external distinction. Law reform is not simply a matter of passing new laws or amending old ones but refers to a conscious effort to change statutes, prevailing precedents, procedures, and practices, including the role and education of lawyers. The usual belief is that the proposed changes will bring positive benefit to society by promoting such goals associated with the law as justice, uniformity, order, and consistency. An overview of law reform identifies at least the following internal factors: the roles of legislatures, commissions, judges, lawyers, and legal educators. The external factors would include the *mentalité* of the times, prevailing ideologies, political culture, interest groups, and the general public. What, for example, have been the specific intellectual influences on the development of Canadian jurisprudence? Judging at least by the absence of any codification movement in the first half of the nineteenth century, no one in power in Ontario seems to have been influenced by Jeremy Bentham, although reprinted articles in law journals do reflect a degree of interest. John Brierley has documented the French origins of the codification movement in Quebec civil law in the mid-nineteenth century.[32] Canada did not produce distinguished legal figures like the Americans James Kent or Joseph Story, whose influence on law in English-speaking countries was extensive. If one looks to the sociological movement in law of the late nineteenth century and considers its implications for the American legal realist movement of the twentieth century, again there has been virtually no observable impact on law reform in Canada until recently.[33] Largely because of the absence of American-style law schools or a legal professoriate in Canada until relatively recent times, critical legal scholarship in Canada has been slow to develop. In 1920 there were only six full-time teachers of law in Canadian universities at a total of five law schools.[34] This is not to suggest that law reform has been or ever should be the exclusive preserve of law professors or lawyers. The external approach acknowledges that there are a number of areas related to law reform where lawyers have not had a monopoly and that a number of statutory changes over time in various areas hardly were regarded as law reforms by lawyers.

In nineteenth-century Ontario many reforms in the law and the legal system pertained to altering the structure and the jurisdiction of the courts.[35] In this sense law reform in nineteenth-century Ontario seems to have been much closer to the English than to the American model. A central issue will be to understand and document the extent of law 'reform' that happened automatically in Canada as a result of the North American environment and of the differences in the scale of human activity between England and Canada. It will also be a significant contribution to the internal history of law reform in Ontario to explain the specific circumstances and inspirations for such statutory changes as the Common Law Procedure Act (1856), the Law Reform Act (1868), and the Judicature Act (1881).

Although some initial work has been done on the history of the Canadian legal profession, it tends to be internal and descriptive.[36] In contrast, Risk has suggested five categories of topics relating to the history of the legal profession:

1 Functions: The kinds of jobs lawyers have done, their knowledge, skills and products, their clients, and their effect, especially on the structure and conduct of business and on the relations between government and the individual.
2 Organization: The distribution of lawyers, both geographically and among government, business, and private practice; the distribution of jobs and clients; and the organization of lawyers into firms.
3 Government of the profession: The attitudes of lawyers and the public towards self government; the structure, powers, policies, and effects of the governing bodies; the means and extent of public accountability, and the actual degree of independence of lawyers in relation to government and large corporate clients.
4 Attitudes and responsibilities about law, the practice of law, and public affairs, of lawyers and the public.
5 Legal education and qualification to practice.[37]

The task of studying the internal and external history of the Canadian legal profession from the perspective of all or one of Risk's suggestive categories is facilitated by the existence of a substantial number of studies for England and the United States. The most relevant English work, Brian Abel-Smith and Robert Stevens's sociological study of lawyers and the courts in the English legal system from 1750 to 1965, is particularly significant because of its broad perspective on the role of lawyers in society.[38] For the United States a series of monographic studies cover the history of the legal profession during the modern period. Gerard W. Gawalt's history of the legal profession in Massachusetts from 1760 to 1840 seems particularly promising, because of its time period, as a model for studying the emergence of the legal profession in the Canadian colonies. The series of sketches in Maxwell Bloomfield's *American Lawyers in a Changing Society, 1776–1876* also demonstrates that the biographical approach can successfully integrate internal and external approaches to legal history.[39]

Given the growth of almost universal tendencies towards formal organization of professions by the late nineteenth century, historians are now studying the legal profession as one aspect of the history of professionalization. All professional groups developed strategies of market control in response to the growing pressure of demand for professional services as the financial stakes grew larger and the age of expertise began.[40] In the United States bar associations or state agencies began in the late nineteenth century to standardize entrance examinations and educational practices for the professions, sometimes regulating practice under the threat of state sanctions, licensing professionals, limiting their number, and in one way or another controlling the production of, and access to, knowledge about law and the legal system. It is not at all clear what impact such developments had in a province like Ontario, where the dominance of the Law Society of Upper Canada over legal education and the practice of law has been almost complete since the early nineteenth century.

In a related vein Jerold S. Auerbach has turned the study of the twentieth-century American legal profession into a controversial topic in *Unequal Justice: Lawyers and Social Change in Modern America*.[41] By asking hard questions about the responsibility of élite lawyers and law firms to the pursuit of equal justice in society and measuring these standards against actual practices, Auerbach has painted an unflattering picture of the leading segment of the American legal profession. This provocative book raises many significant and sensitive issues involved in the practice of law.[42]

Questions concerning the number and role of lawyers in their respective societies are particularly important because they introduce a number of external legal history factors, such as the type of social structure, the availability of advanced education, levels of economic activity, élite formation, fee systems, attitudes to litigation, attitudes towards social mobility, and recruitment patterns for the professions. One of the many intriguing questions in the history of the legal profession is why there have always been more lawyers per capita in the United States than in Canada or the United Kingdom. Although detailed studies need to be made to explain the incidence of lawyers at various times in the past, preliminary indications are that Canada falls between the United States and British patterns, at least in terms of simple numbers of practitioners.

Despite an intriguing series of possible internal and external questions associated with the history of the Canadian judiciary and courts, relatively little research has been done on these topics. What has been the character of the 'Canadian judicial tradition' in comparison with the British and Americans models developed by Robert Stevens and G. Edward White?[43] Competing models of the roles of judges in English-speaking countries include the activist judge in the United States, 'professional' judges versus 'political' judges, and the delicate question of the relationships of judges with legislatures and juries. Recently, scholars have attempted to follow shifts in styles of judicial reasoning in the United States and the United Kingdom during the nineteenth and twentieth centuries. In the United Kingdom formalism continued to triumph over instrumentalism. Abel-Smith and Stevens argue that between 1875 and 1939 British judges 'played an increasingly narrow role ... They became more and more insistent that their role was merely a passive mechanical one ... They became increasingly insistent that they merely declared the pre-existing law and had no way of controlling its development.'[44] Although Morton Horwitz has demonstrated the emergence of an instrumental conception of law in the first half of the nineteenth century in the United States followed by the triumph of formalism in judicial reasoning after 1870, in his latest work Stevens argues that at least the final appeal courts in England were, for much of the nineteenth century, just as instrumental as their American contemporaries chronicled by Horwitz.[45] Thus a Canadian legal historian studying the role of the judiciary in a nineteenth-century province can test two clearly stated but contrasting models, one active, the other passive and formalistic, of the role of the judiciary in the early stages of an industrializing society.

Although it seems likely that the Ontario and English-Canadian pattern will be much closer to the British experience than to the American, older biographies of particular state judges may be useful for the study of provincial jurisdictions in Canada. These include Leonard Levy's expansive study of the early nineteenth-century career of Chief Justice Lemuel Shaw in Massachusetts and John Reid's biography of Justice Charles Doe of New Hampshire in the later nineteenth century.[46] A striking hypothesis advanced by Risk will also have to be tested: 'Our courts have tended to express attitudes and values within narrow limits and through results in technical reasoning, and they have not usually made decisions that have a major impact on society ... Nor have we used courts much to declare values or to focus and make apparent problems, especially diffused problems that affect otherwise relatively power-less groups ...'[47] In this volume Jennifer Nedelsky and Constance Backhouse have presented a case for a view of the Canadian judiciary's role in nuisance and custody cases as being relatively conservative. One could further test the validity at various points in time of Chief Justice Bora Laskin's statement concerning 'the continuing and pervasive influence of English decisions in Canadian courts.'[48] In addition, there are significant questions concerning the patterns of recruitment, selection, and exercise of controls over Canadian judges.

The history of crime and criminal justice is the final category to be examined in this selective discussion of internal and external legal history. It is almost impossible to ignore the interactions of law and society in the context of criminal law and its enforcement, because of its visible, direct impact on the population. Perhaps because the prospects for successful historical integration are thus higher, the social history of crime has become an exciting scholarly field during the last decade. Although historians of England have pioneered this field,[49] the reactionary state of the eighteenth-century criminal law makes their work somewhat less relevant for the understanding of nineteenth-century Canada than existing American or Canadian studies.[50] Fortunately, the history of crime is another area of legal history where some sophisticated Canadian scholarship already exists.[51] Pioneering French, English, and American work becomes even more relevant to Canadian interests in the context of the various reform movements between 1760 and 1860, especially the development and spread of prisons and penitentiaries.[52] John Beattie's documentary study of opinion about the causes of crime and the effectiveness of various punishments in Upper Canada is a valuable beginning for the study of similar issues in the country as a whole.[53]

A person wishing to study the history of the creation of police forces in Canada can also draw upon several excellent studies by American and British scholars. The most useful narrative history of the development of American policing is Samuel Walker's *A Critical History of Police Reform: The Emergence of Professionalism.*[54] There is even an exciting comparative study of police authority in New York and London between 1830 and 1870 by Wilbur R. Miller, which fully illustrates the benefits of both comparative analysis and the law and society approach.[55] In the Canadian context there have been important studies of the history of the RCMP and the emergence of concern for juvenile delinquents.[56] The latter topic has attracted significant scholarship in both the United States and England further illustrative of the internal and external approaches to legal history.[57]

UPPER CANADA AS A CASE STUDY

There are certain basic concerns, questions that arise in the legal history of all English-speaking peoples, that should guide initial study of nineteenth-century Canadian legal history. Canadian legal history, except for the history of New France, extends primarily over the last two hundred years and includes the crucial nineteenth-century processes of industrialization, urbanization, professionalization, and the growth of corporate enterprise. At the most general level legal historians are trying to understand and explain what happened to Canadian law and legal institutions during the extraordinary societal changes of these past two centuries.

In arguing for the utility of focusing in the first instance on the legal history of nineteenth-century Ontario as a case study, I am aware of the risks of attempting to move too cavalierly from the legal history of Ontario to that of Canada. Although one might conceivably substitute any other English-speaking province for Ontario, there are good reasons to start with this province.[58] The Law Society of Upper Canada has exercised a direct and powerful influence on the legal scene since its creation in 1797. The Ontario bench and bar have been and remain influential leaders at the national level, including the exertion of significant influence on the Supreme Court of Canada and the new western provinces through the migration of lawyers in the late nineteenth and early twentieth centuries. The actual nature of the influence of Ontario court decisions on other provinces will have to be tested, as will the idea that the general significance of Ontario's central role in the political and economic development of Canada may have been duplicated in the law as well. Certainly the civil law tradition of Quebec set that province apart and prevented it from playing a prominent national role.

Focusing on Ontario in the nineteenth century also facilitates comparisons with American colonies and states, especially New York. From a Hurstian perspective the respective histories of resource development in Wisconsin and Ontario, for example, seem roughly comparable; even the population figures are within a reasonable range of comparability for the nineteenth century.[59] As well, some interesting differences pose general and specific questions for comparison. For example, an American state features a written constitution, separation of powers, and a seemingly much greater tradition of dependence on law in the ordering of human affairs. Furthermore, during the nineteenth century, American state judges were often elected rather than appointed; Ontario courts, on the other hand, can be regarded as instruments for élite control, especially before 1860. Other differences between an American state and a Canadian province or region raise a basic issue of cause and effect. What should be labelled as differences or simply a consequence of differences? The United

States after all experienced a Revolution, a Civil War, and a strongly entrenched system of slavery, which, far more than legal traditions, accounts for differences between Canadian and American societies.

Nonetheless, the respective powers of nineteenth-century legislatures in state and province pose equally fascinating questions. Did Canadian provinces develop traditions of more government intervention in the economy than existed in certain American states? Or was Upper Canada directly comparable with American canal states such as Ohio, New York, and Pennsylvania? Harry Scheiber has concluded that the nineteenth-century Ohio government 'did play a conscious development role and engaged in calculated planning.'[60] Moreover, the onset of industrialization in the United States was generally earlier than in Canada.[61] American legal and jurisprudential developments may also be regarded as being much more independent and less subject to external influences than in Canada, which, at least at the élite level, thrived on a tradition of general hostility to Americans and positive attitudes towards British values, including constitutional and legal traditions.

Questions about legal change in nineteenth-century Ontario are especially tied to constitutional, political, and economic developments. Obviously the political changes of the century, including the fundamental one, Confederation, greatly affected legal developments in the province. As well, Ontario judges and legislators regularly encountered 'novel' legal problems that had already been settled in more advanced industrial economies. A good example was the adoption in Ontario of the fellow-servant rule, whereby an employee or servant could not sue his employer or master for injuries caused by the negligence of another employee, as a 'solution' to the problem of the costs of industrial accidents. This phenomenon of time-lag decreases further the legal autonomy of Canadian colonies and provinces functioning in an imperial setting.

For Ontario it may be helpful to refer briefly to certain problems of periodization. Political historians often divide the history of Ontario into a colonial era from its creation in 1791 to the formation of the United Province of Canada in 1841, for which period many of the above questions are especially relevant; then the 'commercial' years up to and including Confederation in 1867, and then the last third of the nineteenth century, when Ontario was increasingly becoming an industrialized society. Such periodization for both Ontario and perhaps Canada as a whole will likely prove useful to legal history as well, although this remains to be established firmly by actual research. The enactment of the British North America Act in 1867 seems much more significant for constitutional history than for the legal history of Canada, although this issue raises basic questions about the appropriate relationship between legal and constitutional history which are not treated in this essay. Some secondary literature focusing on social change uses the period from about 1880 to the end of World War I as a unit to discuss the emergence of major societal problems and the attempt to formulate legal solutions to them.[62] Because of the pervasive impact on society of World War I and the Great Depression, both the 1920s and the 1930s form a convenient unit for analysis.

If one uses Upper Canada as a case study in Canadian legal history, following the Hurst model, the following kinds of questions, which are at once simple and complex, come initially to mind. By what kinds of laws did residents of Ontario choose to be governed? What choices did the mother country allow? Who shaped and made the laws? What contributions did ex-American colonists and other immigrants make to the mainstream of legal developments? How did Upper Canadian residents envision the role of law and law enforcement in their society? What legal institutions did they create for their self-government, and what models were followed? What role did the Colonial Office and the law officers of the crown in England play? How did early developments in Upper Canada and Ontario law differ from those of other provinces at an earlier and later date? Were the settlers, or at least the law-makers, consciously reformist or did the New World simply shape their institutions and practices so as to distinguish their opinions gradually from the precedents of their mother countries? To what extent were they inspired by the apparent freedom and opportunity of the New World to make new laws, to do away with laws and legal institutions they might have objected to in England or elsewhere, and to put into effect reformist tendencies in the realm of law? What traditions bound later settlers from the United States or the British Isles in their law-making?

A number of the issues worth close study in Upper Canada's legal history can thus be subsumed under the general rubric of the transmission of English law to the New World. After the initial period of establishment, some of the interesting questions concern the continuing interplay of heritage, external pressures, the frontier, and indigenous developments in the transformation of this law. Such themes recognize that law was not a static entity but rather dynamic. To what extent did the experience of life in the Old Province of Quebec and Upper Canada influence changes in the law and legal institutions? What regional variations developed in Canada?

Upper Canada attained political and legal status with the Constitutional Act of 1791. The first act of the legislature of the new colony in 1792 was to divest itself of the residual influences of French-Canadian law associated with the Quebec Act of 1774 and to introduce English law as the rule of decision for all matters of 'property and civil rights.' In 1800 the legislature determined that English criminal law as it existed in 1792 was to be the law of Upper Canada.[63] In many ways these seem like extraordinary enactments, given the manifest impossibility of introducing all English law and practices into this new world environment. They may also be interpreted simply as typical colonial reception statutes, which at the most basic level they were. It is not even clear what the Upper Canadian legislators conceived of as English law. The charters creating the several American colonies in the seventeenth century stipulated the adoption of English law shaped as closely as possible to the conditions of life in the new world. Apparently some instructions to Canadian colonial officials contained similar terms, as had the charter of the Hudson's Bay Company in 1670. Perhaps the 1792 enactment in particular should be interpreted primarily as an effort to rid the province of any remnants of what was then known as 'Canadian' (ie, Quebec) law and to furnish English-speaking settlers with guarantees of the English laws they wanted.[64]

The thrust to anglicize Upper Canada was at one level very strong; indeed it was the obsession of the first Lieutenant Governor, John Graves Simcoe. Under the Constitutional Act of 1791 the crown could disallow acts of the Upper Canadian legislature within two years, although as Margaret Banks points out in her essay in this volume, it has never been determined how frequently this power was exercised. Both in theory and practice the power to govern Upper Canada largely resided in the hands of British-appointed lieutenant governors.[65] The first Lieutenant Governor, Simcoe, and first Chief Justice, William Osgoode, consciously established courts modelled on those of the mother country, especially by means of the creation of a court of King's Bench, even though this was resisted by some leading residents as unsuitable for a small new province.[66] The judges in Upper Canada were paid directly by the crown.[67] A number of the first judges were sent out from England. Several who arrived in the early nineteenth century, especially Robert Thorpe in 1805 and John Walpole Willis in 1827, engaged in political controversy and were forced to leave the province. It is revealing, however, of the limits of direct English influence on the judiciary that Willis was the first English judge sent out since 1805.[68] Upper Canada gradually obtained great leeway to shape its own legal affairs. Gerald Craig has written that after 1830 the British government 'was anxious to interfere as little as possible in the internal affairs of Upper Canada.'[69]

Despite its colonial status and the reality of imperial control, Upper Canada theoretically was in a position to shape its laws and legal institutions to the Canadian environment, much as the American colonies had done during the seventeenth and eighteenth centuries. Research will have to determine how this actually happened, but it is enlightening to find an Upper Canadian judge in an 1841 decision recognizing that not all English statutes were relevant to conditions in the province. He discussed the 1792 reception statute:

> The intention and meaning of the legislature undoubtedly was that resort should be had to such of the laws of England as are applicable to the state of society in a British colony, which is very different in many respects from the state of society in England ... We consider the statute of 5 Eliz., c. 4 as a local act which was probably adapted to the state of society in England three hundred years ago, but it is not now, and never was adapted to the population of a colony, and was never in force here.[70]

Residents of Ontario have sometimes regarded their province as a bastion of stability and conservative tradition north of the turbulent United States. Thus it is worth noting the extent of political instability in early Upper Canada. Just as well-informed observers around 1800 expected the United States to fail as a united country, so too there was little real reason to expect Upper Canada to survive as a British colony. The War of 1812, the 1837 rebellions, and the 1849 annexation crisis are simply the best-known episodes of extensive turbulence and insecurity in which residents confronted both external and internal challenges. In the legal area there were major trials for treason in 1813 and 1838, the trials of Robert Gourlay, the British visitor and agitator, for criminal libel and sedition in 1818–19, followed by his banishment; and the expulsion from the legislature in 1821 of the American Barnabas Bidwell, who practised law in Kingston.[71] The politicized nature of the various trials and of the system of justice in early Upper Canada in general is perhaps not surprising, since the leading judges often were or had been leading politicians. In the absence of a written constitution, such as existed in American states, there were few checks on the power of the Lieutenant Governor and Executive Council, the Legislative Council, and after the winning of responsible government, the Assembly, on issues that did not explicitly involve the imperial authorities. Yet the dominant impression, which also remains to be tested, is that the judiciary was not subverted, at least in any narrow sense, to serve the ends of partisan politics. The famous damages case which William Lyon Mackenzie won against the scions of the Family Compact would seem to attest to that point. Nonetheless there is little doubt that senior judges accepted the basic tenets of a Tory ideology, economic and social as well as political, and in ways yet to be determined, their interpretations of law reflected Tory values.

A Hurstian approach to the legal history of Upper Canada requires identification in particular of the values that motivated the larger population and shaped the laws and the legal system. The commitment to economic growth and prosperity in Upper Canada seems comparable to that of Hurst's Wisconsin. Gerald Craig has written of the Toronto bishop John Strachan that 'like most Upper Canadians he had dreams of achieving financial security by speculating in land and stocks, and, like most, his speculations proved to be disappointments.'[72] In the first half of the nineteenth century, land, grain, and timber exports were leading sectors of the Upper Canadian economy. J.M.S. Careless records that in pre-Confederation Ontario 'progress, expansion, beckoning destiny – whether Liberal or Conservative, the leading politicians came to share these terms of aspiration with the buoyant, burgeoning society about them.'[73] Clearly, then, the drive for economic growth was prominent in all segments of the population and underlay the diverse political ideologies of the province. Here is an example of a value system that can provide a broader model for historical study.

Related to the need to identify the goals of Upper Canadian society is the importance of writing legal history with an awareness of the appropriate social and economic context, since the focus of legal history, it bears repeating, is history and not law. The risk of writing ahistorical legal history is particularly great when appellate opinions are used as the sole basis for generalization, although they are in limited supply before the mid-nineteenth century. From an economic perspective, for example, the censuses of the 1840s and 1850s in Upper Canada provide valuable insights into class structure and industrial development. Between the 1842 and 1848 censuses the number of sawmills had grown from 897 to 1584, the number of tanneries from 261 to 354, and the number of grist mills from 414 to 553.[74] One cannot write with authority about substantive law treating economic matters, or evaluate the significance of reported cases, without evaluating such data.

A particularly vital question for Upper Canadian legal historians concerns the impact of rapid population growth and large-scale immigration on the legal structure. There were almost 100,000 persons in Upper Canada at the time of the War of 1812. It took the colony of Massachusetts almost one hundred years from the time of its founding to reach that size, mostly on the basis of natural increase. From 1831 to 1840 the censuses of Upper Canada indicate population growth of eighty-two per cent, largely because of immigration. From 1840 to 1848 the population grew sixty-eight per cent.[75] The rate of population growth in Upper Canada in turn largely shaped economic development and suggests that the law responded to rapidly developing conditions. In these circumstances the legal system may have functioned primarily for the ordering of private relationships and the maintenance of social control rather than as a creative initiating force at the leading edge of society. Risk's work indicates that judges in fact favoured progress through private ordering.

Turning from population growth to the nature of immigration, it is noteworthy that between five and ten thousand Loyalists from the United States with a strong commitment to the British Empire and to things British initially settled Upper Canada in the late eighteenth century. Their experience with the American Revolution and its aftermath encouraged in them and their descendants an adherence to a conservative ideology. Yet in terms of actual experience these persons were more acclimatized to a New World than to an Old World environment. They knew American law and legal institutions, not those of the mother country, which may have had particular implications for the expectation of reformed legal institutions and resistance to archaic English practices. At least in terms of the legal system, the initial Loyalists were likely to want to set up an improved version of the kind of society that they had known in the United States.

One must distinguish the Loyalists from those immigrants from the United States who arrived between 1791 and the War of 1812. These so-called 'Late Loyalists' did not come to Upper Canada for political reasons but simply to find free land in this open territory. Settlers from the United States were actively encouraged and became the only real source of immigrants to Upper Canada for the first generation. Although travellers to Upper Canada during these years noted an antipathy to things American, most of the immigrants were in fact from the United States.[76] Craig writes that on the eve of the war of 1812 'although the province's government closely followed British forms, and its leading citizens were consciously and determinedly loyal to the mother country, in many other respects Upper Canada was an American community after being for twenty years in the path of the American westward movement.'[77] The War of 1812 intensified the anti-Americanism of the élite and commitment to things British in Upper Canada, and the imperial authorities no longer wanted Americans as settlers. Yet in the 1820s the Upper Canadian population remained overwhelmingly American in origin. Although resistance to republicanism was in full flower, the discouragement of immigrants from the United States was hard to accomplish and controversial.[78] The so-called 'alien' issue centred around confusing legal questions, in which the somewhat befuddled views of the Colonial Office may have led colonial leaders to rely more on their own legal instincts than on British opinions.

Thus the United States had a significant influence in Upper Canada on ideas of progress, reform, and models for economic development, banking, and even ecclesiastical organization.[79] New York was a particularly influential neighbour. Detailed research will be required to establish whether this American influence extended to statutes and the workings of the courts. In an initial study of legal authorities cited in Upper Canadian decisions between 1791 and 1837, one student concluded that this influence in fact was minimal.[80]

According to the 1842 census approximately one-third of the population of Upper Canada had been born in the British Isles.[81] Of this total, one-quarter was born in Scotland, one-quarter in England and Wales, and one-half in Ireland. What was the impact of these diverse English, Scottish, and Irish immigrants on the legal heritage of Upper Canada? What, if any, ideas about the legal order did the Scots, for example, bring with them? Did immigrant preconceptions and influence differ by class, age, and ethnicity? This large-scale British immigration to Upper Canada, which only began in the 1820s, may have produced a more conservative type of immigrant than their American counterparts.[82] Did this initiate, hasten, or simply reinforce the process of anglicization of the legal system? J.M.S. Careless emphasizes that 'the British stamp on the Ontario community remained preponderant throughout the entire union era. In outline, it was a remarkably homogeneous society, largely British in origin ...'[83] The last phrase is a reminder that in evaluating the continuing impact of population growth and immigration on Upper Canadian legal history, one must ultimately consider the significance of the process by which the population became increasingly native-born. In the 1842 census the percentage of the population born in Upper Canada had reached fifty per cent. In 1848 the figure was more than fifty-five per cent and in 1861 more than sixty-three per cent.[84] In answering such detailed questions, the legal historian will also make an important contribution to understanding our colonial experience.

Writing Upper Canadian legal history does not mean the exclusion of individuals who were leading actors on the legal stage. Some important figures for analysis are William Draper, William Hume Blake, Edward Blake, and Oliver Mowat. Biographical research on judges, attorneys general, leading legislators, and lawyers should also take place within a comprehensive framework. For example, we need to study the actual character of specific law practices in all levels and types of courts, and the quality of legal education furnished by the Law Society of Upper Canada and in law offices. The leading role of lawyers in the political life of Upper Canada also requires more intensive examination from a legal historical perspective.[85]

The extraordinary career of John Beverley Robinson shaped the law and the legal system of Upper Canada at innumerable points between 1812 and 1862 and make him an obvious candidate for legal biography. Born in Lower Canada in 1791, his heritage was Loyalist and Virginian. This led to an anti-Americanism which military service at a young age in the War of 1812 greatly reinforced. As one commentator has noted, 'looking back from the 1840s, he [Robinson] argued that the war had given Upper Canadians a sense of identity, a sense of anti-Americanism and a pro-British sentiment. He ... remained suspicious of American-born settlers and those whose politics were "republican." Indeed, maintenance of the British connection was his major goal...'[86] Although Robinson travelled to Virginia for an enjoyable visit in 1851, the British connection was indeed the dominant one in his life.

Robinson was educated by the Anglican political priest John Strachan and attracted patrons such as William Dummer Powell, Chief Justice from 1815 to 1825. He began to article in law at the age of sixteen in York with the Solicitor General of Upper Canada, D'Arcy Boulton, sr, and then in 1811 with the Attorney General, John Macdonell. Robinson himself wrote of these years of apprenticeship: 'I had read much less than I should have done, but much more than I believe was usual, and so had perhaps the reputation of being studious.'[87] In 1812 he began a successful private practice which continued until his appointment to the bench in 1829. In 1812, at the age of twenty-one and not yet a member of the bar, Robinson was appointed acting Attorney General of Upper Canada, after Macdonell died in battle.[88] He subsequently served as Solicitor General (1815–18) and Attorney General (1818–29). Despite his youth and seeming inexperience, he provided legal opinions to the government and handled major criminal prosecutions as a crown prosecutor and major civil suits as a private attorney.[89] From October 1815 to July 1817 and from early in 1822 until the summer of 1823 Robinson was in England as a keen observer, tourist, and, on the second trip, successful lobbyist for the Upper Canadian government. His stated ambition was to become a member of the English bar, so that he could aspire to appointment by the Colonial Office as an attorney general or a chief justice of a colony.[90] He enrolled at Lincoln's Inn, which was primarily a dining establishment, and was finally called to the bar in February 1823, after completing the requisite number of terms. In England Robinson mixed with the highest legal circles, especially the Solicitor General and Attorney General, and spent a considerable time observing well-known judges and lawyers in the courts at Westminster.[91] He did so with a keen critical sense and none of the exaggerated deference of a colonial. On 5 December 1815, for example, he was shocked to observe 'the gross prevarication' of three successive witnesses in an action for trespass:

> It exceeded any similar exhibition I have seen in Canada, where we have rascals enough, and sad ones. I attribute it, in great measure, to the manner in which causes are tried and witnesses examined here. The style is to browbeat and insult, and uniformly to question the witness's veracity, without respect to his feelings. [Attorney General Sir William] Garrow's manner of examining a witness serves to confound a rascal, and often, I fear, to perplex an honest man. I wonder the abuse is tolerated by a grave Chief Justice on the Bench to the extent it goes.[92]

It seems likely that English exposure reinforced Robinson's sense of Canadian identity, despite his awareness of the opportunities available to pursue a legal career in the mother country.[93] In 1823 he turned down an opportunity to serve as chief justice of Mauritius at a very high salary, 'chiefly for the reason that I believed my services as Attorney General and a member of the Legislature in this large and important colony were much more useful than they were likely to be in Mauritius.'[94]

It is of course well known that in Upper Canada Robinson became a distinguished officer of the crown as Attorney General, successful private practitioner, an elected politician in the 1820s, an influential shaper of Upper Canadian and imperial policy, and a leader of the Family Compact in its fight against responsible government. This aspect of his career has attracted the most attention. Robinson was also Chief Justice of the court of King's (later Queen's) Bench from 1829 to 1862. After his first few years on the bench, a growing sense that judges should be non-political greatly reduced his direct involvement in political affairs. In 1831 he ceased being a member of the Executive Council of Upper Canada. Upper Canadian judges nevertheless remained an arm of the executive to a considerable extent. They did not have American-style judicial independence under the doctrine of separation of powers, nor did they enjoy unlimited tenure of office during good behaviour.[95] They indeed served at the pleasure of the crown. The Chief Justice continued to serve as Speaker of the Legislative Council during the 1830s. But Robinson displayed considerable sensitivity about the appropriate and limited role of judges in Upper Canadian life, as evidenced by his careful statement to the Lieutenant Governor of Upper Canada in April 1838:

> As Chief-Justice, I am, like my brother judges, liable to be called on for reports, opinions, and advice in those cases in which recourse would be had to the judges in England, and in no others. I have no concern in the executive affairs of the colony, and no claim or wish to be consulted on any of them, except when they have so direct a bearing upon the general administration of justice as to make such a reference proper; and the more your Excellency bears this in mind, the better it will be, for it is most desirable that everything should as much as possible be made to pass through its proper channel.[96]

It is indicative of the underdeveloped state of Canadian legal history that Robinson's career as a judge has attracted almost no scholarly attention.[97] It should be possible for someone to write about Robinson in the same way that Leonard Levy used Chief Justice Shaw to prepare a distinguished study of Massachusetts law between 1830 and 1860.[98] It may also be possible to draw comparisons between Robinson and Chancellor James Kent of New York. Robinson's innumerable decisions over the years in various areas of law can also be subjected to the kind of detailed analysis that Horwitz employed in *The Transformation of American Law*. One consequence may well be to confirm the very high regard that Upper Canadians had for their Chief Justice.[99]

So little has been written about Robinson as a judge that only glimpses of his judicial perspective and his influence on the emergence of Canadian law are now possible. In the first instance there is no doubt about Robinson's dedicated commitment to his judicial office. When applying for sick leave in 1838 after almost ten years in office, the Chief Justice could assert that 'I have not, for any private purpose either of business or pleasure, been absent that I can remember for a single day from my duty in the Courts or in the Legislature.'[100] Although Queen's Bench had produced fifteen printed volumes of decisions by 1854, the Chief Justice could state that there had never been any cases in arrears. Again in 1854, Robinson emphasized the scope and indeed novelty of his judicial activities: 'Banks, insurance companies, railway companies, and corporations of all kinds have sprung up, giving rise to new interests, and to a great variety of new legal questons, so that if I were to say that the duties and responsibilities of the office of Chief-Justice have increased fivefold during my tenure of it, I am not sure that I should state more than is true. The number of Assize towns has grown from eleven to thirty.'[101] In a controversial decision allowing the extradition of the slave John Anderson to the United States in 1860 to stand trial on a charge of murder, Robinson, like Chief Justice Shaw in Massachusetts, stated that judges 'must conform to what the law requires and are not at liberty to act upon considerations of policy or even compassion, where duty is prescribed.'[102] Yet at least in some known instances Robinson attempted to make the law compatible with the needs of Upper Canadians, as the following statement in an 1848 decision on sanctity of contracts demonstrates: 'I cannot feel it to be reasonable or warrantable that we should at the present day, be entertaining subtleties, which the courts have rejected in past ages – when a proneness to more subtle reasoning than was suited to the actual affairs of life was their error – disable parties from carrying into effect [their intentions].'[103]

Robinson's career is also a useful vehicle for understanding the dominant political ideologies in Upper Canadian society and the role of élite groups in connection with the legal system. Upper Canadian toryism 'was the political expression of the province's small upper class, the people who considered themselves the natural leaders of society.'[104] Most members of the legal profession and the leading merchants, landowners, and lumbering operators at least on the surface adhered to the tory connection. The implications for the legal system of this conservative tradition have not been properly investigated, despite the pioneering work of Risk.[105] The latter, however, has advanced an interesting argument about Robinson that deserves to be tested further:

> Robinson's beliefs were strongly held and do not seem to have changed, judging from the few documents that remain, but nor do they seem to have affected his judgements, because of the tempering common law tradition that purported to exclude beliefs of this kind, because of the abstractness of so much of the law, and, most important, because political beliefs usually did not dictate any particular result for the kinds of problems the courts considered.[106]

It is sometimes suggested that Robinson adhered to the political ideas of William Blackstone. But what in fact was the political and legal impact of

Blackstone's celebrated *Commentaries on the Laws of England* (1765–9) on leading lawyers and judges in Upper Canada? It would strain credulity to believe that Blackstone could be so popular in the United States yet not be influential in a society that overtly adhered to the British tradition.[107] Yet it is true that the *Commentaries* did not contain much law that lawyers could cite in their cases.[108] In this area Blackstone was overtaken by the emerging tradition of writing treatises, as in the work of Kent and Story, and the publication of law reports in Upper Canada beginning in the 1820s.

Finally, Robinson is a useful point of departure for obtaining insights into the ideology of economic development that prevailed in Upper Canada. In his important statement on *Canada and the Canada Bill,* published in London in 1840, Robinson spoke of the openness of society in Upper Canada: 'In a boundless field, or rather in a boundless wood, no individual among them seemed to have a defined, a settled position in society: there could be no castes or anything approaching to castes, such as the competition and necessities of the crowded countries of Europe tend, more or less, to create. All seem to depend on individual ingenuity and exertion.'[109] In the 1820s Robinson strongly supported the efforts to develop the Welland Canal, and in his later judicial career several significant decisions recognized and assisted the economic developments associated with telegraph and railroad companies.[110] Indeed he and his associates were willing to tolerate a degree of government intervention in support of various major public enterprises that would have been unthinkable in Hurst's Wisconsin.[111] Yet Robinson had ambivalent feelings about economic development. As Terry Cook has written: 'Being so wary of speculation and its results, Robinson urged caution in order that commerce would not force society to accept the standards of crass American materialism. Unsure of these matters himself, he seems to have relegated commercial values to a secondary role in his ideal society.'[112] An analysis of Robinson's decisions in commercial cases will put such judgments to the test.

Robinson continued to visit England as both an Upper Canadian statesman and tourist during his years on the bench. Certain episodes associated with this experience suggest that the Chief Justice was presiding over a relatively sophisticated legal system in Upper Canada. Especially in 1855, Robinson spent considerable time in various courts. After several days in Westminster Robinson made the interesting observation that: 'On the whole, I saw nothing very peculiar in the system here. Like circumstances seem to produce like courses and consequences, here and there (i.e. in England and Upper Canada).'[113] The Chief Justice also met Sir Edward Ryan, a member of the Judicial Committee of the Privy Council, which had just heard an appeal from Upper Canada. Ryan 'was most strong and emphatic in his praise of the ability shown in the judgments sent from Upper Canada in that and the other cases. He said it was a matter of great remark every term. He regretted that I was not present at the argument and judgment, to hear in what terms our judgments were spoken of.'[114]

This brief excursion into the history of Upper Canada serves as a reminder of how difficult it is even to outline any aspect of the legal history of the Canadian past in advance of careful, detailed research.[115] The process currently involves too much groping in the dark. This situation also reinforces my earlier argument about the importance of taking a comprehensive approach to research in the first instance. The final point is that future research on our legal past necessitates greater efforts at preservation and archiving of old and new records relevant to such studies. Preserving source materials and making them available has to remain a major priority for those concerned with promoting the legal history of Canada, so that historians will be able to pursue important avenues of inquiry on all aspects of our legal past.

NOTES

I am indebted to Dianne Newell, Department of History, University of British Columbia, and Mary Stokes of the University of Western Ontario Law School for substantial assistance in the preparation of this essay. R.C.B. Risk, Peter N. Oliver, Neil Semple, and Roger Hall also contributed significantly to its shaping by critical reviews.

1 See Donald Fleming and Bernard Bailyn, eds *Law in American History* (Boston 1972); Bernard Schwartz *The Law in America: A History* (New York 1974); Wythe Holt, ed. *Essays in Nineteenth-Century American Legal History* (Westport, CT 1976); Lawrence M. Freidman and Harry N. Scheiber, eds *American Law and the Constitutional Order: Historical Perspectives* (Cambridge, MA 1978); Stephen B. Presser and Jamil S. Zainaldin *Law and American History: Cases and Materials* (St Paul, MI 1980); David H. Flaherty, ed. *Essays in the History of Early American Law* (Chapel Hill, NC 1969).

2 William S. Holdsworth *A History of English Law* (17 vols, London 1903–72);

Alan Harding *A Social History of English Law* (Baltimore, MD 1966); Brian Abel-Smith and Robert Stevens *Lawyers and the Courts: A Sociological Study of the English Legal System, 1750–1965* (London 1967); Robert Stevens *Law and Politics: The House of Lords as a Judicial Body, 1800–1976* (Chapel Hill, NC 1978); Patrick Atiyah *The Rise and Fall of Freedom of Contract* (Oxford 1979); Anthony H. Manchester *A Modern Legal History of England and Wales 1750–1950* (London 1980); Gerry Rubin and David Sugarman, eds *Law and Economy, 1750–1914. Essays in the History of English Law* (London, forthcoming).

3 Robert F. Berkhofer, jr, has written that:

> The first requirement for a behavioral approach to historical analysis is some basic theory or at least a general orientation to, human behavior...
>
> Every step of producing history presumes theoretical models of man and society, which in turn seem to change in terms of the shifting conceptions of man and society occurring in the historian's own society...
>
> What makes theoretical structures or interpretations scientific and objective is whether or not they can be confirmed or disproven by test of evidence, not whether they should exist or not... So long as historians explicitly phrase questions as precisely as possible to test their interpretations against surviving evidence, then they are scientific. (Robert F. Berkhofer, jr *A Behavioral Approach to Historical Analysis* [New York 1969] 27, 24, 26)

4 Reading and understanding Hurst is not easy, nor am I arguing that he is always right. His writings have only begun to receive critical attention. See, for example, Harry N. Scheiber 'At the Borderland of Law and Economic History: The Contributions of Willard Hurst' *American Historical Review* LXXV (1970) 744–56; David H. Flaherty 'An Approach to American History: Willard Hurst as Legal Historian' *American Journal of Legal History* XIV (1970) 222–34 (hereafter AJLH); Mark Tushnet 'Lumber and the Legal Process' *Wisconsin Law Review* 1972, 114–32; Graham Parker 'The Masochism of the Legal Historian' *University of Toronto Law Journal* XXIV (1974) 313–16 (hereafter UTLJ); Robert W. Gordon 'J. Willard Hurst and the Common Law Tradition in American Legal Historiography' *Law and Society Review* x (1975) 44–55. See also 'A Bibliography of Works by and about Willard Hurst' *Law and Society Review* x (1976) 325–33. There is no figure comparable to Hurst writing modern English legal history.

5 J. Willard Hurst 'Themes in United States Legal History' in Wallace Mendelson, ed. *Felix Frankfurter: A Tribute* (New York 1964) 199–200

6 J. Willard Hurst, 'Old and New Dimensions of Research in United States Legal History' AJLH XXIII (1979) 20

7 J. Willard Hurst *The Growth of American Law: The Law Makers* (Boston 1950) v

8 Ibid. 9

9 J. Willard Hurst *Law and the Conditions of Freedom in the Nineteenth Century United States* (Madison, WI 1956) 6. See also the discussion of this book in the essay by R.C.B. Risk in this volume, 118–19.

10 J. Willard Hurst *Law and Economic Growth: The Legal History of the Wisconsin Lumber Industry* (Cambridge, MA 1964) vii. Hurst's language is typically more opaque than my summary.

11 Ibid. 17, 43

12 Ibid. vii-viii

13 Lawrence M. Friedman *Contract Law in America: A Social and Economic Case Study* (Madison WI 1965); Robert S. Hunt *Law and Locomotives: The Impact of the Railroad on Wisconsin Law in the Nineteenth Century* (Madison, WI 1958); Spencer Kimball *Insurance and Public Policy: A Study in the Legal Implementation of Social and Economic Public Policy, Based on Wisconsin Records 1835–1959* (Madison, WI 1960); James A. Lake *Law and Mineral Wealth: The Legal Profile of the Wisconsin Mining Industry* (Madison, WI 1962)

14 R.C.B. Risk 'A Prospectus for Canadian Legal History' *Dalhousie Law Journal* I (1973) 228

15 Ibid. 229

16 R.C.B. Risk 'Nineteenth Century Foundation of the Business Corporation in Ontario' UTLJ XXIII (1973) 270–306; 'The Law about the Market in Nineteenth Century Ontario' UTLJ XXVI (1976) 307–46; 'The Last Golden Age: Property and the Allocation of Losses in Ontario in the Nineteenth Century' UTLJ XXVII (1977) 199–239; 'Law and the Economy in Mid-Nineteenth Century Ontario: A Perspective' UTLJ XXVII (1977) 403–38, and in this volume, 88–131

17 H. Clare Pentland 'The Development of a Capitalistic Labour Market in Canada' *Canadian Journal of Economics and Political Science* XXV (1959) 450–61 (hereafter CJEPS); Pentland *Labour and Capital in Canada, 1650–1860* (Toronto 1981); Gad Horowitz 'Conservatism, Liberalism, and Socialism in Canada: An Interpretation' CJEPS XXXII (1963) 143–71

18 Carl Berger *The Writing of Canadian History: Aspects of English-Canadian Historical Writing 1900–1970* (Toronto 1976) 216. This volume is a valuable introduction to the major historians of Canada discussed in this paragraph.

19 Risk suggests that this traditional neglect was also inspired by the fact that often leading historians were not on intimate intellectual terms with any university-trained laywers, found no lawyers to talk to in many leading universities, and regarded traditional legal history as incomprehensible. (Conversation, R.C.B. Risk, 26 Sept. 1980)

20 Mr Justice Brian Dickson made this comment during a conference on the Comparison of the Role of the Supreme Court in Canada and the United States, which was held under the auspices of the Canada-US Law Institute at the Case Western Reserve Law School, Cleveland, 20 Oct. 1979.

21 Risk 'Law and the Economy' 433; in this volume, 120

22 G. Blaine Baker 'A Short History of Canadian Conflict of Laws: An Essay in Social Planning' (unpublished manuscript 1979)

23 One of the few scholars to advocate the comparative approach to legal historical studies has been Robert Stevens, who received basic training in both English and American law. (Robert Stevens 'Unexpected Avenues in Comparative Anglo-American Legal History' *Tulane Law Review* XLVIII [1964] 1086)

24 Michael S. Hindus *Prison and Plantation: Crime, Justice, and Authority in Massachusetts and South Carolina, 1767–1878* (Chapel Hill, NC 1980) especially the introduction

25 Gordon 'J. Willard Hurst' 11. See also review by Gordon in *Harvard Law Review* XCIV (1981) 903–18.

26 Lawrence M. Friedman *A History of American Law* (New York 1973) 10

27 Mark V. Tushnet 'Perspectives on the Development of American Law: A Critical Review of Friedman's "A History of American Law"' *Wisconsin Law Review* 1977, 83, 84. See also David J. Rothman 'The Promise of American Legal History' *Reviews in American History* II (1974) 16–22.

28 The Horwitz volume has already led to many lengthy critiques by legal historians. See Stephen B. Presser 'Revising the Conservative Tradition: Towards a New American Legal History' *New York University Law Review* LII (1977) 700–25; S.F. Williams 'Transforming American Law: Doubtful Economics Makes Doubtful History' *University of California Los Angeles Law Review* XXV (1978) 1187–1218; R. Randall Bridwell 'Theme v. Reality in American Legal History' *Indiana Law Journal* LIII (1978) 449–96; A.W.B. Simpson 'The Horwitz Thesis and the History of Contracts' *University of Chicago Law Review* XLVI (1979) 533–601; and David Sugarman's review in *British Journal of Law and Society* VII (1980) 297–310.

29 Morton J. Horwitz *The Transformation of American Law 1780–1860* (Cambridge MA 1977) 254

30 Risk 'A Prospectus for Canadian Legal History' 235

31 As late as 1905, for example, the Ontario government spent slightly more than five million dollars a year and had 700 employees. By 1925 the respective figures were 130 million dollars and more than 4000 employees. (F.F. Schindeler *Responsible Government in Ontario* [Toronto 1969] 15, 23). On the other hand, in an impressive Hurstian analysis of natural resource law in nineteenth-century Ontario, H.V. Nelles has emphasized the positive role of the state (H.V. Nelles *The Politics of Development: Forests, Mines and Hydro-Electric Power in Ontario, 1849–1941* [Toronto 1974] chapter 1).

32 John E.C. Brierley 'Quebec's Civil Law Codification: Viewed and Reviewed' *McGill Law Journal* XIV (1968) 521–89

33 Alan Hunt *The Sociological Movement in Law* (London 1978); Edward A. Purcell, jr *The Crisis of Democratic Theory: Scientific Naturalism and the Problem of Value* (Lexington, KY 1973) 74–94, 159–78; William Twining *Karl Llewellyn and the Realist Movement* (London 1973)

34 Robin S. Harris *A History of Higher Education in Canada 1663–1960* (Toronto and Buffalo 1976) 266; see also John Willis *A History of Dalhousie Law School* (Toronto 1979).

35 One main exception would be changes in penal law and procedure beginning in the 1830s. See J.M. Beattie *Attitudes towards Crime and Punishment in Upper Canada, 1830–1850: A Documentary Study* (Toronto 1977).

36 Dale and Lee Gibson *Substantial Justice: Law and Lawyers in Manitoba 1670–1970* (Winnipeg 1972); James Forbes Newman 'Reaction and Change: A Study of the Ontario Bar, 1880–1920' *University of Toronto Faculty Law Review* XXXII (1974) 51–74; Mark M. Orkin 'Professional Autonomy and the Public Interest: A Study of the Law Society of Upper Canada' (unpublished D.Jur. thesis, York University 1971). As in many other areas of Canadian legal history, Mr Justice W.R. Riddell did pioneer work on the history of the Ontario legal profession. (W.R. Riddell *The Legal Profession in Upper Canada in its Early Periods* [Toronto 1916]; *The Bar and Courts of Upper Canada or Ontario* [Toronto 1928]). Perhaps the best Canadian work to date has been André Vachon *Histoire du notariat canadien 1621–1960* (Québec 1962).

37 Risk 'A Prospectus for Canadian Legal History' 236–7

38 Abel-Smith and Stevens *Lawyers and the Courts*

39 Gerald W. Gawalt *The Promise of Power: The Legal Profession in Massachusetts, 1760–1840* (Westport CT 1979); Maxwell Bloomfield *American Lawyers in a Changing Society, 1776–1876* (Cambridge, MA 1976). See also Stephen Botein 'Professional History Reconsidered' AJLH XXI (1977) 60–79, and Morton J. Horwitz 'The Conservative Tradition in the Writing of American Legal History' AJLH XVII (1973) 275–94.

40 See in general Magali Sarfatti Larson *The Rise of Professionalism: A Sociological Analysis* (Berkeley, CA 1977); Burton J. Bledstein *The Culture of Professionalism: The Middle Class and the Development of Higher Education in America* (New York 1976); Thomas L. Haskell *The Emergence of Professional Social Science: The American Social Science Association and the Nineteenth-Century Crisis of Authority* (Urbana, IL 1977)

41 Jerold S. Auerbach *Unequal Justice: Lawyers and Social Change in Modern America* (New York 1976)

42 For a critique of Auerbach with some Canadian content, see the review by Harry Arthurs in UTLJ XXVII (1977) 513–18; another excellent critical review is Richard M. Abrams 'Lawyers Versus the Good Society' *Reviews in American History* IV (1976) 490–6.

43 Stevens *Law and Politics: The House of Lords as a Judicial Body, 1800–1976;* G. Edward White *The American Judicial Tradition: Profiles of Leading American Judges* (New York 1976). On the rise of an activist model of the American judiciary between 1800 and 1900, see Morton Keller *Affairs of State: Public Life in Late Nineteenth Century America* (Cambridge, MA 1977) 358–70.

44 Abel-Smith and Stevens *Lawyers and the Courts* 121; William E. Nelson 'The Impact of the Antislavery Movement upon Styles of Judicial Reasoning in Nineteenth-Century America' *Harvard Law Review* LXXXVII (1974) 513–66; Harry N. Scheiber 'Instrumentalism and Property Rights: A Reconsideration of American Styles of Judicial Reasoning in the Nineteenth Century' *Wisconsin Law Review* 1975, 1–18; Robert N. Cover *Justice Accused: Anti-Slavery and the Judicial Process* (New Haven 1975)

45 Horwitz *Transformation of American Law*, Stevens *Law and Politics* passim

46 Leonard W. Levy *Law of the Commonwealth and Chief Justice Shaw: The Evolution of American Law 1830–1860* (Cambridge, MA 1957); John P. Reid *Chief Justice: The Judicial World of Charles Doe* (Cambridge, MA 1967); see also Reid *An American Judge: Marmaduke Dent of West Virginia* (New York 1968). For a recent effort to write the biography of a late nineteenth-century judge in British Columbia, see David R. Williams *'... The Man for a New Country': Sir Matthew Baillie Begbie* (Sidney, BC 1977). A focus on judges also necessitates detailed studies of the actual workings of lower level courts, a topic generally neglected to date in Anglo-American legal history. See, however, Robert M. Ireland *The County Courts in Antebellum Kentucky* (Lexington, KY 1972); Mary K. Bonsteel Tachau *Federal Courts in the Early Republic: Kentucky 1789–1816* (Princeton, NJ 1978); and Robert A. Silverman *Law and Urban Growth: Civil Litigation in the Boston Trial Courts, 1800– 1900* (Princeton, NJ 1981).

47 Risk 'A Prospectus for Canadian Legal History' 236

48 Bora Laskin *The British Tradition in Canadian Law* (London 1969) 49

49 See especially D. Hay et al., eds *Albion's Fatal Tree: Crime and Society in Eighteenth Century England* (London 1975); J.S. Cockburn, ed. *Crime in England, 1550–1800* (London 1977); J.M. Beattie 'The Pattern of Crime in England, 1600–1800' *Past and Present* 62 (1974) 47–95; E.P. Thompson *Whigs and Hunters: The Origin of the Black Act* (London 1975); John Brewer and John Styles, eds *An Ungovernable People: The English and Their Law in the Seventeenth and Eighteenth Centuries* (London 1980); and V.A.C. Gatrell, Bruce Lenman, and Geoffrey Parker, eds *Crime and the Law: The Social History of Crime in Western Europe since 1500* (London 1980).

50 Leading recent English and American studies with direct relevance for nineteenth-century Canada would include A.P. Donajgrodzki, ed. *Social Control in Nineteenth Century Britain* (London 1977); David Philips *Crime*

and Authority in Victorian England: The Black Country, 1835–1866 (London 1977); Hindus *Prison and Plantation*; Douglas Greenberg *Crime and Law Enforcement in the Colony of New York, 1691–1776* (Ithaca, NY 1976); Eric H. Monkkonen *The Dangerous Class: Crime and Poverty in Columbus, Ohio, 1866–1885* (Cambridge, MA 1975); Roger Lane *Violent Death in the City: Suicide, Accident and Murder in Nineteenth-Century Philadelphia* (Cambridge, MA 1979).

51 See for example Susan E. Houston 'The Impetus to Reform: Urban Crime, Poverty and Ignorance in Ontario 1850–1875' (unpublished doctoral dissertation, University of Toronto 1974); Beattie *Attitudes towards Crime and Punishment in Upper Canada*; D.J. Bercuson and L.A. Knafla, eds *Law and Society in Canada in Historical Perspective*, University of Calgary Studies in History 2 (Calgary 1979); André Lachance *La Justice Criminelle du Roi au Canada au XVIIIe siècle* (Québec 1978); and André Morel 'La réception du droit criminel anglais au Québec (1760–1892)' *Revue Juridique Thémis* XIII (1978) 499–541; and Louis A. Knafla, ed. *Crime and Criminal Justice in Europe and Canada* (Waterloo, Ont. 1981).

52 David J. Rothman *The Discovery of the Asylum: Social Order and Disorder in the New Republic* (Boston 1971); Rothman *Conscience and Convenience: The Asylum and Its Alternatives in Progressive America* (Boston 1980); Michel Foucault *Discipline and Punish: The Birth of the Prison* (translated from the French by Alan Sheridan, New York 1978); Michael Ignatieff *A Just Measure of Pain: The Penitentiary in the Industrial Revolution 1750–1850* (New York 1978); Andrew Scull *Museums of Madness: The Social Organization of Insanity in Nineteenth Century England* (New York 1979)

53 Beattie *Attitudes towards Crime and Punishment in Upper Canada*; also Rainer Baehre 'Origins of the Penitentiary System in Upper Canada' *Ontario History* LXIX (1977) 185–207

54 Samuel Walker *A Critical History of Police Reform: The Emergence of Professionalism* (Lexington, MA 1977). Walker has also written a brief interpretive overview entitled *Popular Justice: A History of American Criminal Justice* (New York 1980).

55 Wilbur R. Miller *Cops and Bobbies: Police Authority in New York and London, 1830–1870* (Chicago 1977). See also Eric H. Monkkonen *Police in Urban America, 1860–1920* (New York 1981).

56 R.C. Macleod *The NWMP and Law Enforcement 1873–1905* (Toronto 1976); Neil Sutherland *Children in English-Canadian Society: Framing the Twentieth Century Consensus* (Toronto 1976). See also Susan E. Houston 'Victorian Origins of Juvenile Delinquency: A Canadian Experience' *History of Education Quarterly* XII (1972) 254–80.

57 Joseph Hawes *Children in Urban Society: Juvenile Delinquency in Nineteenth-*

Century America (New York 1971); Robert S. Mennel *Thorns and Thistles: Juvenile Delinquents in the United States, 1825–1940* (Hanover, NH 1973); Steven L. Schlossman *Love and the American Delinquent: The Theory and Practice of 'Progressive' Juvenile Justice, 1825–1920* (Chicago 1977); Graham Parker 'The Juvenile Court Movement' UTLJ XXVI (1976) 140–72; Parker 'The Juvenile Court Movement: The Illinois Experience' UTLJ XXVI (1976) 253–306; John R. Gillis 'The Evolution of Juvenile Delinquency in England, 1890–1914' *Past and Present* 67 (1975) 96–126

58 I am indebted to Peter Oliver of York University for many of the points developed in this paragraph.

59 Although Upper Canada was settled two generations before Wisconsin, the population of the latter (305,391) was one-third of Ontario's (952,000) by 1850 and almost identical by 1900, when both had populations just over two million. (U.S. Bureau of the Census *Historical Statistics of the United States: Colonial Times to 1957* (Washington, DC 1960) 12–3; and M.C. Urquhart, ed. *Historical Statistics of Canada* (Toronto 1965) 14)

60 Harry N. Scheiber *Ohio Canal Era: A Case Study of Government and the Economy, 1820–1861* (Athens, OH 1969) 355. See also Oscar and Mary Flug Handlin *Commonwealth: A Study of the Role of Government in the American Economy: Massachusetts, 1774–1861* rev. ed. (Cambridge, MA 1969).

61 See Jennifer Nedelsky 'Judicial Conservatism in an Age of Innovation: Comparative Perspectives on Canadian Nuisance Law' in this volume.

62 Sutherland *Children in English-Canadian Society* passim

63 An Act Introducing the English Civil Law into Upper Canada, 32 Geo. III, c. 1 (UC); An Act for the Further Introduction of English Criminal Law into Upper Canada, 40 Geo. III (1800), c. 1. Such statutes are called reception acts.

64 See Gerald M. Craig *Upper Canada: The Formative Years 1784–1841* (Toronto 1963) 9, 26; and L.F.S. Upton *The Loyal Whig: William Smith of New York and Quebec* (Toronto 1969) 173–86

65 J.M.S. Careless, ed. *The Pre-Confederation Premiers: Ontario Government Leaders, 1841–1867* (Toronto 1980) 5

66 Craig *Upper Canada* 30

67 Ibid. 29

68 Ibid. 60–2, 192

69 Ibid. 204, also 218, 233

70 *Dillingham* v *Wilson* (1841), 6 *Upper Canada Queen's Bench Reports* (hereafter UCQB [os]) 86, at 86–7 per Sherwood J

71 Craig *Upper Canada* 93–9, 115–17

72 G.M. Craig 'John Strachan' *Dictionary of Canadian Biography* IX (Toronto 1976) 762 (hereafter DCB); also Craig *Upper Canada* 110, 159, 164

73 Careless, ed. *Pre-Confederation Premiers* 15

74 Canada *Censuses of Canada 1665 to 1871* IV (Ottawa 1876) 140, 171
75 Ibid. 104, 128, 164, and Craig *Upper Canada* 228
76 Hugh Gray *Letters from Canada Written during a Residence There in the Years 1806, 1807, and 1808* (London 1809, reprinted Toronto 1979) 367; also Craig *Upper Canada* 24–5, 43
77 Craig *Upper Canada* 47, also 64
78 Ibid. 89–91, 95, 111
79 Ibid. 110, 112, 160–2, 170, 198–200, 206–7
80 Fred I. Ernst 'American Influence in Upper Canada's Legal Development, 1791–1837: An Interpretation' (unpublished manuscript 1980)
81 *Censuses of Canada 1665 to 1871* IV 136
82 Craig *Upper Canada* 124–44, 232
83 Careless, ed. *Pre-Confederation Premiers* 15, 16
84 *Censuses of Canada 1665 to 1871* IV 136, 166, 258
85 See John Manning Ward *Colonial Self-Government: The British Experience 1759–1865* (Toronto 1976) 23, 43; J.E. Hodgetts *Pioneer Public Service: An Administrative History of the United Canadas, 1841–1867* (Toronto 1955) 64–5, 82–4; and Careless, ed. *Pre-Confederation Premiers* 12
86 Robert E. Saunders 'John Beverley Robinson' DCB IX 678
87 Major General C.W. Robinson, CB *Life of Sir John Beverley Robinson Bart., C.B., D.C.L., Chief Justice of Upper Canada* (Edinburgh and London 1904) 53
88 Ibid. 39–40, also 54
89 Ibid. 54–7, 136–7, 139–42, 182, 189, 196. Such activities continued until his appointment to the bench.
90 Ibid. 57
91 Ibid. 80–6, 102
92 Ibid. 85
93 Ibid. 92–4, 156–60
94 Ibid. 150–1
95 Craig *Upper Canada* 205–6
96 Robinson *Life of Sir John Beverley Robinson* 224; see also 313–15.
97 The importance of John Beverley Robinson is further suggested by the discussions of his career by several authors in this volume. Attention has been drawn to the possibilities of studying Robinson's ex officio role on a commission that sat as a type of equity court on land claims. See H. Pearson Gundy 'The Family Compact at Work: The Second Heir and Devisee Commission of Upper Canada, 1805–41' *Ontario History* LXVI (1974) 129–46.
98 Levy *Law of the Commonwealth and Chief Justice Shaw: The Evolution of American Law 1830–1860*
99 See Robinson *Life of Sir John Beverley Robinson* 326–8, 334, 396, 456, 458, 460, 464.

100 Ibid. 235; see also 322–4.
101 Ibid. 322–3
102 *In the Matter of John Anderson* (1860), 20 UCBQ 124 at 174 per Robinson CJ. I owe this reference to an unpublished essay on Robinson by Maureen Simpson. The Court of Common Pleas subsequently overturned the Queen's Bench ruling. (Robert C. Reinders 'John Anderson' DCB IX 6–7)
103 *Belcher* v *Cook* (1848), 4 UCQB 401 at 422.
104 S.F. Wise 'Upper Canada and the Conservative Tradition' in Ontario Historical Society *Profiles of a Province* (Toronto 1967) 24
105 Risk 'Law and the Economy' 427–8; in this volume, 113–15
106 Ibid. 428; in this volume, 113–15
107 Compare Laskin *The British Tradition in Canadian Law* 90: 'The American vogue for Blackstone does not appear to have been followed in Canada.'
108 See Risk's essay in this volume, 108.
109 John Beverley Robinson, quoted in Terry Cook 'John Beverley Robinson and the Conservative Blueprint for the Upper Canadian Community' *Ontario History* LXIV (1972) 82
110 Robinson *Life of Sir John Beverley Robinson* 329–30
111 See Wise 'Upper Canada and the Conservative Tradition' 30
112 Cook 'John Beverley Robinson' 89
113 Robinson *Life of Sir John Beverley Robinson* 374
114 Ibid. 375. See ibid. 389 for similar flattering reference by an Englishman to the quality of Robinson's judgments.
115 Recent examples of detailed research that will serve as building blocks for Canadian legal history include the following: William N.T. Wylie 'Arbiters of Commerce, Instruments of Power: A Study of the Civil Courts in the Midland District, Upper Canada, 1792–1812' (unpublished PH D thesis Queen's University 1980); John D. Blackwell 'Crime in the London District, 1828–1837: A Case Study of the Effect of the 1833 Reform in Upper Canadian Penal Law' *Queen's Law Journal* VI (1981) 528–67.

2

Hudson's Bay Company Law: Adam Thom and the Institution of Order in Rupert's Land 1839–54

KATHRYN M. BINDON

The formalization of the administration of justice in Rupert's Land was a process characterized by social and commercial conflict. The area had only one settlement, the Red River colony, in which Europeans, Amerindians, and half-breeds or Métis formed the basis of a frontier community closely connected to the fur trade of the Hudson's Bay Company. The Company was legally responsible for all aspects of the administration of the area. As the colony grew, the need for more formal structures became evident to both settlers and Company officials. This common recognition, however, stemmed from very different concerns. The Company required a more regular judicial system for the maintenance and protection of its monopoly over the fur trade. The community, on the other hand, was sensitive to its own internal social needs and saw the institution of a more traditional legal administration as a means of curbing the Company's authority. Thus the benefits of a systematic introduction of law and order were thought to be very different by those who would impose it and those who would obey it.

The conflict inherent in the situation was apparent in the Company's first judicial appointment. Adam Thom, a Lower Canadian journalist and lawyer, became both legal interpreter and judge for the settlement in 1839. As the first Recorder of Rupert's Land, Thom formulated an appropriate code of laws for the community. As a Company employee and judge, however, he exacerbated cultural and social tensions and provoked the francophone majority of the Red River settlement to articulate many criticisms of the Company's administration. While the court records offer substantial proof of Thom's capabilities as Recorder, the reactions of the community to his behaviour and to his application of the law suggest Thom's failure as a judge. Indeed, through Adam Thom the administration of justice was the means whereby the contradictions of the Company's colonial role became manifest. After 1849 the community repeatedly rejected Thom as a suitable official. In this, the settlers were commenting not only upon the Recorder's application of the law, but also upon the inappropriate linking of the pursuit of justice and commercial monopoly, which underlay the legal organization of Rupert's Land under Hudson's Bay Company rule.

Charles II's Royal Charter in 1670 granted the Hudson's Bay Company exclusive control of Rupert's Land. The area was defined by all waters draining into Hudson Bay. Thus the Charter did not apply to the western part of the prairie interior of British North America or the Pacific coast. During the last years of the eighteenth century, the Company's monopoly was challenged by traders from Montreal who penetrated the northwest via the St Lawrence River-Great Lakes route. Competition for control of the unchartered Athabasca District involved passage of the Montreal voyageurs through Rupert's Land. After conflicts resulted, the British government attempted to impose a legal system on the area by the Canada Jurisdiction Act of 1803. This law authorized the courts of Upper and Lower Canada to deal with those persons 'guilty of crimes and offences, within certain parts of North America, adjoining to the said provinces.' The intent was to resolve jurisdictional problems when crimes were committed in areas not covered by formal legal arrangements. However, the act was vague in terms of its relationship to the chartered rights and territories of the Hudson's Bay Company.[1]

The 1803 act was never enforced, even though the possibilities for violence in the northwest increased in 1811 when a Hudson's Bay Company colony was established on the banks of the Red River. This settlement was the creation of Thomas Douglas, Fifth Earl of Selkirk, whose commitment to emigration schemes for the relief of Scots and Irish peasants had been tested previously in Prince Edward Island and Upper Canada. Selkirk was intrigued by the agricultural possibilities of the northwest, notions that partners of the Northwest Company supported during a visit to Montreal in 1804. Astute accumulation of stock enabled Selkirk to take charge of the Hudson's Bay Company's experiment in colonization and to test his theories about the northwest.[2]

The terms of the agreement with the Company vested Selkirk with title to 116,000 square miles of land in order to establish an agricultural settlement. A token rent of ten shillings and the availability of two hundred potential servants were demanded as annual payment. The intention was that the Earl would provide land in his settlement for retired Company traders, an arrangement the Governor and Committee hoped would lessen the attraction of independent trade for retired Company employees. The granting of Hudson's Bay Company commissions of official employment to all administrators of the Red River settlement underlined the connection of Company and colony.

In 1815 the Company published its first code of penal laws. Thomas Vincent, Governor of the Southern Department of Rupert's Land, notified employees 'that all Crimes, Offences or misdemeanours, which are cognizable by the law of England will in future be punished according to the said Laws.' The code applied only to employees of the fur trade, however, and its limited catalogue of offences strictly related to the Company's monopoly of the fur trade. While it did clarify the Company's intention to maintain its legislative and judicial authority over Rupert's Land, the document also illustrated that such powers would only be exercised when required by commercial priorities.[3]

The first years of the Red River settlement were characterized by conflict. The Northwesters recognized the implications of the colony for the fur trade, and the merchant partners in Montreal promoted a rivalry between the colonists and the Métis progeny of the voyageurs and Amerindians. Selkirk's British settlers and the Northwest Company's half-breed sons persisted as elements within the growing community of Red River, but in 1816 they opposed one another in a commercial war between the London company and the Montreal traders that altered the nature of the fur trade in the northwest. The hostility erupted in armed conflict, and the Governor of the Red River settlement, Robert Semple, was killed at the Massacre of Seven Oaks.

The British Parliament noted the violence. An inquiry concluded that the future of both the Amerindians and the fur trade depended upon the peaceful exploitation of the area. This recognition prompted the imperial government in 1821 to restate the principles embodied in the Jurisdiction Act of 1803. In 'An Act for Regulating the Fur Trade, and Establishing a Criminal and Civil Jurisdiction within Certain Parts of North America,' the original legislation was applied to the territories controlled by the Hudson's Bay Company. However, this law also recognized the chartered rights of the Company in Rupert's Land and thus remained vague. Edward Ellice, one of the Northwest partners and a British parliamentarian, noted that 'there is nothing imperative in the Act of Parliament requiring the Company to send for adjudication anything within their own territories. I take all the provisions of the Act to relate to territories beyond their own boundaries.'[4]

Imperial politicians at this time were concerned that Amerindians be protected from abuses resulting from European commercial conflicts. Thus the law declared that the king could grant exclusive trading rights to the area surrounding Rupert's Land, a provision intended to inhibit the confrontation that had characterized the fur trade to date. On 4 December 1821 the crown awarded a trading monopoly to an amalgamated Hudson's Bay Company and Northwest Company.[5] A Deed Poll, also dated 1821, described the details of the merger. The licence to trade covered a twenty-one-year period, the grantees undertaking to improve the conditions of Indians involved in their commerce. Similarly, the monopoly was contingent upon the prompt punishment of all criminal offences committed by employees of the Company. The precise responsibility for the administration of justice, however, remained ambiguous, a lack of clarity that enabled the Company to reassert its authority in this area.

The idea of Canadian courts acting as the decisive bodies for the northwest was attractive to neither the London nor the Montreal interests. Both had experienced such cases. Court appearances in the Canadas had produced bizarre and confusing sequences of events that had little to do with the legal requirements of the fur trade. Moreover, the transportation of parties and witnesses to York and Montreal was difficult and expensive.[6] Thus the Governor and Committee requested clarification of the imperial government's intentions. Upon being advised that no action was imminent, the Hudson's Bay Company in 1822 passed a series of regulations in which the Governors of the Northern and Southern Departments of Rupert's Land and the Governor of Assiniboia, as the area originally ceded to Lord Selkirk was now called, were deemed competent to administer justice along with their councillors. A sheriff was appointed for each region. Provision was made 'that the Governors in their respective Districts may enroll and arm such numbers of the Company's servants and other male inhabitants ... as they may from time to time deem expedient...' Although capital cases were not anticipated, any such offences would be tried in Upper Canada. The Governor and Council with a jury would try all other criminal cases. However, as one Company official noted, the approach was relaxed: 'If substantial justice is done and the punishments moderate the forms will not so much signify. Everything should be done in open court and juries sworn on proper occasions but I believe it is not necessary that the jury should be 12 if so many unexceptionable persons from the thinness of the population cannot be brought together.'[7] Similarly, punishment was to be 'moderate and reasonable. ... Perhaps solitary imprisonment for short Periods will be the most proper and effectual. In civil or Pecuniary disputes it will be best to endeavour to induce the parties to settle it by arbitration.'[8]

These arrangements were presented to the imperial authorities at once. Lord Bathurst, Colonial Secretary, advised the Governor and Committee that 'until His Majesty shall constitute Courts and Justices ... the Resolutions of the 29th inst. appear well calculated to preserve the peace and good Government of that part of North America under the Jurisdiction of the Hudson's Bay Company.'[9] Bathurst's assessment of the reorganization was apt, because the new system proved adequate for almost fifteen years.

The extreme isolation of the Red River settlement facilitated the Company's task of administering justice and protecting its monopoly. The merger of the rivals became increasingly one-sided as the Hudson Bay approach to the northwest supplanted the Montreal route. The colonists, now dependent upon the Company for all goods and communications, honoured the monopoly. As well, the decade after 1821 was one of peace. The Métis were employed in the restructured fur trade and gradually integrated into the routine of the Red River settlement. Their abilities in the buffalo hunt guaranteed the Company's traders a supply of pemmican; their settlement in Assiniboia gave the Company a sense of control over their activities. The community grew both in numbers and character during the period. Between 1831 and 1835, for example, the population increased from 2422 to 3679 and the number of acres of cultivated land from 2152 to 3405.[10] Moreover, the colony became increasingly francophone as both Métis and former Canadien traders with their native wives made Red River their base in the northwest.

Growth in the settlement was reflected in the emergence of disputes that were beyond the capacity of the rudimentary system of justice established in 1822. George Simpson, by 1835 the senior of the two Governors of Rupert's Land, proclaimed a new administrative approach in conjunction with the reconveyance to the Company by Selkirk's heirs of the land originally granted for settlement. 'It becomes necessary,' he advised the Council of Assiniboia on 12 February 1835, 'to put the administration of Justice on a more firm and regular footing than heretofore, and that immediate steps ought to be taken to guard against dangers from abroad or difficulties at home, for the maintenance of good order and tranquillity, and for the security and protection of lives and property.'[11] The foreign threat was not to the colonists but to the Company's monopoly of the fur trade. American competition prompted the formulation of several laws intended to facilitate protection of the Company's monopoly through regularization of the internal affairs of the Red River colony. Assiniboia was divided into four districts, in each of which a magistrate and any two constables could hear and decide 'cases of petty offence, and of debts under 40' shillings. 'Cases of a more serious nature, cases of debt exceeding 40/, and all appeal cases from the decision of the Justices of the Peace' were to be referred to the Governor and Council, who would sit as a General Quarterly Court.[12] A militia-like police force of sixty men, called the Volunteer Corps, was raised. The costs of the enlarged judicial network and the permanent security force were to be met by a customs duty of four per cent imposed on all goods entering the settlement. Finally, the Council of Assiniboia was enlarged to include the Roman Catholic Bishop of Juliopolis, Monseigneur Provencher, and the Métis leader Cuthbert Grant.[13]

The innovations of 1835 were altered slightly in 1837. Simpson noted to Governor J.H. Pelly of the London office that 'the time has come when it is no longer safe to trust the peace of the settlement solely to the good will of its inhabitants. I, therefore, consider it highly necessary to the security of lives and property that a court of justice, for the trial of civil and criminal cases, with an efficient police to support the civil power should be established.' According to a dispatch from the Governor and Committee, Assiniboia was again divided, this time into three districts. In each, two magistrates were appointed, any three magistrates being deemed to constitute a court 'to hear and decide all cases of petty offence and of debts not exceeding £5.' Again, all other cases would be heard by a General Quarterly Court presided over by 'the Governor or the Hudson's Bay Company's principal representative.'[14]

The period of reorganization was complicated by Simpson's decision to apply for renewal of the Company's trading licence in 1838 rather than 1842. The influential Montreal merchant, George Moffatt, former supporter of the Northwest Company and member of the Legislative Council of Lower Canada, had intimated to Simpson in 1835 that he intended to press for an end to the Hudson's Bay Company's chartered rights in British North America. The Company responded with an early application for renewal supported by detailed descriptions of their commitment to the welfare of the Amerindians and the promotion of colonization in the northwest. The days of conflict were recalled in discussions that reminded London politicians of the impact of rivalry in the fur trade on native peoples. The positive effect of the monopoly was evident, they argued, in the peace of the years 1822–38. The reported growth of the settlement and of its religious and educational institutions suggested that the Company's commitment to the area was more than just commercial. Apart from such persuasive arguments, however, its own recognition that it had no intention of assuming responsibility for the area prompted the British government to renew the licence for another twenty-one-year period, with the addition of a clause specifically requiring the Company to promote settlement.

The administrative reorganization of 1837 was not fully completed until 1839. While the Company had substantially expanded the mechanisms whereby justice was available to, and understood by, the growing community in 1837, the Governor and Committee refined and restated these changes in final form in 1839. George Simpson was named Governor-in-Chief of Rupert's Land. The Governor of Assiniboia, at that time Chief Factor Duncan Finlayson, was supported by an enlarged Council. The district 'Courts of Summary Jurisdiction' were still to 'pronounce final judgement in all civil cases where the debt or damages claimed may not exceed five pounds, and in all trespasses and misdemeanours, which by the Rules and Regulations of the District of Assiniboia ... may be punished by a fine not exceeding ... five pounds.' Cases of 'doubt or difficulty' were still to be referred to the 'supreme tribunal of the Colony,' the Quarterly Court of Assiniboia, which was retitled the 'Court of the Governor and Council of Assiniboia.' A series of regulations were read into the minutes of the meeting in concert with the Company's instruction that written records be kept in an orderly fashion. Trial by jury in the 'Supreme Court' was confirmed in a more traditional way than in 1822, with all landholders qualifying for such duty. Finally, a specifically judicial official, a Recorder of Rupert's Land, was appointed to provide legal advice as well as professional participation in the Court of the Governor and Council.[15] These changes all reflected official recognition of the altered nature of the community as well as a significant formalization of the judicial process of the colony.

Consistent with the legal experience of the settlement and Simpson's sense of the low level of crime in the community, the expectation was that the Recorder would play a relatively low profile role in Red River. The Governor and Committee or the Governor-in-Chief anticipated no contentious encounters. The use of the title 'Recorder' rather than 'Judge' reflected these feelings as well as the necessities imposed on legal organization by the nature of both the community and the Company's chartered powers. It also suggested the variety of legal functions the appointee was expected to fulfil. In Britain, for example, a Recorder was the official responsible for interpretation, advice, and judgment in a number of mayors' courts dealing with a variety of criminal and civil offences. In the colonial context the Recorder's position was even more comprehensive. New York's eighteenth-century Court of Common Pleas, essentially similar to a mayor's court, witnessed the mayor, aldermen, and Recorder hearing cases of diverse origin. The Recorder's duties in this instance were enhanced by his legal training, which set him apart from his fellow court officers. Frequently the Recorder was the only member of the court with any legal background. He thus acted not only as legal advisor, but also as formulator of court rules, general counsel, and author of ordinances.[16]

The Hudson's Bay Company envisioned a similarly varied and comprehensive role for the Recorder of Rupert's Land. While the settlement at Red River was large enough to warrant a more systematic administrative framework, it was still a frontier community in which the imposition of a more rigid judicial structure would have been inappropriate. Thus a court of record held by the Governor and Council was perceived as the most effective way of establishing a system of justice reflecting the particular needs of the community. Moreover, considerable flexibility was required, since the Company's motives in the appointment focused on their need for an advisor who would be willing to argue the legalities of their trade monopoly to the growing number of settlers taking part in a fur trade with their American rivals. Thus the Company's authority 'to make, ordain and constitute such and so many reasonable laws, constitutions, orders and ordinances as ... shall seem necessary and convenient for the good government of the said Company, and of all governors of colonies' was given its most concrete expression in the appointment of a Recorder.[17]

For the Governor and Committee of the Hudson's Bay Company the formalization of a system which united legislative and judicial functions in a body composed almost entirely of Company men was reasonable, since there was little crime in the area that was not related to the trade monopoly. Indeed, there had been only one criminal case prosecuted during the period 1822–39; Company employees were 'respectable men' who required no 'particular discipline.' Similarly, while the Company's obligation to the Amerindian population included protection from the rum trade, it did not require legal interference in tribal affairs. The Company's role was necessarily limited in their regard. As Simpson noted, 'we seldom get hold of them for the purpose of trial, and they are usually punished by their own tribe.'[18] The only remaining group that could provoke the Company to act was the Red River community. Thus the Recorder's rationalization of justice was intended to impress the colonists with the legality of the Hudson's Bay Company's trade monopoly. Company officials were confident that the innovation would be 'productive of salutary advantages to all classes of the rising community.'[19]

ADAM THOM, FIRST RECORDER OF RUPERT'S LAND

Since the Recorder would primarily serve the Red River settlement, the appointment of Adam Thom was intriguing. Born in Scotland and educated at King's College, Aberdeen, he taught school in Britain before emigrating to Montreal in the early 1830s, where he began a career as a publisher and journalist with *The Settler*. The journal, which was committed to informing immigrants of conditions in Lower Canada, lasted only during 1833. Thom continued his career as editor of *The Montreal Herald*, an English newspaper that closely reflected the opinions of the merchant community. Under Thom's editorship *The Herald* became the purveyor of the most extreme elements of British colonial conservatism and francophobia in the province.

Apart from general editorial comment, Thom's views on Lower Canadian affairs appeared in most striking fashion in three series of letters. 'Remarks on the Petition of the Convention and on the Petition of the Constitutionalists by Anti-Bureaucrat' began to appear in April 1835. The content criticized the Ninety-Two Resolutions presented to the imperial parliament by the Parti Patriote in 1834. In July 1835 'On the Canada Committee of 1828' was published. These letters condemned the policy of 'conciliation' pursued in Lower Canada by the imperial government. The final and most notorious material, the 'Anti-Gallic Letters Addressed to His Excellency The Earl of Gosford,' was published under the pseudonym Camillus during 1835 and 1836. The letters focused more incisively upon the 'errors' of the colonial administration, depicting the subjugation of the rights of the British minority in Lower Canada through an ignorance that supported a 'traitorous' French-Canadian majority. Thom attacked French Canadians as anti-commercial and thus anti-progressive, illiterate, and unreliable. Even more provocative than their cultural disabilities was French-Canadian control of the elected legislative assembly through which they 'claimed and obtained power as BRITISH

Adam Thom (1802–90), first Recorder of Rupert's Land

SUBJECTS to exercise it as FRENCH ENEMIES.'[20] According to Thom, the political vulnerability of the British population was compounded by the co-operation of the colonial governor with the Canadiens. 'The narrow spirit of patriotism,' Thom ranted, 'has given place to the diffusive principle of philanthropy. England still expects every son to do his duty; but – oh the march of liberal principles! – she no longer expects her sons to do that duty to herself – she has taken her enemies under her protection.'[21]

Thom's self-appointed task was to inform the British parliament and public of the implications of continued adherence to wrong-headed and dangerously liberal policies. The progress of politics towards open conflict in 1837 reinforced his attitudes. Increasingly anti-French arguments were complemented by Thom's sense that there was a growing need to protect the British community from the imperial government. 'What has France done for Great Britain,' he asked, 'that the latter should at great expense of blood and treasure rear up a French empire in North America, instead of peopling the vacant territory with her own children?'[22] Indeed, the transformation of the British Lower Canadians from loyal subjects to potential revolutionaries was inevitable in Thom's construct.[23] His next and most extreme move was to help to raise an armed group of Montrealers called the Doric Club to maintain the rights of the 'Constitutionalists,' as the British termed themselves.

Apart from his promotion of commercial and political progress, an unreserved antipathy towards French Canadians was the most fundamental and persistent theme in Thom's writings. The first premise of his hostility, the historic cultural inferiority of France to Britain, was supplemented by his experiences in Lower Canada. Thom was convinced that there could be no loyalty from the Canadiens, because the struggle in Lower Canada reflected 'not politics but nationality, not opinion but origin, not principle but blood.'[24] His career as a journalist earned for Thom the title 'un ennemi plus ouvert et plus acharné' of the Canadiens.[25]

In light of his public career in Lower Canada, it is difficult to comprehend the reasoning of the Governor and Committee of the Hudson's Bay Company in their appointment of Adam Thom as legal interpreter and arbiter for the substantially francophone and Catholic community of Red River. However, Thom studied law with James Charles Grant, KC, and was admitted to the Bar of Lower Canada in 1837. While he had not practised extensively, he had done some legal work for George Simpson. A letter from Simpson in 1837 thanked Thom for his services, complimented him on his ability, and enclosed £10 as evidence of gratitude. Thom must also have been recommended to the Governor's notice by retired Company men resident in Montreal, who were impressed with his campaign on behalf of the British party.[26] Moreover, Thom's relationship with a number of influential Montrealers, including George Moffatt and Peter McGill, who were fellow members of the Constitutional Association and financial supporters of his journalism, must also have brought him to Simpson's attention. While no direct evidence exists of the relationship of these parties, the English community of Montreal was a small, intimate group. Simpson's experience with Moffatt's threat to the Company's monopoly might have suggested that the employment of one of the group's spokesmen would obviate future attacks. Similarly, Thom's role as critic of the colonial government had involved him in a spirited defence of the appointment to the bench in 1835 of Samuel Gale, formerly Lord Selkirk's lawyer.[27] Gale's close legal relationship with men involved in the northwest could have brought Thom's writings on the matter to Simpson's attention during one of the winters the Governor spent in Lachine, near Montreal. Finally, Thom's frequent correspondence with Edward Ellice suggests that his candidacy enjoyed some support in London as well as in Montreal.

It is clear that Simpson thought of Adam Thom as soon as the post of Recorder was created. The Governor and Committee were considering a London employee, but Simpson urged them to offer the job to someone familiar with the Canadian judicial system.[28] This had little relevance to the northwest, since the legal system intended for the territory was in no way similar to that of Lower Canada, where Thom had practised for so short a time. Yet by January 1838 a private and confidential letter was sent offering Thom the appointment and outlining the functions and remuneration of the position. Simpson regarded Thom's 'character and abilities' as admirably suited to the task and welcomed his acceptance of the post: 'From all I have seen and heard of you I feel assured you will in every respect do honour to my recommendation of you to the Governor and Committee, who from my report of you, feel that they have been exceedingly fortunate in the appointment they have made.'[29]

Some opposition to the appointment surfaced in April 1838 when an unidentified Lower Canadian warned one of the Hudson's Bay Company officials that should Thom become unhappy in his job, or should a 'misunderstanding' arise between the Recorder and the Company, the judge 'might possibly make some attack upon the Company which would be troublesome and inconvenient to the Governor and Committee.' This caution did not arise from concern over Thom's cultural prejudices, but centred upon his ability to support without complaint policies with which he disagreed. Simpson conveyed the content of the objections to Thom and asked for assurances that nothing relating to the country or the Company would be published without prior permission from the Governor and Committee. At the same time the Governor assured the London Committee that while there was no reason to anticipate any misunderstandings, Thom was a man of honour who would not turn against his employers under any circumstances.[30]

As relieved as the Company may have been by Thom's expressions of loyalty, it was Lord Durham's confidence that was finally convincing. Durham, who should have carefully weighed Thom's abilities against the disadvantages of having a renowned francophobe on his staff, appointed the former journalist Assistant Commissioner of Municipal Affairs for Lower Canada in 1838. The Governor and Committee welcomed the exhibition of such uncritical confidence with enthusiasm. As Simpson wrote: 'I can assure you it affords both the Governor & Committee and myself very great pleasure to learn that you are rendering your aid to Lord Durham in his very arduous duties; and that you are thereby securing to yourself the patronage of that distinguished Nobleman whose energy, decision of character & transcendant abilities we all so much admire.'[31] The justifiably extreme reaction of French Canadians to Thom's appointment to Durham's staff had no effect on Simpson's sense of Thom's acceptability as Recorder.The only indication that the Governor was aware of the cultural matrix into which Thom was being thrust occurred when Simpson advised his appointee that fluency in French was required for the job. 'In saying that I should have much pleasure in recommending you,' wrote Simpson during their first correspondence, 'I presume you are qualified to express yourself with perfect facility in the French Language of the Country ... without which you would not be adapted for the situation.'[32] Durham's signal trust in Thom's ability and merit reinforced Simpson's personal evaluation. The Governor and Committee were satisfied that they were dealing with a responsible officer of the Governor General of British North America, not an unknown Lower Canadian lawyer whose intense feelings about French Canadians might hamper the effective administration of justice in the Red River settlement.

Thom was appointed Recorder of Rupert's Land and Councillor of both Rupert's Land and Assiniboia on 30 June 1839. His first concern was to evaluate the legality of the existing legal machinery. An investigation commenced to examine the competency of 'the general council as constituted under the deed poll [the merger document of 1821], to sit in judgment on any question, to which the Hudson's Bay Company might, directly or indirectly, be a party.' The question was whether a Council of interested parties, that is chief factors, could sit in judgment on questions that involved their employer. Thom studied the documents over a period of almost two years and concluded that the Company's authority in the legislative, judicial, and commercial spheres was supreme. The need to consider the possibility of conflict of interest in judicial proceedings was thereby dismissed. 'In no degree,' wrote Thom to Simpson, 'does the deed-poll prevent the Honorable Company in its sovereign capacity from constituting according to its will and pleasure a Council of Rupert's Land, whether executive or legislative or judicial ... The closing section of the deed-poll reserves to the Honorable Company the absolute control of the whole matter.'[33] Such a finding extended to the rights of the Company in the Council of Assiniboia as well. Thom's first legal investigation thus fixed in his mind the inviolability of the Company's rights in every element of the community's life, a point that would characterize his judicial decisions during his career as Recorder.

Thom was convinced that his presence in the community was reflective of the Company's generosity and its sense of social responsibility. 'The systematic establishment of trial by jury and the practical introduction of fixed and invariable rules of decision,' he wrote in 1840, were already having an effect on the community's morale and standards.[34] The Recorder was committed to enunciating rules and setting precedents that would promote and maintain this peaceful progress. To this end he proposed to the Governor and Committee that he design a code of laws specifically suited to the Red River settlement. While noting that it would be easier for him to introduce the current laws of England into the settlement, Thom offered some 'weighty objections' to such a move. The laws would have to be modified or risk being overly complex and frequently inapplicable. On the other hand, Thom's proposed code would, 'if I could realize my own conceptions ... blend justice with mercy, temper law with equity and reconcile the peculiar circumstances of Rupert's Land with the fundamental principles of the Laws of England.'[35]

The Governor and Committee quickly took up the proposal, although the issue of what would prove acceptable within the community prompted some internal debate at Red River. Thom's response to all criticisms was that a revision was immediately necessary and a part of his official duties:

> Nothing can be more vague than the criminal law of England, as it exists, whether in theory or in practice, among us. I take my version of it from 1670 in theory; but

in practice reason and equity compel me sometimes to admit modern ameliorations ... In theory we all agree that the criminal law of England is, in many respects, inapplicable to the condition of Red River; but in practice one may wish to strike out what another may wish to retain and *vice versa*. This seems to be the reign of discretion to an indiscreet degree.

A draft code was ready by July 1840, and Thom reported the generally positive responses of Governor Duncan Finlayson and various local magistrates. These readers, he wrote to Simpson, 'after a good deal of explanatory conversation on minor points ... unanimously concurred in all my views.'[36]

The draft was not circulated to either Cuthbert Grant of the Métis community or Bishop Provencher. The only dissenting comment was from Sheriff Alexander Ross, who objected that law 'should never be changed save for weighty reasons. The law, as it stood, worked well, and what works well should be let alone.' In October 1840 copies of the proposed 'Penal and Temporary Civil Code' were forwarded to the Governor and Committee in London. Their authorization was necessary before the codes could be declared law, but, as Thom carefully noted, they were under no obligation 'in point of law' to refer any aspect of the proposed system to the imperial parliament for approval. However, he suggested that the Company might consider doing so as a courtesy, 'inasmuch as the licensed and temporary privileges are more vulnerable, than the chartered and perpetual rights' they enjoyed.[37] The Company chose not to refer the documents and approved the Recorder's recommendations without alteration.

Part of Thom's argument in favour of a more formal enunciation of a system of laws had been based upon an analysis of the state of the society he had been appointed to serve. Consistent with Simpson's sense of the need for a more formal judicial administration in 1835, Thom averred in 1840 that it was time for a necessary recognition of the role of law in its more traditional aspect. Thus he argued that there was some urgency for the introduction of his legal revisions:

It is only by commanding the respect of the people, that law can practically exist in Red River; and such respect is not more inconsistent with boldness in doing what is believed to be unreasonable and wrong, than with timidity in doing what is admitted to be reasonable and right. In so simple and natural a state of society, there can be no temptation to frame such laws, as may be mischievous or even doubtful; and to hesitate either to make or to enforce any obviously beneficial regulation from an undefined dread of factious opposition is to abdicate respectively legislative authority or judicial functions.[38]

The Charter was the law of the land, and boldness was demanded if the law was to be upheld.

The combined code was short and straightforward. One of the most notable innovations of Thom's compilation of regulations was what John Bunn, MD, one of the Councillors, termed the 'wiping away the technical disabilities to the giving of testimony.'[39] By this provision, both parties were admitted as witnesses in all cases. Thom's argument for this alteration of traditional rules of testimony centred on 'every juror's knowledge of every suitor's general character':

> By the minute provision of the text, I have tried as far as possible, to obviate anticipated evils. For instance, by examining parties and their consorts first, I have advisedly run counter to the doctrine of admitting certain persons only as necessary witnesses, because such doctrine administers the strongest 'temptation to perjury' to those who are presumed to be the least able to withstand 'any temptation': interested witnesses ought to be the last to know that they have the case at their mercy. But the prevalence of such a doctrine, however unwise may be its application, is an argument in our favor, for, in our primitive state of society, parties are peculiarly likely to be necessary witnesses.[40]

Topics regulated in the Civil Code included pigs, stallions, hay cutting, roads and bridges, fences and 'horse-taking.' The Volunteer Corps police system of 1835 was maintained, as was the four per cent tariff to defray the costs of administration. The rights and obligations of both magistrates and general courts were set out, while provision was made for the protection of property in cases of intestate death.[41] Regarding the Penal Code, Thom pointed out in his annotated draft that he intended to introduce the law of England as of 1 November 1838 with 'provisions [intended] to mitigate the criminal law of England with respect to such offences as are most likely to be committed in Rupert's Land, inasmuch as the penal code of a country, which crowds into unusual and perpetual collision the extremes of wealth and poverty and all the moral incidents of such extremes, must be too severe for the scanty and sparse population of a rudely plentiful region.'[42] The Recorder therefore abolished the distinction between felonies and misdemeanours. Classification of 'substantial' or primary and 'incidental' or secondary crimes was followed by a list of those who could not be tried for criminal offences, such as wives under husbands' influence, children under seven, and idiots. The Penal Code concluded with details of punishments for the offences of bribery, tampering with witnesses, and perjury.[43]

Both codes represented an ambitious and able attempt to create an appropriately modified, traditionally based, statement of law for the frontier community of Red River. 'To form a complete system of jurisprudence,' Thom had noted in the process, 'law and equity, which have grown up in England as supplements of each other, must coexist among us, either to be blended together in one court or to be administered by distinct tribunals.'[44] Thom's intention as reflected in the codes was that both levels of hearing should combine both elements of jurisprudence. The general opinion of local Councillors and London officials was that the Recorder had been very successful. As John Bunn wrote: 'I diffidently, though sincerely, applaud the tone of feeling displayed in the mode of adapting to our circumstances the English system of Jurisprudence and I entertain no doubt but that the ends of justice will be fully met in the practical application of your labours.'[45]

The lack of criticism from the community during the first few years the codes were in effect suggests that this aspect of the formalization of the legal system was generally accepted. The Recorder himself viewed the codes as only part of a process. This 'brief and humble attempt,' he wrote, was 'an anchor in a sea of troubles and uncertainties. Meanwhile, its principles might be tested by experience and expanded into something like a complete system by more minute adaptations of the Law of England to the peculiar condition of Rupert's Land.'[46]

Refinement of the codes began to appear in 1845 when a Commission of Three to examine Parties according to the Principles of Equity was formed. Thom's earlier argument that 'the best evidence is commonly to be found in the breasts of the parties themselves' was still accepted, but the mechanism for previewing testimony was altered. The Council of Assiniboia felt that Thom should be joined in this task by Alexander Ross, sheriff and magistrate, and John Bunn. Three men, rather than the Recorder alone, would present the jury with the findings of interviews with interested parties. Other innovations included an alteration in the collection of customs duties. The collector would receive a percentage of all duties, a technique that was intended to foster a rigorous approach to the job. Similarly, any who refused to pay the duty would be tried by the Quarterly Court. Such commercial offences were related to the chartered privileges of the Hudson's Bay Company and were to be dealt with in future by the supreme arm of the judicial authority. Fines for trading liquor with Indians were increased, while the native peoples were placed under an obligation to press charges against those who supplied them with alcohol. The evidence of an Amerindian would be accepted 'provided, however, that his unsupported testimony shall not be conclusive against any but convicted or reputed offenders.'[47]

The final revision of the codes under Thom's supervision occurred in 1851. Thom, Bunn, and the Reverend Louis LaFlèche prepared a report on the state of the law in Rupert's Land which was presented to the Council of Assiniboia in November. The committee discarded regulations that had not been applied during the previous decade, an attempt at brevity that was complemented by a simplification of the language of the document.[48] The regulations presented in 1851 retained the basic elements of the codes of 1841. Indeed, Thom's original compilation was a very durable document. A legal revision in 1862 produced another code for Red River which drew upon both the substance and format of Thom's earlier work.[49] Thus the achievement of the first Recorder in the important sphere of enunciation of an appropriate legal construct for the settlement seemed satisfactory to both Company and community.

ADAM THOM, COMPANY JUDGE

Notwithstanding his success in compiling a legal system for the Red River settlement, Thom's tenure as Recorder provoked intense criticism and dissent. Ironically much of this developed in response to the Recorder's interpretation and application of the laws contained in his own codes. His objectivity as a formulator of ordinances was clouded by his position as a salaried employee of the Hudson's Bay Company. The conflict between the needs of the Company and those of the community were dramatically reflected in the activities of Thom in his role as judge and legal advisor of the colony.

Sheriff Alexander Ross was one of Thom's first critics. In his history of the settlement, written in 1856, Ross characterized the appointment of a Recorder as having interrupted the flexible approach to justice which had been sufficient prior to 1839.[50] Ross's criticism, however, was less a reflection of hostility towards the regularization of the administration of justice than the result of persistent problems he experienced with Thom. As the Recorder facetiously reported to Simpson in 1840, Ross 'having predicted terrible results from the importation of a lawyer, was sagacious enough to find verification of his prediction in this case of murder at Joe Bird's and in the death by fire of Monkman's daughter and her children in the plains.' Thom was not affected by such hostility and remarked that 'in candour he [Ross] ought to have given me credit for the last year's abundant crop, particularly as, before my appearance, the grub had done much mischief and was threatening more.' Such criticisms were offset in his mind by the Governor and Committee's praise of their Recorder's 'high legal ... attainments and industrious habits.'[51]

By 1842, however, even the London officials were expressing caution in their instructions to the Recorder. On one occasion the Governor and Committee ordered Thom 'to execute justice ... taking care to temper [it] with mercy and not to sentence any one to such a harsh judgement as may be called in question but rather to subject the guilty persons to pains and penalties which cannot be censured.'[52] The Company's notion of the ideal administration of justice was still one that avoided confrontation and maintained a peaceful public image.

What prompted this early caution is not evident, but that the Company had reason to doubt Thom's capacity for mercy again became apparent in 1845. A Saulteau Indian was found guilty of murder by the Quarterly Court and sentenced to death by hanging. The event was the result of a vendetta, not unprecedented among Amerindians of the northwest, which was considered to be beyond the jurisdiction of the Company. The aboriginal defence centred on the opinion, held by Crees, Assiniboines, and Chippewas, as well as Saulteaux, that native peoples were not subject to the Company's judicial authority. Indeed, the only treaty ever concluded in the area had authorized Selkirk to establish his colony but had not implied Amerindian acceptance of the chartered rights of the Company. The absence of any document prompted Thom to interpret the rights of the Company as applying to all inhabitants of Rupert's Land. This case, characterized by irregularities, was used to establish the precedent. In spite of confusion as to whether the right Indian was in custody and in the absence of any counsel, a jury tried the Saulteau. Thom's charge insisted upon severe punishment: 'They would rather have sentenced him to be shot,' wrote Letitia Hargrave, 'but ... that would not be law, & Mr. Thom will sanction no departure from the strict letter of it.' The sentence was carried out even though the Indians in turn threatened to hang Recorder Thom.

This case not only marked a severe change in the leniency that had marked Company-Amerindian relations, it was also in contravention of an agreement sanctioned by the imperial government whereby the jurisdiction of Thom's court was deemed not to extend to capital cases. The Company had posted a bond of £5000 as guarantee of its intention to send major criminal cases for trial to the Canadas, an arrangement that was understood 'perfectly well' in the settlement.[53] Thom's justification of his actions rested on the difficulties involved in transporting cases. 'Every denizen of this vast wilderness of a world,' he wrote, 'has a personal interest in releasing every part of the same from a jurisdiction so absurdly and inconveniently remote as to inflict inevitably on the witnesses more grievous punishment than what the criminal himself may deserve.' The long and costly trip to the Canadas was unnecessary when there was a judge sensitive to the needs of the area established at Red River. While he argued that the change was necessary in the name of 'justice and humanity,' Thom's alteration of the established system of criminal justice struck the community as arbitrary and excessive.[54]

Thom's relationship with the community continued to deteriorate during the 1840s. As a Company employee, Thom was increasingly mistrusted as a judge. The colonists viewed his salaried position as being essentially contradictory to the intent of the legal reforms.[55] This was not an unusual complaint. Accusations of conflict of interest were also levelled against the Recorder of Vancouver, who was 'the brother-in-law of the Governor (who is also a paid servant), and paid by the Hudson's Bay Company, and therefore many cases that come under his notice must clash with the interests of individuals.'[56] The nature of the Company's chartered rights in Rupert's Land compounded the problem. In Assiniboia the legality of the monopoly prompted the Recorder to consistently place the interests of his employers before those of the colonists. Moreover, the nature of the community in Red River evoked in Thom a paternalism that his francophobia underlined. He insisted upon explaining his ideas in tiresome detail, using 'short clauses' and simple language so that the Métis could understand, but he refused to use French in his courtroom.[57]

Thom did not respond to criticisms from the community. He argued that the reformed legal system, which included his own appointment, had 'place[d] ... the administration of justice above the very suspicion of partiality.' Moreover, his opinion of the basic inferiority of the French as a race extended to and was reinforced by the Métis. Thom's notion of place and duty was thus substantiated, allowing him a sense of security in his administration of the colony that underpinned his paternalistic application of the law. He was not concerned with correcting the fundamental contradiction that characterized the judicial administration of which he was a part. The fact that the legal rights enjoyed by the settlers flowed from and supported a commercial entity that was concerned primarily with maintaining a trade monopoly did not mar the veneer of the Recorder's objectivity. As he noted condescendingly in his charge to the grand jury in 1845, 'it is through the ... free gift of the Honorable Company, that you enjoy the only true freedom, the privilege of being governed not by the wavering wills of living men, but by the inflexible impartiality of general rules written in the blood and sweat of the wise and good among your fathers.'[58] All questions of right and wrong and decisions on the application of law were bound by the complex definition of the various abilities and intentions of the Company.

The dangers and drawbacks of such a system became increasingly evident to the settlers in Red River. Early in the decade Thom, whose original codes had suggested a controlled application of justice appropriate to the state of society in the northwest, began to investigate the fine points of the Charter of 1670. His intention was to formulate arguments that would impress upon the settlement the inviolability of the Company's legislative ability, thereby reinforcing his own authority in the colony. A survey of the numerous occasions on which the Charter had been cited by the imperial parliament established its continued validity. Thom then pointed out that the legal system in force under the terms of the Charter was that of 1670. Since the Company had assumed responsibility for the area in the seventeenth century, the laws of the district, until changed, were of that date. Thom wrote that 'the vague generality of the Charter can never be permitted to introduce the English laws of to-day for the present and of tomorrow for the future; nor, in this case, is expediency repugnant to authority; for, surely a fixed rule, which may from time to time be modified to suit our connection, is more convenient than a rule ever varying to suit the condition of others, but never to be varied to suit that of ourselves.'[59] This sense of the social utility of the written law combined with the particular needs of Red River not only justified Thom's alteration of nineteenth-century jurisprudence in his codes but also increased the validity of his attempts to formulate a unique system of justice for the northwest.[60]

However, Thom did not deal critically with this matter until 1851, when he noted that 'independently of their inherent and essential inferiority, [the laws of 1670] are difficult, nay, generally speaking, impossible, to be ascertained, more particularly in such a wilderness as this.' Therefore the revised code of 1851 declared that the laws of England at the date of Queen Victoria's accession were the laws of Rupert's Land.[61] The laws of the settlement would be contemporary, bringing the northwest into the context of the British Empire of 1851 and ending the role of antiquarian expert enjoyed by Thom.

Thom's review of the Charter also involved a clarification of his views concerning the Company's trade monopoly. His resulting argument that any infringement of the chartered rights of the Company was against the law became the source of a major confrontation between the Recorder and the inhabitants. Thom's sense of commitment to his employers was fully aroused by the existence of a trade in furs between Red River colonists and American traders at Pembina. In 1817 Selkirk had remarked upon the ease of trade between Rupert's Land and the United States. The Earl viewed this as an advantage in terms of supplying the colony, but in the 1840s the commercial flow was working in favour of the rival trading operation of Norman Kittson. Red River settlers were benefitting from higher prices for furs and lower costs for goods at Pembina. Traditionally the colonists had been allowed to trap and trade for their own support, but all such commerce was to be conducted with the Company, which paid a fixed and modest price for furs. Lack of competition had enabled the Company to maintain control, but the increasing size and diversity of the community in the 1840s, plus the convenient location of the American posts, fostered a growing challenge to its monopoly.[62]

Simpson's reorganizations of the administration of Rupert's Land and Assiniboia in 1835 and 1839 had been partly in response to the increase in 'petty trading.' While these measures had been effective in curbing competition in the short term, trade with the American posts was carried on openly by the mid-1840s. Thom blamed the growth of the free trade on unsuccessful buffalo hunts and 'an ungrateful combination of cupidity and vindictiveness on the part of ... [some traders] who have carried not only themselves but all such as are ever ready to follow a bad example for the sake of present advantage.' More importantly, unless the Company could 'make such trafficking cost more than it is worth,' the trade was likely to become a 'permanent and inherent' habit.[63]

The mechanics of halting this commerce required delicate handling. In 1844 Governor Alexander Christie of Assiniboia and Thom made a first attempt to curb it quietly. Rather than order seizure of suspect furs, which necessitated giving half to the Queen under the terms of the Charter and would have led to much adverse publicity, Thom suggested that they 'hamper the means' of the smugglers.[64] Both Recorder and Governor were aware that any resolution of the situation could have long-term significance. The Company was not committed to the northwest in the absence of the fur trade. Rather, their monopoly of the trade promoted their interests in the settlement. Accordingly, the London Committee approved attempts by local officials to end the challenge to the monopoly.

The first step was a proclamation issued by the Council that all importers must sign an oath pledging that their goods were not for use in any illegal trade. Failure to comply meant that no goods would be transported in Company ships.[65] All acquiesced, except two local importers, Andrew McDermot and James Sinclair, who were the acknowledged leaders of the free trade movement. The two independent traders demanded their rights as British citizens, to which Thom responded that settlers in Rupert's Land enjoyed rights only insofar as they were not limited by the Charter. Even Thom admitted privately that the matter was complex, and he confided to Simpson that he 'found law and fact inevitably so mixed up together that I may occasionally appear to have stept beyond the limits of my own province.'[66] As Thom may have feared, this served only to isolate him and to identify the two major free traders within the settlement.

The Council now proclaimed other restrictions. Letters were to be marked on the outside with the name of the author and sealed in the presence of Company men, which implied the Company's right to inspect mail as a means of gathering information on illegal trading.[67] In 1845 the Governor and Committee approved a new land deed designed by the Recorder which included 'restrictions on trading or dealing with Indians or *others* under the special protections of the deed with its penal forfeiture.' Land tenure became dependent upon the settler's promise not to deal in furs, not to distribute or import liquor, to resist foreign invasion, and to promote the religious institutions of the colony.[68] The extent to which this drastic form was used is unclear, yet its very adoption was perceived as a serious infringement on the traditional rights of the settlers. The use of land tenure to reaffirm the Company's commercial interests impressed the community as arbitrary and excessive, even though the Company accepted its obligation to protect all settlers in return for acceptance of these terms. Indeed, the settlers viewed protection as a traditional right not previously contingent upon their non-involvement in the illegal fur trade.

Thom and other officials did their best to minimize the opportunity of the colonists to trade in furs. Intending to cut out the Métis middlemen, the Company announced that it would purchase furs only from the original trapper. Then in June 1845 Thom attempted to introduce a twenty per cent import duty on American goods that would have made the cost of trade with rival companies prohibitive. The proposal was aimed at non-Company traders within the settlement. Thom was using his intimate understanding of the Charter to find justification for interference in matters of taxation in the name of the Company monopoly. While the new tax was not applied, its basic intent was identified with the Recorder and further established Thom as an enemy of the Métis. Alexander Ross noted in 1856 that 'the odium it created lives to this day,' and a petition from the Métis to the Canadian government in the 1850s identified the increased duty as a major factor in their opposition to the Company's 'fictitious' Charter.[69]

In spite of these efforts, the Company's commercial control was becoming weaker. At the urging of Kittson and Father Georges Belcourt, a missionary at Pembina, the Métis fur traders sought legal status for their commerce. A petition to the Crown in 1846 argued against the Hudson's Bay Company's unfair trade monopoly and also drew attention to the unsatisfactory state of the administration of justice in the settlement. On the advice of Christie and Thom, London interpreted the petition as presaging serious conflict within the Red River colony and ordered the Sixth Royal Regiment to the area to preserve order. The regular troops were costly to maintain, because the imperial government had insisted that the Company absorb half their expenses. The presence of troops was also unnecessary; they were replaced by a company of half-pay pensioners under newcomer Major William Caldwell in 1847. At the same time Caldwell was appointed Governor of Assiniboia, the first non-Company man to occupy that position.[70] This change was taken as a signal of fuller understanding on the part of the Company of the community's need for some independence in its government, although it did not in any sense interrupt Thom's efforts to re-establish the monopoly.

Caldwell was not impressed with either the court system or his legal advisor. However, his lack of experience in both administration and the fur trade placed him at a disadvantage in his attempts to administer the law under the terms of the Charter. 'I was judge and everything,' he advised the Select Committee in 1857, although he could fulfil his responsibilities only 'as far as my ability enabled me to perform them in the state in which I found the place.' Thom countered Caldwell's complaints that the Recorder's powers were excessive and dismissed the Governor as having no sense of the particular requirements of the Red River settlement. Thom complained to Simpson that Caldwell consistently failed to seek the Recorder's aid and advice in managing the affairs of the community and thus disrupted the established pattern of administration.[71]

The change of governor did not alter the economic challenge posed by the 'illicit' trade in furs. The traders became increasingly doubtful of the validity of the chartered trading privileges; the Recorder became more convinced of the necessity of curbing the pretensions of the Métis in order to preserve peace and order in the settlement. Both sides had their respective opinions validated by the events of 1846–7. Continuing their campaign for legitimization of their enterprise, the Métis submitted another petition to the imperial government that demanded an inquiry into all aspects of the Company's administration of the northwest. William Kennedy and James Sinclair, as leading free traders, and Alexander

Isbister, the British-educated half-breed son of a Company employee, were identified as the leaders of this challenge to the Company's chartered authority in the legislative and judicial, as well as commercial, spheres.

The petition sparked an investigation rather than a military action. In 1848 the imperial parliament asked Lord Elgin, Governor General of the Canadas, to inquire into the affairs of the settlement. Major Caldwell was required to poll residents in an attempt to assess the validity of the complaints of the Métis. No changes resulted from the investigation, although it became in itself another cause for complaint. Thom was satisfied that the examination of residents had been thorough, but there was evidence to suggest that it was neither complete nor objective. Colonel John Crofton, for instance, was asked to comment after only a few months in the settlement as commander of the Sixth Regiment. His assurance to Lord Elgin that 'the government of the Hudson's Bay Company is mild and protective, and admirably adapted ... for the state of society existing in Rupert's Land, where Indians, half-breeds, or Europeans are happily governed and live protected by laws which I know were mercifully and impartially administered by Mr. Thom' was accepted in London but not in Red River. Similarly, of those canvassed in the settlement Thom noted that the Bishop of Juliopolis and James Sinclair had not responded to Caldwell's questions, and that only Andrew McDermot had replied unfavourably. This limited inquiry was not an honest reflection of the community's critique of the Company.[72]

Nonetheless, the British government dismissed the charges. Isbister's credibility as a Métis spokesman was seriously undermined, although Thom persisted in accusing him of spreading rumours that Charles II had secretly revoked the Charter of the Hudson's Bay Company. William Kennedy, Isbister's ally and uncle, was dismissed as a 'stupid rogue ... the dupe of his own newborn fanaticisms.'[73] This response to the petition, therefore, confirmed both the Recorder and the traders in their analysis of the problems facing the settlement. Thom thought that his position as legal interpreter was vindicated, while the Métis felt that the Company's control was even more dependent upon Thom's efforts to support the Charter. Moreover Thom was much more than a symbol of the commercial monopoly of the Hudson's Bay Company. It was in the Recorder that the Métis first found elements of cultural antagonism that helped shape their feelings of identity into a strong sense of community.

Thom's actions during the 1840s inevitably reminded the settlers of the stories they had heard about his Lower Canadian career. The Rebellion of

1837 had evoked considerable sympathy for the patriote cause in the northwest. Louis Riel the Elder had reported Thom's authorship of the 'Anti-Gallic Letters' and his role with Durham. Rumours carried by French-Canadian labourers and clerics who visited or settled in Red River during the early 1840s reinforced these old memories. Thom's Protestant and English prejudices, reflected in his refusal to speak French, suggested to the Métis that his attitudes had not changed since the 1830s. His unilingual policy was even more offensive, since he was capable of speaking French. In 1849, for example, Thom finally agreed to use French in court when it became necessary in order to keep his position.[74]

The Métis were nevertheless disturbed by Thom's excesses in the English language. Sheriff Ross noted that the Recorder's pedantic insistence upon detailed instruction in each point of law, no matter how trivial or inappropriate, offended the Métis. Eden Colvile, Governor of Rupert's Land in Simpson's absence, remarked that 'the people like honesty & common sense quite as well as all Thom's long dissertations on General Principles.'[75] Thom, impervious to such criticisms, persisted in his campaign to enlighten the primitive society of Red River. The lack of persons qualified to challenge his interpretations and his air of 'confidence in his own views' exaggerated the Métis' sense that Thom could manipulate the law in the interests of the Company. The people feared, according to Ross, that the Recorder 'could turn black into white, and white into black.'[76]

Thus Thom and his legal administration signified cultural as well as commercial opposition for the Métis, whose growing hostility to the Recorder began to mar his effectiveness. At the same time his actions became more overtly anti-French. The resolution of the trade monopoly developed into an even more complex matter, and the personality of the Recorder became part of the issue. This was the state of opinion when four Métis were arrested in 1849 for possession of illegal furs. The Métis discerned Thom's hand behind the action. It was a logical step in the Company's campaign to maintain its trading rights, although the traders ignored the probable role played by Governor Caldwell and Chief Factor John Ballenden in deciding to test the question in open court.

The trial was scheduled for 17 May 1849 with Thom and Caldwell presiding and Ballenden as prosecutor.[77] That the day was Ascension Day, a Catholic holy day, further aroused the hostility of the Métis against the panel of Company men assembled in the name of Company justice. After attending early mass, the Métis, exhorted by Riel to assert themselves, gathered outside the court to protest the trial. Armed and hostile, they challenged the Company in the person of the Recorder. Again it was no longer just the monopoly, but the judicial and legislative authority of the Company, that was the focal point of Métis discontent.

James Sinclair entered the court to present the Métis' demands, including the right to trade freely in furs, the removal of all restrictions on American imports, and the improvement of the administration of justice through the removal of Recorder Thom. Unperturbed by these events, Thom insisted upon the strictest order in his courtroom and in typical fashion adhered to procedural rules that were quite out of context in the situation. Refusing to accept Sinclair and the Métis as a'delegation of the people,' although allowing them to sit as jurors, he thus placed the Métis once again in a position in which he as the fount of justice explained their duties to them. In his summation Thom reminded the jurors of the chartered trade rights of the Company.

The verdict went against Guillaume Sayer, the first of the four to be tried, because testimony offered by his son under the Recorder's unique regulations removed any doubt that the furs in his possession were not intended for the Company's warehouse. A recommendation for mercy was taken seriously by Ballenden, who in the hopes of avoiding trouble from the crowd that remained outside the courthouse accepted the verdict of guilty as sufficient statement of principle and asked for no punishment. Sayer was set free and allowed to keep his furs, and the crowd assumed that their right to trade freely had been confirmed. After a long struggle, then, the public test of the legality of the monopoly and the Charter had compromised rather than confirmed the Company's rights.

The trial did clarify the Métis' position. They exhibited a significant degree of politicization and began to articulate demands that reflected their sense of identity as well as their commercial needs. Upon his arrival in the colony shortly after the trial, Governor Simpson was presented with a petition demanding Thom's removal and calling for political, cultural, and economic equality for Métis settlers. The criticism of the Recorder was not premised upon a rejection of the need for an organized legal administration. Rather it implied that the community expected independence and objectivity in its judicial administrators. The document reiterated the need for the use of French in judicial proceedings, the recognition of free trade in principle, and the extension of Métis political representation.[78] It was a fundamental rejection of Thom's activities and the consequent manipulation of the law of the community to support the monopoly of the Company.

Simpson was greatly disturbed by the trial and the petition. The Métis had argued forcefully against the conflicts inherent in Thom's roles as judicial authority, legal interpreter, and Company employee. The Governor, however, responded initially in terms that indicated adherence to his original recommendation:

> With Mr. Thom's entire concurrence, I replied to the petition that the inhabitants of Red River Settlement had no right to dictate to the Company with respect to its choice of a Recorder of Rupert's Land or of its legal adviser ... In regard to this application on the part of the Canadians and French Half-breeds, I would respectfully suggest that the Settlement, in default of being satisfied with the gratuitous aid of Mr. Thom's services, should be left to find a professional man for local purposes at its own expense.[79]

The debate continued for some months, during which Simpson remained firmly allied with Thom.

In a private gesture the Recorder offered to withdraw his public services until normal conditions prevailed. Reluctant to concede to any Métis demands, however, Thom soon changed his mind about withdrawing and warned the governor that 'any concession on that point [the demand for his dismissal] would be fatal to the Company's authority in this country, discouraging every friend and emboldening every foe. There could be nothing, which these people would hesitate to demand, if The Company ... should listen to a clamour for the removal of one, whom even the agitators themselves feel to have been neither the least faithful nor the least zealous nor the least able of The Company's servants.' The opposition of the Métis in fact highlighted Thom's value. He rejected the personal elements of the critique. 'I have no fear,' he continued, 'and what is more, the people do not suppose that I have any.'[80] The Company at this point apparently agreed that dismissal of their appointee would have implied agreement with Métis arguments, because Thom's services were retained.

On 31 May 1849 the Council of Assiniboia held a special session to discuss, in Thom's presence, 'the restoration of the tranquility of the Settlement.' After examining the position of the Métis, the Council announced that 'the personal liberty of Mr. Thom must be held equally inviolable with that of every other citizen, and that those attempting any infringement on the same must bear the consequences.' A sense of mutual vulnerability was evident in the Council's expressed hope that Thom's agreement 'to address the Court in both languages, in all cases involving either Canadian [ie, French-Canadian] or Halfbreed interests' would quiet the opposition. The request for representation could not be acted upon, although the Council announced it would 'gladly make a recommendation to the Committee of the Honorable Hudson's Bay Company on the subject.' Similarly, the issue of free trade was avoided, since any alteration in the Charter could only be made by the Queen in Parliament.[81]

Thom' s position as Recorder was finally undermined by his behaviour in two cases in 1850. The first, *Matheson* v *Thom,* was a provocative and confusing diversion for the settlement. Matheson had built a veranda on Thom's house, but the Recorder refused to pay him on the grounds that a written bill had never been presented. Thom forced Matheson to sue for payment to teach him a lesson in business practice. While the record of the case describes a very straightforward hearing with Cuthbert Grant on the bench, the case was punctuated with a series of personality conflicts and demonstrations of prejudice that scandalized the colony. Thom was intent upon demonstrating his legal abilities and proving to the Métis that he was not intimidated by their threats. He objected to the composition of the jury, noting that all jurors should be English. French-speaking jurors, even if bilingual, would be unable to comprehend the nuances of the Recorder's case. He further objected that he could not be tried in his own court and attacked Grant for procedural errors. Thom then stalked out of the courtroom, an act of contempt that would have been punished severely had he been presiding. Less concerned about the majesty of the law, however, Grant did not react to this outrageous behaviour. He simply accepted Thom's acknowledgment of the debt as conclusive. Thom then felt that he had to underline the fact that his actions had not been motivated by any shortage of funds but rather by his desire to illustrate his unique value to the community. He proceeded to pay Matheson more than the £25 claimed. However, the case confirmed the Métis in their evaluation of Thom's prejudices and arbitrary views on the law. His criticism of francophone jurors and his disregard for Grant contributed to the Métis' growing sense that Thom must be replaced.[82]

When Eden Colvile arrived in Red River in August 1850, he was presented with yet another demand for Thom's dismissal. The recent events of the *Foss* v *Pelly* libel suit in July had convinced the community that they must act. The case centred on gossip about the alleged adultery of Chief Factor Ballenden's wife Sarah and Captain Christopher Foss, second-in-command of the Company of Pensioners. The talk had spread until Mrs A.E. Pelly, wife of a Company accountant, had snubbed Mrs Ballenden in the mess. Thom urged Foss to challenge the story on behalf of Mrs Ballenden. Foss, whom Caldwell relieved of his official duties because of the scandal, agreed to seek redress from the husbands of the gossiping women. He charged Pelly and the mess cook, John Davison, with slander. The latter party was named to prevent his appearance as a witness for the defence.

Caldwell was concerned about Thom's advisory role and discussed the propriety of his hearing the case with Bishop Provencher. The prelate warned the governor that any appearance by Thom in court would likely result in a disturbance and confirm the Métis' suspicion that any trial conducted by Thom would be judged according to the Recorder's personal feelings rather than any objective rule of law. Caldwell then approached Simpson for advice, with the result that Sir George warned Thom that his appearance in the trial 'might endanger both your life and property.'[83] Simpson added, politely but persuasively, that 'the state of public feeling' was such as to warrant Thom's resignation from the post of Recorder of Rupert's Land. Thom responded aggressively, certain that the case required his legal expertise, and proceeded to act in the conflicting capacities of counsel for the plaintiff and judge. As Letitia Hargrave reported the event:

> Mrs. B. was sent from her husbands house & confided to the care of Mr Recorder Thom, who was judge in the case & in whose family she remained till the proceedings were over. Foss came boldly out, Mrs B. appeared in court as a witness & harangued the public accusing Pelly of having a pique at her because she had rejected 'his advances' the previous winter, he being one of her husbands clerks. Pelly declared that she is wrong & that she, not he, had made 'the advances' – This she, as the Bench Report says, *calmly* denied on oath. Mr. Thom charged Mrs Cochran the clergymans wife & Mrs Black with perjury because they had given evidence that they had seen Mrs B. and Capt F. behaving in a very free style.[84]

This case exemplified the Métis' various criticisms of Thom and the administration of justice in the settlement. Having previously advised Captain Foss, Thom should have disqualified himself as judge. However, he felt bound in his capacity as Company counsel and officer of the court to conduct the trial in a manner that met his standards of professionalism. 'Thom's conduct on the trial,' wrote Colvile, 'seems to have been as unlike a judge as anything could be.' His evaluation was that Thom's behaviour in the case had been ambivalent and also improper. Caldwell, who had nominally presided, described the unfolding of the 'notorious' case for the Select Committee of 1857:

Who charged the jury and delivered the sentence of the court upon that occasion? – Mr. Thom got into court that day by permission from those who had previously prevented him from attending ... Mr. Thom pointed out the nature, and charged the jury as to the extent of the penalty, and the jury gave the verdict; they gave a grand sum of £300. Mr. Thom then pointed out that that would not do; that they were to discriminate between the Pellys and Davison, and to specify a given sum to each part. Did he act on that occasion as advocate? – I am afraid that he acted both as advocate and judge.

In advising the jury, Thom had insisted upon excessive damages to symbolize Mrs Ballenden's innocence. Caldwell considered the amount to be 'beyond my means of imposing a fine,' and Foss's public forgiveness of Davison highlighted the problem faced by Pelly in raising £200 to pay his fine.[85]

The success of the trial prompted Colvile to be sympathetic to Mrs Ballenden. 'I am inclined,' he wrote, 'to think that she has been more sinned against than sinning. In fact it seems a dreadful place for scandal, and these persons and their wives are very strait-laced.' But the victory did little to alter the governor's attitude towards Thom who, he felt, 'for a clever man, [is] endowed with marvellously little judgment.'[86] Thom, however, viewed the verdict as further proof of his objectivity and value to the settlement. 'It does, however, amuse one,' he wrote to Simpson, 'to find it preferred as a charge against a judge, that he, though alleged to be unpopular, has never been thwarted by a single jury ... [Of] the danger of my sitting, you would appear to have been misinformed by Major Caldwell. It is not me, but himself, that my appearance has damaged.'[87]

By January 1851 Thom's success was severely qualified. The 'ill used woman' of September had taken up residence with Foss. Simpson pointed out that Thom's unswerving support of Mrs Ballenden had caused 'much ill will and mischief' in the settlement and reminded the Recorder that there had been much doubt about the case all along. 'I placed no reliance on any whitewashing, however dexterously it might be done,' he wrote to his Recorder. 'You will no doubt now admit I was in the right and you were in the wrong, or rather I should say your out and out support of what you assumed to be the cause of an insulted female was secured by means of deception and intrigue – in fact that you were duped.' [88] The Métis warned Colvile that Thom would not be allowed to attend the fall court. The Governor acquiesced in the hope that the protest would die down but noted that 'if we have another Court in February I am clear for having him in *coûte qu'il coûte*.'[89] The idea of administering justice without professional legal advice was discomfitting to the Council of Assiniboia.

The Governor and Committee in London were becoming increasingly sceptical of the value of their Recorder. Thom's steady flow of complaints about his salary, which was lower than that of a Chief Factor, had long-since qualified the Company's initial enthusiasm about their appointee. 'Having given the most attentive consideration to ... the voluminous correspondence, which has formerly passed on this subject,' the Company advised Thom that 'were your remuneration to be in proportion to your talents there might be little difficulty in acceding to your wishes; but the decision of the Governor and Committee must be regulated by the extent of the duties to be performed and the other circumstances of the case.'[90] When this factious correspondence was supplemented by the continued hostility of the community in Red River, the Company began to sense that Thom was a liability to the peaceful administration of the northwest. His presentation of the codes had been satisfactory in every detail, as were his various attempts to reinforce the monopoly, but the interposition of Thom's cultural antipathies, which aroused the settlers to demand his removal, prompted the Company to revoke his appointment as Recorder of Rupert's Land on 10 April 1851. Thom argued that 'it is not against Mr. Thom, but against The Company, that the ultimate aim [of Métis demands] is intended.' He was incensed that his brave vindication of the commercial and judicial rights of his employer was being repaid by an action which only 'strengthened their [Métis] determination to work their own will.'[91] Similarly, Thom was appalled that the details of *Foss* v *Pelly* were cited as cause for dismissal; he blamed Caldwell for any irregularities. Finally, Thom pointed out that since his appointment as Recorder had interrupted a promising career in Lower Canada, he felt entitled to occupy the position as long as he desired 'as indemnity for ... lost prospects at the bar.'[92]

Simpson finally sent Thom a detailed indictment of his recordership. The appointment had been made solely on the Governor's recommendation, not because Thom was a famous Lower Canadian lawyer. A Canadian contact had advised Simpson that Thom would undoubtedly accept the position because his future in the colony was uncertain, ' inasmuch as, although you were studious and possessed of abilities of a superior order

... still your want of facility in public speaking was a serious drawback to your success.' Simpson recognized after Thom had been Recorder for only a short time that the appointment had been ill advised, due to Thom's 'ignorance of the French language ... unfortunate temper and ... overbearing manner.' Thom's consequent unpopularity had disturbed the peace in the colony and impeded the administration of justice. Simpson left Thom wondering, as did others by this time, why it had taken so long for the Company to replace him.[93]

The revocation of Thom's appointment as Recorder did not remove him from the councils of Rupert's Land or Assiniboia. Similarly, the cessation of his public duties did not mark the end of his advisory duties. The Company appointed him Clerk of the Court of Assiniboia and thereby retained its legal advisor in Red River. Yet the situation remained unsatisfactory. Although Colvile attempted to convince the Métis that Thom 'was now the servant of the Court instead of Master as heretofore,' the new arrangement 'in no way conduced to the peace of the settlement, or contributed to rendering him [Thom] more popular.' Caldwell deemed the arrangement 'a farce.' He finally had to order Thom to stay completely away from court. By the spring of 1851 Thom's official duties consisted of correspondence and letter-copying.[94]

During this time Thom co-operated with John Bunn and Louis LaFlèche in preparing a report on the state of law in Rupert's Land. As previously noted, the committee was charged with updating and removing those 'antiquated absurdities' that were contained within the earlier codes because of the nature of the Charter of 1670. While he did not change his argument that the essence of the law of Rupert's Land was to be found in the Charter, Thom did support a significant alteration in the code of 1841. Because he could no longer enter the court he was required to provide written interpretations of legal points. In this the Council felt that the simple application of more contemporary and familiar principles of law should operate. 'If Mr. Thom is, henceforward, to give formal opinions in writing,' they noted, 'he must either shock the common sense of the community, with antiquated absurdities in all their naked deformity, or assume to himself a responsibility, or, rather an authority, which ought not to fall to the lot of any individual whatever.'[95]

Nor were Thom's current services enthusiastically endorsed by members of the Council. Despite significant alterations in his duties and authority, he had managed to retain his annual wage of £700. Colvile felt that 'there is no office you could give him that he would not accept, provided always that he got the same amount of pay.' Members of the

Council argued that Thom should be paid off with an annuity; they felt 'a decided objection to the Fur Trade continuing to pay £700 a year for the performance of duties that are merely nominal.'[96] Moreover his presence was considered to be provocative. Colvile wrote that although 'we have had no serious offences to try since I have been in Red River and it is a duty which I by no means relish as my knowledge of law is unfortunately very limited,' he would not 'endanger the present happy tranquillity of the Settlement by requesting Mr. Thom to come into Court.'[97] This was the final acknowledgment of his failure in the settlement. The Métis continued to threaten him, and his role in the administration of the settlement no longer existed.

In the spring of 1853, then, Thom put in writing the substance of a recent conversation with Eden Colvile. He would resign as of 1 June 1854 and his salary would continue for two weeks. The Company would purchase his house for £500 after he had left for England at Company expense. In the fall of 1854 Thom boarded ship at York Factory and left Rupert's Land without apology.[98]

Adam Thom's career as Recorder of Rupert's Land must be evaluated on two levels. Despite his perseverance in a highly personal economic and cultural vendetta with the francophone community of the northwest, his legal efforts were effective and lasting. Apart from the revised code of 1862, Thom's interpretation of the meaning of the Charter for the administration of the settlement was revived by Justice A.C. Killam who in 1886 argued in an appeal case, *Sinclair* v *Mulligan,* that the laws of Rupert's Land in the 1850s were the laws of England in 1670. While the decision invoked different reasons for the interpretation, it nevertheless revealed again the complexities of the principles which the Recorder had grappled with during the 1840s and confirmed much of Thom's view of the laws of Red River.[99]

Thom's official relationships in both Lower Canada and the Hudson's Bay territory had betrayed a strong sense of duty to official bodies, but his actions had always been prompted by something more than simple loyalty to his employer. His belief in racial traits and the heritability of fundamental cultural characteristics, combined with a world view that conceded economic and political progress only to those who were nationally predisposed to enjoy it (that is, the British), underlay his behaviour in Red River. His objectivity as a legal officer was clouded by his desire to 'civilize' the settlement, an urge that denied the validity of the Métis culture or community. Similarly the negative reaction of the Métis to

Thom was not a reaction to law and order, but rather a statement of their disagreement with the Recorder's assumptions about their community and its requirements in a judicial system. The need for law and rules of governance was accepted. It was the partial administration of such conventions by an overtly biased judge that was rejected. The Métis reacted to the elements in Thom's character that enabled him to act as though he were dealing with more than questions of right and wrong. They rejected his services, so graciously provided by the Company, in an argument that underlined their community's need for a more objective and sensitive administration of justice.

The Honourable Company's role in the affair was complex. In that its major concern was the maintenance of a commercial monopoly through the imposition in 1839 of a formal application of legal rights granted in 1670, its judicial reforms must be viewed as intimately connected with the desire to make a profit. Thus it is apparent why no action was taken to remove the Recorder before 1851, when his offensive behaviour was compounded by administrative ineffectiveness. The Company learned an invaluable lesson from their first Recorder, however. In what appears to have been a conscious effort to ensure the peaceful evolution of the colony, the Governor and Committee appointed a very different man as Recorder of Rupert's Land in 1854. Francis Godschall Johnson had been educated at St Omer's in France, indicating that he was sympathetic to and familiar with both the French language and the Catholic religion.[100] The Company, it seems, had apprehended the risks involved in not thoroughly examining potential employees in such matters.

For his part, Thom realized that he was hated by most of the settlers but refused to make any concessions in his approach to the execution of his duties. He exacerbated the situation by refusing to speak French and graphically illustrated his contempt for the Métis in *Matheson* v *Thom*. His excesses in *Foss* v *Pelly* were symbolic of his attitude, which implied an essential attack on the abilities of the Métis, and aided in focusing the attention of both the colonists and the Company on his prejudices. Indeed, the Métis owed much to Thom. He compelled them to enter the political arena in the first place. His attitudes, translated into the seemingly straightforward issue of trading rights, posed larger questions of Métis rights and abilities vis-à-vis the governing authority. Their response to these questions, embodied in petitions in 1846, 1847, 1849, and 1850, presented an increasingly articulate and political sense of their community. The Métis were successful in their protests. Their reactions to future attempts to impose inappropriate structures, including that of the government of Canada in 1869, reflected the lessons learned in their experiences with Adam Thom. The first Recorder represented a point of view that prepared the Métis to meet any threat to the maintenance of their identity and their community.

The legacy of the introduction of a formal system of law in Rupert's Land thus was complex. While the law successfully withstood Thom's personality, his success in this sphere was tinged with a sense of personal defeat. His private assessment of the revised code of 1851 revealed an unhappy feeling of betrayal in the larger objectives of his appointment. 'The revised code of local regulations' he complained, 'which was carried, will go forth to the world under the sanction of three names, two French and Catholic, as the indivisible majority, and one English and Protestant, as the helpless minority. Can this state of things be permitted in a community, of which the disfranchised section contains one half of the population, nine tenths of the wealth and ninety nine hundredths of the intelligence?'[101]

Thom linked his personal loss with the ultimate demise of the Hudson's Bay Company in the northwest. The Recorder never appreciated the dichotomy that had characterized his actions but viewed his various legal and personal pronouncements as stemming from the same fundamental impulse. His firing, then, prompted Thom to speculate that the system of government in the area would not remain long after his departure. 'It hitherto has been,' he advised Simpson, 'and still is, in its mercantile character alone, that the Hudson's Bay Company governs this country ... and, as soon as the people shall have advanced beyond the capabilities of this paternal tutelage, The Hudson's Bay Company's political power is sure to be either abridged or abolished.'[102] Prompted by bitterness, this judgment related to Thom's profound sense that the Company had failed in its most important task in the northwest, the anglicization of the territory.

Any portrait of Thom in the northwest must necessarily be tempered by his relationships with the growing community of the Red River settlement. While he has been treated as a minor figure in the histories of both Lower Canada and Rupert's Land, Thom's contacts and appointments were of immense significance when viewed from the perspective of the consistency of his prejudice. His presence in both regions was characterized by fundamental assumptions of French inferiority and British superiority that coloured the character of his legal actions. Those who have studied his career solely in terms of his legal accomplishments have described an official history of Thom's recordership that ignores the impact of his personality on the colony. Indeed, in most of these studies the community loses its social dimensions. As Thom's obituary in the *Western Law Times* noted: 'A halo of romance is thrown round his name when we pause to think of the vast extent of his jurisdiction, and the wild and peculiar people over whom that jurisdiction was exercised.'[103]

To understand his career from an historical perspective, however, one must look beyond the codes and law reports and recognize the social context of Thom's judicial administration. Those to whom he was responsible, in this sense the settlers of Red River, were not impressed with the Recorder's abilities. A more compelling summary of both Company law and the Recorder of Rupert's Land was given by William Caldwell, who when asked if Thom 'gave satisfaction' to the northwest, replied 'Not to the people.'[104]

NOTES

1 An Act for extending the jurisdiction of the Courts of Justice in the Provinces of Lower and Upper Canada 43 Geo. III (1803), c. 138

2 Good accounts of the establishment, growth, and development of the Red River settlement are contained in the following: A.S. Morton *A History of the Canadian West to 1870–71, being a History of Rupert's Land (The Hudson's Bay Company's Territory) and of the North-West Territory (including the Pacific Slope)* 2nd edition (Toronto 1973); E.H. Oliver, ed. *The Canadian North-West: Its Early Development and Legislative Records, Minutes of the Councils of the Red River Colony and the Northern Department of Rupert's Land* 2 vols (Ottawa 1914); and E.E. Rich *The History of the Hudson's Bay Company 1670–1870* Vol. II: *1763–1870* (London 1959).

3 'Hudson's Bay Company Code of Penal Laws' 1 Sept. 1815, in Oliver, ed. *Canadian North-West* 1285–7

4 Great Britain *Sessional Papers* Session II 1857 'Report from the Select Committee on the Hudson's Bay Company: together with the Proceedings of the Committee, Minutes of Evidence, Appendices and Index' 548 question 6014 (hereafter 'Report of the Select Committee')

5 The licence was issued to the Hudson's Bay Company and William McGillivray, Simon McGillivray, and Edward Ellice. See Rich *Hudson's Bay Company* 404; Morton *History of the Canadian West* 629.

6 George Keith, a Northwester, wrote to George Simpson of the Hudson's Bay Company on 24 Sept. 1820 'that a constable of Montreal should arrest a

person in the Indian Territory of British North America and detain him a Prisoner ... is certainly an absolute mockery of all Law and Justice.' (E.E. Rich, ed. *Simpson's Athabaska Journal* [London 1938] 96). A good account of Lord Selkirk's difficulties with Canadian courts may be found in G.M. Gressley 'Lord Selkirk and the Canadian Courts' in J.M. Bumsted, ed. *Canadian History before Confederation: Essays and Interpretations* (Georgetown, Ont. 1979) 278–93. See also 'Report from the Select Committee' 59, 60 questions 1020, 1040 evidence of Sir George Simpson.

7 'Resolutions passed at a general Court of the Hudson's Bay Company ... 29 May 1822' in Oliver, ed. *Canadian North-West* 219–21; A. Colvile to J. Halkett 31 May 1822 in ibid. 221

8 Governor and Committee to W. Williams, G. Simpson, and A. Bulger 1 June 1822 in R. Fleming, ed. *Minutes of Council Northern Department of Rupert's Land, 1821–1831* (Toronto 1940) 333–4; A. Colvile to A. Bulger 31 May 1822, J.H. Pelly, T. Langley, and A. Colvile to A. Bulger 1 June 1822 in Oliver, ed. *Canadian North-West* 222–3

9 Lord Bathurst to J. Berens 31 May 1822 in Morton *History of the Canadian West* 630

10 Oliver, ed. *Canadian North-West* 74. In announcing his intentions to the Council Simpson noted that the population of the settlement was 5000, a figure that is not supported by available census data. See 'Minutes of the Council of Assiniboia' (hereafter 'Minutes') 12 Feb. 1835 in Oliver, ed. *Canadian North-West* 267. Rich *Hudson's Bay Company* 787 notes that Simpson recorded approximately 2000 white and 3000 Indian settlers at Red River in 1837.

11 'Minutes' 12 Feb. 1835 in Oliver, ed. *Canadian North-West* 267. One resident described the state of the settlement as follows: 'The settlement was rather in a disturbed state – various commotions having arisen in course of the winter chiefly among the Half-breeds – some of these at times assumed a very alarming appearance, but all passed over so far without any active violence being committed – men's minds are nevertheless in a very unsettled state – and unless some speedy measures are adopted ... my firm belief is that both the Settlement and the Fur Trade will fall to pieces on our hands within a very brief term of years – and perhaps get our throats cut in the bargain – .'Donald Ross to James Hargrave 13 Mar. 1835 in G.P. de T. Glazebrook, ed. *The Hargrave Correspondence* (New York 1938) 188–9

12 'Minutes' 12 Feb. 1835 in Oliver, ed. *Canadian North-West* 270; A. Martin 'The Rise of Law in Rupert's Land' *Western Law Times* 1 (1890) 94 identifies 1835 as the date of the inauguration of the General Quarterly Court, but notes that 'it was not until the advent of Recorder Thom in the spring of 1839, that

the General Quarterly Court was formally and regularly established.' This assertion is based upon the subsequent and similar reorganizations of 1837 and 1839.

13 Originally fixed at 7.5 per cent, the duty was reduced to 4 per cent upon appeal by the settlers to the London office. (Rich *Hudson's Bay Company* 532; 'Minutes' 12 Feb. 1835 in Oliver, ed. *Canadian North-West* 267–70). Simpson was prompted to reorganize the administration of justice in part because of his own reluctance to spend more time in the settlement. Prior to 1835, as Alexander Ross noted, 'all points hitherto in dispute were settled by the Governor himself, or not settled at all.' (Rich *Hudson's Bay Company* 531)

14 G. Simpson to J.H. Pelly 1 Feb. 1837 in Martin 'The Rise of Law' 94; 'Dispatch of the Governor and Committee' 15 Feb. 1837 in Oliver, ed. *Canadian North-West* 279–81; F. Read 'Early History of the Manitoba Courts' *Manitoba Bar News* x (1937) 454–5. Simpson advised the Select Committee of 1857 that the Company considered a commission as factor equivalent to a commission as magistrate ('Report of the Select Committee' 67 questions 1191–2).

15 'Minutes' 13 June 1839, 4 July 1839 in Oliver, ed. *Canadian North-West* 283–92. A. Thom *A Charge Delivered to the Grand Jury of Assiniboia, 20th February 1845* (London 1848) 24 discusses the affirmation of trial by jury at this stage.

16 See R.B. Morris, ed. *Select Cases of the Mayor's Court of New York City, 1674–1784* (Washington 1935) 47–50.

17 'Royal Charter Incorporating the Hudson's Bay Company, 1670' in Oliver, ed. *Canadian North-West* 144–6

18 'Report of the Select Committee' 59, 61 questions 1024, 1060–1 evidence of Sir George Simpson. Simpson's statistical evidence was hazy. At this point he said: 'There was never a criminal case within my recollection previously to 1839, except the case to which I am alluding, in Mackenzie's River.' See also Read 'Early History' 454.

19 Governor and Committee to Chief Factors, Chief Traders of the Northern Department 7 Mar. 1838, Public Archives of Canada, Hudson's Bay Company Records A. 6/24 consulted with permission of the Hudson's Bay Company (hereafter PAC HBC)

20 *Montreal Herald* 30 July 1835. For a more complete biography see K.M. Bindon 'Adam Thom' in *Dictionary of Canadian Biography* XI (Toronto 1981) and K.M. Bindon 'Journalist and Judge: Adam Thom's British North American Career 1833–1854' (unpublished MA thesis Queen's University, Kingston 1972).

21 A. Thom *Canadian Politics* (Montreal 1836) 'Anti-Gallic Letter' No. XIX 61–2

22 *Montreal Herald* 30 July 1835

23 Thom *Politics* 'Anti-Gallic Letter' No. LIII 198–200

24 *Montreal Herald* 15 Dec. 1835
25 *La Minerve* 27 Apr. 1837: 'the most frank and tenacious foe'
26 G. Simpson to A. Thom 22 Sept. 1837 PAC HBC D.4/23; G. Bryce *The Makers of Canada: Mackenzie, Selkirk, Simpson* (Toronto 1910) 242
27 Thom *Politics* 'Anti-Gallic Letter' No. XLII 156–7
28 G. Simpson to A. Thom 21 Apr. 1838 PAC HBC D.4/23
29 G. Simpson to A. Thom 4 Jan. 1838, 4 July 1838 PAC HBC D.4/23
30 G. Simpson to A. Thom 24 Apr. 1838 PAC HBC D.4/23
31 Ibid.
32 G. Simpson to A. Thom 4 Jan. 1838 PAC HBC D.4/23
33 A. Thom to G. Simpson 8 Feb. 1841 PAC HBC D.5/6. See D.H. Brown 'Unpredictable and Uncertain: Criminal Law in the Canadian North West before 1886' *Alberta Law Review* XVII (1979) 503.
34 A. Thom to E. Ellice 14 Apr. 1839 PAC *Durham Papers* MG 24 vol. 28; A. Thom to G. Simpson 29 May 1840, 27 July 1840 PAC HBC D.5/5
35 A. Thom to G. Simpson 29 May 1840, 27 July 1840 PAC HBC D.5/5
36 A. Thom to G. Simpson 31 July 1840 PAC HBC D.5/5
37 A. Thom to G. Simpson 29 May 1840, 15 December 1840 PAC HBC D.5/5
38 A. Thom to G. Simpson 27 July 1840 PAC HBC D.5/5
39 J. Bunn to A. Thom 1 Jan. 1841 PAC HBC D.5/5
40 A. Thom 'Witnesses, Their Competency' Appendix A to Penal Code PAC HBC D.5/5
41 A. Thom 'Observations on the Law and the Judicature of Rupert's Land' PAC HBC D.5/5, E.16/1; 'Minutes' 8 June 1841 in Oliver, ed. *Canadian North-West* 293–305
42 Thom 'Observations' PAC HBC E.16/1
43 Ibid.
44 A. Thom to G. Simpson 30 Oct. 1840 PAC HBC D.5/5. The need for flexibility in the codes is readily apparent when the varied nature of legal matters dealt with in Red River is considered: 'The relations with domestic help, the occasional boisterous times at weddings, the crying out of lost oxen at the church doors, regulations of the buffalo hunt, drinking habits, all stand discovered in the records of the court. The cases tried cover every species of offence, – adultery, libel, theft, escape from custody, assault, murder, leaving holes in the ice, supplying Indians and halfbreeds with beer and whisky, deserting employer's service, worrying of lambs by dogs, attempted rape, trespassing, cutting down and carrying off wood, setting fire to the plains, seduction, breach of promise, violation of trade, restrictions in furs, defamatory conspiracy, perjury, appeals from Petty Courts, concealing birth of child, breach of contract, opening packages en route from York Factory, selling

spirits on Sunday, breach of revenue laws, attempting abortion.' (Oliver, ed. *Canadian North-West* 80). Thom recognized the demands that would be placed upon his codes and thus aimed for a blend, rather than a strict replication, of the traditional forms of British law.

45 J. Bunn to A. Thom 1 Jan. 1841 PAC HBC D.5/5

46 A. Thom to G. Simpson 30 Oct. 1840 PAC HBC D.5/5; 'Minutes' 25 June 1841 in Oliver, ed. *Canadian North-West* 295–306; Read 'Early History' 465; Brown 'Unpredictable and Uncertain: Criminal Law in the Canadian North West before 1886' *Alberta Law Review* XVII (1979) 506

47 'Minutes' 3 Apr., 19 June 1845 in Oliver, ed. *Canadian North-West* 314–15, 317, 331–2

48 'Minutes' 1 May, 27 Nov. 1851 in Oliver, ed. *Canadian North-West* 366, 369

49 'Minutes' 11 Apr. 1862 in Oliver, ed. *Canadian North-West* 485–502; D. and L. Gibson *Substantial Justice: Law and Lawyers in Manitoba 1670–1970* (Winnipeg 1972) 30; R. St George Stubbs *Four Recorders of Rupert's Land* (Winnipeg 1967) 15–16; Read 'Early History' 465; Brown 'Unpredictable and Uncertain' 506

50 A. Ross *The Red River Settlement: Its Rise, Progress, and Present State. With Some Account of the Native Races and Its General History, to the Present Day* (London 1856) 223. Ross was recognized as one of the two men of 'abilities or acquirements' to hold the job of sheriff during the Company period (A. Martin 'The Sheriffs of Assiniboia' *Western Law Times* I [1890] 153). Despite their mutual hostility Thom and Ross served together on the Commission of Three to Examine Parties to Written Agreements according to English Principles of Equity (1845), the Committee of Finance (1847), and the Board of Works (1847). See Oliver, ed. *Canadian North-West* 61, 64, 314.

51 A. Thom to G. Simpson 31 July 1840 PAC HBC D.5/5; Governor and Committee to D. Finlayson 4 Mar. 1840 PAC HBC D.6/25. The Monkman deaths were the result of a prairie fire, while the murder at Bird's was never solved. Thomas Simpson 'in a fit of insanity, shot two of his travelling companions (John Bird & Antoine Legro), under the impression that these unfortunate men intended to murder him for his papers, and about 12 or 15 hours after, terminated his own existence, by the same means.' (D. Finlayson to J. Hargrave 18 Dec. 1840 in Glazebrook, ed. *Hargrave Correspondence* 329). Hargrave's wife elaborated: 'there must have been a quarrel, particularly as there was an old grudge between the Red River half-breeds and him [Simpson].' (L. Hargrave to Mrs D. Mactavish 2 Feb. 1841 in M.A. MacLeod, ed. *The Letters of Letitia Hargrave* [Toronto 1947] 93).

52 Governor and Committee to A. Thom 19 Mar. 1842 PAC HBC D.6/25

53 'Treaty between Selkirk and Chippewa, or Saulteau, Killistine or Cree Chiefs'

in Oliver, ed. *Canadian North-West* 1288–9; L. Hargrave to Mrs D. Mactavish 30 Nov. 1845 in MacLeod, ed. *Letitia Hargrave* 211–12; 'Report of the Select Committee' 59 question 1022 evidence of Sir George Simpson 278, 280 questions 4983, 5022, 5027–9 evidence of John McLaughlin; Ross *Red River* 331

54 Thom *Charge to the Grand Jury* 16–17

55 This sense of conflict of interest is noted in Ross *Red River* 223; M. Giraud *Le métis canadien: son rôle dans l'histoire de l'ouest* (Paris 1945) 907; and Alexander Begg *History of the North-West* (Toronto 1894) 255.

56 'Report of the Select Committee' 193 question 3611

57 Ibid. 278 question 2981 evidence of John McLaughlin 301 questions 5427–8 evidence of Lt-Col. W. Caldwell; obituary of Adam Thom *Western Law Times* I (1890) 44; A. Thom to G. Simpson 23 July 1844 PAC HBC D.5/12

58 Thom *Charge to the Grand Jury* 24, 26

59 Ibid. 12. Brown 'Unpredictable and Uncertain' 507n considers the explanation to have been delivered in 1848. It is fully presented and developed, however, in the *Charge* of 1845.

60 Thom *Charge to the Grand Jury* 3–17; Ross *Red River* 383; Martin 'The Rise of Law' 75, 97; Thom 'Observations' PAC HBC E.16/1; Read 'Early History' 465, 469

61 'Report of the Select Committee' 59 question 1018 evidence of Sir George Simpson; 'Minutes' 27 Nov. 1851 in Oliver, ed. *Canadian North-West* 369–79

62 Thom 'Observations' PAC HBC E.16/1; Thom *Charge to the Grand Jury* 12–13; J. Pritchett, ed. 'A Letter by Lord Selkirk on Trade between Red River and the United States' *Canadian Historical Review* XVII (1936) 420–1. See also A.C. Gluek, jr *Minnesota and the Manifest Destiny of the Canadian Northwest* (Toronto 1965) 47–57.

63 A. Thom to G. Simpson 2 Jan. 1845 PAC HBC D.5/13. John Rowand described the problems of competition to James Hargrave in a letter of 20 June 1843: 'Guns is [sic] now given to 10 Robes each in former times an Indian who would have been bold enough to ask a Gun for that number of Robes he would have been turned out of the shop with a kick in the B.S. – We may thank the Americans for spoiling the trade as it is. When our Indians do not see those people, there is no change in the trade' (Glazebrook, ed. *Hargrave Correspondence* 441).

64 W. L. Morton introduction to E.E. Rich, ed. *London Correspondence Inward from Eden Colvile, 1849–1852* (London 1956) lix. While the Recorder authored these various actions, Thom always ensured that Governor Christie appeared to be their source. That Thom was recognized as the true instigator is implied by Rowand in his letter to Hargrave of 20 June 1843: 'When Mr. Toms [sic]

goes he will not be regretted all the people at R.R. hate the Gentleman it would not require much for the half breeds to send him off. (it would be so much wages *saved*) – ' (Glazebrook, ed. *Hargrave Correspondence* 442).

65 Morton introduction lx-lxi; A. Christie to Secretary, Hudson's Bay House 31 Dec. 1844 PAC HBC A.11/95

66 A. Thom to G. Simpson 2 Jan. 1845, 10 Mar. 1845 PAC HBC D.5/13; A. Christie to Secretary 31 Dec. 1844 PAC HBC A.11/95; Morton introduction lxv-lxvi

67 See J.J. Hargrave *Red River* (Montreal 1871) 88 and Rich *Hudson's Bay Company* 535.

68 A. Thom to G. Simpson 23 July 1844 PAC HBC D.5/12; Morton introduction lix

69 'Minutes' 19 June 1845, 30 July 1849, 27 Nov. 1851 in Oliver, ed. *Canadian North-West* 319, 353, 376; 'Minutes of the Council of Rupert's Land' in Oliver, ed. *Canadian North-West* 1304–5; 'Report of the Select Committee' 437–9 'Petition of the Inhabitants and Natives of the Settlement Situated on the Red River'; Ross *Red River* 385

70 'Minutes' 31 May 1849 in Oliver, ed. *Canadian North-West* 352–3. Morton introduction lx states that Thom and Christie repeatedly asked Simpson for troops; Thom denied it. See Ross *Red River* 365–6; G.K. Raudzens 'A Successful Military Settlement: Earl Grey's Enrolled Pensioners of 1846 in Canada' *Canadian Historical Review* LII (1971) 289–403.

71 'Report of the Select Committee' 300 question 5410 evidence of Lt-Col. W. Caldwell; A. Thom to G. Simpson 19 Mar. 1850 PAC HBC D.5/27

72 Crofton is quoted in G. Bryce *A History of Manitoba: its Resources and People* (Toronto 1906) 135; A. Thom to G. Simpson 28 Mar. 1849 PAC HBC D.5/24

73 A. Thom to A. Christie 2 Oct. 1847 PAC HBC A.12/3; A. Thom to G. Simpson 3 Mar. 1849 PAC HBC D.5/24

74 Morton introduction lx; Ross *Red River* 378; Giraud *Le métis* 906; 'Minutes' 31 May 1849 in Oliver, ed. *Canadian North-West* 352

75 E. Colvile to G. Simpson 22 May 1851 in Rich *Eden Colvile* 209

76 Ross *Red River* 384–5; Morton introduction lx; Giraud *Le métis* 906

77 For a detailed account of the trial see Morton introduction lxxiv-lxxxv and Ross *Red River* 372–86.

78 'Minutes' 31 May 1849 in Oliver, ed. *Canadian North-West* 352

79 G. Simpson to Governor and Committee 30 June 1849 PAC HBC A.12/4

80 A. Thom to G. Simpson 19 Mar. 1850 PAC HBC D.5/27

81 'Minutes' 31 May 1849 in Oliver, ed. *Canadian North-West* 352; Morton introduction xcii

82 R. St George Stubbs 'Law and Authority in Red River' *The Beaver* (1968) 17–21 discusses the various events of this trial.

83 G. Simpson to A. Thom 3 July 1850 PAC HBC D.4/42

84 L. Hargrave to Mrs D. Mactavish 29 Aug. 1850 in MacLeod, ed. *Letitia Hargrave* 255–6

85 'Report of the Select Committee' 300, 302 questions 5443–5, 5458 evidence of Lt-Col. W. Caldwell

86 E. Colvile to G. Simpson 19 Sept. 1850 PAC HBC D.5/28

87 A. Thom to G. Simpson 1 June 1840 PAC HBC D.5/28

88 G. Simpson to A. Thom 20 Apr. 1851 PAC HBC D.4/43; E. Colvile to G. Simpson 19 Sept. 1850, 7 Jan. 1851 in Rich, ed. *Eden Colvile* 197, 201

89 E. Colvile to G. Simpson 27 Nov. 1850 in Rich, ed. *Eden Colvile* 199

90 There is a large correspondence on this subject. See, for example, G. Simpson to Governor and Committee 28 Oct. 1847 PAC HBC A.12/3; Governor and Committee to A. Thom 1 June 1844 PAC HBC A.6/26; Governor and Committee to A. Thom 3 Apr. 1849 PAC HBC A.6/28; G. Simpson to Governor and Committee 28 Oct. 1847 PAC HBC A.12/3.

91 A. Thom to G. Simpson 4 June 1851 PAC HBC D.5/30

92 A. Thom to G. Simpson 19 Mar. 1850, 23 July 1851 PAC HBC D.5/27, D.5/31; E. Colvile to A. Barclay 4 June 1851 in Rich, ed. *Eden Colvile* 58; G. Simpson to A. Thom 10 Dec. 1851 PAC HBC D.4/44. Thom's obituary in the *Western Law Times* I (1890) 44–5 noted: 'A very complicated case of great importance – *Foss* vs. *Pelly* – having arisen, Mr. Thom again resumed his office for the purpose of the trial. The Governor, however, disagreeing with Mr. Thom on his finding, probably because he would not find as the Governor wanted, managed either to secure his permanent removal or to force him to resign.'

93 G. Simpson to A. Thom 10 Dec. 1851 PAC HBC D.4/44

94 'Report of the Select Committee' 301 question 5438 evidence of Lt-Col. W. Caldwell

95 'Minutes' 27 Nov. 1851 in Oliver, ed. *Canadian North-West* 370; Stubbs *Four Recorders* 40

96 E. Colvile to G. Simpson 14 July 1851 in Rich, ed. *Eden Colvile* 231; E. Colvile to Governor and Committee 21 July 1852 in Rich, ed. *Eden Colvile* 160. Some of these Council members would have been shareholders in the Company and thus resented Thom's salary.

97 E. Colvile to A. Barclay 16 Mar. 1852 in Rich, ed. *Eden Colvile* 121

98 A. Thom to E. Colvile 28 June 1853 PAC HBC D.5/37; J. Ballenden to A. Barclay 16 Aug. 1854 PAC HBC A.11/96; Stubbs *Four Recorders* 42

99 Read 'Early History' 469; Brown 'Unpredictable and Uncertain' 497

100 'Obituary' of Francis Godschall Johnson *Western Law Times* V (1894) 63. Johnson was called to the Bar in Montreal in 1839 and appointed Recorder of Rupert's Land on 3 Feb. 1854.

101 A. Thom to G. Simpson 16 Aug. 1852 PAC HBC D.5/34
102 A. Thom to G. Simpson 1 June 1850 PAC HBC D.5/28
103 Obituary of Adam Thom *Western Law Times* I (1890) 46
104 'Report of the Select Committee' 301 question 5425 evidence of Lt-Col. W. Caldwell

3

The Law and the Economy in Mid-Nineteenth-Century Ontario: A Perspective

R.C.B. RISK

INTRODUCTION

This essay* is a study of the courts, the common law, and the economy in Ontario between 1841 and 1867, and it is the last of a series of four. The first three were about particular and substantive topics: the corporation, the market, property, and the allocation of losses.[1] This one is intended to give perspective and to emphasize legal institutions and processes.

Of course, dates cannot specify a period that is both unified and different from the times that preceded and followed it. But 1841 and 1867 mark important constitutional changes, and the period between them includes political, religious, educational, economic, and social changes that shaped the future of Canada. These changes have been extensively described and interpreted by historians, but the law has been virtually ignored. This article and its companions are a product of a belief that law also can usefully be studied.

Before 1791 the area that was to become Ontario was part of the British colony of Quebec. In 1791 it was made into a separate colony, Upper Canada. In 1841 it was united with Lower Canada and became part of a new colony, the Province of Canada, although its law, especially the courts and the law about the economy, was substantially independent from the civil law system of Lower Canada. In 1867, at Confederation, the two were divided, and Upper Canada became Ontario and Lower Canada became Quebec.

THE ECONOMY

In 1841 the population of Ontario was 480,000, settlement was dispersed, and the urban centres were small; for example, Toronto, which was by far the largest town, had a population of only 14,000. In 1867 the population of Ontario was 1,525,000, little land was left for settlement, and urban centres had expanded. Toronto's population had increased to over 50,000, and small industries had been established. The major themes of the economy were the natural resources, transportation, and dependence upon Britain and the United States.

The natural resources were forests, land, and rivers and lakes. Originally, most of the land was covered by forests. In the south during the beginnings of settlement these forests were regarded primarily as an obstacle to be cleared, often by burning, and the wood was used only to make potash for export and small amounts of lumber for local use. A specialized timber industry began in the Ottawa Valley early in the nineteenth century, encouraged by Britain's war-time needs and economic policies. The Napoleonic wars threatened the supply of timber from the Baltic and prompted tariff preferences that became part of the mercantile system. The industry flourished during the 1820s and 1830s, but in the late 1840s overproduction and the removal of the preferences contributed to a short slump. Recovery came in the early 1850s. The United States replaced Britain as the dominant market, and sawn lumber replaced wasteful squared timbers as the dominant product. The myriad rivers and streams that flowed to the Great Lakes and the St Lawrence were the major means of transporting the logs to mills and to markets and were a source of power for mills, although a shift to steam power, especially in the large mills, began during the 1850s. The forests appeared to be limitless. Extensive cutting spread across the province and above the north shore of Georgian Bay, and little concern was expressed for supply in the future.

For agricultural purposes the province was divided by the Pre-Cambrian Shield, which stretched across the north and the east. Much of the Shield was rock and water, and most of its soil was thin and inhospitable. Most of the land south and west of the Shield was fertile, although not as fertile as the rich land in the mid-west of the United States. Most of this land was settled by 1850, and the value of agricultural products began to exceed the value of the forest products in the late 1850s. At the outset as settlers struggled to become established, the usual crops were vegetables for the settlers and their families, and grains, especially wheat, for sale. Hundreds of mills powered by the rivers and streams were built to mill the wheat to flour. After 1840 accumulations of capital and cleared land, improvements in transportation and marketing facilities, and increasing demand from urban centres and the United States combined to cause a slow shift away from wheat to mixed farming. Many of the products were exported to Britain and, especially after the early 1850s, to the United States.

The transportation system took these products to market and brought settlers to the frontier. It was shaped by changing technologies, especially the invention of the steam engine, and by the vision, which had continued from the fur trade, of controlling the trade of the mid-west United States as well as Canada. In the early nineteenth century the dominant objective was to improve water transport on the St Lawrence system by building canals, and in the 1840s the system was completed from Lake Erie to the Atlantic. Soon afterwards, in the early 1850s, a railroad boom began. Before 1850 only a few miles of track had been built in the British colonies. At the end of the boom, a decade later, over 2000 miles had been built, and southern Ontario was crossed by competing railroads, especially the Grand Trunk and Great Western. The canals and the railroads served Ontario's transportation needs as well as could have reasonably been hoped and the railroads were the exciting symbol and the reality of a shared progress. But the vision of control of the mid-west was never realized. The Erie canal, the railroads of the northeast, and New York City were all too powerful to be overcome.

Throughout, Ontario was dependent primarily upon Britain and secondarily upon the United States for markets, settlers, financing, and technology and ideas. Economic policy in Great Britain during the early nineteenth century encouraged the production and export of natural resource products by granting liberal tariff preferences, especially for wheat, flour, and timber. The triumph of free trade in England changed preferences during the late 1840s, but did not, despite fears of the late 1840s, close the English markets. Trade with the United States increased greatly and between 1854 and 1866 may have been encouraged by reciprocity in natural products. The early settlers came from the United States, but after 1815 almost all came from Europe and most came from Great Britain, and Ontario lost more settlers to the United States than it received. Most of the financing came ultimately from Britain, although much of it came from Montreal, an intermediate metropolitan centre. Most capital investments were purchases of bonds. A small amount of investment from the United States began during the 1850s and was usually purchases of shares in business. The technology and ideas ranged from the steam engine and agricultural implements to ideas about political economy – including ideas about law.[2]

THE COURTS

At the time this essay begins, about 1840, the courts had existed for over four decades.[3] But considering the purposes of the study, and the structure, work, and processes of the courts, this period includes not only the conclusion of a formative period but much of its development. In 1791, when Upper Canada was created, the only courts were decentralized and informal and administered largely by laymen. In 1794 the Court of King's Bench was created,[4] as part of Governor Simcoe's plan to make Upper Canada the 'image and transcript' of England. An appeal could be taken from this court to the governor-in-council and ultimately to the Privy Council. For over thirty years, no court existed to administer equitable jurisdiction, although proposals for one were often made.[5] In 1837 the Court of Chancery was established,[6] and it too was in substance a copy of the English model. Weaknesses of this court and an increasing volume of cases led to major changes in 1849. Another common law court was created, the Court of Common Pleas; the Chancery was expanded in size and stature; and the Court of Error and Appeal was created.[7] William Hume Blake, the Solicitor General, was the major architect of these changes.[8] He became Chancellor in 1849 and will loom large later in this essay.

During these first forty or more years the courts decided the disputes that were brought to them, but the surviving records and the slim published reports suggest that they did not decide a representative, large, and continuing volume of disputes about commercial transactions and economic issues, and they decided only a few cases involving major issues of principle. Attitudes towards process were being shaped from the outset, but a set of working principles was not settled. Much of the change occurred between about 1845 and 1855, and even the appearance then of continuing and comprehensive reports is suggestive.

The judges appointed to these courts were members or representatives of powerful groups. Fifteen served between 1840 and 1860. A substantial proportion – at least one-third – were members of loyalist families, had fought in the war of 1812, and had been educated by John Strachan. Only a little more than half had been born or matured in Canada, but almost all had received their legal education, such as it was, in Ontario and had practised extensively there. More than half had participated extensively in politics. The senior judges of each of the three courts were dominant: John Beverley Robinson, the Chief Justice of the Queen's Bench, James Macaulay, the Chief Justice of the Common Pleas, and William Hume Blake, the Chancellor. During one important and representative period, from 1850 to 1855, Robinson and Macaulay wrote judgments in virtually all the reported cases and wrote the judgment for the court in over seventy-five per cent. Chancellor Blake did not write such a large number of judgments but dominated because of the distinctive and original power of his mind.

The kinds of cases decided by these courts were very different from the kinds of cases decided by their successors more than a century later. The five largest groups were (1) the internal management of the work of the courts, (2) property, (3) the market, (4) enforcement of claims against debtors, and (5) municipal institutions. Among these five, internal management was by far the largest group; it included cases about pleadings, procedure, and appeals and other kinds of controls over lower courts. The market included cases about contracts, commercial paper, and security; property included cases about boundaries, conveyancing, leases, interpretation of wills, and administration of estates; claims against debtors included enforcement of executions against individual debtors, priorities among executions and other claims, assignments for the benefit of creditors, and bankruptcy; and municipal institutions included elections and the powers of municipalities. The facts and the problems presented by these cases were typical of the facts and problems of the society. For example, the contracts cases give a comprehensive description of the typical transactions and problems of the grain market: milling, brokers, financing, transportation, insurance, and standards. This reflection of reality in the cases was far greater than it is at present, because other tribunals did not exist to administer particular aspects of the economy, functions had not become administered by internal decisions in large and integrated corporations rather than by transactions among independent bodies, and standardization of transactions and forms had not made many transactions routine and therefore not a matter for courts.

The judges seemed to know and to understand these facts and problems, and, more particularly, seemed to know and to understand the typical functions, transactions, and problems of the economy. Again, the degree of knowledge and understanding was much higher than it is more than a century later. One reason may be the backgrounds of the judges. Lawyers were not nearly as specialized in the nineteenth century as they became later, and they tended more to a general practice, which gave them an extensive contact with their worlds. A much larger reason is the greater simplicity of institutions and transactions. For example, the financing of the Grand Trunk Railway was simple from the perspective of more than a century later, and much more simple than the financing of a small shopping centre. Two important examples of this knowledge and the understanding are the work of the Queen's Bench in the grain trade and the work of the Chancery in contracts about land. A more particular example is *Brunskill* v *Rigney,*[9] in which a factor sought to set off a claim, and Justice John H. Hagarty said 'it would be contrary to the well established course of merchantile dealing and calculated to destroy confidence in sales such as the one before us, which are of almost daily occurrence, if the plaintiff could be allowed to set up this answer...' In *Bryson* v *Clandinan,*[10] a claim for a commission as well as interest was made on a loan to a lumberman, and Chief Justice Robinson said 'we have abundant reason to know that such arrangements are not usual in carrying on the lumber business...'

The procedures the courts used were taken almost entirely from the procedures used by the courts in England. The procedures of the common law courts were different from the procedures of the Chancery and need extensive discussion. The major elements were the forms of action and pleading. The forms were the kinds of claims that could be made. A plaintiff had to choose one and make a claim, for example, of trespass or assumpsit or replevin. If the facts did not justify the form chosen, the action failed, even though another form might have given success on the same facts. The rules about pleading were designed to make the parties produce a single and precise issue of law or fact. For example, the times at which all material facts occurred had to be alleged, and issues had to be isolated in separate and independent pleas. If one party did not follow the rules, the other could force an amendment or, depending upon the kind of mistake, have the action dismissed. Both the forms of action and the rules of pleading had origins centuries before and originally had been functional responses to particular needs: the limited interventions of the royal courts, the emergence of the jury, and the division of trial between the formation of the issue in London and the use of the jury throughout England. Centuries later, change had transformed the original needs, but these procedures had continued, and during the early nineteenth century they reached a peak of complexity, abstraction, and confusion. Judges and lawyers had learned these procedures both as particular rules and as a way of thinking and believed they were necessary and needed to be rigorously enforced. Reform began in the mid-nineteenth century, but in a limited way, and was not completed until late in the century.[11]

The cases about these procedures were by far the largest single group of cases in the reports. An assessment of numbers and proportions is difficult to make, because many cases involved both substantive and procedural issues. Also, merits often were settled by decisions about procedure, especially decisions about pleadings, and often it is difficult or impossible to determine whether a decision had this effect or not. But after making reasonable allowances for these cases, over thirty per cent of the reported decisions of the two common law courts were about procedure. In the Queen's Bench the proportion was consistently slightly above thirty per cent, and in Common Pleas the proportion was larger at the outset and then declined. Among these cases, only a few were about the choice of forms of action, most were about scattered cases about times, forms, and jurisdiction, and the largest group were cases about pleading. In the Queen's Bench the proportion of cases about pleading was again consistent and slightly above ten per cent, and again, in the Common Pleas the proportion was higher at the outset and declined.

The pleading cases were by far the most complex and abstract. In the late twentieth century perhaps only a specialist in corporate taxation with both perspective and a sense of humour can comprehend the intensity of the dogma, the union of absurdity and reality, and the union of good faith, intelligence, and blind mindless conviction. Empty requirements of form were preserved; precedent and abstract logic overcame the merits of individual claims; and strict and critical interpretations overcame apparent intention. Examples of the extremes of this process would be persuasive only through their virtual incomprehensibility. Modest examples can be more useful, and the struggles about the need for allegations of dates in claims to enforce commercial paper demonstrate also the unwillingness of the courts to depart from authority and to make law. The general rules of pleading required a date to be alleged for the happening of each material fact. In *Bank of Upper Canada* v *Lewis*,[12] the bank made a claim against Lewis as the endorser of a note. Lewis pleaded that at the time the note came due, the maker had much more than the amount of the note in an account with the bank, and 'then' directed the bank to take the amount of the note from this account. The bank asserted that the plea was inadequate, because of the lack of a date, and succeeded. The word 'then' permitted the inference that the direction had been given after the action had begun. These facts were unusual, but time and notice were always issues in endorsement and notice of non-payment. The general rules were modified by statute to permit allegations that after a note was made, an endorser 'afterwards duly endorsed,' and that 'due notice' of non-payment was given.[13]

In *Grant* v *Eyre*,[14] the holder pleaded that the note was 'duly endorsed,' and the Court of Queen's Bench concluded unanimously that the omission of 'afterwards' made the plea inadequate, simply because the statutory form was not literally complied with, even though a note could be endorsed before it was made. In *Commercial Bank* v *Cameron*,[15] the Bank pleaded that the defendant, an endorser, had 'notice' of non-payment. The Queen's Bench divided equally about the adequacy of the plea and especially the need for 'due.' Both Robinson, who had been unhappy with the result in *Grant* v *Eyre*, and Justice Archibald McLean believed it unnecessary, because 'due' was hardly a substitute for the date that the new form had made unnecessary. They distinguished *Grant* v *Eyre* on the ground that 'notice' and 'due notice' had been held to have the same meaning, even though 'duly endorsed' and 'afterwards duly endorsed' might not. Justices James Macaulay and Jonas Jones decided it was necessary because it was included in the form. Robinson eventually joined them to confirm *Grant* v *Eyre* and make a rule for the future. In *Gooderham* v *Garden*,[16] literal compliance was not required. The holder of a note pleaded that it was made to the payee and 'then duly endorsed.' Robinson held that 'then' denoted a succession of events and was 'equivalent' to 'afterwards.' But in *Beaty* v *Jarvis*[17] form and rigour prevailed again. The holder of two notes pleaded that both were made and 'afterwards duly endorsed.' Robinson said that: 'This seems to have been an experiment in pleading. It would have been better to follow the beaten track, as nothing can well be more unnecessary than to supply occasion for a demurrer to a declaration upon a promissory note.' The plea was inadequate, because it did 'not import that the note later made was endorsed after it was made.' These rules about pleading doubtless squandered the time and energy of intelligent lawyers and caused much injustice by suppressing or delaying consideration of the particular merits of cases.

The judges did not assess or describe their attitudes towards their functions in any general way, nor did any thoughtful observers. Therefore generalizations must be made retrospectively from scattered comments, working documents, and results. The general attitude or implicit assumption was that the function of the courts was primarily, if not entirely, to adjudicate disputes according to the settled principles of the common law and the terms of statutes. The judges perceived little or no power or responsibility for change and creativity. This attitude, which included attitudes about the sources and limits of judicial reasoning, was expressed most clearly in the use of precedent. Any legal system seeks continuity and consistency, but the institutional arrangements made to achieve this objective and the degree of allegiance to the past vary greatly.

In England the doctrine of precedent was in a slow and confused transition.[18] In the late eighteenth century reason and general principle were perceived to have some independent effect. In 1774 Lord Mansfield said: 'The law of England would be a strange science indeed if it were decided upon precedents only. Precedents serve to illustrate principles and give them a fixed certainty.'[19] During the nineteenth century individual precedents came to have greater authority, and in the late nineteenth century their authority reached a peak. During the middle of the century the Ontario courts occasionally invoked principle and reason,[20] but principle was abstract generalization from the accumulation of decided cases, and reason was the process of making these generalizations and determining whether any particular case was included in them. Neither integrated social need or context with the cases in any general or substantial way. Individual precedents controlled the outcome of cases, unless they were inconsistent with principle,[21] and this possibility of inconsistency was not often considered and less often realized. Often precedents were followed even though they were acknowledged to be clearly unfair, and required results inconsistent with 'the moral justice of the case'[22] or reached 'with unfeigned reluctance.'[23] Equity included some general principles that permitted fairness and context to affect results, but these considerations never prevailed over settled precedent. The courts realized that the common law had been created by courts and did change, but this realization was not a part of their working philosophy. They were prepared to acknowledge that change was needed, but assumed it must be made by the English courts or the legislature. 'The legislature may of course place the law on a different footing, if they think it proper to do so, but we have no authority to change it.'[24] Only one judge, Chancellor Blake, seemed to feel a responsibility for the continuing utility of the law.

But the courts did not assume that their function was entirely the application of settled doctrine to particular disputes. They often perceived that the common law was inconsistent, unsettled, or unclear, and responded deliberately.[25] Occasionally the response was an expression of a choice between the possibilities presented by an inconsistent or incomplete tangle of cases. These choices were usually made by considering the internal appeal of the general principles or some simple sense of fairness or need. More often, when the common law seemed to be unsettled or unclear, the response was a considered declaration of general principles. This function was especially apparent in cases involving problems about the market. Robinson and Chancellor Blake gave the most useful explanations. In *Chisholm* v *Proudfoot*,[26] the Queen's Bench considered the obligation of vendors of flour. The case could have been decided by reference to a case decided the year before, and upon the narrow ground that a brand on the particular barrels was an express warranty. However, Robinson said:

> But from the great importance of the question, we have thought it right not to satisfy ourselves with resting on that decision, or upon the judgement which was given in it upon the question of implied warranty, where the person selling the article is the person who manufactured it. Upon a review of the authorities we have come to the conclusion that in this case, independently of the brand upon the barrels, there was evidence given to the jury which, if believed, would warrant them in finding an express warranty.

In *Bank of Upper Canada* v *Smith*,[27] he said: 'It is of much importance that the law should be duly administered on settled principles in regard to commercial transactions of this nature, occurring so constantly and in which so many persons are interested.' Chancellor Blake made his most illuminating statement in *Hook* v *McQueen*,[28] which involved the consequences of delay in making payments owing under an agreement to buy land.

> Rules deducible from English authorities cannot be applied, without considerable modification, to a country where the habits of society and the condition of property are so widely different; and to no branch of equitable jurisdiction is the observation more applicable than to the one now under consideration. The uncertainty produced by these causes, which was felt to be a great evil, I believe, both by the public and the profession, it has been my constant endeavor to correct to the utmost of my ability, by stating in each case, too minutely it may be, the grounds upon which my judgment has proceeded; and in this particular instance I have no disposition, certainly, to depart from this practice – for it seems to be of great importance that the spirit in which this branch of the law is to be administered should be ascertained with as much accuracy as the nature of the subject will admit.

The courts seem not to have made these declarations as a mask for avoiding precedent and changing law. The common law system inevitably involved uncertainty about particular issues, even important and recurring ones, and the declarations were usually no more than what they appeared to be. The courts believed that they were elaborating general principles and not exercising any creative power. Their efforts were probably in part a reflection of a general concern for certainty and generality, but both the context and terms of the declaration suggest that the primary purpose was to enable businessmen to plan and manage their affairs. Planning could be more effective if uncertainties were diminished and the requirements for effective action made clear.

A good example of the attitudes towards precedent, and an introduction to the obligation to follow English precedent and the use of cases from the United States, is the struggles with the need for a seal to enforce contracts made by corporations. The general rule, which was well established by many English cases, was that a promise could not be enforced by or against a corporation, unless the corporation had made the promise by using its corporate seal. The Ontario courts rarely discussed the justification for this rule, and the few discussions were short and abstract and essentially assertions of the rule itself: the only way a corporation, considered either as a group or an abstract entity, could express consent was by a seal, and the seal was necessary evidence of the consent.

Whatever its theoretical or functional justifications may have been, the application of the rule to some situations caused difficulty and apparent misfortune. Exceptions had emerged in English cases, but were vague and continuing to be formed, and took different forms in different courts and at different times. The Ontario courts never doubted and rarely expressed their obligation to follow these English cases, although in *Hamilton* v *Niagara Harbour and Dock,*[29] Robinson said 'our adherence to the principles of the English common law is a duty imposed upon us by written law, and is therefore more strongly obligatory than it may be acknowledged to be in the courts of the United States,' and in *Marshall* v *School Trustees of Kitley,*[30] Justice William B. Richards said 'we are bound by the authority of the cases decided in England, and until the law is entitled differently, we must carry it out in the mode indicated by those decisions.' Many of the judgments of the Ontario courts were extensive discussions of these English cases, and even though the law seemed unsatisfactory, the courts denied themselves any creative powers, except the power to choose among the uncertain or conflicting authorities. The legislature seemed to be the sole law-making power. In *Hamilton,* Robinson said:

'This doctrine of the liability of corporations does seem to require some legislative revision'; and in *Marshall*, Justice McLean said that the law was unsettled, and 'it appears to be equally unsettled in England ... and seems to require legislative interference.' In *Pim* v *Municipal Council of Ontario*,[31] Chancellor Blake said: 'It may be that the evil calls for legislative interference, but ... courts of justice are bound to place their decisions upon some principle intelligible to the public and sufficient for their guidance,' but even he was not willing to go beyond what seemed authorized by English cases. Courts in the United States had exercised a much greater law-making power and had made their law apparently more rational and fair by expanding enforcement regardless of the use of a seal.[32] The courts in Ontario knew about these decisions and admired them,[33] but were never tempted to stray from their perception of their constitutional obligations and functions.

The simplest exception permitted enforcement of contracts made routinely and often in the performance of the business of the corporation. Its justification was convenience or even necessity, and it presented only the inescapable problem of deciding which contracts it included.[34] The other major exception was enforcement to give compensation for benefits conferred (contrasted to enforcement of an unexecuted promise to perform). It was the most unsettled issue and was doubted and even denied by some English cases and courts. The Queen's Bench, led by Robinson, recognized it,[35] justifying their results by resort to English cases and their own reluctance to permit benefits to be received without payment. The Common Pleas reasoned in a more formal way, and denied it.[36] The Court of Error and Appeal confirmed the Queen's Bench,[37] in a judgment written by Chancellor Blake, who said: 'I do not disguise from myself that this opinion is opposed to many cases in the Exchequer, and much that is to be found elsewhere, but when these decisions are in such manifest and painful conflict, it becomes the duty of the court to adopt that conclusion which appears on the whole most consistent with the principles of justice.'

In *Whitehead* v *Buffalo and Lake Huron Railway*,[38] Blake suggested that he was willing to use a more liberal approach and enforce all contracts of corporations 'within the scope of their charter,' 'a principle which, if adopted, would have the effect of placing this important class of commercial contracts upon the same footing here as in the United States – a footing at once intelligible and adapted to the age and country in which we live.'

This approach was consistent with the language and results of some recent English cases, but on appeal to the Court of Error and Appeal,[39] Robinson asserted that these cases did not clearly upset the traditional and opposed authority, and that 'I am not in favour of acting ... until we can see that the other courts in England take the same course, or until we find that the principle ... is confirmed in the House of Lords...'

THE COMMON LAW – AND SOME LEGISLATION

The content of the common law corresponded to the structure of the courts and the disputes they decided: it was primarily rules about the conduct and claims of individuals, respecting usually the conduct of other individuals and occasionally the government. It had been made by the English courts and seemed to be substantially settled by 1840. Few large changes were made before the late nineteenth century, and much of it has remained intact later in the twentieth century. For the purposes of description and analysis, it can be considered as rules about powers and rules about the allocation of liability. The powers took three forms: (1) powers to make agreements for exchanges, (2) powers to make agreements to achieve common objectives, and (3) powers to use the natural resources. The powers to make exchanges were the law of the market, especially contracts, commercial paper, and security. The law of contracts enabled individuals to make enforceable promises about the conduct of their affairs in the future. The requirements were generally simple and were usually satisfied by the conduct of businessmen in making a bargain. No substantial restrictions were imposed on the purpose or the fairness of the contracts; some requirements about form were imposed by legislation, but they were not onerous, and most of them were fairly easily standardized. The law of commercial paper enabled obligations to pay to be made in a form that made them easily and reliably transferable, and the law of security enabled obligations to pay to be secured by personal obligations, goods, or land. The power to make agreements to achieve common objectives was the power to create partnerships. They could be made by simple agreement or conduct and could be used for a wide range of purposes. The natural resources were the land, rivers, and forests. The power to use them was primarily the law of property, and it was most complex and refined about the land. It permitted the creation and transfer of interests in land, particularly the fee simple, which was the usual interest of an owner, and which gave an owner an exclusive and comprehensive power to determine the use of land and to restrain any interferences with this use. An owner could decide whether to make a farm from a forest, whether to plant a crop or let the land lay fallow, or whether to sell it to a new owner. The law about the rivers gave extensive powers to use them for transportation, especially transportation of logs, and allocated powers to use them to generate power among the riparian owners, in proportion to the potential of the flow past each one's property.

Economic activity occasionally caused losses that were not allocated by contract. The general rule was that compensation must be paid for losses caused deliberately or by negligence. However this obligation did not extend to some kinds of losses, especially losses caused by the railroads. Legislation that authorized activity, for example the construction and operation of a railroad, was interpreted to authorize the losses that the activity must cause, for example the inconveniences of operation. Legislation gave extensive power of expropriation for the railroads, and although a requirement for compensation was virtually always included, it did not include all the losses caused by the taking. The safety of humans may have had less protection than property: general attitudes and particular decisions about individual responsibility required employees to assume the apparent risks of their jobs, including the negligence of fellow employees.

The common law was extensive, but it was not all of the law about the economy. Legislation was enacted for five major purposes: the establishment of supplemental terms to facilitate the working of the market, the creation of corporations, the allocation of land and forests, the creation, financing, and operation of transportation facilities, and the creation of terms for international trade. The legislation about the market generally did not amend common law doctrine. Instead it established rules and institutions that did not exist in the common law and that were beyond the power of the courts to create, for example standards and arrangements for inspection of raw materials, bankruptcy and insolvency, and most important, arrangements for accommodating the competing interests of purchasers and secured creditors of goods and land. The legislation about the corporations was statutes that created individual corporations and statutes that enabled individuals to create standard forms of corporations by satisfying specified requirements. These statutes were the beginnings of the eventual domination of business enterprise by the corporation, but at the time the partnership was used much more often and for a wider range of purposes. The legislation about the transportation facilities included creation of corporations to undertake roads, canals, and railroads; grants of franchises to construct and operate; powers of expropriation; limited liability for shareholders; and most important, extensive financial support that often become substantial or even formal ownership. It also included direct provision of facilities, especially canals, roads, and timber slides.

Much of this legislation was enacted around 1850, and its appearance coincides roughly with the change in the cases in the reports. In 1848 a reform government headed by Baldwin and LaFontaine took office, and its record is remarkable. During the first session in 1849 the Rebellion Losses Bill, which gave compensation to inhabitants of Lower Canada for losses incurred during the rebellion of 1837, was the most dramatic public issue. The assent by the Governor General was a crucial symbol of responsible government and the immediate cause of riots and the burning of the parliament buildings. The session produced other legislation of great and immediate public importance that is not included in this study, for example legislation about government guarantees of railroad bonds, schools, and municipal government. The reform of court structures has already been briefly described. As well as all this, legislation was enacted about registration of chattel mortgages, creation of limited partnerships and road corporations, and the use of the rivers for floating logs. The next session in 1850 produced legislation about free banking, creation of manufacturing corporations, and allocation of timber. The third session in 1851 produced a general railroad act and legislation about basic property principles. Throughout these three years, other less important statutes about the economy were enacted. Moreover, the railroad boom was reflected not only in general and financing legislation, but in the creation of increasing numbers of individual railroads, and the number of all kinds of corporations began a large and sudden increase.

The reasons for this outburst of legislation are complex. The increasing volume and complexity of commercial transactions is probably the ultimate reason but it does not explain the sharp limits to the timing, especially the beginning. The Reform government had considerable unity and a comfortable majority and had been preceded by years of weak and divided governments. It was followed by complex reorganizations of political alignments, and eventually by the depression of the late 1850s, and the paralysis of government that contributed to Confederation.

VALUES

All of this law, common law and legislation together, expressed values or attitudes towards economic activity which can be best described in three themes: the encouragement of private initiative, change, and the public and private interests. The most powerful and pervasive value was the facilitation and encouragement of private initiative. The primary effect of the law about the market, business organizations, and property was to enable individuals to take initiative about economic affairs. The expression of this value was most clear in the law about the market and business organizations, and was most blurred by competing values in the law of property, which gave an individual immunity from interference by others and therefore from the initiative of others. Its strength was demonstrated by both the scope of the powers and the simple requirements for their exercise. The scope of all three kinds was comprehensive and extensive and permitted virtually all reasonably conceivable purposes and conduct.

Three minor values overlapped the encouragement of private initiative. The first was that each individual should have responsibility for his own fate. This value was often, but not always, a corollary of the encouragement of private initiative, and it was expressed most clearly by the courts in their unwillingness to consider the fairness of bargains and in their allocation of liability for physical injuries, and again property gave protection. The second of these minor values was the protection of useful private effort, which was demonstrated most clearly in cases about compensation for improvements made to land by purchasers and squatters. It is a small example of a value that was overcome in some contexts by competing values and other influences: it did not appear in claims for compensation for improvements made by mistake about ownership or boundaries because of settled English authority and the value of property as an exclusive right, and it did not appear in cases about claims against trespassers because of the settled limits of trespass.

The last of these three minor themes was the most important. It was the degree of dispersal and equality of economic power, particularly the extent of property that could legitimately be owned by an individual, and the legitimacy of substantial or monopolistic control over a resource or market. The record is sparse, confusing, and often ambiguous. The law about the market may have assumed that a rough equality of bargaining power would usually exist, but it imposed no limits on accumulation or use of power. The expressed policies about allocation of land were usually that most of the land would be granted to and owned by individual settlers, but official practice and the lack of any effective limit on market acquisitions of property permitted some individuals to accumulate large holdings. The terms of licences to cut timber included restrictions designed to prevent individuals from accumulating large and unused resources, and the common law that regulated the use of the rivers for transporting logs and for power suggests a fear of monopolistic control of a crucial resource. Fear of monopoly was also expressed in the debates about corporations, even apart from the transportion corporations, for which the very grant of a franchise was often effectively a grant of a monopoly. The general incorporation statutes and the lack of any controls over accumulation of power eventually permitted corporations to acquire immense power, but long after 1867. In short, much of the law assumed a substantial dispersal and equality of power, and some particular terms tended to make this assumption a requirement, but it expressed no consistent general tendency, except for the lack of any general restrictions on accumulation or use of power. The powers of the railroads, and some large owners of land and wholesale traders were conspicuous, but no reliable general assessment has been made of the dispersal and equality of power. Doubtless accumulations were not as large as those that began fifty years later.

The private powers supported by the legislation were powers to make economic change. They did not require change or attempts at change; instead they simply authorized whatever conduct was chosen, if conduct was chosen at all. However, the prevailing belief was that the powers should, and would be, used to achieve progress. The law about the market was a power to make countless routine commercial transactions and to fashion new kinds of transactions. The law about business organizations was a power to gather crucial economic power to make change, and the law about property was a power to exploit the natural resources and to change a countryside. Of the three, property again was the most blurred and ambiguous, because it was also a power to make no productive use and to resist aggressive invasions that might have been productive. The tendency of these powers to encourage change was complemented by the law about allocation of losses. At crucial points activity designed to make substantial change, for example the clearing of land and construction and operation of transportation undertakings caused loss, but causing loss did not alone create liability; instead the liability depended upon proof of negligence or was entirely denied by statutory authority.

The courts and the legislature did not make any extensive statement of public and private interests, nor did any other source of expression. The attitude must be gathered from acts and from fragments of thought, but it was nonetheless real, consistent, and effective. The public interest was material productivity and progress, and it was to be achieved primarily through private initiative, encouraged by government support. The private interests, guided by an 'unseen hand,' generally coincided with the public interest. Chancellor Blake invoked this unity in *O'Keefe* v *Taylor*[40] by asserting that protection of settlers' efforts was necessary, 'not only to the attainment of justice in individual cases but to the general welfare.' But conflicts occurred and were usually problems for courts to resolve. In *Phillips* v *Redpath and McKay*,[41] Robinson said 'private interest and convenience must ... be made to yield to the public welfare'; in *Dean* v *McCarty*,[42] he said that burning wood to clear land was 'indispensable, not merely to individual interests, but to the public good'; in *Hill* v *Ontario, Simcoe, and Huron Railroad Union*[43] Justice Robert E. Burns said the legislature must have intended railways to be used 'for the public benefit, even though some individual interest should suffer.' No simple generalization can be made about the results of these conflicts because of the pressures of other values and other influences, but the public interest tended to prevail where individual effort seemed likely to create a useful facility or to accumulate capital, although legislative authority was needed to prevail over property claims.

The allocation of risk in the market was influenced by the same public interest. The general measure of damages for breach of contract denied recovery for all losses caused by breach and encouraged market transactions by giving a general rule and assurance against unforeseeable liability. In decisions about the liability of telegraph corporations the courts demonstrated an inclination to protect a new and important communication facility against the apparent threat of crushing and disproportionate liability. The bankruptcy statutes and the limited liability of corporations limited the claims of individual creditors to enable individual businessmen to be productive and to enable corporations to accumulate capital.

These three elements of values – private initiative, change and stability, and public and private interest – are all consistent and to a considerable extent are the same terms and results considered from different perspectives. They make a comprehensive public philosophy: economic progress, especially exploiting the natural resources, was good and was to be achieved primarily by individual initiative facilitated by government support, but individual aggressiveness was limited: property interests generally gave owners the right to be unproductive, except for land needed for transportation facilities.

INFLUENCES

Law, like any other large and complex social institution, is a product of complex influences and processes, and choice and interpretation are ultimately expressions of purposes and understandings of change. The major immediate influence has been values or beliefs about the proper terms and limits of law. The common law was made by judges. Decades and centuries of change have demonstrated that the choices of its terms have not been substantially constrained by settled doctrine and the rules of precedent. It has generally expressed the values of the judges, and these values have been those of powerful social groups. The values expressed by judges are likely to be shaped by the society in which they live. Mavericks are not likely to be appointed judges, and the expectations and institutional pressures of the job of judging tend to make the results and rules acceptable, although often the values expressed by judges have been values of past generations or a limited class or group, and resistance to change or to expansiveness has made obligations to precedent into apparently impersonal obstacles to change. Legislation has tended more to express current values, because the power and the legitimacy to make change are more simple and apparent.

During the mid-nineteenth century in Canada, a set of values about the economy was widely shared and was substantially the same as, or consistent with, the values expressed by the law.[44] These values were products of English liberalism, qualified by legacies from the Loyalists and the English Tories, and by the Canadian geography. They were pragmatic, and usually expressed in action and debate about particular issues, rather than extensive general statements, but they were strongly held, uniform, and consistent. Individual initiative and responsibility were respected and encouraged, as moral obligations and as the most efficient foundations of the economy. Material progress was desired and seemed to be continuously attainable, but it was to be pursued with restraint and not turbulently or aggressively. The government should participate in the economy, to support individual effort to overcome the limitations imposed by a sparse population and the harsh geography. During this period, these values did not shape the common law in more than small ways, because it had been shaped in England during centuries, but they gave strong support. The courts shared these values, although near the end of the period a gap seemed to be widening between the increasing complexity and scale of commercial activity and the attitudes and experience of the judges. The need for certainty to enable economic activity was slowly becoming a rigidity and formalism that would make the courts unable to respond to change and need in the late nineteenth century.

The search for ultimate influences entangles values and economic structure, and the search is complicated by the realization that much of the relation between law and economic structure can be tautological. Private ownership and private power are contracts and property unrestrained by governmental regulation, and the question, why did the fee simple exist? is ultimately the question, why did private ownership exist? Whatever other interpretations may be made, one general conclusion is important for understanding the legal process: values and economic structure formed a consistent context that shaped the structure and context of the law.

Three more particular and immediate influences are important for study of this law during this period: the law of England and the United States, the legal institutions, and the frontier.

Formal obligation, and preferences produced by loyalty, habit, convenience, and ambition made the laws of England and the United States a large influence. This influence, especially of the law of England, overlaps greatly with the influence of values. In England values had influenced law and were expressed in law, and the influence of English law on Ontario law was an influence of English values. Also, the expression of the values through law tended to reinforce them and to contribute to the shaping of values in Ontario. From this perspective, law was a massive means of communication, not simply of legal doctrine, but of ideas and values. Despite this overlap, the independent influence of the law of these other jurisdictions needs to be isolated, especially for a study of legal history, and especially because formal obligation and habit might have made the law diverge from contemporary values.

A distinction must be made between the courts and the legislature. For the courts, faithfulness to the precedents of English courts was a constitutional obligation which was supported by loyalty, habit, and convenience. The constitutional obligation was established in 1792 by one of the first statutes of the colony: 'In all matters of controversy relative to property and civil rights, resort shall be had to the Laws of England as the rule for the decision of the same.'[45] This obligation was continually reinforced by the disposition of appeals from Ontario courts to the Privy Council, which decided cases from Ontario according to English law. The support of loyalty was a product not only of the usual loyalty of the colony, but also of the traditional education and associations of the legal profession, and the powerful appeal of being part of the massive traditions of the English legal system. Habit and convenience were weaker and more subtle influences. Habit was a product of constant reference and was, perhaps, loyalty without spirit. Convenience was simply the availability of a vast, coherent, and useful body of law. A pioneer community could not create, and was not likely to seek to try to create, an adequate body of law through its own independent efforts and resources. The result was that the general outlines and most of the detail of the common law in Ontario was the same as common law in England. Occasionally the courts expressly acknowledged the obligation and the influence,[46] but its most impressive and eloquent witness is the results and the routine discussion and acceptance of English authority in countless cases in all three courts.

Despite this influence from England, cases from the United States, especially from the Supreme Court and the northeastern states, were discussed and used. The extent of this use was small in absolute terms, and small in proportion to the use of English cases, but it was larger than it has been at any time afterwards. The use was not inconsistent with constitutional obligation and did not significantly betray loyalty, because the cases from the United States tended to be used if no English cases seemed to govern an issue. The United States offered a rich accumulation of experience about problems that were distinctive to a North American economy, and, just as important, experience that was easily accessible through the texts of Story and Kent, which also included discussion of English cases. Blackstone's *Commentaries* are often assumed to have greatly influenced the minds of nineteenth-century lawyers in the colonies. Doubtless they did, but the nature of the influence was distinctly limited. The *Commentaries* gave the general outlines of much of the common law and much useful learning about the English constitution, and they were a major symbol of the English legal traditions, but the record of the law reports and journals demonstrates that during this period they were rarely used for deciding specific problems about the law that governed the economy. The reason is simply that the *Commentaries* contained almost nothing, especially contrasted to Story and Kent, about contracts and the corporation, or about the property and loss allocation problems that were pressing in Ontario. In *Bank of Montreal* v *DeLatre*, Robinson said:

> The defendant's counsel, in the argument, referred to American authorities, and it is always advisable and useful on questions of this nature to look for information in that quarter, for in applying legal principles to mercantile contracts and

dealings, and the remedies upon them, the American Courts have generally gone before those in England in introducing such relaxations as have seemed necessary for the convenience and safety of those engaged in commerce; and they have, in some instances gone further, without the aid of legislative enactments, in moulding the principles of common law to suit supposed exigencies, than English Courts of Justice have yet ventured to go...

With this view I have looked into whatever Mr. Justice Story has collected on the subject in his work on promissory notes and on agency.[47]

But he eventually considered the English cases, 'as we are bound to do,' and concluded that they governed the issue. In *Street* v *Commercial Bank of the Midland District,* he said:

The American courts ... find no insuperable difficulty in relieving themselves from the mere force of English authority, when they think adjudged cases at variance with general principles. We are clearly bound by such authority, when we can shew no dispensation from it ... The tribunals of the United States ... have in the decisions of the English courts a pattern which they may work by ... We have in them a pattern which we must work by, unless where the legislature has sanctioned a deviation...[48]

Compared to the common law, the legislation was substantially less influenced from England. The legislature had no constitutional obligation to use English models, and the emotional appeal of the English legal system was far less strong for statutes than it was for the common law. The distinctively Canadian needs and wants that seemed to affect law and require differences were usually appropriately the subject of legislation, not common law. This appropriateness was a consequence of the nature and limits of the common law generally, and not the particular content of English common law; for example, creation of arrangements for the allocation of natural resources was a function for legislation, not common law. The influence from the United States, especially New York, was larger, especially for legislation about the market and corporation. Some comments in debates suggest that models from the United States were appealing simply because they seemed to be a means to achieve the envied prosperity with which they were apparently associated. The legislation that made the terms for allocation of the land and timber was not influenced by external models, because English models did not exist, and because the policy was different than the policy that shaped the legislation in the United States.

The influence of legal reasoning and legal institutions is difficult to assess. It is difficult to imagine any rational mind believing that legal reasoning and legal institutions, whatever these phrases may include, have been the only influences on law. It is almost equally difficult to imagine a rational belief that they have had no influence at all. For the common law, two particular possibilities need to be discussed: precedent and the implications of settled doctrine, and procedure. Courts make common law by deciding individual cases and working from case to case and have a tendency and an obligation to follow cases and settled doctrine. The nature and extent of the obligation has changed over time and has been continuously debated, but clearly the control of precedent and the implications of settled doctrine depend greatly upon both the context and the attitude of each judge. Considering the other possible influences on law, the general expectation is that whatever these attitudes may be in any particular time and jurisdiction, this process of reasoning has had little effect on making the general shape of law. The scope of its influence is generally limited to making particular form and detail, and, through the obligation to precedent, to making doctrine continue after its shaping context has passed. For example, the implications of settled doctrine were a slight influence in the making of the fellow-servant rule early in the nineteenth century, but the dominant influences were likely values, even though the particular nature of the values is debatable. But late in the century, the weight of precedent was so large that no court in England or North America was likely to escape the rule, even if the need for escape had been clear and acknowledged.

The influence of procedure, particularly the forms of action and pleading, is even more difficult to assess. Doubtless it was more subtle. Thinking about law as an abstract set of rules ordered entirely by precedent and their own self-sufficient logic may have been encouraged by constant working with doctrine and assertions of fact, not to decide a case and the fate of real and present people, but to decide whether an issue was properly found and posed. Also, a tendency not to consider remote and general implications of decisions may have been encouraged by the constant concern to make a precise issue between the parties.[49]

The purposes of the structure and procedures of the legislature were more complex and diverse than the purposes of the procedures of the courts. For a study of their effect on the form and content of statutes, the significant characteristics were a lack of staff, and scanty and erratic arrangements for use of committees and controlling debate. The result was to emphasize a tendency to formulate and consider legislation without extensive knowledge of purposes, alternatives, and implications, and to consider only immediate and pressing issues. More particularly, for example, the construction of some of the legislation, especially some of the legislation copied from New York, was careless; some of it was internally inconsistent, and some of it was adopted without consideration of its implications and limits. Much of the legislation about railroads and natural resources was conceived and discussed considering primarily immediate and particular pressures, without regard or even knowledge of long-term needs and capacity.

The 'frontier' is a vague term. It is used here to denote the distinctive geography and resources and the pervasive newness and developing character of the country. These characteristics made Ontario greatly different from England, and it is tempting to presume that they had some large and pervasive influence on the law, and to make some 'frontier' interpretation. Such an interpretation can be made, but it cannot be simple and dramatic.

The influence on the common law was small, and the problem is not to make a frontier interpretation, but explain why one cannot be made. The frontier conditions were pervasive and shaped problems and the terms of transactions in distinctive ways through the economy; for example, problems were created about the interpretation of agreements to cut timber, about giving notice over long distances to endorsers of commercial paper, about the use of rivers, and about clearing land. But the general rules used by the courts to govern these problems were the common law that was originally made in England, and were not significantly influenced by these conditions. Occasionally and perhaps dramatically some frontier conditions influenced the application of general doctrine, for example, the grant of specific performance to sell saw logs, or to a purchaser of land who was in possession and who was clearing the land, but was in default in making instalment payments, but in these cases the doctrine was not modified: its terms permitted or required consideration of particular conditions.

For the law of contract, partnership, and property the only significant impact was the recognition of useful effort, the uneasiness about the English law of waste and, most important, the use of the rivers for transportation. One reason for this lack of substantial influence was the strength of the other influences, especially the law of England, but this does not explain why this law was not inappropriate for use in the frontier conditions. Generally, little tension existed between the law and the perceived economic needs that were created by the frontier conditions.

The only apparent and persistent strains were in the law about sale of land. The more important reason is the abstract character of this law. Its terms generally did not include any distinction or requirements for particular parties, purposes, or places. The private powers were, in effect, blank powers to be used in whatever way individuals wished. The law of contract did not include any terms or requirements that differentiated between an agreement to import cotton into Manchester and an agreement to build a railroad bridge in Hamilton. The power of the fee simple did not differentiate between use of land in Sussex and the use of land in western Ontario.

The law about allocation of losses was not abstract, but it too was not substantially affected by the frontier conditions. They were mentioned in only a few cases, and the most interesting was *Dean* v *McCarty*,[50] which considered the liability for damage caused by a fire that was started to clear a settler's land. The pervasive need to clear the land was recognized, but the standard used to determine liability was negligence, which was a general standard that had been settled earlier in England – and applied to liability for fires. This standard, and the denial of liability for activity that had been authorized by legislation, did not impose liability on private conduct for some of the losses that it caused. The influence of English law and the values about individual responsibility, progress, and property combined to make this law, even though the apparent needs to develop the country would have seemed to justify greater limitation on liability, and occasionally did in the United States.

The frontier conditions did create distinctive needs for law, but the response came from legislation, not common law, because the needs were appropriate for legislative responses, not common law. The very existence and the general purpose of most of the legislation about the economy were products of these influences. Geography created the apparent needs for the transportation facilities that many of the statutes were enacted to provide; the major facility, the railroad, caused a small flood of statutes; and the need to allocate resources created the need for a few but important allocation statutes. The particular content of these statutes was not influenced nearly as much. The abundance of the resources affected some terms, but values and traditional associations seem to have been a much larger influence on content.

TWO POSSIBLE HEROES

Two judges were more visible, interesting, and influential than the others: John Beverley Robinson, Chief Justice of the Court of Queen's

Bench, and William Hume Blake, the Chancellor. Of the two, Robinson played a much larger role in the history of the colony. His parents were Loyalists who came from the United States to New Brunswick. They moved to Kingston in Ontario in 1792, when he was barely a year old. A good education, influential friendships, and sheer ability gave him opportunities and advancement. He began his legal education, which was simply articling, in 1807, participated briefly but auspiciously in the War of 1812, and was made acting Attorney General in 1812, before he had even become a lawyer. He was made Solicitor General in 1815, and Attorney General in 1818. In 1820 he was elected to the Assembly and continued to be a member until 1828. Throughout the 1820s he was a principal member of a small group of supporters and advisors of the government. In 1829 he was made Chief Justice of Upper Canada, then during the 1830s lost most of his political power.[51]

He was a conservative, in a sense that mingled ideas of the Loyalists and late eighteenth century Tory England. He believed in property, class, and religion, and he viewed his public service as a response to an obligation. He believed in Blackstone's balanced constitution, especially an appointed upper house, and deplored the claims of democracy, especially the excesses of democracy he saw in the United States. He had the conservative's organic concept of society, and this concept and his deep religious beliefs imposed a perspective on the utility and the limits of law:

> the impartial administration of the law will under the blessing of Providence enable us to lay a sure foundation for the enjoyment of social happiness and rational freedom in as abundant a measure as the nature of man will permit.
>
> What can laws avail without morals and without religion? A conviction of the sacred truths of Christian revelation supplies at the highest [situation?] to human laws and the fairest as well as the strongest [instance] for obeying them...[52]

He believed that economic and material progress was beneficial and should be encouraged by government – for example, he was one of the original and strong supporters of the Welland Canal – but the progress should be controlled and gradual and achieved through effort, not speculation. Attitudes about the economy and about political power and the composition and alignment of groups changed after the 1820s, and a broad liberal-whig consensus emerged. Robinson's beliefs were strongly held and do not seem to have changed, judging from the few documents that remain, but nor do they seem to have affected his judgments, because of the tempering common law tradition that purported to exclude beliefs

John Beverley Robinson (1791–1863), Attorney General of Upper Canada 1818–29, and Chief Justice of Upper Canada 1829–62
Oil portrait by George Théodore Berthon (Osgoode Hall, Toronto)

of this kind, because of the abstractness of so much of the law, and, most important, because political beliefs usually did not dictate any particular result for the kinds of problems the courts considered. Belief in private property and the indifference of the market was a belief that tended to express and support attitudes about classes and distribution of wealth but they were common to all political thinking and groups.

An outstanding characteristic of Robinson's work as chief justice was his great conscientiousness. He served for thirty-three years, and throughout these years he continuously wrote careful judgments for most cases, for himself or for the court. The result is an immense mass of judgments which is difficult to approach because replete with the technicalities of common law procedure and discussions of English cases. He shared the prevailing assumptions and attitudes about the nature of the common law and the obligations of a judge and seemed to embody and express them more consistently and clearly than any other Canadian judge. His judgments include some short statements of dissatisfaction with doctrine, the need for certainty, and economic need and policy, that were more numerous than the general appearance of the judgments suggest. These were the products of a strong and forthright mind and did not affect the reasonings or outcomes except in the few cases for which the precedents permitted a choice.

Chancellor Blake was born in Ireland in 1809. He received a liberal education at Trinity College, Dublin, and studied medicine for a few years, although he did not become a doctor. He immigrated to Ontario in 1832, and briefly tried pioneer farming near Strathroy. He moved to Toronto in 1834 and began his legal education, articling, twenty-seven years later than Robinson and nine years older. He quickly became a successful lawyer, and was one of the leading counsel during the 1840s and the pre-eminent Chancery counsel. He was also appointed professor of law at King's College in Toronto, and thus became the first law teacher in Ontario. He became involved in politics during the 1840s as a member of the Reform party. He was elected to the Assembly in 1848 and became Solicitor General in the Baldwin-LaFontaine Reform government, although not a member of the cabinet. His brief political career had two major features. The first was a brilliant and intemperate speech defending the Rebellion Losses Bill and attacking the Tory members, which aroused John A. Macdonald to challenge him to a duel. The second, less dramatic but more useful, was his important role in reorganization of the courts in 1849.

Blake was appointed Chancellor of the reorganized Chancery in 1849, and one of the reasons for his appointment was probably to give him a retreat from the rough-and-tumble world of politics for which a sensitive and volatile temperament and delicate health made him inappropriate. He kept the office until 1862, but failing emotional and physical health greatly reduced his participation after the mid-1850s. His major judgments were all written in the early 1850s, when he was in his early forties. The nature of his weaknesses cannot be known from a distance of over a hundred years, but whatever they were, they clearly restricted his potential career and contribution.[53]

Like Robinson, Blake was deeply religious and staunchly loyal to Britain, the British constitution, and British ideas, although his loyalty was to liberalism and not Robinson's toryism. His public speeches stressed freedom; Robinson stressed duty. His distinctive characteristics as judge were sheer intelligence and perception, openness, a passion for fairness, and a determination to shape the law to Canadian needs and conditions. One statement from *Attorney General* v *McLaughlin*[54] is representative of many others. 'For if it be the duty of courts of equity in England to modify their rules and practice to meet the growing wants of society, *a fortiori*, must we labour to render those rules effectual for the ends of justice in our social condition, differing as it does in many respects so widely from that of England.' But Blake never doubted the obligation to follow English authority and never claimed any power or responsibility to make law. 'The case to which I have adverted is an authoritative declaration of the law of England, which we do not feel ourselves at liberty to disregard. If the law upon the subject requires alteration, that is a matter proper for consideration of the legislature; we are to administer the law, not to alter it.'[55] In the cases in which his plea seemed effective, either the distinctive conditions became the particular considerations for the application of general principles, or the English authority seemed to be divided or confused enough to permit a choice of an appropriate result. Two examples are especially illustrative and demonstrative. In *Farwell* v *Wallbridge*,[56] he granted an injunction to restrain taking saw logs – a 'staple' – rather than leave the plaintiff to claim damages, so that mills would not remain 'unproductive.' In *O'Keefe* v *Taylor*, a purchaser of land under an instalment agreement was given specific performance despite his failure to make payments on the dates specified in the agreement, because the vendor had acquiesced in delay by permitting time to pass. One long passage is an impressive assertion of Blake's faith in progress, the unity of the public and private interests, his determination to think about Canada, and his ultimate respect for English authority:

we are about to define the position of multitudes by whom a country is being peopled – by whose enterprise and labour the wastes of this vast province are rendered subservient to the purposes of civilization with unexampled rapidity ... it is of vital importance, not only to the attainment of justice in particular cases, but to the general welfare, that in this court, the numerous titles which depend exclusively upon this jurisdiction for their validity, should not be shaken by the introduction of doctrines, which, however suited to other states of society, have no application in our present social condition ... But were we to apply the rule to be deduced from some of the English cases which were cited, especially some of the latter cases, upon the subject of delay, without reference to the totally different social condition of this country, we should not only produce great practical evil and injustice, but should also, in my opinion, very much misapply a doctrine which in England would never have been laid down under the circumstances in which we are placed ...[57]

The results may not have been dramatic, but the determination to think about Canada was unique. He would surely have applauded the eloquent appeal to terminate appeals to the Privy Council made in 1875 by his son Edward, the Attorney General of Canada:

The lives, liberty and property of the Canadian people are practically subject to their own laws; these laws they make, unmake and alter at pleasure. If they are fit to make, they should be fit to expound the law ... [Canadian courts] possess local knowledge and experience ... and ... at any rate, such as they are, they are our own ... the daily learning and experience which Canadians living under the Canadian Constitution acquire, is not theirs [the Privy Council's], nor can it be effectively instilled into them for the purpose of a particular appeal ...[58]

The division between common law and equity prevented Robinson and Blake from considering many of the same problems, but the overlaps of jurisdiction and the comprehensive jurisdiction of the Court of Error and Appeal led to disagreement about three illustrative problems. The need for a seal has already been described. The second disagreement was about waste. Robinson believed that a tenant could not clear forests from land to make a farm,[59] but Blake hinted that the result might be different.[60] The difference suggests Robinson's respect for English authority, and Blake's determination to consider Canadian conditions and needs, especially the need for development. The third disagreement was about the kind of evidence needed to permit a grantor to show that conveyance was intended to be a mortgage. Blake was satisfied with convincing evidence of any kind,[61] and Robinson imposed a substantially more stringent requirement.[62] The difference suggests Robinson's concern for certainty and respect for form and documents, and Blake's strong and instinctive desire to seek individualized fairness.

Both Robinson and Blake must be major figures in any comprehensive study of the Canadian judiciary. Robinson led the common law courts throughout a long and important period and he was one of the early makers of a tradition that has become dominant among Canadian judges: deference to authority, denial of any significant creative power, and denial of any general attitudes beyond fidelity to statutes and the accumulation of precedent. Blake's influence and distinctive attitudes have not been widely shared, and the Canadian judiciary has been less distinguished than it might have been.

THE UNITED STATES: CONTRASTS AND COMPARISONS

Comparisons and contrasts to the law in the United States can illuminate the law in Ontario, and can be made by using two brilliant books written about the law during the nineteenth century in the United States: Hurst, *Law and the Conditions of Freedom*,[63] and Horwitz, *The Transformation of American Law*.[64] Both describe an instrumental attitude towards law that emerged at the turn of the century. Hurst says:

> We are all Republicans, we were all Federalists, in possessing a common instrumental belief which shaped the nineteenth-century legal order. Jefferson and Hamilton, Jacksonian and Whig, were alike confident that men could materially control their environment through the legally mobilized power of the community.[65]

and Horwitz says:

> By 1820 the legal landscape in America bore only the faintest resemblance to what existed forty years earlier. While the words were often the same, the structure of thought had dramatically changed and with it the theory of law. Law was no longer conceived of as an eternal set of principles expressed in custom and derived from natural law. Nor was it regarded primarily as a body of rules designed to achieve justice only in the individual case. Instead, judges came to think of common law as equally responsible with legislation for governing society and promoting socially desirable conduct. The emphasis on law as an instrument of policy encouraged innovation and allowed judges to formulate legal doctrine with the self-conscious goal of bringing about social change. And from this changed

perspective, American law stood on the verge of what Daniel Boorstin has correctly called one of the great 'creative outbursts of modern legal history.'[66]

Hurst undertakes to study a wide range of law and experience, and his book is a landmark in showing and shaping the scope of legal scholarship, especially legal history. The social context for the law was turbulent expansion, and a faith in individual liberty, creativity, and material progress. The two major objectives or 'working principles' for law were the 'release of individual creative energy' by giving freedom to act and enforcement for private planning, and control of the environment to increase the range of effective choices and activity for individuals. The principle of release of energy was expressed primarily through contract, property, and the corporation. Contracts gave individuals wide scope for making private agreements that the state would enforce, and the corporation could be used for a wide range of private business purposes. Property was not the right to privacy and immunity from government interference that had developed in England in the seventeenth and eighteenth centuries. It was a power to act. 'We were concerned with protecting private property chiefly for what it could do; as one looks at the facts of cases and pays somewhat less attention to the sonorous language of judicial opinions, he is impressed that what we did in the name of vested rights had less to do with protecting holdings than it had to do with protecting ventures.'[67]

The principle of control of the environment was expressed primarily in protecting free movement of goods and finance within and among the states, creation and financing of transportation facilities, especially the railroads, distribution of the public lands widely and cheaply; provision of credit facilities, especially banks; and encouragement of industry, especially through tariffs.

Horwitz emphasizes courts and common law, and provides a more intensive analysis. He reinforces and expands some of Hurst's themes and introduces some new ones. Throughout, one general conclusion is dominant: during the first half of the nineteenth century, the courts transformed the law, and created law for an economy of individual wills, competition, and innovation. Contract was transformed by the abandonment of controls over the fairness of the exchange and the emergence of enforcement of bargains that were simply expressions of individuals wills. Negotiability of commercial paper became generally accepted, and the corporation became generally available as a form for private business undertaking. Property was transformed 'from a static conception entitling an owner to undisturbed enjoyment, to a dynamic, instrumental, and more abstract view ... that emphasized the new paramount virtues of productive use and development.' The rules about allocation of losses encouraged important activities, especially the railroads, by not imposing liability for some of the losses they caused. Limitations were imposed on the kinds of losses for which compensation would be given after expropriation, the limitations of nuisance and the defence of statutory authority were accepted, restrictions were imposed on the power of juries, and, most important, negligence emerged to replace more strict grounds of liability. About the middle of the century innovation ceased, and formalism replaced instrumentalism. The objectives of commercial and entrepreneurial interests had been accomplished.

> Law, once conceived of as protective, regulative, paternalistic and, above all, a paramount expression of the moral sense of the community, had come to be thought of as facilitative of individual desires and as simply reflective of the existing organization of economic and political power ... The rise of legal formalism can be fully correlated with the attainment of these substantive legal changes. If a flexible, instrumental conception of law was necessary to promote the transformation of the postrevolutionary American legal system, it was no longer needed once the major beneficiaires of that transformation had obtained the bulk of their objectives. Indeed, once successful, those groups could only benefit if both the recent origins and the foundations in policy and group self-interest of all newly established legal doctrines could be disguised. There were, in short, major advantages in creating an intellectual system which gave common law rules the appearance of being self-contained, apolitical, and inexorable, and which, by making 'legal reasoning seem like mathematics,' conveyed 'an air ... of ... inevitability' about legal decisions.[68]

Summaries are inadequate to suggest all the riches of these two books and the debate their interpretations can create, but they are a useful beginning for making some interesting comparisons and contrasts, even though the diversity among the states forbids precision. By the mid-nineteenth century, the organization and structure of law and most of the terms of doctrine were substantially the same in Ontario and the United States, and a lawyer from one jurisdiction would have had little difficulty understanding and coping with the differences. The differences were generally discrete and limited, and generally demonstrated a greater willingness in the United States to authorize innovation, change, and competition. For example, courts in the United States were more receptive to innovation in financing and security, and managed to remove much of the requirement of the seal for contracts made by corporations. The differences may seem largest in the law about property, but some untangling and perspective is necessary to assess their nature and extent. Comparisons about allocation of land and timber are difficult to make because of the diversity among the states, but the allocation in Ontario was probably more restrained and less clearly impelled by the ambition to permit economic development. But the land was allocated in fee simple, and once the process of allocation was complete, countless individuals had extensive power to use and transfer. The major differences in this law about the fee simple were about compensation for improvements made by mistake, the existence of dower in unimproved land, and, perhaps, waste, and they are small contrasted to the widespread use of the fee simple. The use of the rivers is the last aspect of property. The rights to use for navigation, especially the transport of logs, were roughly the same, although in Ontario the legislature declared the rights generally, and the courts alone would probably not have gone as far as the courts did in the United States. The rights to use for power were substantially different. In the United States legislation generally deprived an owner of an injunction to restrain flooding caused by an adjoining mill-owner for the purpose of increasing power, and common law permitted extensive interference with the natural flow and permitted an aggressive riparian owner to accumulate much or all of the power of a river.

The two countries shared much that made their laws the same: the inheritance from England, and similarities in economics, resources, and geography. Also, the abstract character of the law about the market and much of property made some differences of context immaterial. The differences were products of different attitudes towards economic activity, the greater respect for English authority in Ontario, and, perhaps, occasionally the intensity of perceived need. For example, the difference in the use of rivers for power clearly was influenced by a greater willingness in the United States to sanction innovation, productivity, and aggressive conduct, but perhaps it also was influenced by differences in the perceptions of need: in Ontario water power must have seemed relatively much more abundant than in New England.

The result is large similarities, and some differences. The assessment of the extent of difference and the emphasis on differences or similarities depend upon purposes and perspectives. The differences probably had little effect on, or reflected little of, the differences in the way the economy was ordered or its productivity. These differences were large, but they were more a product of the resources, and expressed more in the uses made of the law, not its general terms. But for the purpose of studying a legal system, the differences loom larger, as an expression of the willingness of the legal system, especially the courts, to reflect and make changes in the the limits of their functions and traditions.

The 'instrumental' attitude of the courts in the United States during the first half of the century was a willingness to make and change law and depart from precedent, and an openness in considering needs, context, and the process of change. In Ontario Chancellor Blake's judgments about the distinctive Canadian conditions are impressive, and occasionally Chief Justice Robinson was openly restless about perceived limitations, but the overwhelming impression from hundreds and thousands of cases is that the courts generally were willing to accept and apply whatever seemed to be settled law, and felt no responsibility for change. Reading volumes of reports from beginning to end, without selecting cases for some purpose, for example, to determine doctrine, is a tedious experience. The first few volumes of the Common Pleas reports are especially painful. Countless cases are decided by reciting English cases and general propositions of doctrine, and seem utterly divorced from any context in space and time. Even after the shift to formalism began at mid-century, courts in the United States discussed functional issues more openly and were more willing to consider change.

This difference in thinking about law existed beyond courts. Apart from discussions about the constitution, such as discussions about responsible government, law was virtually not discussed or thought about, beyond analysis by lawyers that paralleled the work of the courts. A few texts were published, but all were essentially guides to court structure and procedure. A journal appeared, the *Upper Canada Law Journal*, but it usually published only the analysis of lawyers, reports of cases, and reprints of material from English journals and, occasionally, journals in the United States. The few articles that might be indexed as speculation or thinking about law generally are conspicuously superficial and barren.

Another and closely related difference is more subtle, yet fundamental. In the United States, much more than in Ontario, the legal institutions, especially the courts, were used, and were expected to be used, to debate and shape values about the society, including values about the economy. De Toqueville's observation that 'there is hardly a political question in the United States which does not sooner or later turn into a judicial one'[69] still seems profound, especially from the perspective of Canada. This difference is not simply the difference of the instrumental tradition of the courts. It is a wider difference in the perception of law and legal institutions, and ultimately in constitutional tradition.

An example of all these differences is the law about exclusive franchises for public utility undertakings. Early in the nineteenth century, in the United States, the power to grant exclusive franchises was clearly acknowleged, and such franchises were justified as giving the certainty and stability needed to attract private investment in public utilities. The franchises that were granted were given generous interpretation; for example, a grant of a power to charge tolls was held to imply a grant of an exclusive franchise. During a generation, attitudes changed, and the change was marked by the *Charles River Bridge* case, decided by the Supreme Court in 1837.[70] The Charles River Bridge corporation was created in 1785 to build a bridge across the Charles River and was given a power to collect tolls. It was an extremely profitable undertaking, until a competitor, the Warren Bridge corporation, was authorized to build only a few hundred feet away. The Charles River Bridge corporation claimed that it had been given an exclusive franchise, which the legislature could not revoke. The court agreed that such a franchise could be given, but refused to imply one if none was expressly granted. In the background, and clearly acknowledged, was the possibility that if exclusive franchises were implied, existing bridge, canal, and road corporations would seek to hold the expanding railroads to ransom. Chief Justice Taney wrote: 'Let it once be understood, that such charters carry with them these implied contracts ... and you will soon find the old turnpike corporations awakening from their sleep, and calling upon this court to put down the improvements which have taken their place. The millions of property which have been invested in railroads and canals, upon lines of travel which had been before occupied by turnpike corporations, will be put in jeopardy.' Throughout, the law and the issues were openly perceived and discussed in terms of economic policy and need. The result was part of the change in attitudes towards property and the increasing and explicit emphasis on innovation and economic utility, and also part of the emergence of the corporation as a way of organizing for private business activity and the passing of its use as a way of organizing private and public interests to achieve public purposes.

In Canada, the apparent needs and technologies for transportation were substantially the same. About two hundred corporations were created before 1860 to undertake canals, roads, bridges, and railroads. Like the Charles River Bridge corporation, they were a union of private capital and effort with public power to achieve essentially public purposes, although the attempt to describe their functions in terms of public and private elements imposes a division that may have emerged clearly only afterwards and that cannot capture the unity of purposes. Only a few were expressly given exclusive franchises, and a few were expressly subjected to the possiblity of competitors. Almost all were created without any undertaking at all.

The only extensive body of law about franchises was about ferries, even though they were far from being the most important or most debated kind of transportation undertaking. From the outset, the government granted franchises to ferries, exercising a prerogative power that was well established in England. Legislation assumed the existence of this power, and provided elaboration and regulation, and eventually transferred much of it to the municipalities.[71]

The courts upheld the prerogative power without hesitation or question, and Robinson declared, 'It is not for the benefit of the crown, as distinct from the benefit of the public that the prerogative is ever exercised.'[72] The interpretation of the legislation seems generally to have been generous to the exclusiveness of the franchises, although not enough cases were decided to make a strong pattern.[73] In particular, the franchises were assumed to be exclusive, even though their terms did not include this right. The attitudes and analysis were usually in terms of property. In *Regina* v *Davenport*, the facts have some similarities to the *Charles River Bridge* case, although the differences make the similarities almost amusing.[74] The government made a grant to Davenport of a ferry across the Detroit River, and ten years later made another grant for the same route to Baby. The crown claimed rent from Davenport and failed. The court could not conceive that the two ferries might compete and analyzed the problem in terms of successive grants of the same property. Because Davenport's right was 'at pleasure' it was revoked by implication by the grant to Baby.

In short, and in contrast to Canada, in the United States the problems of exclusive franchises for transportation undertaking were perceived as issues to be resolved by the legal institutions, especially the courts, and the economic issues and ambition were considered openly. In Canada, competition among the undertakings was not as extensive, because the more limited resources restricted duplication of undertakings, an extensive system of privately owned roads had not been created before the railway boom began, and, perhaps most important, the government provided, controlled, or financed a much larger proportion of the facilities. But despite these differences, the railroad promoters sought, obtained, and used competing franchises. The decisions about these franchises were made by the legislature without any control by the courts and were the products of conflicting ambitions and claims about economic needs.

PERSPECTIVE

This essay has been primarily a study of the courts in Ontario during the final stages of their emergence as major and mature legal institutions. During this period distinctive attitudes towards their functions and process were settled and have continued to be dominant. Even within the limits imposed by principle and realistic expectation, the courts have been deferential to apparent authority, unwilling to initiate change, and inclined to consider issues in terms of precedents and doctrine. The most important influence was England, and the obligation to follow English authority seemed greatly to restrict the power to create and to make much of the analysis of problems into a concern for the existence and scope of authority. Eventually obligation became habit. But authority can often be avoided, and no authority was available for many problems. Obligation and habit were strongly supported by the loyalty of the colony, which was especially strong among the governing classes, and the strong appeal of English legal tradition to the lawyers. All these elements combined to make our courts – and our entire legal community – a legal colony, forbidden and eventually unwilling to consider its own legal destiny openly. The courts in Ontario during this period did not participate in change and innovation, even vicariously as spectators and beneficiaries on the sidelines. The English law seemed to have reached a relatively settled stage by 1840, and the English courts were in the midst of a long and complex shift from creativity to formalism, for example from Mansfield to the House of Lords of the late nineteenth century. Horwitz describes a similar shift in the United States (and perhaps the reasons are common). This timing tempts the speculation that the lack of any large creative element during this crucial stage helped shape the traditions for the future.

NOTES

* Reprinted with minor changes from *University of Toronto Law Journal* XXVII (1977) 403–38

1 R.C.B. Risk 'The Nineteenth Century Foundations of the Business Corporation in Ontario' *University of Toronto Law Journal* XXIII (1973) 270–306 (hereafter UTLJ); Risk 'The Golden Age: The Law about the Market in Ontario in the Nineteenth Century' UTLJ XXVI (1976) 307–46; and Risk 'The Last Golden Age: Property and the Allocation of Losses in Ontario in the Nineteenth Century' UTLJ XXVII (1977) 199–239
Much of the analysis and generalization in this essay is based on material in these three articles. Extensive references to them would be unwieldy, and would give little convenience and no authority. Therefore references to particular material in them will generally be omitted, and references will be given only for material that is not included in them, and individual cases discussed in the text.
Throughout this essay some propositions are made about numbers and proportions of judges and cases. They are based simply on counting, and notes could only repeat the text or give an unjustified aura of precision by specifying more particular numbers. Therefore, none will be given.

2 Nothing in this section is intended to be original or debatable. Some of the books about the economy of the period are J.M.S. Careless *The Union of the Canadas* (Toronto 1967), A.W. Currie *The Grand Trunk Railway of Canada* (Toronto 1957), W.T. Easterbrook and H.G.J. Aitken *Canadian Economic History* (Toronto 1961), G.P. de T. Glazebrook *A History of Transportation in Canada* (Toronto 1938), R.C. Harris and J. Warkentin *Canada before Confederation* (New York 1974), A.R.M. Lower *The North American Assault on the Canadian Forest* (Toronto 1938), A.R.M. Lower *Great Britain's Woodyard* (Montreal 1973), R.S. Lambert and P. Pross *Renewing Nature's Wealth* (Toronto 1967), and G.N. Tucker *The Canadian Commercial Revolution 1845–1851* (New Haven 1936).

3 Very little has been written about the history of the courts in Ontario, and most of the writing that has been done is anecdotal. The single most useful source of information is W.R. Riddell *The Bar and the Courts of the Province of Upper Canada, or Ontario* (Toronto 1928).

4 34 Geo. III (1794), c. 2. An eloquent protest was made by a member of the Executive Council, Richard Cartwright; see E.A. Cruikshank, ed. *The Correspondence of Lt Governor John Graves Simcoe* II 265 (Toronto 1924). The court quickly adopted English procedures. For example, in 1805 it made a rule that 'the practice of this said Court do conform in all possible respects to that laid down in Tidd and Sellon,' which was a standard English guide to practice.

5 For some descriptions and references, see John Delatre Falconbridge 'Law and Equity in Upper Canada' *University of Pennsylvania Law Review* LXIII (1914)

1, and William R. Riddell 'Early Proposals For a Court of Chancery in Upper Canada' *Canadian Law Times* XLI (1921) 740.
6 7 Wm IV (1837), c. 2
7 12 Vict. (1849), cc. 63–4
8 See, for example, a pamphlet written by Blake in the form of a letter to Baldwin in 1845, 'A Letter to the Honourable Robert Baldwin upon the Administration of Justice in Western Canada,' and succeeding correspondence between the two in the Baldwin Papers in the Toronto Public Library and the Blake Papers in the Ontario Archives.
9 (1857), 6 *Upper Canada Common Pleas Reports* (hereafter UCCP) 509
10 (1850), 7 *Upper Canada Queen's Bench Report* (hereafter UCQB) 198. For similar statements by Chief Justice Robinson see *Ballard* v *Ransom and Jackson* (1832), 2 *Upper Canada Queen's Bench Reports* (Old Series) (hereafter UCQB [OS]), *Parker and Dunbar* v *Roberts* (1846), 3 UCQB 114, *Bradley* v *Crane* (1847), 4 UCQB 122, *Brown & McDonell* v *Browne* (1852), 9 UCQB 312, *Higby* v *Cummings* (1853), 10 UCQB 222, *Tilt* v *Silverthorne* (1854), 11 UCQB 619, *Tumblay* v *Meyers* (1858), 16 UCQB 143, and *Bank of Montreal* v *Reynolds* (1866), 25 UCQB 352.
11 Nothing in this paragraph is intended to be original or debatable. Two standard references are F.W. Maitland *The Forms of Action at Common Law* (Cambridge 1936), and William S. Holdsworth *A History of English Law* IX (Boston 1926) 263–335.
12 (1847), 3 UCQB 325
13 3 Vict. (1840), c. 8
14 (1845), 2 UCQB 426
15 (1847), 3 UCQB 363
16 (1855), 12 UCQB 521
17 (1855), 12 UCQB 540. Some other examples of a concern for form, strict reading of pleadings, and rigorous logic, taken from the *Queen's Bench Reports*, are *Tanner* v *D'Everado* (1846), 3 UCQB 154, *Ambridge* v *Foster* (1846), 3 UCQB 157, *Cook* v *Mair* (1847), 3 UCQB 478, *Maddock* v *Stock* (1847), 4 UCQB 118, *Perry* v *Grover* (1849), 5 UCQB 331 and 468, *Gourlay* v *Gunn* (1849), 5 UCQB 566, *Brown* v *Hawke* (1849), 6 UCQB 275, *Blanchfield* v *Birdsall* (1850), 7 UCQB 141, *Aikin* v *Howcutt* (1850), 7 UCQB 143, *Hutchinson* v *Munroe* (1851), 8 UCQB 103, *McLeod* v *McLeod* (1852), 9 UCQB 331, *Powell* v *Currier* (1852), 9 UCQB 352, *Worthington* v *Municipality of Haldimand* (1853), 10 UCQB 217, *Summers* v *Geary* (1853), 11 UCQB 134, *Commercial Bank* v *Muirhead* (1854), 12 UCQB 39, *Roys* v *Cramer* (1854), 12 UCQB 165, *Abel* v *Leonard* (1854), 12 UCQB 192, *Harris* v *Fraser* (1855), 12 UCQB 402, and *Ross* v *Heron* (1855), 12 UCQB 467.
18 See Sir C.K. Allen *Law in the Making* (Oxford 6th ed 1958) 206–30, Sir A.R.N.

Cross *Precedent in English Law* (Oxford 1961) 17–30, and J.P. Dawson *The Oracles of the Law* (Ann Arbor, MI 1968) 77–99.

19 *Jones* v *Randall* (1774), 1 *Cowper's King's Bench Reports* 37, at 39; 9 *English Reports* 954, at 955

20 See, for example, *Bank of British North America* v *Ross* (1844), 1 UCQB 199, and *Aikin* v *Howcutt*, above note 17.

21 See, for example, *McCuniffe* v *Allen* (1850), 6 UCQB 377, *Lott* v *French* (1853), 10 UCQB 385, and *Wilson* v *Municipality of Port Hope* (1853), 10 UCQB 405.

22 *Henderson* v *McLean* (1858), 8 UCCP 42

23 *Tisdale* v *Dallas* (1861), 11 UCCP 238

24 *McCuniffe* v *Allen*, above note 21

25 See, for example, *Breeze* v *Baldwin* (1837), 5 UCQB (OS) 444, *City Bank* v *Ley* (1844), 1 UCQB 192, *Matthewson* v *Carman* (1844), 1 UCQB 259, *Bank of Upper Canada* v *Parsons* (1847), 3 UCQB 383, *Jennings* v *Robertson* (1852), 3 *Grant's Chancery Reports* (hereafter Ch) 513, *Coleman* v *McDermott* (1856), 1 *Grant's Upper Canada Error and Appeal Reports* 445, and *Brunskill* v *Rigney* (1857), 6 UCCP 509.

26 (1857), 15 UCQB 203

27 (1847), 3 UCQB 358

28 (1854), 4 Ch 231

29 (1842), 6 UCQB (OS) 381

30 (1855), 4 UCCP 373

31 (1859), 9 UCCP 302

32 See Edwin Merrick Dodd *American Business Corporations until 1860* (Cambridge, MA 1954) 93–109.

33 See, for example, *Hamilton* v *Niagara Harbour & Dock*, above note 29, *Clark* v *Hamilton & Gore Mechanics' Institute* (1854), 12 UCQB 178, and *Marshall* v *School Trustees of Kitley*, above note 30.

34 See, for example, *Blue* v *Toronto Gas and Water* (1849), 6 UCQB 174, and *Raines* v *Credit Harbour* (1843), 1 UCQB 174.

35 *Clark* v *Hamilton & Gore Mechanics' Institute*, above note 33. See also *Lyman* v *Bank of Upper Canada* (1852), 8 UCQB 354, *Turley* v *Grafton Road Company* (1852), 8 UCQB 579, and *Bartlett* v *Municipality of Amhurstberg* (1856), 14 UCQB 152.

36 *Marshall* v *School Trustees of Kitley*, above note 30. See also *Stock* v *Great Western Railway* (1859), 9 UCCP 134. The citation suggests that this case came before the *Pim* case, below note 37, but the result and passages in the judgment suggest that it came after.

37 *Pim* v *Municipal Council of Ontario* (1859), 9 UCCP 304. After *Pim*, see applications in *Perry* v *Corporation of Ottawa* (1864), 23 UCQB 391, *Maynard* v *Gamble*

(1863), 13 UCCP 56 and 467, and *Whitehead* v *The Buffalo and Lake Huron Railway* (1859), 7 Ch 351, affirmed 8 Ch 157.

38 Above note 37

39 Ibid.

40 *O'Keefe* v *Taylor* (1850), 2 Ch 95

41 (1830), *Draper's Upper Canada King's Bench Reports* 68

42 (1830), 2 UCQB 448

43 (1856), 13 UCQB 503

44 See Careless, *Union of The Canadas;* M.S. Cross *The Frontier Thesis and the Canadas* (Toronto 1970); Harris and Warkentin, *Canada before Confederation;* G. Horowitz *Canadian Labour in Politics* (Toronto 1968) 1–23; H.V. Nelles *The Politics of Development* (Toronto 1974) chs 1 and 2; H.G.J. Aitken 'Defensive Expansionism: The State and Economic Growth in Canada' in H.G.J. Aitken, ed. *The State and Economic Growth* (New York 1959) 79–114, reprinted in W.T. Easterbrook and M.H. Watkins, eds *Approaches to Canadian Economic History* (Toronto 1967) 182–221; S.F. Wise 'Upper Canada and the Conservative Tradition' in Ontario Historical Society *Profiles of a Province* (Toronto 1967) 20–32; Laurence S. Fallis 'The Idea of Progress in the Province of Canada 1841–1867' (PHD thesis University of Michigan 1966); and A.W. Rasporich 'The Development of Political and Social Ideas in the Province of Canada 1848–1858' (PHD thesis, University of Manitoba 1971).

45 32 Geo. III (1792), c. 1, s. 3

46 The cases cited in the discussion of precedent, the need for a seal, and pleading are all examples of express respect for English authority. Some others are *Watkins* v *Nicolls* (1845), 1 UCQB 473, *Bank of Montreal* v *Grover* (1846), 3 UCQB 27, *Davis* v *Barnet* (1853), 10 UCQB 501, *Loomer* v *Marks* (1853), 11 UCQB 16, *The Queen* v *Hespeler* (1854), 11 UCQB 222, *Arnold* v *Higgins* (1854), 11 UCQB 447, and *Sinclair* v *Robson* (1858), 16 UCQB 211.

47 (1849), 5 UCQB 362

48 (1844), 1 Ch 169 (Executive Council)

49 This tendency was especially apparent in cases of allocation of liability. For example, a seller's liability for defective goods, a shipper's liability for lost or damaged goods, and liability for accidents were generally perceived as problems of assessing the conduct and fault of individuals. The few comments about the telegraphs were distinctive.

50 *Dean* v *McCarty* (1830), 2 UCQB 448

51 Very little has been written about Robinson. See C.W. Robinson *Life of Sir John Beverley Robinson* (Edinburgh and London 1904) (a biography by his son), Terry Cook 'John Beverley Robinson and the Conservative Blueprint for the Upper Canadian Community' *Ontario History* LXIV (1972) 79–94,

E.A. Cruickshank 'John Beverley Robinson and the Trials for Treason in 1814,' *Ontario History* xxv (1929) 191–219, and the biography (by R.E. Saunders) in *Dictionary of Canadian Biography* IX (Toronto 1976) (hereafter DCB) 668–79.

52 These two passages are taken from a collection in the Ontario Archives of Robinson's addresses to grand juries. The first is dated 16 Sept. 1834 and the second 12 Sept. 1840. I am indebted to Ms Maureen Simpson for these references.

53 Even less has been written about Blake than about Robinson. See an incomplete and unpublished manuscript by a great-grandson in the Blake papers in the Ontario Archives, the biography by D. Swainson in DCB IX (1976) 55–60, and John Blackwell 'William Hume Blake and the Judicature Acts of 1849: The Process of Legal Reform at Mid-Century in Upper Canada' in this volume.

54 (1849), 1 Ch 34

55 *Cameron* v *McRae* (1852), 3 Ch 311

56 (1851), 2 Ch 332

57 Above note 40

58 A memorandum to the Colonial Secretary about appeals to the Privy Council, dated 9 Mar. 1876, and reprinted, in part, In L.A. Cannon 'Some Data Relating to the Appeal to The Privy Council' *Canadian Bar Review* III (1925) 469

59 *Weller* v *Burnham* (1853), 11 UCQB 90

60 *Chisholm* v *Sheldon* (1850), 1 Ch 318

61 *Le Targe* v *De Tuyll* (1852), 3 Ch 369

62 *Greenshields* v *Barnhart* (1851), 3 Ch 1 (in appeal); *Holmes* v *Matthews* (1852), 3 Ch 379. This issue is discussed at greater length in Risk, 'The Golden Age: The Law about The Market.'

63 J. Willard Hurst *Law and The Conditions of Freedom* (Madison, WI 1956)

64 Morton J. Horwitz *The Transformation of American Law* (Cambridge, MA 1977)

65 Ibid. 33

66 Ibid. 30

67 Ibid. 24

68 Ibid. 31, 253–4

69 J.P. Mayer and Max Lerner, eds *Democracy in America* (New York 1966) 248

70 *Charles River Bridge* v *Warren Bridge* (1837) 36 US (11 Pet.) 420

71 37 Geo. III (1797), c. 10, 8 Vict. (1845), c. 50, 9 Vict. (1846), c. 9, 20 Vict. (1857), c. 7, 22 Vict. (1859) c. 41

72 *Kerby* v *Lewis* (1842), 6 UCQB (OS) 207

73 See *Jones* v *Fraser* (1843), 6 UCQB (OS) 426, *Ives* v *Calvin* (1847) 3 UCQB 464, *Higgins* v *Hogan* (1850), 7 UCQB 401, *Hickley* v *Gildersleeve* (1861), 10 UCCP 460, and *Smith* v *Ratté* (1868), 15 Ch 473 (in appeal).

74 (1858), 16 UCQB 411

4

William Hume Blake and the Judicature Acts of 1849: The Process of Legal Reform at Mid-Century in Upper Canada

JOHN D. BLACKWELL

The nineteenth century was a period of legal reform throughout the English-speaking world. Some insights can be gained into the process of reform by an examination of the circumstances surrounding the introduction of what were known in Upper Canada as the Judicature Acts of 1849. The individual most responsible for this reform was William Hume Blake (1809–70), a significant figure in Canadian legal history, and one who has been described as Upper Canada's 'only potential judicial hero.'[1] Blake's role is significant not only because of his contribution to Canadian judicial reform, but also in terms of the impact of the reform, which clearly reflected the interests of the province's legal élite. Blake and the élite he represented regarded Upper Canada's judicial structure as tired and outmoded. Well aware of the political necessity of improvements in the legal system, they also acted out of a genuine concern for the requirements of the public good.

The issue of legal reform emerged in the early 1840s. At that time there was increasing criticism of the unpopular Vice-Chancellor, Robert Sympson Jameson (1798–1854). After continued controversy, the legislature of the Province of Canada appointed a commission in 1843 to report on the operation of the Court of Chancery, which dated only from 1837. Prominent among those named to the commission was William Hume Blake, a leading member of the provincial bar and professor of law at King's College, Toronto.

BACKGROUND: ENGLAND AND UPPER CANADA

The English Court of Chancery and its body of equity law evolved over centuries in a supplementary relationship with the common law and its courts. Recognizing such hardships as accident, mistake, and fraud, equity provided relief in certain cases where the strict letter of the common law granted a plaintiff only monetary damages or sometimes admitted no claim at all. In some cases an injured party was more interested in controlling the offender's behaviour than collecting monetary compensation; the Court of Chancery's remedies of specific performance and injunction met this need. Unlike at common law where the strict rule of precedent sometimes led to injustice in individual situations, in equity the precepts of fairness and conscience allowed the Chancellor greater freedom to determine each case on its own merits. Chancery developed its own procedure for initiating proceedings whereby a suitor filed a written bill or petition asking for the Chancellor's favourable decree, rather than issuing a writ as a plaintiff did at common law. The Court also evolved different rules of evidence; it was presented in written form instead of orally. Chancery's jurisdiction developed only in some areas, including the supervision of trusts, the guardianship of infants and lunatics, the administration of the estates of deceased persons, the moderating of the common law's strict enforcement of mortgages, the handling of bankruptcy cases, and the drawing up of accounts for commercial partnerships in which disputes arose. Real property was of prime concern in many cases, and from an early date the landed class used the court to protect its interests. However, well before the early nineteenth century Chancery's machinery had become formalized and encumbered, its officers were exploiting their positions, and the twin horrors of delay and expense drove away many potential litigants. It was not uncommon for a case to last twenty years and for legal fees to consume the matter at issue.[2]

The Legislative Assembly of Upper Canada adopted aspects of the English judicial system on an ad hoc basis to meet the limited requirements of a pioneering society. The judges of King's Bench, the senior Upper Canadian court established in 1794, travelled periodically on circuit with commissions for the trial of civil and criminal matters. In specified cases appeal lay to the Governor and Executive Council and even to the King and Privy Council. Neither route was very satisfactory, the first being made up primarily of laymen and the second too remote and costly. At the local level the General Quarter Sessions of the Peace and the Justices of the Peace, both established in the old province of Quebec in 1764, dealt informally with minor civil and criminal matters and municipal administration. The local Courts of Requests after 1792 and above these, the District Courts after 1794, heard small civil matters such as the recovery of debt. After 1793 the district Surrogate Courts handled estates of the deceased and the provincial Probate Court heard appeals.[3]

Prior to the belated creation of the provincial Court of Chancery in 1837 only the Surrogate and Probate Courts and the Courts of Requests exercised a portion of equity's jurisdiction. The provincial secretary performed the routine administrative common law or 'ordinary' duties of Chancery, such as the issuing of writs for parliamentary elections and of commissions to judges. As Keeper of the Great Seal of the province, the Lieutenant Governor was considered *ipso facto* Chancellor, but most occupants of the former office were soldiers professionally unequipped to preside in a Court of Chancery. The absence of this court and of the exercise of its extraordinary or equitable jurisdiction, perhaps the result of Chief Justice William Osgoode's early resignation in 1794 before he could draft appropriate legislation, led to repeated efforts to establish an equity tribunal. At least two judges actively sought a position on the proposed equity bench. The growing commercial class in particular desired an equitable jurisdiction which would provide greater certainty in their daily business transactions, for instance, a means of foreclosing on mortages and of enforcing specific performance of contracts for the sale of real property. Authorities in London, who opposed the addition of another salary to the imperial Civil List, urged the creation of a Court of Chancery on the prerogative principle: the Lieutenant Governor should preside. By 1827 this concept had lost favour, and Whitehall proposed colonial legislative action. Rather than granting equitable jurisdiction to the common law courts, the Upper Canadian government presented a bill in 1828 for the creation of a separate Court of Chancery. However, strong public apprehension of the evils of the infamous English Chancery blocked its passage.[4]

The issue did not die, however, and in late December 1832 a Select Committee of the Assembly reported on the expediency of establishing a separate Court of Chancery and presented 'the draft of a Bill for that purpose.' The report observed that 'such a Tribunal ... is imperiously called for, and cannot be delayed, without subjecting His Majesty's subjects ... to the denial of Justice...'[5] Relying on conjecture, the committee stoutly opposed the transfer of equitable jurisdiction to King's Bench. 'In a very few years,' they suggested, 'this blending of duties would be found inconvenient, and the performance of them unsatisfactory, if not impracticable.' The report enumerated nine crucial areas where no court had jurisdiction: enforcing the accountability of trustees and executors; repealing letters patent issued erroneously; redeeming mortgaged estates; enforcing specific performance of agreements; protecting the estates of infants, lunatics, and idiots; settling disputes in accounts between co-partners; restraining against awards corruptly made; compelling discovery of evidence; and giving relief against inequitable proceedings at law.[6] Sensitive to public apprehension, the committee cautiously suggested limiting the equitable jurisdiction to cases of the greatest necessity, unlike England, and allowing the legislature to augment the court's powers only as circumstances required. The report deflected criticism of the proposed expense by arguing that this essential judicial body warranted the necessary appropriation of funds. This analysis provided little room for deviation from the English model, although the appended draft bill included some enlightened measures, such as requiring witnesses to give oral testimony. Unfortunately the proposal reached only second reading. Yet the need persisted. In 1835 Chief Justice John Beverley Robinson expressed his consternation in a judgment: 'we are absolutely without the means of exercising an equitable jurisdiction, having no Court of equity of any kind or for any purpose.'[7] Because of its technical nature, the problem was easily forgotten amid the furor over such volatile issues as responsible government and clergy reserves.

After the 1836 election the Tory Solicitor General, Christopher A. Hagerman, introduced another Chancery Bill, which aroused much attention. The provincial judiciary was favourable and perhaps its approval alleviated some of the public's fears of the notorious delays and expenses of Chancery. After fierce and extensive debate the bill secured passage on 1 March 1837.[8] Basically an elaboration of the 1832 bill, the enactment created for Upper Canada a separate non-itinerant Court of Chancery with the Lieutenant Governor as Chancellor. A single judge, styled 'the Vice-Chancellor of Upper Canada,' was to exercise the Chancellor's legal and equitable judicial powers. This formula nicely combined the prerogative and legislative bases for establishing a new Court of Chancery. Its jurisdiction included 'like power and authority' as the English Court of Chancery in all cases of fraud, accident, and account; in all cases relating to co-partnerships; in all matters relating to trusts, executors and administrators, mortgages, dower, awards, infants, idiots, lunatics and their estates; with power to compel the discovery of concealed evidence and specific performance of agreements, to prevent multiplicity of suits, to stay waste and inequitable proceedings at law, and to decree rightful letters patent from the Crown and to repeal those granted erroneously or improvidently. The new provincial tribunal also acquired authority in cases of alimony which were under the purview of ecclesiastical courts in England. For all these matters there had previously been virtually no judicial remedy in Upper Canada. Dower was an important addition to the proposed 1832 jurisdiction, but still conspicuously absent and indicative of the new court's somewhat limited field of operation was the power to grant injunctions. The court was to follow English rules of decision, and the Vice-Chancellor was to establish the court's rules of practice. The act also provided certain officers for the court, stipulated who might practise therein, made provision for appeal, and established a fee schedule for procedural services. After four long decades the transplant of the basic elements of the English legal and judicial system was complete.

The 1837 creation soon proved inadequate to meet the requirements of the burgeoning province. During the first twelve years of its existence, the Court of Chancery faced widespread criticism. One of the principal causes was the Englishman Robert Sympson Jameson, the province's first Vice-Chancellor. Jameson has generally received a brief and negative 'press,' but not with entire justification.[9] A host of obstacles contributed to his unpopularity. His personal disposition was one of extreme caution and reserve; his strict adherence to legal precedent reflected an intrinsic conservatism, probably reinforced by his mentor, Lord Eldon. Having had little practical experience in the law and having to deal with several outstanding members of the bar in the new court, Jameson also faced serious professional disadvantages. He alone had the enormous task of hearing the whole provincial caseload in Chancery under a system of antiquated and cumbersome proceedings inherited from English equity. The Upper Canadian bar's resentment of imperial appointees and the home government's growing indifference towards the restless province's affairs made Jameson a prime and solitary target. Although the court sat only in Toronto, except briefly in Kingston when Jameson also served as speaker of the Legislative Council between 1841 and 1843, Chancery had substantial business and a clientele from across the province. From mid-1841 to late 1844 alone the court heard 463 suits but settled only 155.[10]

CONTEMPORARY MODELS

Potential solutions to these problems lay outside the province's boundary. Some Upper Canadians were aware of the varied and tangled

American experience with equity.[11] Suspicion of any prerogative court of chancery began in the colonial period, even though there was a general acceptance of equitable doctrines. Efforts for judicial reform, especially in equity, were achieving success by the late 1840s. New York led the way in the codification of law, equity, and procedure. The champion of the movement was David Dudley Field (1805–94). William Sampson, a Protestant Ulsterman and an admirer of the Code Napoleon, first popularized the idea in America during the 1820s, advocating the certainty and simplicity of codification. Many developing western states adopted Field Codes or a variant, but a number of eastern states retained separate courts to administer an equitable jurisdiction. Even in New York acceptance of codification was slow and limited. Amendments to the original Field Code of Civil Procedure (1848) quickly dampened the reform by adding complexity; it was still not possible to join all claims in a single civil action. The profession and the courts resisted the procedural merging of law and equity whereby one civil law action replaced separate actions at law and suits in equity. As well, enthusiasm for this reform waned in the face of greater enthusiasm for codification of other areas such as the criminal law. In spite of considerable opposition, partial codification was widespread by 1900. Businessmen in the growing market economy favoured the greater certainty which codification brought to the law. The reforms, however, were somewhat illusory; it was one thing merely to reorganize the law, its procedures, and rules of pleading and practice, quite another to alter it substantively. Frequently, the 'merging' of law and equity resulted in one court administering the two old and unreformed systems and in rules of equity prevailing where they collided with those of the common law.[12]

Morton Horwitz has argued that the American merger of law and equity represented 'the formalization of equity,' that is 'the final and complete emasculation of Equity as an independent source of legal standards' by subjecting it to 'formal rules.' Using the rubric of 'law as science,' the nineteenth-century treatise writers regularly attacked equity 'as inherently discretionary and "political".' Horwitz has also noted that 'Justice [Joseph] Story's "scientific" treatise on *Equity Jurisprudence* (1836),' for instance, 'marks a major step in the transformation of Equity from an eighteenth century system of substantive rules derived from "natural justice" to a nineteenth century positivist conception of Equity as simply providing a more complete and inclusive set of procedural remedies.' In short, 'the movement to merge Law and Equity begun by the Field Code of 1848 ... represents another instance of the subjection of an already internally eroded tradition of substantive justice to an increasingly formal set of legal rules, which were themselves now stridently justified as having nothing to do with morality.'[13]

Equitable developments followed a different course in nineteenth-century England. The profession only gradually initiated law reform. After a long crusade Jeremy Bentham (1748–1832) brought the evils of Chancery practice to public notice by the 1820s. Others rallied to the cause, including the press and popular writers such as Charles Dickens. The first Chancery Commission (1825) was a sham of apology, dominated by the profession; reform came only with lay representation in the process. Parliament began slowly to remedy some problems of personnel and structure in Chancery, the worst offender, but not until 1843 were there any significant procedural improvements. 'There was a gradual merging, if not of the substantive doctrine of common law and equity, at least of their more useful remedies and procedures.'[14] Marked progress began in 1852 with the Chancery Procedure Act. Chancery was finally able, for example, to decide points of law which arose in equity cases instead of referring them to the common law courts. These developments anticipated in only a small way the union of the two jurisdictions under the first Judicature Act of 1873 but marked a significant return to simplicity and flexibility.[15]

For Blake, as we shall see, American developments marked too radical a shift from the tradition of English law. What would become of the flexibility and adaptability, indeed the genius of the law, in a rigid and absolute code? He believed that 'the admixture of law and equity [was] so much to be deprecated on every account.'[16] Keeping in mind local conditions and requirements, Blake took his inspiration for judicial reform in the 1840s from the conservative English tradition. He also had the benefit of the experience of other British North American provinces. The civil law tradition of Quebec was virtually irrelevant, because the system had no separate body of equity as such, but in the Maritimes the Governor, by virtue of possessing the Great Seal, had jurisdiction in equity and sat as Chancellor. In Nova Scotia, for example, the Governor was assisted by professional lawyers and later sat only in appeal. The court's practice seems to have been modelled after that of the Irish Court of Chancery. By 1833, however, a Nova Scotian commentator complained of the provincial court's 'reverence for antiquity. ... The Court of Chancery in England has become a national grievance from its expense and delays, and some of the colonies and many of the United States have no Court of Chancery, being disposed rather to submit to many of the strict rules of common law in ordinary cases, and in important questions to resort to legislative Acts.'[17] Although the Nova Scotia court obtained power to amend its procedures and though its caseload increased, the legislature abolished the tribunal in 1856 and transferred its jurisdiction to the Supreme Court. This process had begun in 1849 with a series of legislative committees. But the merger of law and equity was imperfectly executed and in 1864 the assembly re-established a Court of Equity; it survived until 1881, when the Judicature Act again fused the two jurisdictions.[18]

WILLIAM HUME BLAKE: THE REFORMER AND HIS MILIEU

William Hume Blake was born in County Wicklow, Ireland, in 1809. The son of junior members of two distinguished landed families, he was obliged to make his own way in the professional world. Blake attended Trinity College, Dublin, and took his BA in 1830. Having abandoned medicine and only begun theological studies, the newly-wed Blake joined a group of friends and relatives who chartered a ship to Upper Canada in 1832. After a short effort at pioneering near the present-day town of Strathroy, he moved to Toronto in 1834 and became a student-at-law in the office of Simon E. Washburn (1793–1837), a prominent liberal Toronto barrister. Perhaps because Washburn had articled under Dr W.W. Baldwin, another Irishman and father of Robert Baldwin, Blake quickly entered the moderate reform camp. Although he came late to the law, and the informal system of articling may have provided a generally inadequate legal training, the intense law clerk, ably supported by his ambitious wife and cousin, Catherine Hume Blake, overcame these obstacles. He possessed many of the qualities of an outstanding lawyer, including 'great powers of eloquence ... untiring industry and a commanding presence.'[19] After his call to the bar in 1838, Blake formed a partnership with Joseph Curran Morrison (1816–85), formerly a fellow student in Washburn's office and later a prominent judge, and George Skeffington Connor (1810–63), his brother-in-law, who had practised in Dublin. The firm soon became known as a 'flourishing concern' and its founder earned a reputation as one of the leading counsellors of the day, especially in the recently-established field of equity. Blake served also as judge of the Surrogate Court of the Home District from 1841 to 1846 and as solicitor for the Law Society of Upper Canada from 1840 to 1845.[20]

Blake's appointment in March 1843 as first professor of law at King's College reflected his rapid rise in the legal profession. Although the Law Society did not require a degree and gave holders few concessions, this

William Hume Blake (1809–70), Chancellor of Upper Canada 1849–62
Unsigned and undated oil portrait attributed to George Théodore Berthon
(Osgoode Hall, Toronto)

early experiment supplemented the haphazard training provided by apprenticeship. The professorship afforded an opportunity for the successful and busy practitioner to develop as a legal theorist. One eminent student later recalled his mentor's independence of thought. 'The lecturer never quailed before any decision, English or Canadian. If he thought the judgment unsound reasoning, he did not hesitate to say so and urge the students to examine for themselves.'[21] His efforts as educator served to further both his interest in current developments and his desire to adapt the law to provincial circumstances. Moreover, the position was a handsome credential which elevated Blake's prestige among his brothers at the bar and eventually served as a useful platform from which to urge judicial reform.[22]

Blake's attention gradually shifted to politics. Although he always remained a staunch advocate of order and loyalty, his inherited conservative outlook evolved into that of a moderate reformer. His political credo may be traced to another Protestant Irishman, Edmund Burke, who had advocated solving problems 'by allowing the people to express their opinions freely and by translating popular grievances into reformist legislation';[23] but neither Burke nor Blake was a democrat. In the early 1840s the Upper Canadian legal profession included many supporters of moderate reform. Most of Blake's close legal associates, including his partners and R.B. Sullivan, Robert Baldwin's cousin, were Irishmen whose watchwords were freedom and responsible government. Although radical elements of the Reform party's pre-Rebellion ranks continued to cause the party some embarrassment, its leadership came increasingly into the hands of a group of 'Irish' lawyers under Robert Baldwin.[24] Many of the extreme reform leaders like William Lyon Mackenzie were discredited by the events of 1837 or were conveniently absent in American exile during the 1840s. Under the leadership of William Henry Draper, the Tories also shifted from an extreme to a more moderate and conciliatory position. But just as party lines remained extremely fluid in the new legislature of the United Canadas, so too the Upper Canadian bar was highly fragmented. In fact, the group defies neat generalization. As is the case today, there was a considerable gap between the influential élite in Toronto and the rest of the profession scattered in outlying areas. Political as well as social differences served to create pronounced rifts in the Upper Canadian legal fraternity.

Blake's own political commitment and involvement grew along with his convictions about the need for judicial reform. Throughout the protracted effort for reconstruction he acted primarily as 'a professional spokesman' representing an essentially urban and upper middle class interest.[25] But Blake also had his own reasons for advocating changes. In the election following the resignation late in 1843 of the short-lived Baldwin-LaFontaine government, he tried unsuccessfully to win a seat as the party's candidate. During a subsequent 1844 Simcoe by-election against John Beverley Robinson's brother, Blake maintained that the Tory Chief Justice's judicial intimidation had deprived the former of sympathetic support from the bar, because of fear about the outcome of a case pending before Queen's Bench.[26] Although Blake made it clear at this time that he regarded the provincial bench as the preserve of the old Tory Compact, he asserted nonetheless that 'there was no man in the Province whom he more unfeignedly respected'[27] than arch-conservative Chief Justice John Beverley Robinson. Of the much-maligned Vice-Chancellor Jameson, only vague hints of Blake's private opinion survive. These do not provide evidence of a personal vendetta against Jameson; nor do they show an intention to oust the Vice-Chancellor to free the post for personal occupancy.[28]

For many years the general public with varying degrees of justification and comprehension had complained of unwieldy tribunals, especially Chancery, and of an avaricious and cunning legal profession. Such views were particularly prevalent among radical reformers. Unfortunately the extremely partisan newspapers of the decade do not necessarily provide an accurate gauge of social attitudes towards the judiciary, the law and the profession, although the dominant impression is one of widespread dissatisfaction. W.N.T. Wylie, who has examined public opinion at this time, observes that 'considerable suspicion of the legal system and profession was a traditional factor in Canadian politics, though this is not often mentioned by historians.' There was distrust 'of a centralized and complex system of justice. A recurring theme in early nineteenth century Canadian experience was the attempt of the legal profession to assert its special right to design the legal system and the challenge of this right by individuals fearful of being exploited by the profession and distrustful of professional expertise.'[29] Even Blake's own associate, Skeffington Connor, privately corroborated this impression: 'I was all Saturday in Chancery. That's the business I like. The speaking colloquial, the pace slow and dignified, the pay handsome, and a gentlemanly understanding among the Practitioners to make it handsomer.'[30] Little wonder that public opinion was quick to ascribe ulterior motives to the legal fraternity's talk of reform.

Whatever the accuracy of the public's perception of evils in the profession and the judiciary, this apprehension created very real and enduring fears. Even after the passage of the Judicature Acts in 1849, the *Examiner*, a Toronto newspaper of moderate reform stance, recited the old lament: 'the law craft is all powerful in the Assembly, and it has shown at least as much anxiety to foster and enlarge its peculiar privileges as to protect defenseless ignorance and helpless poverty against the encroachments of powerful knavery.' The secret of the lawyer's craft was simple. 'Hitherto a language and a host of useless forms peculiar to the legal tribe has been used to make law a profitable mystery – a kind of congeries of mere technicalities, the more plausibly to draw upon the resources of the litigants, and to enrich the practitioners.' The person, concluded the outraged editor, 'who will bring about such a reform in Canada as to make justice simple, cheap, and accessible to the poorest in the land will deserve an enduring monument to his memory.'[31]

THE HALTING MOMENTUM FOR CHANGE

Fortunately for Blake, the Chancery Commission to which he was appointed was established in 1843 before the fall of the Baldwin-LaFontaine government. His colleagues on the commission included Chief Justice Robinson, Vice-Chancellor Jameson, Justice James Buchanan Macaulay, the senior puisne of Queen's Bench, and Robert Easton Burns and James Christie Palmer Esten, two prominent equity lawyers. Operating under a broad mandate to investigate the workings of Chancery, they eventually produced two reports. The first appeared in April 1844; it was not published and now seems lost.[32] The second and final report of 25 January 1845 reaffirmed the commission's earlier findings that the chief problem in Chancery, the expense, could be alleviated only by 'shortening the pleadings, and simplifying the proceedings.'[33] This action would also render suits in Chancery 'less dilatory.'

After a detailed review of the inadequate provincial equitable jurisdiction prior to 1837, the commissioners observed that the legislature had had 'a clear field for experiment.' It might, for example, have taken the course of 'authorizing the Court[s] of Common Law to give effect to equitable considerations in cases tried before them.' Yet 'the legislature of Upper Canada in 1837, determined to adopt a system as nearly as possible similar to that which exists in England. They left the Courts of Common Law to discharge their proper duties as before, and created a Court of Chancery wholly distinct from and independent of them.' The commissioners concluded that this decision 'was most in accordance with the real and permanent interests of the Province' since it permitted the most complete application of equitable principles. Another fortunate result was that the law would be closely tied to that of 'the Parent State,' the breadth of whose legal tradition would in turn provide a solid guide for the growth of Canada's own jurisprudence. In reaching this conclusion the commissioners did not address the fact that a developing society had its own particular problems and that these did not necessarily require full-blown duplicates of English judicial machinery for their resolution.

In fact, the commissioners appear to have had no hesitation at all about following the English model. In the conservative manner of their profession they argued with some force that any 'attempt to substitute an entire new system' would be highly undesirable because it would put everything into question: 'departing very widely from the English system, and casting ourselves loose from precedents and authorities.' The commissioners further asserted that even suggesting such a departure fell outside their mandate. The legislature had already given the Vice-Chancellor the power to adapt English practice to provincial circumstances; he had the added advantage of observing the effects of recent reforms in English Chancery. But these changes were generally structural rather than procedural and had little relevance in Upper Canada. American influence cannot be detected in this report.[34]

The commissioners conceded that the old bogies of Chancery, expense and delay, had resurfaced. Delay was 'unavoidable from the nature or objects of equitable jurisdiction.' Some rules might be adjusted to expedite proceedings without injuring suitors' interests, but the investigators reported no backlog of Chancery cases. The main problem was the expense of proceedings in equity.

After considering the statutory tariff table in Chancery, the commissioners observed that these fees could not be reduced 'without evident injustice to those by whom the business is to be done.' The commission then considered 'making such alterations in the pleadings and practice as will lessen the labour. It is only by such measures ... that any very important reduction can be made in the costs of Chancery proceedings ...' The commissioners noted that in England, after the diligent consideration of those best qualified, that is, eminent members of the legal profession, little alteration in the machinery of Chancery had resulted. The Canadian investigators inferred that the English had not deemed it wise to sacrifice the interests of suitors to economy and 'expedition.' In conclusion the commissioners found it ... most expedient ... to endeavour to take a middle course, and so to curtail the proceedings and reduce the costs, that, while the resemblance to the English Chancery practice shall be preserved in essentials, the suits shall be brought as regards expense, within a limit somewhat in proportion to the value of the business to be transacted, without affecting to make the Court of Chancery that kind of cheap tribunal, that parties may be tempted, by the facility of access, to abuse its purposes...

The government accepted the commission's initial recommendations for streamlining the pleadings, practice, and proceedings in equity.[35] These included such frequent business as the foreclosing of mortgages, in which the commissioners estimated the changes would reduce the cost of a suit by one-half. In their second report the investigators proposed further rules for diminishing 'the length and consequently the expense of Petitions' in Chancery. Realizing that their mandate would end by July 1845 and that wider alterations in the workings of Chancery required continued and consistent supervision, the commissioners recommended that the legislature establish 'a continuing authority ... for amending and modifying the new practice.' The report advocated no structural changes in Chancery, such as a larger bench. The government, preoccupied with other matters, took no immediate action on receipt of the commission's findings.

Despite the attractive rhetoric, the limited proposals of the 1845 report obviously represented in large part the views of senior lawyers. A strong representation of Chancery practitioners on the commission was probably a necessity in reporting on such a specialized and complex subject. The commmissioners well appreciated 'that it may be imputed to them, that their connection with the business of the Court prevents them from exercising an unbiased judgment.'

Indeed there is little doubt that the views of the commissioners reflected prevailing professional attitudes. In its inaugural issue the *Upper Canada Jurist* mirrored the commission's homage to the English model of jurisprudence and regretted that 'we have by no means availed ourselves of the advantages which have been offered to us, by the adoption of those changes in the law in England, which, in their practical working, have been attended with most satisfactory results.' The editors did not advocate blind imitation of 'all the changes made in the law in the mother country, but we would have no time lost in appropriating those that had worked well already. The nearer we keep to the English system, the more likely we are to ensure to our laws the highest degree of perfection.' After all, 'it is to English books that we turn for authorities, and by English forms and precedents that we are mainly guided.'[36]

POLITICAL LOBBYING

The early months of W.H. Draper's new moderate Conservative administration which took office in 1844 witnessed an acceleration in the controversy over alleged shortcomings in the administration of justice. In response the government maintained that it had no intention of amending or repealing the act establishing the Court of Chancery.[37] Whereas some groups, such as the radical reformers, called for drastic changes, including the abolition of Chancery, senior members of the bar for the most part advocated an expansion of the superior court system to better facilitate an increased caseload and also to provide efficient, prompt, and less expensive local appellate jurisdiction. Despite the conservatism of these suggestions, they were not solely for the profession's advantage; lawyers were themselves weary of the complicated and sluggish old system. For instance, in 1842 young Oliver Mowat of Kingston observed that practice in Chancery was onerous and offered little remuneration: 'much ... is undesirable about the unceasing attention which a Chancery practice requires. We are not so well paid for what we do as the Common Lawyers are, our clerks are of not half the use to us that theirs are, our responsibility is far greater than theirs, the assistance we receive from one another far less than they receive: and lastly,' but perhaps most importantly, 'all our profits in the end appear to be but nominal.'[38]

The bar soon acted on its concerns. In June 1844 a member of the legal profession petitioned Governor General Metcalfe for consideration of judicial reform. Later that year Robert Easton Burns headed another effort; William Hume Blake assisted Burns in drafting the second petition, which other leaders of the profession endorsed. In this document, addressed to the House of Assembly, the essential elements of the wider judicial reforms of 1849 first took shape. Burns had recently acted as counsel in proceedings where Queen's Bench had treated Chancery as an inferior court. He was genuinely concerned about the apparent weakness of the latter tribunal; clearly the old English rivalry between common law and equity by this time had spread to Canada.[39] The Burns petition went well beyond the recommendations of the Chancery Commission. Burns and his associates now advocated the creation of another superior court of common law, each to have three judges, the addition of two justices to the equity bench, and the establishment of a Court of Appeal from these three high courts. These measures, the petitioners argued, would exorcise many 'evils' from the whole judicial body. The additional judges would provide more expeditious and less expensive hearing of cases at first instance and of those on appeal, which would then take place in the province.

In late January 1845 Robert Baldwin, the leader of the fragmented Canada West reform opposition, laid the petition before the House, where it was read just as the tumult was subsiding over a bill to appoint a reporter in Chancery. On the 27th Blake, who by this time was orchestrating the various efforts for judicial reform, sent Baldwin a candid, detailed, and rather testy letter on the subject: 'I had hoped to have found in you a strenuous upholder of our plan, not only on account of your political acumen ... but also on account of your experimental knowledge of its [Chancery's] evils.' After commenting on Baldwin's evident lack of enthusiasm for the measure, he also chided him for his misleading public explanation of the petition: 'You speak of the plan as formed for the sole purpose of getting rid of a judge [Vice-Chancellor Jameson]. But that is by no means a fair representation of our view. It is my firm conviction that our bar is not in a condition to furnish a single judge fitted to discharge [by himself] the duty of Vice-Chancellor.'[40]

Blake emphasized that the paramount problem was the lack of a satisfactory appellate tribunal at common law: 'The improvement of our Chancery Court is however the *smallest part* of the plan in my estimate. The position of our common law court from which there is no appeal [except to the Judicial Committee of the Privy Council], is truly alarming ... the danger to liberty from this despotic tribunal [Queen's Bench] is most imminent.' Blake spoke from bitter experience. 'To calculate its effect upon the bar alone would be impossible. It is the thought of offending judges whose decrees are absolute, and who thus hold the fate of transgressors in their hand which has driven the bar,' and here Blake perhaps exaggerates, 'into the ranks of our [political] opponents ... Give us the court of appeal, and you do more to liberalise the people and the bar than can be well conceived.'

Blake did not let the matter rest with a private letter to the reform leader. Something of the sense of urgency felt by the advocates of change is suggested by the fact that they forgot for the moment some of the conservatism of their profession and resorted to the popular English lobbying device of the day, the publication of a pamphlet. Clearly Blake believed intensely that the time was ripe for Baldwin to push for judicial reform. In an open letter to Baldwin on the administration of justice in Canada West, Blake endorsed and expanded upon the Burns petition to the House of Assembly. Although he exercised more reserve in this public statement than in his private letter to Baldwin, this forty-page pamphlet was Blake's most elaborate comment on the subject.[41] In it he stressed two principal problems in the existing structure of the judiciary: the absence of a practical common law appellate tribunal and the inadequacy of having only one judge on the provincial equity bench. It was the profession, he insisted, and not the general public, which had the best opportunity to be aware of such problems and had the responsibility for urging necessary reform.

Blake devoted about half of his 1845 pamphlet to the urgent need to establish a proper appellate court. The courts, he claimed, must have not only 'able and impartial judges, but ... [ones who] feel that they act in the presence of an observing people, and in an independent bar, *who are permitted at every step to bring their decision under review.*' The present 'appeal ... to the Governor in Council ... [and] to Her Majesty in Council ... is so ruinously expensive, and requires for its completion so great a portion of time, that it amounts in effect to a total denial of justice.' Such a court should sit in this country, not only because of the resulting decrease in expense and delay, but because its decisions would carry the added moral sanction of justice seen to be done.

Blake then fixed his attention on the shortcomings of the Court of Chancery. Whereas five judges gave their 'united consideration' to questions brought before Queen's Bench, the Vice-Chancellor *alone* determined all questions in his court. This situation was especially alarming because the questions of fact and the doctrines applied in equity were of much greater complexity and the issues involved larger monetary values than those at common law. According to Blake, it was impossible to find among the fledgling colonial bar men sufficiently experienced to superintend the Court of Chancery singlehandedly and so to command public and professional respect. This difficulty in Canadian Chancery could be traced to the faithful transfer of English practice, where one judge sat in Chancery, but it might be easily corrected by expanding the local bench.

Having outlined these judicial problems, Blake proceeded to champion the legal profession's solution. He argued for the creation of a second superior common law court and the augmentation of the equity bench, with each of the three courts having three judges. 'By bringing the united wisdom of three judges to bear upon the matters in controversy ... the applicability of precedents, and the validity of arguments ... would be closely sifted, and severely tried ... [and] inevitably result in decisions commanding the respect of both the suitors and the bar.' Above this reformed structure of superior courts, to better provide for justice, there ought to be an Upper Canadian appellate body composed of several judges from the new courts. For Blake the advantages of the profession's proposals were self-evident, although he conceded that 'a sense of the *imperious necessity* of the alteration, does not seem to have as yet impressed itself upon the public mind.' Yet his own inquiries had uncovered weighty endorsement for the changes: 'the learned judges ... view with favour the proposed alteration, which would divide the arduous duties, at present imposed on the Equity Judge; and would relieve the common law tribunal of ... a sense of the finality of its judgments.' The judiciary and the public may not have been equally enlightened as to the probable benefits of the proposed changes but the latter well appreciated the even greater obstacle of their cost. Even supporters of the petition recognized that the public would object to an increase in the expense of administering justice. Blake argued forcefully that a £3000 increase in public taxation was a small price for remedying these ills and providing individual suitors with inexpensive access to the court.

Although Blake had addressed his thoughts primarily to legislators, the legal profession undoubtedly took note of his views. Blake would hardly have presented such a daring and comprehensive treatment of the situation, involving recommendations which moved well beyond the second Chancery report (which appeared almost concurrently), without the assurance of substantial support from his colleagues. Yet the pamphlet's impact on the wider public was probably minimal, even though George Brown's pro-reform *Globe* did report on 11 February 1845 that 'Mr. Blake's masterly pamphlet ... has excited general interest ... [T]he state of things pointed out by that letter is truly alarming. The Administration of Justice ... is still ... in the hands of men over whom there is no practical check.' The Toronto editor endorsed Blake's exposé so far as it went, but politely criticized his failure to address adequately the most pressing judicial problems: 'we cannot help wishing that he had fully discussed, rather than hinted at, what appears to us the worst feature of the present system ... "the dangerous consequences to liberty, which ... result from placing the administration of the law practically beyond [public] controul." ... Had such a plan been adopted by Mr. Blake, we have no doubt that the public voice would have forced the Ministry into some measure.' The article ended on an impassioned note, suggesting the newspaper's wish to use the issue to attack the Draper government. 'Who can regard our condition without the utmost alarm? ... The law is not only administered, but *made*, by men whose judgment can in no way be examined ... if the Government decline to take ... up [the measure] ... it is earnestly hoped that Mr. Baldwin will bring his influence and experience to bear upon the subject.'

Robert Baldwin, however, remained cautious. Despite Blake's entreaties and perhaps doubtful of some aspects of the proposals, he would not commit his party to the thorny issue of judicial reform: 'though I may not be at once carried away by the ... [illegible word] zeal that you [Blake] seem filled with and may see occasion for some circumspection both in respect of the measure itself & the time and manner of having it brought forward[,] you must not therefore conclude that I am either indifferent to the importance of the subject or undervalue your excellent letter [pamphlet] upon it,' And he added, more encouragingly, 'I trust ... that within a reasonable time[,] if not as soon as your warm imagination would lead you to expect[,] the evil will be remedied. But the plan involves a grant of money that *must* emanate from the Govt[,] so that what you seem to contemplate could not be done without [it].'[42]

But even before Baldwin had a chance to write this reply, the impatient Blake had fired off another note to his leader, urging that the time was right to promote judicial reform in the legislature.[43] 'It has been hinted to me ... that if Mr. Baldwin would refrain from taking up the question touching the administration of justice, as a party measure, the Government would assent to a committee ... of enquiry. But with the understanding that the enquiry shall be restricted to the necessity of *changes in the Court of Chancery*.' Blake then analyzed the political climate: 'Now I should think that no objection could be made to the amicable consideration of this subject by both sides of the House ... But fully alive as I am to the importance of some change being made in the equity Court, I cannot forget that the evils arising from the position of our Court of common law, are of much more serious moment.' Blake concluded by reiterating the chief intent of the Burns petition: 'Our object was to obtain a court of appeal for the "Inquisition" [Queen's Bench] ... if both parties are to unite, let it be to carry the whole measure, not a petty part of which may suit the inconvenience [*sic*] of Ministers.'

On 14 February 1845 Baldwin replied from Montreal to Blake's latest detailed prompting. Now he agreed at least in principle with the proposals but he retained serious tactical reservations: 'I have a great objection to the system of tinkering upon the subject of the Judiciary, and

... I scarcely know how I should be able to bring myself to consent to one part only of the question being taken up.'[44] Baldwin well appreciated the political ramifications of that strategy: 'if we consent to take up the Court of Chancery as an isolated question, will we not be in effect postponing the other indefinitely[?]' Baldwin preferred another solution. 'Let the Govt. ... take up the question as they ought to do and come down with a measure calculated to dispose of it upon comprehensive and permanent principles. That is the way to act both for their own honor & the public good.'

INTERLUDE AND DELAY

The unwieldy House turned only slowly to the divisive issue of judicial reform. There seems to have been a general acceptance of the continuing need for an equitable jurisdiction, but no consensus as to whether a separate court should administer it. W.R. Riddell (1852–1945), the prolific pioneer of Ontario legal history, has maintained that 'the [legal] Profession at large [which was well represented in the Assembly] viewed the proposition of a single Court administering Law and Equity with alarm as revolutionary and destructive of sound principles.'[45] It seems more likely, however, that the opposition came from the radical element of the Reform party which regarded American solutions as the panacea for most Canadian problems and was suspicious of prerogative privilege vested in the Court of Chancery. In many American states equitable and legal jurisdictions were united under one court.[46] More conservative members of the legislature may have hesitated to raise the issue of Chancery and provide a political opening for the radicals.

Early in 1845 a Select Committee began to study the recent presentations on Chancery: Burns's petition, the second report of the Chancery Commission, and an enumeration of recent suits in Chancery. A year later the Assembly clarified the court's jurisdiction over the estates of lunatics and idiots by granting the court a jurisdiction comparable to that of the English Lord Chancellor. The key political debate over Chancery in 1846 came in late May when the House resolved to go into committee of the whole to consider the expediency of abolishing the court. Although members hotly disagreed over the measures required to remedy the alleged evils in the Upper Canadian judicature, especially Chancery, they did acknowledge the importance of the matter. Nevertheless, the view prevailed that the problem would be better met in the subsequent session.[47]

For the most part 1847 and the first half of 1848 brought little apparent activity towards judicial reform. A notable exception was the publication in 1847 of a pamphlet by John Godfrey Spragge, a prominent member of the provincial bar and Master of the Court of Chancery. Although his comments dealt with the provincial judiciary in general, Spragge made a point of defending the Court of Chancery and attempting to refute commonly held misconceptions. 'There are those who say we may safely abolish equitable jurisdiction, for we did very well without it before the Court of Chancery was established. I take leave to deny both the conclusion and the premises. The want of equitable jurisdiction was much felt, and considering the many cases in which remedial justice is administered in equity, it is impossible that it could be otherwise.' On the contrary, he argued, 'no stronger evidence is needed of the want of such a jurisdiction having been felt than the circumstance of an act being passed to introduce it, as part of the law which without it was imperfect, and in many instances worked injustice. It was from no love of a Court of Chancery that it was introduced, but in spite of many and strong prejudices.' Spragge freely acknowledged that the machinery of Chancery had to be overhauled; he also pointed to the lack of an effective indigenous appellate court. Finally, he asserted that 'it is the duty of the State to make proper and sufficient provision for the due administration of justice ... it is the worst economy to grudge what is necessary for such a purpose.'[48] Nevertheless the Draper government, at that time hard pressed on many other fronts, still did not turn its attention to judicial reform.

Retaining a keen interest in politics and reform, Blake directed the majority of his energies in 1846–7 to the demands of his legal practice, professorial responsibilities, and private concerns. He had rapidly made a name for himself in Toronto and reaped handsome rewards, but the price had been great. Overexertion, due to an almost obsessive desire for success, began to impair his health. In mid-September 1847 Hume, his wife Catherine, and their elder son, Edward, sailed to Europe for an extended holiday. Eventually Blake learned of the reform victory of 24 January 1848 and of his own election to the Canadian House of Assembly. As the new member for the East Riding of York, where with Baldwin's assistance he had won easy nomination the previous February, Blake had to return to Toronto at once. He was finally entering politics as an elected participant.[49]

Fortunately for the cause of legal reform, Attorney General Baldwin then appointed Blake to the office of Solicitor General for Canada West in

April. Blake was now ideally placed to effect the changes he regarded as necessary to remedy the shortcomings of the superior courts. The numerous and ill-defined duties of a solicitor general in the mid-nineteenth century permitted him a voice in many important legal and administrative matters. During his brief term Blake was responsible for an enormous quantity of non-political business of the office, but his active involvement in the political activity of the tumultuous session was of more moment.[50]

LEGISLATIVE REFORM

The proroguing of parliament in late March 1848 provided Blake with nine months for consultations and drafting bills.[51] 'Working day & night,' the Solicitor General began to shape the specifics of his judicial reforms. He first sought the opinion of the senior provincial judges. Blake then wrote to Baldwin giving 'the results' of these free and candid discussions.[52] The Solicitor General reported first on the reform of Chancery: 'The Cheif [*sic*] Justice [Robinson] is decidedly adverse to a multiplicity of Judges in equity. It is he thinks incompattible with the satisfactory discharge of the peculiar duty of an equity Judge, and has never been adopted to his knowledge. He is adverse to this change in toto, but at all events would not attempt the change until the appointment of a single judge,' a successor to the unpopular Jameson, 'had failed to give satisfaction to the Country. In this latter view Mr. [Justice James Buchanan] McCaulay [*sic*] concurs ... He sees nothing incompattible in the multiplicity of judges and only dissents from the proposed changes under the impression that the amount of business would not justify so large an establishment.' There was also the possibility of uniting the two jurisdictions. 'Mr. [Justice Archibald] McLean is in favor of a court of common pleas with equitable jurisdiction. The Cheif [Justice] dissents ... but Mr. McCaulay leans to that view.' Here Blake could not resist editorializing: 'nothing but necessity would induce me to adopt that suggestion. Possibly I might prefer it to a continuance of our present monstrous system of a court without appeal. But I would rather countenance one court of equity with one judge and erect a separate court of appeal as mentioned by the Cheif.'

Blake then turned to the judges' opinions on the proposed Court of Common Pleas: 'The Cheif Justice would not assent to any change which would alter the constitution of the present court of Queens Bench ... the reason which really disinclines him so strongly to a second court of common law is the apprehension of the removal of one to Kingston. Upon this point I had to reason against the probability.' But Chief Justice Robinson pointed to 'the certainty with which local interests have uniformly sooner or later prevailed ... I found all opposed to the second common law court. And certainly the removal of one to Kingston would be in my judgment so great an evil that I would submit to present evils rather than encounter it.'

The Solicitor General then treated the several views on the formation of a new appellate tribunal. 'The Cheif ... would leave the court of equity & law unchanged *in constitution* and would erect a new court of appeal consisting of the three ablest men to be found. Thus the judicial establishment would not be larger than under the system proposed by yourself [Baldwin] and the dangers [to liberty] ... would be avoided.' There were after all political factors to consider: 'the new proposition would expose us to new difficulties. The business of the Court of Appeal would be inconsiderable ... The appointments would seem *sinecures.*' But under this arrangement, cautioned Blake, 'our Common law establishment already sufficiently burthened would shortly be insufficient to meet our growing business. And our equity would be kept in the hands of a single judge.'

In late September 1848 the Solicitor General again sought Baldwin's opinion on the specifics for the planned judicial reforms. Time was running out. After two short and seemingly hesitant notes from Baldwin, Blake expressed his resolve to carry out his original plan: 'As to the courts my opinion remains unaltered. I am not afraid to undertake the justification of placing three judges in equity, so far as this Court & its business is concerned. The incompatibility of having a multiplicity of judges in a court of equity, I am prepared to encounter. But ...,' and this was crucial, 'will the establishment seem in the public view disproportionate[?]' Blake decided in the affirmative. 'I have considered it and think the balance is in favour of the alteration. But on whatever side the right lies[,] some change must be made, and that without much further delay.'[53]

The legal fraternity for its part continued to urge the Solicitor General to take measures of reform. During a mid-November meeting at Osgoode Hall members of the Upper Canadian bar resolved that 'for ... the purpose of instituting an efficient and inexpensive Court of Appeal, it is highly desirable that the plan formerly proposed, of constituting two Courts of Superior Common Law Jurisdiction, each presided over by three Judges, with the Court of Chancery presided over in like manner, should be adopted.'[54] Early in 1849 the profession, represented by Skeffington

Connor, presented another petition to the Assembly urging the adoption of measures for placing the Superior Courts in Upper Canada on an efficient foundation.[55]

It was a victory for Blake that the Speech from the Throne on 18 January 1849 referred to the government's ambitious slate of proposed legislation, including the revision of the senior courts in Upper Canada. Unfortunately vicious partisan squabbling consumed a good part of the early session, making progress difficult. Most explosive was LaFontaine's unexpected proposal for compensating those in Lower Canada who had suffered property losses in the Rebellion of 1837–8. Privately Blake opposed the measure of the Attorney General East as politically inexpedient, but once the bill came to the floor he felt duty-bound to defend it.[56] On 15 and 16 February 1849 Blake delivered one of the most memorable orations in the United Province's history. He deflected the Tories' charge of disloyalty by picturing them as abject and selfish sycophants ruled by narrow attitudes and self-interest. Giving an extended account of the historical development of responsible government in England and Upper Canada, he hammered this impassioned theme at the stunned Tory ranks for hours.[57] His impulsive behaviour almost resulted in duels with Sir Allan MacNab and John A. Macdonald and could easily have cost Blake his political career. The Rebellion Losses issue, however, was no small victory; the Reformers won the day and at the same time instituted responsible government.

With that out of the way, Blake's own moment had finally come. As Solicitor General West he was personally responsible for the three major Upper Canadian judicial and legal reform bills which he presented to the House on 13 March: a bill for the more effectual Administration of Justice in the Court of Chancery of the late Province of Upper Canada; a bill to make further provision for the Administration of Justice, by the establishment of a Superior Court of Law, and also a Court of Error and Appeal in Upper Canada, and for other purposes; and a bill to improve the Law of Evidence in Upper Canada.

The Chancery bill proposed the reconstitution of the equity court along the lines desired by the profession.[58] The bench was to have a Chancellor, with 'rank and precedence next to the Chief Justice of the Court of Queen's Bench,' and two Vice-Chancellors. The bill increased the court's jurisdiction by allowing it to try the validity of wills and testaments, that is, for both real and personal property. It endorsed the recommendations of the Chancery Commission (1843–5), which had advocated simplifying the pleadings and practice of the court to diminish costs and to expedite justice. The court's benchers and officers were to receive salaries from the Consolidated Revenue Fund; all fees paid into court were to go to that fund.

The other Judicature bill provided for a second Superior Court of Law.[59] 'The establishment of an additional Superior Court of Common Law jurisdiction would facilitate the satisfactory disposal of business, and would otherwise tend to promote the public advantage by affording the means of constituting an efficient Court of Appeal within Upper Canada.' The bench of the new Court of Common Pleas was to have a Chief Justice, with 'rank and precedence next to the Chancellor of Upper Canada,' and two puisne judges. After the passage of the bill only a Chief Justice and two puisne judges would preside over Queen's Bench; the other two puisne judges were to be transferred to the Court of Common Pleas, so that both Superior Courts of Common Law would have three judges. Common Pleas was to have equal and concurrent jurisdiction with Queen's Bench and to follow its mode of procedure. All laws and orders applicable to Queen's Bench were to apply to Common Pleas, and the judges in each court were to sit in rotation. Judges and officers of both courts were to paid by salary. The bill set out the terms of sittings for the two courts in Toronto and provided for triannual issuance of civil and criminal itinerant commissions to try cases in the outlying counties. The measure also specified detailed procedural matters. Judges were to have authority to make general rules and orders to implement the act.

Clauses thirty-seven through forty-six of the bill provided for the establishment of a provincial Court of Error and Appeal to replace the old Court of Appeal. The Chief Justice of Queen's Bench, or his immediate subordinate on that bench, was to preside at Error and Appeal and the judges of Queen's Bench, Common Pleas, and Chancery were to join him at full sittings of the court. The tribunal was to sit in Toronto and to 'exercise an appellate civil and criminal jurisdiction ... [for] appeal ... from all judgments of the ... Courts of Queen's Bench and Common Pleas, and ... from all judgments, orders and decrees of the ...Court of Chancery.' The judges of the new Court of Appeal were to make, subject to the approval of parliament, general rules and orders to govern all proceedings and to regulate costs in the court. The bill also required the posting of securities and restricted appeals to Her Majesty in Council.

The third bill was a major procedural advancement to improve the law of evidence in Upper Canada and so to facilitate 'the inquiry after truth.'[60] In order to provide fuller disclosure of facts in civil and criminal cases, those adjudicating issues 'should exercise their judgment on the credit of witnesses adduced, and on the truth of their testimony.' The bill further asserted that 'no person offered as a witness ... [was to] be excluded by reason of incapacity, from crime or interest, from giving evidence ... [in any] proceeding, civil or criminal.' Witnesses were to give evidence on oath. According to the bill, 'objections should apply to the credibility, and not to the admissibility, of the evidence.'[61] Formerly much time and money had been wasted in determining whether or not witnesses should be excluded on the basis of interest from giving evidence, and their frequent exclusion had brought much injustice. Parties to an action, however, were still to be excluded from giving evidence. Blake's Evidence Act was clearly modelled after an earlier British statute, which Lord Brougham, late Lord Chancellor, had hailed as 'the greatest measure that has been carried, under the head of judicial procedure ... since the Restoration.'[62]

The immediate controversy over the Rebellion Losses Bill distracted journalistic coverage from the less spectacular issue of judicial reform.[63] Yet within a week detailed reports of the Solicitor General's bills, especially the one to reform Chancery, appeared in the press. Blake's central and partisan involvement in the Rebellion Losses confrontation brought him abuse and reduced his credibility. The Toronto *British Colonist*, a moderate Conservative paper, did not spare its wrath. After a scathing attack on 'this very important gentleman's very absurd speech on the rebellion losses,' the *Colonist* gleefully alleged an apparently early and 'mysterious appearance' of the printed judicial bills as 'another evidence of the determination of the Executive Government to legislate by surprise, to withhold from the public all information of their intention until the period arrives when they are fully prepared to carry out their privately arranged plans, and then to force them through Parliament, regardless of public opinion, – or rather, without affording the public an opportunity of forming any opinion regarding them.' Ironically the paper followed this political and dishonest invective with an objective account of 'the general features of the new Judicature Bills for Upper Canada' and criticized the expense, not the principle, of the plan 'in these days of empty treasury.'[64]

The pro-Reform Toronto *Globe* on the other hand lauded the Solicitor General's bills and pointed to English developments as models:

> We understand that it [the Chancery Bill] has given much satisfaction to the profession and have no doubt it will be equally acceptable to the public ... The amendments of Equity practice and pleadings already adopted in England, and ... those on the eve ... of being adopted there ... will guide the steps of the new court

in adapting such amendments to the circumstances of this country ... we may look forward with confidence to the equity jurisdiction of Upper Canada being established on the most satisfactory basis. The demand for equitable remedies is daily increasing.[65]

The *Globe* editorial also considered the chief disadvantage of implementing the bills, their cost, but on balance found in their favour: 'The first duty of a community is to provide an efficient system of judicial administration ... so far as we can learn, the country will be put to little additional expense in the matter. All the fees are to be paid into the Consolidated Fund. These without adding ... to the expense of suitors, will ... furnish a very considerable portion of the expense which the creation of new judges will occasion.' The account concluded by praising the comprehensive nature of the Judicature Bills:

That system, composed of three co-ordinate courts of superior jurisdiction, furnishes by the union of the nine judges, an efficient court of appeal *within* the province, a desideratum long earnestly sought by the profession. With such a system in operation for a short time, no one ... will leave the courts with an impression ... that his country does not afford him the means of obtaining justice – an impression which, whether well or ill founded is most injurious to the peace and welfare of society.

The progress of the three bills through the House was sporadic. Second reading was delayed, and as late as 8 May Baldwin remained ambivalent about the legislation; in response to a question the Attorney General West stated that 'he was not prepared to say whether [the] Government intended to proceed with the new Judicature Bills this session or not.'[66] The violent attack on the administration in late April had apparently shaken Baldwin's confidence. He was perhaps also contemplating the impending battle over the secularization of King's College, which started in earnest on the eleventh. Yet 15 May finally produced a second hearing for the three bills. The Assembly ordered that the Evidence Bill be engrossed immediately and sent the two Judicature Bills to the committee of the whole House. The next day the Assembly considered each of the proposed judicial reforms. Four members, including John A. Macdonald of Kingston, opposed the plan. However, 'Mr. Sol. Gen. Blake replied in a long ... speech, in which he powerfully advocated the necessity of the utmost care and attention in the construction of Courts of Justice, eulogizing the conduct of the Judges in England, which he said,' with no small generosity, 'had for a long course of years been unimpeachable; and denouncing as the cause of all mis-government in any country, not so much the mis-constitution of the government as the maladministration of the law in the Courts of Justice.'[67]

The Assembly quickly concluded consideration of the judicial reforms. On the eighteenth the members of the House, perhaps surprisingly, approved with little or no controversy the payment of additional judges and court officers from the Consolidated Revenue Fund. The Solicitor General had overcome with relative ease the greatest practical obstacle to judicial reform. On the twenty-first and twenty-second the Judicature Bills encountered their last opposition before passage. George Sherwood, a High Tory from Brockville, proposed that the Chancery Bill be returned to committee 'with an Instruction ... to provide for the Administration of Justice in the Court ... by one Judge only.' The House rejected the motion and on division passed the bill by a solid vote of thirty-five to five; only one of the latter was a lawyer. Sherwood's colleagues also overwhelmingly rejected his motion for more comprehensive reform based on radically different principles. He urged that 'the ... [other Judicature] Bill ... be recommitted to ... Committee ... with an Instruction to ... report upon the propriety of increasing the Jurisdiction and efficiency of the present Local and Inferior Courts in Upper Canada, with a view to reduce the expenses of litigation ... and to relieve the Court of Queen's Bench from a great portion of civil business.'[68] On the twenty-second the House approved the measure by resolution. The Legislative Council passed the several bills without amendment and on 30 May, the last day of the session, Lord Elgin gave them royal assent.

AFTERMATH

The judicial reforms of 1849 did not produce an immediate surge of public confidence in the courts or the legal profession. If anything, doubts, whatever their bases, seemed to be reaffirmed. In early December the Toronto *Globe* responded to the widespread dissatisfaction with a reflective and supportive editorial on the new Judicature Acts:

> The *Examiner* and one or two other Journals have arraigned the conduct of the Administration in regard to the Judiciary measures of the last Session, and denounced that part of the general scheme by which the Court of Chancery has been reconstructed as 'a flagrant abuse'[;] they accuse the Government of taking the country by surprise, and using their parliamentary majority to perpetrate an

expensive judicial system without affording time for public discussion; and they allege that all this has been done as a conspiracy of professional men in and out of parliament, and with the corrupt purpose of providing for their adherents.[69]

The *Globe* contradicted these claims, claims which probably reflected the public's continuing suspicion of the legal profession:

The changes required in our judicial system had formed the subject of discussion both in and out of Parliament, long prior to the late Session ... they were regarded as a test question at the late elections ... they received the sanction of public opinion ... when perfected by the alterations, purposely and wisely left to the judges to make, they will be eminently satisfactory ... the Government have earned a just claim to public gratitude, for the introduction of ... as perfect a system for the administration of justice as our social condition permits or requires.

The editor pointed to the necessity for a Court of Appeal in place of 'appeal to a *political unprofessional* body like the Executive Council,' defended Chancery, and attempted to debunk popular misconceptions about the legal profession:

The *Examiner* argues as if Lawyers alone had an interest in the continuance of this Court [of Chancery] ... But if the *Examiner*, instead of talking of the Court of Chancery, as nursery children talk of ghosts, would lay before the country a statement of the evils which that Court is intended to remedy, we fancy that Farmers of Canada [West, many of whom were radical Reformers] would see ... clearly ... what interests would be best served by its abolition. We feel that evil influence of the legal gentlemen in public affairs ... but we are not prepared to join in the mad-dog cry raised against the whole bar, which numbers in its ranks many of our best and most honourable citizens.

Another criticism levelled at the Judicature Act was its complexity and tendency to centralize the system. Opponents of the changes argued that equitable principles could be applied with less expense and difficulty in a common law court than in a separate court of equity, where precedent and not 'moral justice' guided decisions.[70] The same critics were not above twisting a fact or two. They asserted, for example, that the government had exacerbated judicial evils by enlarging the membership of the equity bench, thus breaking with English practice where one judge had sufficed; but clearly one judge had not proven adequate on the parent bench. There was also a regional aspect to the criticism. Many lawyers outside

Toronto did not practise in Chancery and may have gladly supported the abolition of the non-itinerant court.[71] As well, 'one of the disadvantages ... [Chancery] had to bear up against was that the great majority of Lawyers shrunk from the labour required in its practice, and betook themselves to the easier paths of the Common Law.'[72] In general, advocates of the simplification persuasion – for instance, simplification of laws and broadening of local courts' jurisdictions – regarded the American example as more appropriate than the English to Canada's young and impoverished condition.[73] The conservative Toronto *Patriot*, however, loyally defended the Upper Canadian judicial status quo: 'We maintain that the popular voice frequently does select the presumptuous noisy ignorant demagogue in preference to the studious, quiet, well-informed man ... The country magistracy in the United States are contemptible because the average education and moral tone of the men who *elect* them are very inferior to those of the class who *select* our magistracy.'[74]

The all-important question of who would sit on the new Chancery bench troubled the profession for some months, since a poor choice would jeopardize the success of the reforms. George Ridout, a prominent Toronto lawyer, addressed the matter in a letter to Attorney General Baldwin in late March 1849: 'There is no confidence in Mr. J. [Jameson] and I ... believe that if the Judiciary Bills should fall through this Session, that there will be a petition from the Bar here praying for his removal and the appointment of another. That person doubtless would be Mr. Blake, & if one Judge only must preside, he would be preferred, but ... the decision of three impartial men must always command the most respect.'[75] Such was the general preference of the bar. 'A Court composed of Mesrs. Blake[,] Esten & Spragge I think would give satisfaction.' Baldwin had originally hoped that Marshall Spring Bidwell, the exiled moderate Reformer, would take the post, but he was busy practising law in New York and does not seem to have received Baldwin's offer.[76] In early September 1849 Baldwin wrote to his Solicitor General formally offering him the Chancellorship.

Blake's acceptance further fuelled suspicions of self-interest. Tory and radical Reformer detractors easily misconstrued the situation in their claims that Blake had specifically modelled the Chancellorship for himself. In fact, Blake was one of the best qualified men for the post. He was a leading Chancery lawyer, an experienced judge and, of course, he also happened to be a prominent member of the governing party. Although judicial positions of the time were often regarded as patronage plums, there is no reason to suspect that Blake regarded the comfortable salary of £1250 as handsome. Although he himself had set the sum high enough to attract competent men, he had earned much more in private practice. Blake probably was attracted far more by the prestige of a judicial office, second only to that of the Chief Justice, and by the opportunity of being in a position to implement the reforms for which he had fought for so long. Another consideration was his declining health, although he was only forty years of age. In the cirumstances he must have been pleased to leave the contentious political forum and return to the relative serenity of the courtroom. Although his exit from the Ministry represented a significant loss of talent, Baldwin was perhaps relieved by the idea of having the impetuous Blake safely out of political harm's way.[77]

Blake accurately anticipated the response of many. 'I have been haunted,' he wrote to Baldwin, 'by the thought that my acceptance of the office may bring discredit upon your administration as though it were carried on for private ends.' He later added: 'The circumstances are sufficient to warrant a good deal [of] talk.'[78] In fact, the Chancellor long felt 'the storm of abuse' he endured after his appointment.[79] Other eminent lawyers, such as Robert Easton Burns, Robert Baldwin Sullivan, and James C. Palmer Esten, joined the benches of the reconstructed superior courts but, being less directly involved in the judicial reforms, were not objects of criticism. Even after Blake died, enterprising politicians of both stripes continued to allude, periodically and almost ritualistically, to the ex-Chancellor's alleged self-interest in accepting the office.[80] Indeed, one cannot deny that the case for self-interest, however circumstantial, at least exists.

The controversy over the Court of Chancery eventually overtook Attorney General Baldwin and injured his political career. Despite personal reservations, Baldwin loyally stood by his Solicitor General during the extended legislative program of judicial reform. By 1850 the Reform party's radical wing (soon known as the Clear Grits) grew impatient with the government's moderate pace. With the Grits demanding more radical social and political changes, the Reform party by 1850 had begun to splinter. One continuing cause of radical unease was the enlarged Chancery, stationed as it was entirely in Toronto. Seven outlying municipal councils petitioned the Assembly for the abolition of Chancery and the extension of equitable jurisdiction to the court of Queen's Bench. These requests came to naught and early in the session of 1850 the Assembly also rejected another proposal for the abolition of Chancery.[81]

In late June 1851 William Lyon Mackenzie, recently returned from the United States to resume the role of maverick-agitator in the Assembly, moved the appointment of a Select Committee to report by bill or otherwise for the abolition of Chancery and for the transfer of equitable jurisdiction in certain cases to the common law courts.[82] The radical Reformer asserted that a court of equity was unnecessary and expensive, but this latter charge at least was largely unjustified.[83] Baldwin firmly opposed Mackenzie's motion, arguing that the restructured court was functioning in an improved manner and ought to be given an opportunity to vindicate itself. The House defeated the motion by a narrow margin of thirty-four to thirty. However, a majority of Upper Canadian members (twenty-five, seven of whom were lawyers) supported Chancery's abolition. Although the motion may have been only 'a gesture to secure radical votes, not a move to defeat the government,' Baldwin, always obsessed about matters of honour, saw resignation as his only option. As Attorney General he deemed himself personally responsible for the legislation, even though Blake had been its author.[84] LaFontaine, Attorney General East and acknowledged leader of the government, also retired at the session's end. The two vacancies cleared the way in the autumn of 1851 for a major political reconstruction under the subsequent Hincks-Morin Reform ministry.

These events did not destroy the validity of Blake's reforms. Before the next election a well-argued pamphlet appeared which supported Baldwin's viewpoint and addressed the matter of the proposed abolition of Chancery. Referring to the recent controversy, Charles W. Cooper, Blake's former student and already a noted attorney, condemned 'the amount of ignorance betrayed by those who attacked, and the very weak defence offered by those who defended the Court [of Chancery] as now constituted ... The arguments in favor of the proposed measure [to abolish Chancery] are all based on facts as they existed before the remodelling of the Court, and either in ignorance or disregard of the reforms.' There existed, however, reason for optimism. 'That the prejudice created by past abuses is strong we are aware, but that confidence in the present tribunal is daily increasing, is evident from the increased business occupying its attention; the matters adjudicated upon in open Court, of greater or less importance, average about one hundred cases a month, and are constantly becoming more numerous.' The pamphleteer concluded: 'let judicious reform be exercised where it is needed; but it is easier to destroy than to create. Let those then beware who either from ignorance, recklessness, or for party purposes, would endeavor to foster an imaginary grievance that they may gain popularity by its pretended removal, even at the expense ... of justice.'[85]

CONCLUSION

Blake's chancellorship brought both praise and criticism, while his declining health all too quickly eclipsed a promising career on the bench. As the first presiding judge of the revamped Court of Chancery until his retirement in 1862, he personally supervised its reformation. Relying on his own integrity, ability, and strong personality, Blake brought greater efficiency and economy to the court and its procedure; equity was truly his forte.[86] Legislation of 1857 establishing a circuit for Chancery greatly increased its availability to citizens outside Toronto and answered much of the political criticism. By 1860 the editor of the court's *Orders* noted that 'Chancery business is not now, as formerly, confined to a few offices in Toronto. Many country practitioners, who a few years ago would have entered the regions of equity with great distrust, have now undertaken, to some extent at least, the conduct of chancery suits.'[87]

R.C.B. Risk, who has surveyed Blake's judicial decisions, concluded that 'his distinctive characteristics as judge were sheer intelligence and perception, openness, a passion for fairness, and a determination to shape the law to Canadian needs and conditions ... But,' he added, 'Blake never doubted the obligation to follow English authority and never claimed any power or responsibility to make law.' That role was for the legislature. 'The results may not have been dramatic, but the determination to think about Canada was unique ... Blake's influence and distinctive attitudes have not been widely shared, and the Canadian judiciary has been less distinguished than it might have been.'[88] This evaluation seems persuasive except perhaps on one point. D.B. Read, the late nineteenth-century legal historian, claimed that Blake had greater 'independence of mind ... His chief characteristic was disregard of case law, where case law came in conflict with principle ... Wherever the English law ... failed to impress him with its justice as applied to the state of things in Canada, he threw aside old precedents, to establish Canadian rights.'[89] But this interpretative difference is one of degree only; most important is the recognition that Blake was one judge who at least attempted to adapt the law to Canadian circumstances.

William Hume Blake, as Read has suggested, was probably 'the greatest Law Reformer ... in public life' in his day.[90] His grasp of judicial needs was truly comprehensive. He initiated, shaped, and implemented the changes he believed necessary to meet the requirements of Upper Canadian jurisprudence. In bringing about this adaptation of the English legal tradition, he utilized every role available to him as lawyer, commissioner, pamphleteer, lobbyist, confidant, professor, politician, cabinet minister, and judge. His involvement in this broad spectrum of activities brought to the fore an essentially moderate political philosophy. 'The cause of order, of good government, of British connection' formed the touchstone of his career.[91] Firmly in the spirit of nineteenth-century liberalism, he advocated an extended popular influence in government, yet never strayed from a devout adherence to constitutional, evolutionary, and orderly development. He was no sympathizer with the techniques of the radical school of reform.

His most important work as a reformer, his fathering of the Judicature Acts of 1849, reflected these values. By helping to adapt English law and courts to Upper Canadian needs, he set in place the framework for the development of an Anglo-Canadian jurisprudence. After 1849 provincial residents enjoyed a fuller judicial system, one able to meet their needs more efficiently and economically. Blake's reforms did not drastically disrupt the status quo and generally represented the wishes of a very conservative legal profession. But it was Hume Blake who took the initiative in the matter and patiently followed the tedious business through to its conclusion. His work benefitted both the public and the profession. In retrospect one may argue, for instance, that the Court of Common Pleas was an unnecessary creation and therefore represented a flaw in the reforms; in fact, cases eventually had to be allotted alternately to Common Pleas and Queen's Bench in batches of twelve.[92] But the former at least provided additional manpower for the much-needed Court of Appeal. The virtual silence about the functioning of the Courts of Appeal and Common Pleas and for that matter, the Evidence Act, attests to their success. Although Chancery was not Blake's initial priority, equity became his most celebrated reform because of his long involvement in that contentious area.

That Blake's judicial reforms were not more far-reaching may be traced in part at least to the provincial *mentalité* of the time. In assessing the behaviour of the mid-nineteenth-century courts, Risk has posited that

> the most important influence was England, and the obligation to follow English authority seemed greatly to restrict the power to create and to make much of the analysis of problems into a concern for the existence and scope of authority.

Eventually obligation became habit ... [These] were strongly supported by the loyalty of the colony ... especially ... among the governing classes, and the strong appeal of English legal tradition to the lawyers. All these elements combined to make our courts – and our entire legal community – a legal colony, forbidden and eventually unwilling to consider its own legal destiny openly.[93]

However alluring, this generalization is misleading in its implications. Upper Canada did not become a perfect reflection of England, even in legal matters. Differing circumstances dictated legal adaptation in some orderly evolution to meet changing social conditions. If England often seemed to lead the way in Upper Canadian law, this was understandable because the former being the more advanced had to solve many common problems beforehand. The United States had broken away at a much earlier point in English legal development and felt compelled to find its own answers. Perhaps in the final analysis Upper Canada's response to its legal dilemmas reflected a lesser need to chart a separate identity and the wisdom to maintain the essentials of a time-proven familiar tradition of jurisprudence rather than a mere aping of the English judicial and legal scheme. Yet the province did not ignore the American model. Its influence, as Risk clearly demonstrates, appeared in legislation, the traditional vehicle of reform in the common law system. The overall result was a synthetic Upper Canadian legal entity.

Ironically Blake's renovation of the provincial judiciary provided the basic elements for the eventual consolidation of equitable and common law jurisdictions under the Ontario Judicature Act of 1881.[94] A similar English development partially influenced by Field's reforms in New York led the way in 1873.[95] The Court of Chancery became the Chancery Division of the High Court of Justice for Ontario. Each of the three Divisions, including Queen's Bench and Common Pleas, acquired 'full legal and equitable jurisdiction' but were 'like three separate and distinct Courts'; the Court of Appeal remained intact.[96] Together the High Court of Justice and the Court of Appeal constituted the Supreme Court of Judicature for Ontario. The structural merger of the courts and their jurisdictions did not, in fact, result in a corresponding substantive amalgamation of law and equity. The act did, however, simplify and unify procedure and pleading in all divisions so that in deciding a case one court could conveniently and simultaneously utilize the rules and remedies of both equity and law.[97]

To comment at this point on the merits of administering equitable jurisprudence in a separate or combined court, in a codified or noncodified system, would be imprudent.[98] One cannot be very certain without a great deal more investigation whether the fusion of law and equity actually had positive social ramifications or preserved or enhanced the effectiveness of equity. There was little doubt in the nineteenth century about the necessity for an equitable jurisdiction; the question was how best to exercise it. Shortly after the reforms of 1849, one lawyer had idealistically asserted that 'in whatever Court ... [equitable] jurisdiction may be vested, is a matter of comparatively little importance to the lawyer or to the student, or even to the public, provided that it be a Court competent for the purpose, and such as to satisfy the wants, but not to form a disproportionate drag upon the resources of the country.'[99] This was the desideratum of various proponents of reform. The advocates of fusion thought that route would be most expedient, and the perception, or perhaps more accurately the anticipation, of its alleged benefits long persisted. Few if any had a clear idea of what 'fusion' would in fact entail. Its supporters rarely specified whether they meant administrative or substantive changes. Equity was such a complex subject that only a handful of specialized lawyers really understood it. Lay legislators and especially the general public often had only disjointed notions of equitable issues. The pages of *Hansard*, not to mention the newspapers, abounded with specious and uninformed statements on the subject.[100]

This charged and uncertain situation makes an accurate evaluation of the administration of justice, especially in Chancery, very difficult. Perhaps the most important consideration is the impression that equitable remedies, and with them, wider means of justice, seem eventually to have become more accessible to the province's population. Although somewhat removed from the reforms of 1849, the later nineteenth-century developments owed much to a now largely forgotten Irishman who had first arrived in the town of York as an 1832 legislative committee was pondering the expediency of establishing a long-overdue Court of Chancery. William Hume Blake's central place in this protracted series of events provides an instructive, although one suspects extraordinary, illustration of the process of legal reform at mid-century.

NOTES

The author would like especially to express his appreciation to Professor Donald Swainson, Department of History, Queen's University, who initially suggested studying this topic and offered valuable assistance throughout.

1 R.C.B. Risk 'A Prospectus for Canadian Legal History' *Dalhousie Law Journal* I (1973) 244. Risk has since added the name of John Beverley Robinson to this list.

2 J.D. Blackwell 'William Hume Blake and Judicial Reform in the United Province of Canada' (master's thesis, Queen's University 1980) 8–17 (available at the library of the Public Archives of Ontario and the Great Library, Osgoode Hall, Toronto); see also A.H. Manchester *A Modern Legal History of England and Wales 1750–1950* (London 1980) 135–7.

3 Blackwell 'Blake and Judicial Reform' 18–28

4 W.R. Riddell *The Bar and Courts of the Province of Upper Canada or Ontario* Part II: *The Courts* (Toronto 1928) 160–5, 169–78; W.R. Riddell 'The "Ordinary" Court of Chancery in Upper Canada' Ontario Historical Society *Papers and Records* XXII (1925) 222–38; J.D. Falconbridge 'Law and Equity in Upper Canada' *The Canadian Law Times* XXXIV (1914) 1130–40; W.R. Riddell *Upper Canada Sketches: Incidents in the Early Times of the Province* (Toronto 1922) 51, 147–53; Alan Wilson 'John Walpole Willis' in *Dictionary of Canadian Biography* X (Toronto 1972) 704–7 (hereafter DCB)

5 *Journals of the House of Assembly of Upper Canada* (1832–3) 66 and *Appendix* 79–80

6 Also absent was the power to issue an injunction. Its omission from the jurisdiction of the provincial Court of Chancery, eventually created in 1837, was probably due to the influence of the cautious Chief Justice Robinson (Falconbridge 'Law and Equity' 1132, 1139).

7 Quoted in ibid. 1134. In Aug. 1830, the Reverend William Bell of Perth had also noted that 'the judge of assize ... in his charge to the grand Jury ... regretted that there was no *equitable* court in the province: a circumstance which has been regretted by a great many others' (Queen's University Archives, Rev. William Bell Papers, diary, vol. 7, p. 71. Larry Turner of Kingston generously provided this reference).

8 *Statutes of Upper Canada* 7 Wm IV (1837), c. 2; Riddell *Courts of Upper Canada* 167–8, 177

9 Blackwell 'Blake and Judicial Reform' 36–9, 59–60

10 Public Archives of Ontario (hereafter PAO) Record Group (hereafter RG) 22, 05-99-24A vol. 183 *Court of Chancery Causes for Hearing Book, 1838–1854,* and 05-119-06 vol. 9 *Central Office Chancery Letterbook, 1838–1840; Journals of the Legislative Assembly of the Province of Canada* (1844–5) *Appendix* I.I.I.

11 Although little concrete evidence survives of Blake's familiarity with American equity, he was probably aware of these developments; his letters and writings refer virtually exclusively to English experience. He sold most of his library in 1856 (*The Daily Globe* 1 Oct. 1856), but it is known that in 1843 he

purchased a copy of the second edition of James Kent's *Commentaries on American Law* (New York 1832). (G.B. Baker located this set at the Columbia University Law Library and kindly brought it to my attention. Baker, who has read the *Minutes* of Convocation of the Law Society of Upper Canada, 1797 to 1890 [hereafter LSUC] also notes that Joseph Story's *Commentaries on Equity Jurisprudence, as Administered in England and America,* first published in 1836, was required reading for provincial bar admission examinations *after* 1854). Two items in the PAO pamphlet collection (*Re-organization of the Judiciary* ... [New York 1846]; D.D. Field *What Shall Be Done with the Practice of the Courts?* ... [New York 1847]) and the holdings of the contemporary legislative library (*Catalogue of Books in the Library of the Legislative Assembly of Canada* [Kingston 1842]) corroborate Upper Canadians' general awareness of the legal situation to the south, especially in New York. Yet the few provincial law journals of the time, such as *The Upper Canada Law Journal,* 'usually published only ... material from English journals and, occasionally, journals in the United States' (R.C.B. Risk 'Law and the Economy in Mid-Nineteenth-Century Ontario: A Perspective' *University of Toronto Law Journal* XXVII [1977] 435; in this volume, 122).

12 The American literature has many specialized studies of equity, but no one has attempted a comprehensive review. This brief survey is based on: S.N. Katz 'The Politics of Law in Colonial America: Controversies over Chancery Courts and Equity Law in the Eighteenth Century' in Donald Fleming and Bernard Bailyn, eds *Law in American History* (Boston 1971) 262–5, 282–3; Maxwell Bloomfield 'William Sampson and the Codifiers: The Roots of American Legal Reform, 1820–1830' *American Journal of Legal History* XI (1967) 234–52 (hereafter AJLH); E.C. Surrency 'The Courts in the American Colonies' AJLH XI (1967) 271–4; and L.M. Friedman *A History of American Law* (New York 1973) 21–3, 24, 130–1, 340–58

13 M.J. Horwitz *The Transformation of American Law, 1780–1860* (Cambridge, MA 1977) 265–6

14 Brian Abel-Smith and Robert Stevens *Lawyers and the Courts: A Sociological Study of the English Legal System, 1750–1965* (London 1967) 41

15 R.L. Severns 'Nineteenth Century Equity: A Study in Law Reform' Pt II, 'Maturity and Reform' *Chicago-Kent Review* XIII (1935) 317–27; J.D. Gregory 'The Centenary of the Judicature Act' *University of Toronto Faculty Law Review* XXXI (1973) 103–5; Lord Chorley 'Procedural Reform in England' in Alison Reppy, ed. *David Dudley Field: Centenary Essays* (New York 1949) 99–100; Augustine Birrell 'Changes in Equity, Procedure, and Principles' in *A Century of Law Reform* (London 1901) 177–202; Manchester *Modern Legal History* 137–43, 173–4, 403–6

16 Metropolitan Toronto Library Board (hereafter MTLB) Baldwin Papers William Hume Blake (hereafter WHB) to Robert Baldwin 7 Sept. 1848
17 Quoted in C.J. Townshend 'History of the Court of Chancery in Nova Scotia' *Canadian Law Times* XX (1900) 76
18 Ibid. 14–22, 37–42, 74–80, 105–17; Falconbridge 'Law and Equity' 1138; Riddell *Courts of Upper Canada* 161; J.A. Clarence Smith and Jean Kerby *Private Law in Canada: A Comparative Study* (Ottawa 1975) 159, 161, 219, 221, 223, 225
19 D.B. Read *The Lives of the Judges of Upper Canada and Ontario, From 1791 to the Present Time* (Toronto 1888) 268, 270. Read's recollections, although not without error, provide a valuable first-hand account of some early provincial legal figures. He had studied law under Blake at King's College.
20 D.W. Swainson 'William Hume Blake' DCB IX 55–60; Blackwell 'Blake and Judicial Reform' 40–58, 142, 173–4; *Minutes* of Convocation LSUC II 306, 602
21 Read *Lives of the Judges* 273
22 Blackwell 'Blake and Judicial Reform' 68–73
23 J.D. Livermore 'Towards "A Union of Hearts": The Early Career of Edward Blake, 1867–1880' (PH D dissertation, Queen's University 1975) 37
24 Elgin to Grey 10 May 1848 private in A.G. Doughty, ed. *The Elgin-Grey Papers, 1846–1852* (Ottawa 1937) I 161
25 D.W. Swainson 'William Hume Blake' 12, unabridged typescript of an article prepared (1974) for volume IX of the DCB
26 MTLB Baldwin Papers WHB to Baldwin 27 Jan. 1845
27 *Debates of the Legislative Assembly of United Canada* ed. Elizabeth Nish (Montreal 1970-) VIII 849–50 (20 Feb. 1849) (hereafter *Debates of United Canada*)
28 Blackwell 'Blake and Judicial Reform' 115–17
29 W.N.T. Wylie 'Toronto and the Montreal Annexation Crisis of 1849–1850' (Master's thesis, Queen's University 1971) 91, 93–4
30 PAO Blake Family Papers (addition) Skeffington Connor to J.C. Morrison 26 Oct. 1845 (typescript copy)
31 *Examiner* 15 and 22 Aug. 1849 cited in Wylie 'Annexation Crisis' 95–6
32 Public Archives of Canada RG 5 C1 vol. 128 file 7622 (hereafter PAC)
33 *Journals of the Legislative Council of the Province of Canada* (1844–5) *Appendix* J.J. (no pagination)
34 William Holdsworth *A History of English Law* (7th ed. London 1956) I 442–5. Before he left office in 1844, Baldwin had encouraged consideration of both the American and English experience in equity. On 8 Sept. 1843 the Governor-General-in-Council endorsed Baldwin's suggestion that 'it would be of great advantage, were the Commission to extend its inquiry into the establishment of Courts of Equity, in the several American States, and also in the changes which have been advised in the Court of Chancery in England ...

the Government will furnish such reports and books as the Commissioners may find necessary in the course of their investigation, such expense not to exceed fifty pounds.' (PAC RG 5 C1 vol. 114 60/6308)

35 PAC RG 5 C1 vol. 128 file 7622 W.H. Draper to the Provincial Secretary 22 May 1844

36 'Law Reform' *Upper Canada Jurist* I (1844–5) Part I 20, 23–4 (hereafter UCJ). This legal journal soon evolved into the *Queen's Bench Reports*.

37 *Debates of United Canada* IV 243

38 Oliver Mowat to John Mowat 29 July 1844 in Peter Neary, ed. '"Neither Radical Nor Tory Nor Whig": Letters by Oliver Mowat to John Mowat, 1843–1846' *Ontario History* LXXI (1979) 106. In fact, Mowat was soon reaping a handsome reward for his labours (ibid. 88).

39 Ibid. 111–12; Riddell *Courts of Upper Canada* 185, 193 notes 7 and 8. A printed copy of the Burns petition is appended to WHB *A Letter to the Hon. Robert Baldwin, from Wm. Hume Blake, A.B., Professor of Law in the University of King's College, upon the Administration of Justice in the Western Province* (Toronto 1845) 5, 38–40. The *Minutes* of Convocation LSUC for the 1840s contain much routine business such as admissions but reveal little about the profession's attitudes.

40 MTLB Baldwin Papers WHB to Baldwin 27 Jan. 1845. During the mid-1840s Blake was one of Baldwin's principal advisors in Toronto (PAC LaFontaine Papers Baldwin to LaFontaine 7 May 1847 private).

41 WHB *Letter to Baldwin on the Administration of Justice* passim. 'I have omitted to notice other and more important tho' less obvious considerations, because I feared that bringing them into discussion would injure our cause.' (MTLB Baldwin Papers WHB to Baldwin 27 Jan. 1845)

42 PAO Blake Papers Baldwin to WHB 6 Feb. 1845

43 MTLB Baldwin Papers WHB to Baldwin 5 Feb. 1845

44 PAO Blake Papers Baldwin to WHB 14 Feb. 1845

45 Riddell *Courts of Upper Canada* 186

46 Doughty, ed. *Elgin-Grey Papers* II 620, 749; P.G. Cornell *The Alignment of Political Groups in Canada, 1841–1867* (Toronto 1962) 28

47 Blackwell 'Blake and Judicial Reform' 93–7

48 J.G. Spragge *A Letter on the Subject of the Courts of Law of Upper Canada, Addressed to the Attorney General and Solicitor General* (Toronto 1847) 12, 26

Blackwell, 'Blake and Judicial Reform' 99–101. Blake's ailments included an inherited 'nervous' problem, gout, and eventually diabetes.

Ibid. 102–5

G.E. Wilson *The Life of Robert Baldwin* (Toronto 1933) 242, 262. Other prominent members of the bar, such as Robert Easton Burns and John Godfrey Spragge, probably influenced Blake's scheme but their contribution is unclear from surviving documentation. Riddell states that the Chancery Bill of 1849 was as much the work of Spragge as Blake, but provides no evidence for this assertion (Riddell *Courts of Upper Canada* 196 note 26).

52 MTLB Baldwin Papers WHB to Baldwin (28 July and) 7 Sept. 1848. (The reader should note that original spelling has been retained in quotes throughout this essay and that the use of *sic* is minimal.) Several months later Justice Macaulay sent Blake some technical notes on the draft judicature bills which the latter had circulated. Unfortunately only the enacted versions seem to survive (PAC RG 13 B1 vol. 1391 Macaulay to WHB 20 Mar. 1849).

53 MTLB Baldwin Papers WHB to Baldwin 10 Oct. 1848

54 Quoted in Toronto *Globe* 15 Nov. 1848

55 *Debates of United Canada* VIII 164, 278

56 PAO Blake Family Papers (addition) WHB to R.B. Sullivan (Provincial Secretary) 3 Apr. 1849 (typescript copy)

57 WHB *Separate Report of Mr. Blake's Speech on the Rebellion Losses* (Montreal 1849)

58 Later enacted as *Statutes of Canada* 12 Vic. (1849), c. 64

59 Ibid. c. 63

60 Ibid. c. 70

61 Read *Lives of the Judges* 280. The measure proved very effective. For a concise survey of the evolution of the law of evidence, see J.H. Wigmore *A Treatise on the Anglo-American System of Evidence* (3rd ed. Boston 1940) I 234–41.

62 Quoted in 'Law Reform' UCJ I (1844–5) Pt I 22; *Statutes of the United Kingdom* (hereafter *Stat. U.K.*) 6 and 7 Vic. (1843) c. 85

63 C.F.J. Whebell 'Robert Baldwin and Decentralization 1841–9' in F.H. Armstrong et al., eds *Aspects of Nineteenth-Century Ontario* (Toronto 1974) 48

64 *British Colonist* 20 Mar. 1849

65 *Globe* 21 Mar. 1849

66 *Debates of United Canada* VIII 2175

67 Ibid. 2323

68 Ibid. 2378–9; Blackwell 'Blake and Judicial Reform' 133–8

69 *Globe* 11 Dec. 1849. In fact, the judicial reform had been an electoral issue in 1848. (*Debates of United Canada* x 604, 605)

70 Wylie 'Annexation Crisis' 96–7

71 Ibid. 97; Riddell *Courts of Upper Canada* 203

72 *Globe* 11 Dec. 1849

73 Wylie 'Annexation Crisis' 98

74 *Patriot* 16 Feb. 1850 cited in Wylie 'Annexation Crisis' 131 (emphasis added)

75 MTLB Baldwin Papers Ridout to Baldwin 28 Mar. 1849

76 Wilson *Robert Baldwin* 263; Egerton Ryerson *The Story of My Life* ed. J.G. Hodgins (Toronto 1883) 417

77 Blackwell 'Blake and Judicial Reform' 141–4

78 MTLB Baldwin Papers WHB to Baldwin 14 and 25 Sept. 1849

79 PAO Blake Papers WHB to Edward Blake 22 Aug. 1868

80 Blackwell 'Blake and Judicial Reform' 146–8

81 Wilson *Robert Baldwin* 272–4; *Journals of the Legislative Assembly of Canada (1850)* 5, 13, 46, 54, 70, 117. For example, L.-J. Papineau criticized judicial appointments from among the administration. (*Globe*, 23 May 1850)

82 Wilson *Robert Baldwin* 283; Riddell *Courts of Upper Canada* 200, 202; Elgin to Grey 28 June 1851 private in Doughty, ed. *Elgin-Grey Papers* II 832; F.H. Armstrong and R.J. Stagg 'William Lyon Mackenzie' DCB IX 506

83 Following the Judicature Acts of 1849, there was no significant increase in the cost of the administration of justice in Upper Canada until 1852; the new expenses were not, it appears, significantly attributable to the Court of Chancery (*Réponse à une demandant de l'Assemblée Législative du 12 mars 1860, demandant un état des frais de l'administration de la justice dans le Haut et le Bas-Canada [1841 à 1859]* [Québec 1860]).

84 Wilson *Robert Baldwin* 284–90. Some historians have overestimated Baldwin's role in the judicial reconstruction of 1849. (See, for example, J.M.S. Careless, ed. *Pre-Confederation Premiers: Ontario Government Leaders, 1841–1867* [Toronto 1980] 136, 141, 161, 254). This misinterpretation probably originates with Francis Hincks's self-serving, distorting influence on the writing of J.C. Dent's *The Last Forty Years: Canada since the Union of 1841* (1881) (Elizabeth Nish 'How History is Written: The Hincks to Dent Letters' *Revue du centre d'étude du Québec* II [1978] 32, 70). At the time of his resignation, Baldwin clearly credited Blake with authorship of the legislation (*Debates of United Canada* x 605; also MTLB Baldwin Papers Baldwin to John Ross 28 June 1851 [typescript copy]). The Assembly's 1851 debate over Chancery recounted in some detail the history of the judicial reforms of 1849 and evidenced a growing awareness of foreign legal systems (*Debates of United Canada* x 562ff.).

85 [C.W. Cooper] *Remarks on the Proposed Abolition of the Court of Chancery (from the Columns of The Chronicle and News)* (Kingston 1851) preface, 17, 19: 'Many of those voting with Mr. Mackenzie are themselves lawyers practicing in other districts: they are themselves scarcely aware of the changes that have taken place, and have not taken the pains to make themselves acquainted with the very simple system of practice necessary to enable them to conduct their own causes; but this is not likely to be the case long…' (ibid. 15) David R. Keane, who has completed a group profile of early university students in Toronto, confirms that Cooper attended Blake's lectures in law.

86 For contemporary assessments of Blake's chancellorship, see Blackwell 'Blake and Judicial Reform' 154–68; see also commentaries on chancery practice in volumes IV and V (old series) of *The Upper Canada Law Journal*.

87 T.W. Taylor *Orders of the Court of Chancery for Upper Canada, With Notes*

(Toronto 1860) iii. Blake served briefly in 1864 on the bench of the Court of Error and Appeal, another legacy of his judicial reforms, but soon had to retire because of poor health. Apart from his work on the Railway Postal Service Commission in 1865, Blake's last few years passed quietly among his family and in healthful European havens (Blackwell 'Blake and Judicial Reform' 166–72).

88 Risk 'Law and the Economy' 429–31; in this volume, 116–18

89 Read *Lives of the Judges* 282

90 Ibid. 280

91 Toronto *Mirror* 8 Nov. 1844, from an address to the electors of Simcoe

92 This is the opinion of H.R.S. Ryan, Professor Emeritus, Faculty of Law, Queen's University.

93 Risk 'Law and the Economy' 438; in this volume, 125

94 *Statutes of Ontario* 44 Vic. (1881) c. 5. At one point, even Edward Blake advocated fusion. (Richard Snelling *Articles on the Court of Chancery and the Fusion of Law and Equity, Contributed to the Toronto 'Leader' in 1868* [Toronto 1871] 26–7) There has been one recent survey of these later developments (Mary Stokes 'Myth and Legal Reform: The Life and Times of the Courts of Chancery in Upper Canada, 1837–1881' (unpublished essay, University of Western Ontario 1980)).

95 H.G. Hanbury *English Courts of Law* (3rd ed. London 1960) 142ff.; Friedman *History of American Law* 346. The Act (*Stat. U.K.* 36 and 37 Vic. [1873] c. 66) came into force in 1875 but did little to reduce expense and delay (Manchester *Modern Legal History* 149–50). Although knowledge of foreign developments increased in Ontario, English experience remained the principal model (T.W. Taylor *Commentaries on Equity Jurisprudence Founded on Story* [Toronto 1875] preface; A.H. Marsh *History of the Court of Chancery and of the Rise and Development of the Doctrines of Equity* [Toronto 1890] passim).

96 Riddell *Courts of Upper Canada* 220, 231–3

97 Gregory 'Judicature Act' 105; Clarence Smith *Private Law* 143

98 M.K. Singleton 'New Light on the Chancery Side of Virginia's Evolution to Statehood' *Journal of American Studies* II (1968) 150 note 2

99 Robert Cooper *The Rules and Practice of the Court of Chancery of Upper Canada* (Toronto 1851) v

100 In 1851 during an attack on the *provincial* Court of Chancery, William Lyon Mackenzie resorted to quoting the opinions of Mrs Anna Jameson (R.S. Jameson's estranged literary wife), Oliver Cromwell, and John Wesley (*Debates of United Canada* x 563).

5

The Law of Master and Servant in Mid-Nineteenth-Century Ontario

PAUL CRAVEN

Mid-nineteenth-century Ontario law characterized the employment relationship as one of contract, whereby the employer (the 'master') undertook to provide wages in return for faithful and obedient service by the worker (the 'servant'). Such contracts might be expressed in verbal or written agreements, or they might be implied by the conduct of the parties. In either case, the promises that constituted the contract could be enforced by the courts. The law provided two distinct mechanisms for the enforcement of employment contracts. First, masters and servants could sue each other in the common law courts through civil actions for breach of contract, unpaid wages, wrongful dismissal, and so forth. This mechanism had several disadvantages. It was expensive and time-consuming and was rife with uncertainties, because the common law system was a tangle of procedural rules and lawyers' technicalities. Moreover, the available remedies were restricted. The chief remedy at common law was money in damages for breach of contract.[1] The common law would not enforce specific performance of the employment contract: it would not compel absconding workers to return to their jobs, or employers to reinstate workers whom they had improperly fired.

Several of these deficiencies were supplied by the second mechanism for the enforcement of employment contracts, the Master and Servant Act of 1847, which provided cheap and expeditious access to a variety of remedies.[2] The Act gave local magistrates jurisdiction to hear and adjudicate complaints by workers that their employers had mistreated them or failed to pay wages that were due, and by employers seeking to have recalcitrant workers disciplined. Workers who had been mistreated could be released from contractual obligations to their employers, while the claim for wages was analogous to a civil action for the collection of a debt, to be remedied by an order for payment. The sanctions available against misbehaving workers were rather different. The Master and Servant Act made breach of contract by an employee a criminal offence for which he could be arrested, summarily prosecuted, and punished by fine or imprisonment. In the 1847 legislative debate on the Act Attorney General Henry Sherwood insisted that it was 'aimed at punishing servants for not acting up to their engagements, not at coercing them in the discharge of their duty.'[3] In practice, however, the criminal provisions of the Act were frequently used to enforce specific performance of the employment contract, as magistrates gave convicted servants a choice of either returning to work or going to jail.

In making different modes of recourse available to workers and employers respectively, the Master and Servant Act reflected the fact that the employment contract was one between unequals, between the man of tangible resources and the man whose principal asset was his capacity for labour. Thus the *Canada Farmer* rebutted the view of a contemporary that employers might be made subject to the Act's criminal provisions by observing that 'common sense will tell him upon a moment's thought that such a law would be absurd and oppressive. If the master sins, he has *property* which can answer.'[4] By contrast, the ultimate security for the propertyless employee's good behaviour was his personal liberty.

This is the first of two essays intended to account for the Master and Servant Act's passage and eventual repeal and to describe the manner in which it was administered. After a brief discussion of the common law of the employment contract, this essay focuses on the statutory and legal history of the Act against the background of Ontario society at mid-century. The sequel will propose an explanation of the manner in which the Act was administered and explain its repeal in 1877 on the basis of a detailed quantitative analysis of master and servant cases in the Toronto police court. It is hoped that together the two essays will elucidate some of the problems in the legal and social history of the employment relationship in Ontario's transition to industrialism.

THE EMPLOYMENT CONTRACT AT COMMON LAW

An examination of reported decisions in the courts of Queen's Bench and Common Pleas reveals that the common law of the employment contract changed very little, if at all, from the late 1820s, when the first published cases were decided, to the late seventies.[5] Since the common law understanding of the employment relationship was one aspect of the legal environment within which the Master and Servant Act emerged, and since there is evidence that magistrates made some use of common law tests in their enforcement of the Act, it is worthwhile summarizing what that law entailed.[6]

Contracts of employment might be express agreements, frequently in writing, or implied. An implied contract was presumed from evidence that work had been performed and accepted, although the presumption could be rebutted by evidence of an express agreement that the services were to be provided gratuitously. There were exceptions however, the most important of which had to do with work performed by one member of a family for another. Here the law seems to have reflected the significance of the family as an economic unit in what was still predominantly a society of agrarian smallholders. Thus in one case which came before the courts no contract of employment was implied between a woman who lived for years with her father, looking after him in the ultimately disappointed expectation of an inheritance, and his estate. Describing her suit as one 'of very dangerous tendency,' Chief Justice John Beverley Robinson commented that 'this young woman could not be living any where else more properly than with her aged and infirm parent; and if she did acts of service, instead of living idly, it is no more than she ought to have done in return for her clothes and board, to say nothing of the claims of natural affection which usually lead children to render such service.'[7]

Similar considerations applied to the suit of a son against his mother, claiming that she had offered him $1000 if he would remain home and work her farm for four years. Robinson argued that 'there are strong reasons of policy, as regards the due maintenance of domestic relations, against the supporting of such a contract as binding on the parent.'[8] Nor was a sister any more successful in suing her brother for wages she claimed to have earned during several years of work on his farm, for 'nothing was more natural than an unmarried young woman should live with and keep house for her brother, especially while he was also unmarried, and that without the idea of hiring or wages entering into the mind of either. It would be we fear a mischievious doctrine to lay down that in every case in which a niece, or cousin, or sister in law is proved to be living in a farmer's house, treated in every way as one of the family, and assisting in the work of doing all or most of the house-work, she could, in the absence of any evidence whatsoever as to hiring or wages, be held entitled to the direction of a judge that the law in such a case implied a promise to pay.'[9]

The presumption that work performed by one family member for another did not imply an employment contract could be rebutted, however, by evidence of a wage agreement. When a son sued his father's estate for work he had performed and provided a witness to a discussion of wages, Judge (later Chief Justice) John Hawkins Hagarty somewhat reluctantly sent it to the jury with the comment that 'we fully agree with all that has been said about the extreme care with which both Courts and juries should scrutinize all claims like that before us.'[10] On the other hand, the presumption sometimes extended beyond members of the immediate family. While a minor stepdaughter could successfully sue her stepfather for both wages and the value of the board, lodging, and clothing she had supplied to her mother, his wife,[11] the courts held that a woman who had looked after a merchant's shop in the hope that he would marry her could not sue him for wages on an implied contract of employment when he married someone else.[12] Perhaps the strangest case illustrating the difficulty of determining whether an employment contract was to be implied among parties who were almost, but not quite, relatives, was *Wilkinson* v *Lawson* (1878). It was a well-established principle of the common law that when a master married his servant the contract of employment ceased to exist, and there could be no subsequent action for wages. But what if their marriage was bigamous? Chief Justice Hagarty held that since it was the former servant who was already married when she married her master, she had forfeited her claim to wages. He went on to suggest even broader possibilities: 'Nor could it be held that if the relation of master and servant were established, the mere fact of the plaintiff allowing the defendant to treat her as his concubine, would bar her claim. It would be a question for the jury whether her assuming such position, and the position and authority of a wife in the management of the defendant's household, etc., had established another implication rebutting the former one of hiring.'[13]

When a contract of employment was implied, the law presumed that certain conditions were to govern the relationship. The presumption that a 'general hiring' was for a full year could be read into such contracts, although it was capable of being rebutted by evidence that hirings in a particular line of work were normally for a different term. When a ship's captain sued for a year's wages on a general hiring, the court accepted correspondence between himself and his employer as evidence that the contract was for the shipping season only.[14] A foreman in a printing office, hired in March 1857 at $10 per week, quit his job in October 1859 when his wages were over $500 in arrears. He sued for the back wages, claiming that the hiring was a weekly one; his employer rejoined with the claim that the hiring was general, the term was year by year, and consequently the foreman could not sue for wages earned since March 1859 because he had defaulted on the contract by quitting before the year was out. Chief Justice William Henry Draper approved the action of the trial judge in submitting the question whether this was a yearly hiring to a jury, which found it to have been weekly: 'If they had found that the hiring was general, I should not have thought the verdict contrary to evidence; but I cannot say there was not evidence to sustain the conclusion that the hiring was by the week.'[15] But where a jury sought to compromise matters in this sort of dispute, its verdict was overturned on appeal.[16]

The question of term was important, for if an employee voluntarily left his service before the contract expired, he could not claim back wages. As Chief Justice Robinson explained, 'courts of justice have expressed themselves strongly on the importance to society of enforcing such engagements, by making parties bear the legal consequences of breaking them.'[17] On the other hand, 'no-one disputes the right of a master to dismiss his clerk for misconduct during the currency of and in the course of employment.'[18] An employee dismissed for cause could not hope to recover for the amount of wages he would have earned had he been allowed to serve out his term, although he was entitled to damages if his claim for wrongful dismissal was upheld.

When the contract of employment was expressed in writing, the law held that its written provisions must be strictly interpreted and could not be varied by verbal or customary understandings. This gave rise to numerous problems, the majority of which seem to have been resolved to the advantage of the employer. Raines sued the Credit Harbour Company on a contract to pay him £85 a year so long as he should continue in its service as harbour master. He complained that he had been wrongfully dismissed, that he remained ready and willing to work, but that the company refused to keep him in its service. Finding that the contract failed to specify a term, Robinson held that Raines had not 'laid a sufficient foundation' for his claim for a year's wages and suggested that the law was unclear as to whether an employee in Raines' position could rely on the presumption of an annual hiring or must restrict his action solely to the express terms of the contract.[19]

However, the contract of employment implied the employer's power to dismiss for cause, whether or not that power was explicitly stated. For example, the owner of the *London Prototype* hired an editor 'to give his sole time and attention to the editorial management' of the paper for a year at the salary of £200, payable quarterly. At the end of the third quarter, he was fired and refused payment of the last £50. He then sued for wrongful dismissal, arguing that the owner's claim that he had 'conducted himself in ... an improper, offensive and disobedient manner' was no answer, since it did not allege a specific breach of the written contract. Chief Justice Draper upheld the dismissal: 'I have no doubt that in the relation existing between the plaintiff and defendant ... there *might* arise circumstances in the conduct of the plaintiff [such as] writing in a manner offensive to the defendant personally, or advocating views and opinions contrary to the avowed principles, political or otherwise, of the defendant, and of those who were his supporters, and took his paper, and persisting in doing so against remonstrance and positive prohibition, to the injury of the defendant, which would justify the dismissal.'[20]

The power to dismiss for cause aside, written contracts appear to have been strictly interpreted. Roche and Walsh had both signed this agreement:

> I do hereby agree and bind myself to Walsh & Co. to act as bookkeeper, salesman, or traveller, for the term of five years, in consideration of the following sums annually ... The undersigned also further agrees to pay the sum of $10 per month for board, which will be deducted from the above sums; his washing and other personal expenses to be paid by himself. This agreement to commence from the 1st February, 1876, and ends 1st February, 1881.

When Walsh dismissed him, Roche sued for breach. Walsh did not contend that he had cause to dismiss Roche, but argued that there was nothing in the specific words of the agreement that bound him to employ Roche for the full five years. Walsh's argument was accepted, for 'an implied contract by the defendant to retain the plaintiff cannot be presumed, and there is nothing like express language binding the defendant to any such engagement.'[21] Despite the apparent lack of mutuality, the courts held to the view that while employees under such contracts were bound to serve out the whole term and were liable in damages upon failure to do so, their employers were not similarly bound to retain them.[22]

To sum up, the courts in mid-nineteenth-century Ontario viewed the employment relationship as one of contract. In the absence of an express agreement or evidence to the contrary it was presumed that an engagement was for a year's term. It was also presumed that family members were not party to an employment relationship. There was a contractual duty upon the employee to work faithfully and upon the employer to pay wages for the term of the contract. The employee could be dismissed for cause during the life of the contract and would not be entitled to wages for the balance of the term. Non-payment of wages was not cause for the employee to leave his employment: he must continue to work faithfully until his term was up, although he could sue his employer for back wages owing. Written contracts of employment were narrowly construed to relieve the employer from any implied undertaking, but the presumption that an employee could be dismissed for cause was read into written contracts which lacked an express provision to that effect.

The conclusion is inescapable that when master and servant stood before the high courts of law, the former was the more likely by far to have his claim upheld. The law favoured the employer's part of the bargain. But with the significant exception of the cases involving family members, the great majority of the employment contract cases to reach the superior courts did not touch on the most common types of wage labour. Farm hands, canal navvies, lumberers, labourers, and domestic servants were conspicuous by their absence, either as plaintiffs or defendants. The employees who appeared were ships' captains, clerks, managers, and quasi-professionals. Of course, there is an inherent bias in a study of higher court cases, because claims would have to have been of some magnitude to justify the expense of time and money involved in appealing a case. It is not known to what extent workers and employers of various descriptions engaged each other in civil litigation at less elevated levels. It seems likely, however, that employers recognized the futility of suits in damages against workers, who for the most part would not have had the wherewithal to pay, while for their part most wage workers could hardly have had much hope in risking relatively large sums on the uncertain gamble of actions at common law. Pending far more detailed investigation of this question, it is reasonable to assume that of the whole population of potentially justiciable claims arising from contracts of employment, only a very small and unrepresentative proportion ever reached the courts.[23]

THE ENGLISH STATUTES IN ONTARIO

Long before a detailed conception of the employment contract entered the English common law, statutes had been devised to regulate the relations of employers and employees. The first of these appeared in 1349, in response to the labour force dislocations occasioned by the Black Death.

Taking advantage of the severe labour shortage, bound labourers deserted their feudal obligations in search of higher wages. The Statute of Labourers was intended to restore wages to their earlier levels and reinforce traditional employment relations. Justices of the Peace were empowered to compel every able-bodied man and woman below the age of sixty and without an independent income to work for any master who required his or her services, at wages that were not to exceed the levels customary before the plague. Any servant who left his employment before the expiry of its term, without permission or reasonable excuse, was liable to imprisonment.[24]

This law was extended in the sixteenth century by the very detailed provisions of the Elizabethan Statute of Artificers. Its underlying policy was continued by several eighteenth-century statutes that are sometimes referred to collectively as the Master and Servant Act. These gave Justices of the Peace summary jurisdiction in disputes between masters and servants, with a right of appeal from their decisions to the Quarter Sessions. Servants could seek an order compelling the payment of wages due them, while masters' complaints about the wrongdoing of their servants could result in the docking of their wages or imprisonment.[25]

Were any (or all) of these English statutes in force in Ontario? Like the Ontario Act of 1847, the English master and servant statutes had both civil and criminal aspects. English criminal law was in force in Ontario by virtue of the Quebec Act of 1774 and an Upper Canadian reception act in 1800, while English civil law was introduced into the province in 1792, when the first legislature of Upper Canada determined that 'in all matters of controversy relative to property and civil rights, resort shall be had to the Laws of England as the rule for the decision of the same.'[26] On the face of it the English master and servant statutes would appear to have become part of Ontario law, yet in 1847, in the preamble to the Ontario Act, the legislature declared that 'no Statute is in force to regulate the duties between Masters and Servants or Labourers in that part of the Province formerly Upper Canada.' It appears that prior to 1847 some at least of the English statutes were treated as being in force in Ontario, although the evidence so far available suggests that they may not have been used extensively. By 1847 a series of high court decisions, which are reviewed below, had raised serious doubts about whether the English master and servant laws, in either their civil or criminal aspects, were to be considered part of the law of Ontario. The legislature responded to these doubts by enacting the Master and Servant Act, identical in its policy to the eighteenth-century English statutes, although differing somewhat in detail.

Research to date has uncovered but one account of a successful prosecution under the English statutes. In November 1839 a Colonel O'Hara of the Toronto Adjutant General's office, himself a magistrate, brought his domestic servant, Mary Anne Fraser, before George Gurnett, a magistrate and former mayor of Toronto. O'Hara complained that Fraser had left his service before the end of the month for which she had engaged. Gurnett found 'that the girl had broken her engagement, without having sufficient cause, legally, to justify her in doing so, and therefore had rendered herself amenable to the punishment in such cases by law prescribed: viz. Imprisonment.' Gurnett attempted to persuade O'Hara not to insist on the full severity of the law, because the only accommodation in the Toronto jail was 'filled with women of the most abandoned and loathsome character, and I felt great reluctance at the idea of exposing this young girl to the contamination of such society which would probably prevent her from getting a respectable situation afterwards, and might ruin her future prospects in life.' When O'Hara proved adamant, Gurnett committed Fraser to the custody of the jailer with instructions that she was to work in the kitchen and be kept from the company of the other women. The following day he was approached by a local upholsterer who told him that his instructions had not been followed. His informant was willing to take Fraser into his own family on condition that she be released immediately, since 'if she remained a week in such society, he could not think of taking her again into his house, nor did he think anyone else could.' Gurnett released Fraser into the upholsterer's custody. When O'Hara heard of this, he began writing enraged letters to the Lieutenant Governor's Civil Secretary. Gurnett's explanation was at length accepted, and O'Hara retired from the fray, sarcastically remarking, 'vivent les sans culottes.' The case is interesting both because it demonstrates that a master and servant law was considered to be in force before 1847, and because it suggests a reluctance on the part of at least one influential magistrate to enforce it strictly.[27]

Additional evidence that the English statutes were considered to be in force in Ontario before 1847 can be found in handbooks published for the instruction of the magistracy. These were private undertakings, carrying no official warrant. The first seems to have been W.C. Keele's *Provincial Justice* (1835). In a preface to the 1843 edition, Keele claimed that before his work first appeared Ontario magistrates 'were unprovided with any work of reference, to guide them in the discharge of their duties, except the Provincial Statutes, and a few scattered volumes of Burns' Justice, and other Law works, excellent in their kind, but designed for the Parent Country, and therefore containing a vast deal of matter wholly inapplicable to this Province.'

Keele's first edition abstracted four of the eighteenth-century statutes with a commentary based on English case law and supplied a set of forms for complaints, warrants, and committals under these acts. He did not refer to the Elizabethan statute under the heading, 'Servants,' but dealt with it at length in his section on apprenticeship. The 1843 edition repeated this material, but in 1851, after the passage of the Master and Servant Act, Keele dropped his references to the eighteenth-century statutes and replaced them with an abstract of the new legislation and a set of forms. So far as Keele was concerned, then, the eighteenth-century statutes were part of Ontario law at least to 1843, as was the Elizabethan statute with respect to apprentices.[28] Finally, five of the superior court decisions reported before 1847 touch on the English statutes. Of these, three are apprenticeship cases, and the remaining two do not decide the 'reception question' – whether the English law was in force in Ontario – for masters and servants.

The earliest of these cases, *Whelan* v *Stevens*, was decided on appeal in 1827. Whelan had been hired by a farmer to work for a month on the land, supplying his own team of oxen. When he left before the expiry of his term, the farmer brought Whelan before a local JP, Stevens, who convicted him of a breach of the eighteenth-century statutes (here grouped as 'the Statute of Labourers') and sent him to jail. Whelan then laid an action against Stevens at the Bathurst Assizes to set aside the conviction on the ground that since he was to supply a team, he was not a labourer within the meaning of the acts. The court found that Whelan was not a labourer within the meaning of the statutes and released him.[29] The case is significant for two reasons. First, it indicates that an Ontario high court in the 1820s considered the eighteenth-century statutes to be in force, although they did not apply to one very common form of employment. Second, it indicates the policy underlying the master and servant legislation: Whelan was not a labourer liable to criminal prosecution for breach of contract because he brought *property*, his oxen, to his employment, property that could presumably be made to answer for his breach in civil proceedings. (His contract might be classified not as one of service, but as a contract for services: in modern labour law parlance, he might be called an independent contractor rather than an employee.) The question whether a worker who brought property in the form of his tools or even his artisanal skill to his employment was covered by the 1847 legislation would be settled only by an 1855 amendment: the mediaeval understanding of the wage labourer as an impoverished and likely criminal vagrant died hard.

In 1846, just a year before the passage of the Master and Servant Act, another reference, which can only be interpreted as being an allusion to the English statutes, was made in an Ontario court. An employee sued his employer for assault and battery, wounding and kicking, and tearing his clothes. The defendant claimed that he had merely been administering the moderate correction of his servant to which he was entitled at law. The court rejected this defence. Justice Archibald McLean expanded on the majority judgment by stating that while moderate correction might be permitted in the case of a minor servant or apprentice, 'the beating of a servant of full age cannot be justified, and will form a sufficient cause or excuse for departure, or for discharge from service by a magistrate upon complaint.' In saying this, McLean relied on Burns's *Justice of the Peace*, the standard English work which, as Keele had commented, contained a good deal of law inapplicable to the Ontario setting. Nevertheless, the reference to the magistrate's jurisdiction to release a servant from his obligations to a cruel master can only mean that McLean considered the English statutes to be in force in Ontario in some form, because magistrates had no such jurisdiction at common law.[30]

The remaining three cases turned on the reception of the Elizabethan statute in its bearing on contracts of apprenticeship. They are significant because they illustrate the problem of adapting English law to Ontario conditions, and because they raised doubts as to whether the English statutes were in force.

In *Fish* v *Doyle*, decided in 1831, an apprentice defended himself against a charge of unlawfully absenting himself by claiming that his articles of apprenticeship, which set his term at three years, were void since the Elizabethan statute specified a term of at least seven years. Chief Justice Robinson held that the question whether the statute was in force was irrelevant because the contract could still be enforced at common law. But he went on to say: 'In my opinion these provisions were never part of the law of this province; I have no objection to express that opinion, although it is not necessary for the decision of this question.'[31]

Ten years later, in *Dillingham* v *Wilson*, Judge Henry Sherwood formally considered the reception problem in light of the statute which introduced English civil law to Ontario in 1792: 'The intention and meaning of the legislature undoubtedly was that resort should be had to such of the laws of England as are applicable to the state of society in a British colony, which is very different in many respects from the state of society in England ... We consider the statute of 5 Eliz., c. 4 as a local act which was probably adapted to the state of society in England three hundred years ago, but is not now, and never was adapted to the population of a colony, and was never in force here.'[32] Both *Fish* and *Dillingham* were civil actions for damages, the first for breach of the contract of apprenticeship, the second for enticing the apprentice away from his service. As Keele pointed out in a note to the 1843 edition of *Provincial Justice*: 'The question of criminal jurisdiction under the statute did not arise, and may therefore be presumed to be undecided.'[33]

The final case of the trilogy, *Shea* v *Choat* (1846), resolved the question. Choat, an apprentice tinsmith, deserted the service of his master, who had him arrested and brought before a magistrate. When he was convicted and sent to jail he launched an action for false imprisonment, relying on *Fish* as authority that the Elizabethan statute was not in force, and arguing by extension that the eighteenth-century statutes (in particular 20 Geo. II, c. 19) were 'only a continuation of the statute of Elizabeth,' and therefore not in force. His master argued in reply that some parts of the statute could be in force even if others were not. Chief Justice Robinson ruled that the Elizabethan statute was not in force, remarking that 'it cannot possibly admit of doubt that its provisions are inapplicable to any state of things that ever existed here: a clause here and there might be carried into effect in this colony, or anywhere, from the general nature of their provisions; but that is not sufficient to make such a statute part of our law, when the main object and tenor of it is wholly foreign to the nature of our institutions, and it is therefore incapable of being carried out substantially and as a whole into execution.' If the Elizabethan statute was not in force, Choat's arrest and imprisonment were improper, since the eighteenth-century statute (20 Geo. II, c. 19) prescribed proceedings before two justices, not one, and on summons rather than arrest, in cases involving apprentices. Robinson did not finally determine whether the eighteenth-century act was in force in Ontario: 'My inclination at present is, that the statute, in its general scope and bearing, is not applicable to this province; but considering the latitude of construction given to it by the court in [an English case] I am not prepared to hold that it is not in force.'[34]

In summary, at least some of the English statutes were considered to be part of Ontario's law before 1847. It remains unclear precisely which sections of these statutes were treated as being in force, and it is unclear as well how widely the statutes were applied. The defence counsel in *Shea* v *Choat* noted that Keele thought the English law applied to Ontario and further argued that 'the magistrates in almost every part of the province have been in the habit of considering these statutes in force, and have acted upon them in many instances, without their authority being called in question.' His account was scarcely disinterested, however, and in any event the court rejected his argument. The evidence that these statutes were not extensively applied is largely negative, and the question must await further investigation.

In 1846, as we shall see, the legislature apparently believed that there was a master and servant statute in operation in Ontario. In 1847, presumably in the wake of *Shea* v *Choat*, it believed that there was not and remedied the lack with new legislation. But the reception question remained somewhat clouded, at least in technical terms. While Robinson had been unwilling to render a final determination of the question in Shea's case, the headnote to the published decision reported that 'the statute 20 Geo. II., c. 19, is in force.' As late as 1878, long after the legislature had determined that no English statute was in force to regulate the relations of master and servant, and hard on the heels of the Dominion parliament's decision that ordinary breaches of the employment contract were to be treated solely as civil matters, a magistrates' manual cited *Shea* v *Choat* as authority that 'the 5 Eliz., chap. 4, is not in force in Ontario, but the 20 Geo. II, chap. 19. is...[35]

THE MASTER AND SERVANT ACT 1847

A bill 'to regulate the duties between Master and Servant, and for other purposes therein mentioned,' was presented to the assembly on 27 April 1846 by the Reform member for Quebec City, Thomas Cushing Aylwin. He said that the bill, which he had not prepared, 'related particularly to the contracts between parties engaged in the trade on the Ottawa River, where there is a large business carried on in the manufacture of lumber. It was badly situated, far from any courts of justice, for the punishment of criminals. [It was impossible to bring] parties to justice for crimes committed, especially on the Lower Canada side of the river.' It would appear from the debate which followed that Aylwin's bill was intended to apply solely to Lower Canada, presumably because it was believed that the English master and servant legislation was in force in Upper Canada.[36] It seems likely that the bill was intended to give magistrates summary jurisdiction on the English model in order to overcome the difficulties associated with the scarcity of court facilities. In any event, the short debate focused on the granting of bail to persons accused in the Ottawa district, even of such offences as murder and bank robbery, on condition that they present themselves at Montreal for trial. In mid-May the bill was referred to a select committee, reported, and committed to the House, but it was not considered again during the session.

About a year later, on 17 June 1847, the Conservative member for Frontenac (and later Solicitor General West), Henry Smith, presented a bill 'to enforce the fulfilment of engagements between Master and Servant' in Upper Canada. The bill seems to have been introduced in consequence of the decision in *Shea* v *Choat*, for Smith told the House on 5 July that 'there was no English statute in force in Upper Canada on the subject, and the present measure was intended to supply the deficiency.' It was 'intended chiefly to apply to servants in the lumbering business, with whom so much difficulty occurred; but it would embrace household and out-door servants generally.'[37]

The *Globe* summarized Smith's bill on 14 July, calling it a 'brutal Bill' that showed 'what a precious set of tyrants and prosecutors of women are the gentlemen on the ministerial side of the House!'[38] It made servants who left their employment during the term of their contracts liable to fines of up to £5 and imprisonment for up to two months. Costs were to be allowed and where fines were not paid the offender could be committed to jail at hard labour.

There was nothing in the scheme as originally presented that protected the servant. During the debate Reform leader Robert Baldwin complained that the bill was 'one-sided – all for the master ... It was certainly imperfect; for while professing mutual protection, it did not protect the servant in a single instance.' The *Globe* elaborated:

> As Mr. Baldwin very justly observed, it professes to be a Bill to enforce good faith between masters and servants but in truth, it only enforces it *from the servant*, the master is bound to nothing ... Who does not know that in the never ending disputes between master and servant, the master is generally at least as much to blame as the servant? And who does not admit that compulsory service is worse than useless – that servants must be kept to their duty by self-interest and good treatment, and not by terrors.

In this last, the *Globe* was echoing the protest of Baldwin's supporter in the Assembly debate, William Hamilton Merritt, who opposed the principle of the bill because 'there was no use in endeavouring to compel an unwilling servant to perform his contract. He thought that work was ill performed which was done under coercion; when a servant desired to leave, it was the master's interest to get rid of him.' Smith and Solicitor General John Hillyard Cameron responded to these protests by promising amendments to 'render the bill binding on both sides.' The Master and Servant Act did incorporate protections for the servant against mistreatment and the non-payment of wages. Such provisions had, of course, been included in the eighteenth-century English statutes.

Besides Smith's passing reference to the lumber workers, the only substantive discussion of difficulties arising between workers and their employers was contributed by the assembly's caricature of the Anglophile gentility, Colonel John Prince:

> The Bill might appear unnecessary to members who lived in the *civilised* parts of the Province; but he, who lived a hundrd [*sic*] and fifty miles beyond the confines of civilization [ie, Sandwich, now Windsor], thought it very important that the Bill should pass. He lived in the wild Western country, where he had a plain farmer's home [a Regency cottage on a large holding of park lots], and in that home he found one of the greatest annoyances, an annoyance many honourable members could not conceive, was the difficulty of getting and keeping servants. It would frequently happen to him that he would engage a fine buxom lassie as a servant girl who would agree with him by the month, and after she had entered his establishment, would turn round and inform Mrs. Prince, for he never interfered in those matters, that she would take instant leave of her place, because she wasn't called a 'help' instead of a servant, or invited to the family table instead of being left to dine in the kitchen. His was an old English family, and he was very old-fashioned in his notions, and did not admire those American ideas of independence, moreover, he could not accustom his tongue to the word 'help,' in preference to the old and scriptural name of servant. He did not like to be subjected to the caprices of the fine young girls. He spoke of the majority of them, for many of them were very pretty, although some few were frightfully ugly ... The only cure he saw for the evil he described was, to send any young lady he saw so acting for a month to jail, and he therefore cordially supported the bill.[39]

The Master and Servant Act passed on 21 July 1847 and received royal assent a week later. It provided that written contracts of employment, together with verbal agreements for a term of not more than one year, were to be binding on both parties. Employees who refused to work, left their master's employ, refused to obey his lawful commands, neglected his service, or injured his property were liable to punishment, as were any persons (tavern and boarding-house keepers were specifically mentioned) who induced 'servants or labourers to confederate for demanding extravagant or high wages, and prevent their hiring.' Tavern and boarding-house keepers were further prohibited from keeping servants' clothing in pledge for debts greater than £1/10 currency. These criminal provisions were to be enforced by the magistracy, who would receive complaints, call the accused before them, proceed in 'a summary and expeditious manner,' and impose penalties of up to £5 fine and one month's imprisonment. Costs were to be assessed, and offenders could be committed to jail if fines went unpaid. Offenders might be prosecuted, convicted, and punished in the District in which they were found, whether or not that was the District where the offence was committed, the employer resided, or the contract made.

A second set of provisions applied to servants' complaints against employers. The Act entitled workers to complain to the magistracy of 'misusage, refusal of necessary provisions, cruelty, ill-treatment or non-payment of wages' by their masters. The Justice would summon the master to appear before him 'at a reasonable time' in order to determine whether or not the summons was obeyed. If the servant's complaint was upheld, the Justice could discharge him from his contractual obligations and direct payment of any unpaid wages up to a limit of £10; costs could also be assessed against the master. Failing payment of wages or costs, a warrant of distress could be issued against the master's property. Finally, the Act provided for a right of appeal to Quarter Sessions against any 'conviction or order for the payment of wages, or order for the dismissal from service,' provided certain technical requirements were met.

The Master and Servant Act closely resembled its English predecessors in its general scheme, although its punitive provisions were not quite so harsh and the details of administration differed slightly. The Ontario legislation preserved the crucial distinction between breach of the employment contract by the servant and by the master. The former was a criminal offence to be punished by law, while the latter was a matter for civil remedy. So while accused servants could be arrested, accused masters could only be summoned to appear at a reasonable time. While neglectful servants could be imprisoned, cruel masters might forfeit their contractual rights. While servants could be jailed for failing to pay a fine or costs, masters were liable to the forced sale of property.

The doubts cast on the reception of the English statutes by the courts' decisions in *Shea* v *Choat* and its predecessor cases are important in explaining why the legislature passed a Master and Servant Act in 1847. But those doubts do not exhaust the need for explanation. Clearly, the legislature must have felt a continuing need for a special master and servant law: this deserves further exploration. Moreover, the courts had decided that the English laws were not in force, because they were inapplicable to the social conditions of nineteenth-century Ontario. Yet when the legislature fashioned the Act, it followed the 'inapplicable' model very closely. Even in the wake of the reception cases, then, it remains to be explained why the legislature considered *any* master and servant law to be necessary, and why it chose to follow the English model in particular. Unique and definitive answers to those questions are not available, but it will be helpful to sketch a fairly general account of the 'labour problem' as it existed in mid-nineteenth-century Ontario.

THE 'LABOUR PROBLEM' IN MID-CENTURY ONTARIO

The legislative debate on the master and servant bill singled out timberers and household servants. There was, however, no intent to restrict the Act's reach to these particular groups. Nothing in the wording of the statute limited it to the lumberjacks and domestics; it was applied far more broadly. When it appeared that some magistrates entertained doubts about the Act's applicability to skilled tradesmen, because it spoke of 'Servants or Labourers,' an 1855 amendment removed those doubts.[40] The special mention of domestic servants and lumber industry workers had *symbolic* importance: these two groups epitomised the interrelated difficulties of supply and discipline that constituted the 'labour problem' in mid-nineteenth-century Ontario.

When Colonel Prince regaled the legislature with his domestic upsets, he was sounding a familiar refrain. Complaints about the availability and adequacy of household servants echoed throughout the memoirs of genteel visitors and settlers. For Anna Jameson, a vegetable diet consisting wholly of potatoes was but a minor inconvenience beside the 'more serious evil,' the scarcity of good servants. Thomas Langton complained that 'we could get no experienced servant from the more settled part of the country, and we had seen specimens of the new arrivals which were very discouraging.' For his sister Anne the want of good servants was 'the peculiar and unavoidable trial of the backwoods [which] colours the stream and directs the current of all one's ideas.' Catharine Parr Traill advised immigrating gentlewomen to learn the arts of household management, because servants would be hard to get and harder to keep, while

Susanna Moodie provided the definitive catalogue of evils accruing to those foolish enough to bring out servants with them:

They no sooner set foot upon the Canadian shores than they become possessed with this ultra-republican spirit. All respect for their employers, all subordination is at an end; the very air of Canada severs the tie of mutual obligation which bound you together. They fancy themselves not only equal to you in rank, but that ignorance and vulgarity give them superior claims to notice. They demand the highest wages, and grumble at doing half the work, in return, which they cheerfully performed at home. They demand to eat at your table, and to sit in your company, and if you refuse to listen to their dishonest and extravagant claims, they tell you that 'they are free; that no contract signed in the old country is binding in "Meriky"; that you may look out for another person to fill their place as soon as you like; and that you may get the money expended in their passage and outfit in the best manner you can.'[41]

The shortage of domestic servants and their consequent high wages and insubordination stood for a more general concern about problems of labour supply that extended back at least to the 1820s. Robert Gourlay's proposals that Ontario become the outlet for Britain's surplus labour and capital were part of this concern, as was, for example, the advice tendered to the Lieutenant Governor in 1829:

The want of that service which at home is supplied by apprentices, has been long felt in this province, as well by artificers, as by Householders and agriculturalists. In this present limited state of our Population, and at the exorbitant rate at which labour in every department is paid, to procure a supply of boys and girls as apprentices would be rendering the Province an essential service. It happens opportunely at this juncture that, the redundant population of G Britain, the difficulties of its manufacturing districts, and the alarming accumulation of its poor rates, opens a way for obtaining an ample supply of Children from the age of 9 and upwards.[42]

In view of the labour shortage, it was especially galling to see the parade of new immigrants pass through Canada on their way to take up American homesteads. 'It certainly is a melancolly [*sic*] instance of our remissness, or a striking proof of our modesty,' complained 'Senex' to the Bytown *Gazette*, 'that hundreds of emigrants pass through the Rideau Canal on their way to the West, in quest of employment, ignorant of the vast field wherein their labour could be usefully and profitably expended here;

there is an outcry every spring and fall that agricultural operations are impeded for want of a due supply of servants, or carried on at a ruinous expense.[43]

By the early 1840s these concerns had been systematized in the colonization theory of Edward Gibbon Wakefield. Influenced by Gourlay, he had come to conclude that the colony's prosperity depended on its ability to attract development capital from the mother country, and that the ability to attract capital depended in turn on the presence of a pool of wage labour. Labour supply in the colony could be maximized by fixing land prices at a level low enough to attract the agricultural settler who had capital of his own, but high enough to channel impoverished immigrants into the wage labour market for at least so long as it would take them to accumulate the funds necessary for agricultural settlement. Wakefield had accompanied Lord Durham to Canada, and his views permeated the discussions of land policy in the Durham *Report*. Moreover, his theory received legislative expression in the Land Acts of 1831 and 1841. By the early 1840s, then, concern about labour supply in Ontario had become explicitly Wakefieldian, concentrating on the manipulation of land policy to ensure the creation of a class of landless labourers.[44] The assimilation of Wakefieldian views by the Ontario ruling élite was attested to in a statement by banker and Legislative Councillor William Allen, in 1840:

The greatest drawback to the employment of Capital in this country ... consists in the *high price of wages*, and the *extreme difficulty of procuring the labor* requisite for its profitable employment in *any* pursuit; and more especially in the *agricultural* ones. Everything therefore, that tends to lessen the *quality of labor in the Market*, will tend also to *exclude capital from it*. But the main cause of the scarcity of hired labor in a new Country is the *Cheapness of Land*, and it seems to follow, as an irresistable conclusion, that the *Free gift of Lands*, must increase that scarcity an hundredfold.[45]

But if Ontario's economic prosperity was thought to rest on the creation of a labouring class, the emergence of such a class was seen at the same time as a threat to the province's social stability. The propertyless had no stake in the social order and no interest in its maintenance. The insubordination of Susanna Moodie's servants was one indication of this, while graver fears were expressed to the Lieutenant Governor by an anonymous 'Observer' during the rebellion period:

Of late most of the emigrants from the States have been labours [sic] or Mechanicks, but of the two the last are the worst, for they import with them the depravity of the towns and villages, and a degree of intolerable upsetting impudence and conceit which they dignify with the name of independence and being half taught and well clad they imagine themselves equal to the first in the land and because they are not treated as such, their hearts boil over with envious Malignity which they would go any length to gratify. To effect their purpose they have recourse to falsehood Slander and rebellion in hopes either to reduce their Superiors to their own level or overthrow the institutions and the laws which protect life and property, that they might massacre them, and for no other reason, but that the Very things they Should admire Men for, creates their boundless hatred.

In this correspondent's view, the root of the problem was the nationality of the 'labours and Mechanicks.' His solution was to import as many British workers 'as will reduce the wages at once, and the depraved scum of the United States called Mechanicks will no longer have an inducement to trouble us ... and a great proportion of them will leave us.'[46]

American wage workers were not the only, nor even the principal, threat to the social order, however. Irish workers in the Ottawa valley timber industry furnished the most potent illustrations of social havoc wreaked by the propertyless throughout the thirties and early forties. While the lumbermen's rebellion peaked with the 'Shiners' War' of the late thirties, Aylwin's abortive master and servant bill of 1846 and the plea of an 1847 Bytown grand jury that an efficient police force be established to counter 'the frequent assaults of a lawless mob who by their conduct put all law and authority at defiance,' indicate the continuing problem of labour discipline in the industry.[47] About a year after the Master and Servant Act was passed, the *Globe* reprinted the following from the Bytown *Gazette*:

During the past week, a number of cases have been tried before the Town Council, under the Act for the better regulation of duties between Master and Servant. The complaints were for breaches of contract on the part of men, who had left their employment contrary to the terms of their arrangement. The defendants were fined in sums ranging from £1 to £5, and costs, with imprisonment until paid. The evils arising from breaches of contract, by men running away in defiance of their agreements, have been felt to a very serious extent by the lumberers on the Ottawa, and the punishment of a few offenders will have a most salutary effect, by teaching them that they cannot, with impunity, longer indulge in a practice which has been attended with great loss and injury to those engaged in the lumber trade.[48]

By the mid-forties, moreover, the reputation of the Ottawa valley lumbermen for riot and indiscipline was well on its way to being surpassed by that of the hordes of impoverished Irish employed in canal-building. The story of the construction of the Ontario canal system is in large part the narrative of violent confrontations between groups of Irishmen competing for work, and between the Irish and the canal contractors over wages and the availability of work.[49] In 1845 the legislature passed 'An Act for the better preservation of the Peace, and the prevention of Riots and violent Outrages at and near Public Works while in progress of construction,' and it was continued and extended six years later.[50] The famine immigration of 1847, which deposited nearly a hundred thousand totally impoverished Irish on the resources of the colony, swelled the problem almost to the breaking point.[51]

Fear of the social unrest accompanying a mass movement of the propertyless into the locality inspired Judge James Robert Gowan to instruct Simcoe's constables in the criminal law in 1852, 'more especially now, as the progress of extensive public works in this County will bring into our sober law-respecting community, a class of persons who will not have the same interest we have in maintaining peace and order, and who *are not noted for their appreciation of either*.'[52] A similar connection between lawlessness and wage labour was evident in the explanation of an upswing in incendiarism given to the grand jury at the 1847 Gore Assizes by the Chief Justice: 'It was sometimes committed to defraud Insurance Offices, but was much more generally the result of vicious feeling, or produced by quarrels between employer and servant.'[53]

On the one hand then, Ontarians believed that the creation of a pool of propertyless labourers was essential to future prosperity; on the other hand, they feared the threat that the propertyless posed to social order. This apparent contradiction could have been resolved by resort to outright repression, as in some small degree it was, but for an increasingly significant number of Ontarians the key to social salvation and economic prosperity was moral reform, particularly as institutionalized in the evolving system of universal compulsory education. The growing urban middle class and prosperous farmers, who provided the social basis for the schools movement of the 1840s and 1850s equated poverty with criminality and ignorance with vice. Common schools were to be the vehicle for transforming the children of the poor into respectable and responsible citizens of the prosperous urban society then emerging.[54]

It is tempting to speculate that criminal legislation like the Master and Servant Act was considered necessary to control the irredeemable present generation: their children would be 'saved' by the schools. Whatever the merits of this conjecture, it is apparent that the more prosperous members of the Ontario community were prepared to believe in the inherent lawlessness of the wage labourer. It was not merely convenient that the disobedient worker be treated as a criminal: it was reasonable and just.

AMENDMENTS AND REPEAL

The Master and Servant Act originally gave no clear definition of master and servant. In 1855, perhaps because the justices had been interpreting its original intent too narrowly, the legislature found it necessary to remove the 'doubts [that] have been entertained' about the Act's scope by providing specifically that it was to apply to 'Journeymen or skilled Labourers in any trade, calling, craft or employment, and to their Masters, that is to the tradesmen or persons employing them as such Journeymen or skilled Labourers, as fully to all intents and purposes as to other Servants and Labourers and their Masters or persons employing them...'[55]

If the Act had been interpreted too narrowly before – restricted, it would seem, to unskilled labourers – there is some evidence that in the aftermath it was sometimes applied rather too broadly. One correspondent complained to the *Upper Canada Law Journal* that 'magistrates think they have the power to bring almost every kind of work within the ... Act. I have known suits before magistrates, for threshing done by a threshing machine; upon contracts with railroad companies and other corporations, for wages earned months after the employment ceased, etc.' The editors replied that they had heard similar tales and warned that 'magistrates should be very careful lest they "burn their fingers" in assuming jurisdiction. ... The law was not intended for the recovery of *debts*.'[56] The magistrates' manuals made the same point and supplied tests to distinguish between the contract of service and the contract for services, the employment relationship and that of the independent contractor. Richard Dempsey recommended that magistrates not 'entertain any complaint as for wages, where the arrangement between the parties is by the job or contract or savours of such, as for instance, cutting wood by the cord, splitting rails at so much per 100, working threshing machines, painting, etc., by the job, instead of so much per day.'[57] Here the nature of the relationship was seen to be fixed at least in part by the mode of payment; John McNab seems to have been closer to the nub of wage employment in proposing that 'perhaps the best test as to whether the relation of master and servant or labourer exists, is to ask whether or not the employer can cause the person doing the work to leave one description of work and attend to or perform another.'[58]

The *Canada Farmer* had foreseen a second problem in the interpretation of the Act: 'if a servant refuses to perform his agreement at any time *before he actually commences work*, the master will have no remedy, whatever may be the inconvenience he suffers, and it may sometimes be very great, because the refusal was not "after the commencement of such employment".'[59] By the 1855 amendment, the Master and Servant Act applied to all 'engagements entered into for the performance of any service or work,' whether or not they had been 'actually ... entered upon.' Henceforth the relation of master and servant was to be deemed to exist upon concluding a bargain and not merely once the work had begun.

In the 1859 statute consolidation, the Act was amended in a few purely technical respects – amounts formerly set out in currency were now set out in dollars; the term 'district' was replaced by 'county'; and so on – and the jurisdiction of the Justices in cases under the Act was made to conform to the general legislation on summary proceedings.[60] Nevertheless, uncertainties remained.

Among these was a procedural question that went to the heart of the Act's policy that the worker's breach was criminal while breach by the employer was at worst a civil wrong. In nineteenth-century criminal procedure, the accused could not give sworn evidence in his own defence, while more generally the law did not permit any party individually named on the record to give evidence in any proceeding, criminal or civil. In 1862 the editors of the *Law Journal* were asked whether a servant who brought action against his master for non-payment of wages was competent to testify. Admitting that there was no authority on the question, they concluded that such evidence probably was admissible, first because the magistrates' court was not a court of record, and second because of 'universal practice. We know of no case in which such testimony has been excluded. We know that it has been received in every proceeding of the kind of which we have any knowledge.' Moreover, they pointed out that actions for wages were 'more in the nature of a civil than a criminal proceeding.'[61]

This analysis meant in effect that while in proceedings for wages both parties could introduce evidence, the accused servant could not respond on oath to his master's charges in actions on his breach, for the general rule in criminal procedure applied to summary proceedings before magistrates as well as to courts of record. This was remedied by an 1865 amendment providing that 'whenever the Justice shall take the evidence of the complainant in support of his or her claim, the said Justice shall be bound to take the evidence of the defendant also, if tendered.' This change might be taken to indicate that the fundamental inequity of the Act was somewhat tempered, at least procedurally. The same amending legislation extended the reach of the Act by making it possible to launch actions as much as one month after the employment contract ended, 'as though the engagement between the parties still subsisted.' This may have been more to the advantage of unpaid workers than deserted employers.[62]

While the 1865 amendment may have somewhat tempered the criminal burden, the master's failure to pay wages was coming to be seen as something less than a breach of contract. The issue was joined over the question of whether a magistrate's order for the payment of wages amounted to a 'conviction' of the master. In an 1862 case the court of Queen's Bench held that a proceeding for unpaid wages was 'nothing but a summary mode of enforcing and collecting a debt, and the money so ordered to be paid *to the servant* for wages does not come, we think, within the meaning of the word "*damages*"...' But a year later the Huron and Bruce Quarter Sessions quashed an order for wages on technical grounds, complaining that 'it is departing from the common law to give Magistrates jurisdiction in matters properly belonging to civil tribunals.'[63] Is it overly cynical to note that in the former case the master's success depended upon the order not being considered a conviction, and in the latter on the opposite, and that both masters won? It can at least be said that there was some uncertainty among the judiciary. Thus in 1862 the *Law Journal* was able confidently to assert that an order for wages was not a conviction. Two years later it had to confess some doubts as to whether an action for wages was 'in the nature of civil process for the recovery of a debt' or 'a *quasi* criminal proceeding.'[64]

No such doubt obtained on the other side: a servant was liable to *punishment* for breach of contract, as the *Law Journal* informed a puzzled inquirer:

Gentlemen: – Magistrates in new counties being frequently at a loss for advice upon questions pertaining to their duty, may I take the liberty of asking your opinion upon the following case, which came before us: –

A. summonses B. to appear before magistrates. In evidence it appears that A. was engaged by B. to work for five months for a stipulated sum. A. serves a portion of time, and then, without leave, absents himself from the employment of

B. Is the contract violated? and is B. bound to pay A. for the term of time he has served? Upon the facts stated by our correspondent, we are of opinion not only that A. has no right to recover against B. for the portion of time mentioned, but that, under [the Master and Servant Act] A. is liable, upon complaint of B., to be punished for leaving B.'s service before the expiration of his term of engagement.[65]

Much uncertainty and difficulty resulted from magistrates' unfamiliarity with proper proceedings under the Act. In *Perrin* v *Neil* (1863), the Elgin Quarter Sessions overturned a conviction by the Mayor of St Thomas because the defendant was not a servant but an apprentice, and therefore not covered by the statute. *Cummins* v *Moore* (1875), arising ten years after the 1865 amendment, overturned a conviction because the action had been commenced more than a month after the termination of the engagement. Most egregious of all, in *Regina* v *Milne et al.* (1875) a conviction was quashed because of three justices sitting together to hear the case, one took it upon himself to enter the conviction against the decision of the other two. The court commented sternly on his conduct: 'Even if the strict letter of the law had given him the exclusive right of determination, it cannot increase either the respect or the confidence of the public in the administration of justice, that such right should have been exercised, in opposition to the opinion of the two other Justices who, without objection on his part, heard the case with him.' In each of these cases it was an order against a master that was quashed.[66]

In 1877 the Dominion parliament repealed the criminal provisions of the Master and Servant Act and its counterparts in other provinces, saying that 'breaches of contract, whether of service, or otherwise, are in general civil wrongs only, and not criminal in their nature; and it is just that breaches of contract of service should in general be treated like other breaches of contract, as civil wrongs, and not as crimes...'[67] Repeal came in response to urgent lobbying by the trade unions, who were able to point to the success of their English counterparts two years earlier in having the analogous British legislation repealed.[68] In 1880 appellate jurisdiction under the Act was transferred to the Division Court,[69] and in 1914 a new consolidation of the Ontario law governing contractual relations between employers and employees appeared, still under the title, 'An Act respecting Master and Servants': the terminology has continued in use to this day.[70] What has survived, in essence, is a mechanism for the recovery of unpaid wages by summary proceedings before a magistrate, and in this respect section 4 of the current Ontario statute is remarkably similar in language to its predecessor of 1847. What has disappeared, at least from the Master and Servant Act, is the special penalty attaching to the erring employee.

Before leaving the statutory history of the Act, however, it must be noted that parliament did not wholly repeal the criminal provision. 'Certain wilful and malicious breaches of contract, involving danger to persons or property, or grave public inconvenience,' were still to be punished as crimes by fines or imprisonment.[71] But while some breaches of contract by workers might still be considered crimes, wage workers as a class were no longer to be considered potential criminals held in control by fear of punishment.

THE MASTER AND SERVANT ACT IN OPERATION: THE GALT POLICE COURT 1866–77

No assessment of the significance of the Act would be complete without some account of actual experience with its working at the hands of local Justices of the Peace. This is not an easy task, however, not least because there existed no central registry of proceedings by the magistracy whose courts, it has already been said, were not courts of record. Nonetheless, justices were required to supply a return of convictions to the Quarter Sessions, and while such returns seem rarely to have been copied into the Quarter Sessions minute books, they were sometimes published in local newspapers.[72] During the thirty years that the Act was in force, some three thousand justices exercised jurisdiction in Ontario. A minute fraction have left personal papers, and of those few a small fraction again have left materials bearing on the practice of the Act.[73] There was a right of appeal to Quarter Sessions from proceedings under the Act, and the surviving minute books do record that court's proceedings systematically. Unfortunately their informational content is far from rich. This excerpt from the minutes of the Home District Quarter Sessions is typical:

> The Appeal of William J. Mitchell, from the conviction of Ira White Esquire under the Masters & Servants Act, Notice of Appeal, with the proceedings of conviction by the Magistrates, were put in.
>
> Swore Ira White Esq. & James Mitchell.
>
> The Court Ordered that the Conviction be quashed, but without Costs.[74]

For the most part, then, magistrates' papers, newspaper accounts, and Quarter Sessions minutes are incidental evidence of some usefulness but shed insufficient light on proceedings under the Act.

The most extensive set of records and supporting documentation bearing on the practice of the Master and Servant Act is the Toronto Police Register of Criminals, a record of summary proceedings before the stipendiary police magistrate, or, until 1850, the Mayor and aldermen sitting in their magisterial capacity as the urban equivalent of rural Justices of the Peace. Taken together with the Toronto warrant registry and the police court columns of the daily press, the Register of Criminals makes available for quantitative examination several thousand proceedings under the Act from its inception to its repeal. Similar, if less extensive, material exists for Hamilton as well. These records will be discussed and analysed in a sequel to this essay.

The richest qualitative source of information on the day-to-day practice of the Act identified to date is the five-volume record of proceedings in the Galt police court from 1857 to 1870.[75] Unlike the Toronto and Hamilton registers, the Galt volumes contain detailed minutes of evidence taken by the JPs in the course of their proceedings. The number of cases is not large, but the information provided on most of them is without parallel in the other known records.

The Galt records are more or less continuous from 1857. One master and servant case was recorded in that year, but from then until 1866 none appear. Between 1866 and 1877, forty-eight proceedings under the Act can be identified (although some of them may have come under the analogous legislation respecting apprentices instead), representing on the average between five and six per cent of the court's annual case load. Of these forty-eight cases, twenty-five were proceedings by servants for unpaid wages, and the remainder actions by masters against insubordinate or absenting employees. Actions by masters were slightly more frequent earlier in the period; actions for wages arose slightly more often later on.

Almost the full range of wage employments typical of a small southwestern Ontario market town in the period are represented: farm labour; domestic service; construction trades and labour; store clerks; small factories. Most proceedings took place before a single justice, commonly the Mayor, but occasionally two or three magistrates sat together. In most cases, neither party was represented by counsel; in the remainder, masters were more frequently represented by lawyers than were servants. Proceedings were summary and expeditious; they were rarely adjourned, and never for more than a day. The justices often seem to have encouraged settlements between the parties; if they could not be arranged the law took its course. In one wages case, Mayor Adam Ker, sitting as one of two justices, himself took the stand to explain his involvement in settlement negotiations. He testified that the sum involved was so small that he had not considered it worth preparing the necessary documents but spoke to the employer about making a settlement. When the employer refused to do so, Ker 'had nothing to do but to take an information.' The master was ordered to pay the wages and the statutory costs, the latter amounting to almost twice the value of the former.[76]

The first requirement in proceedings was normally that a contract of employment within the scope of the Act be proved. Thus cases were dismissed when a verbal agreement for a term of three years was alleged, when a servant seeking unpaid wages testified that he had been working for the defendant 'off and on' since the fall, when the employment relationship had terminated more than one month before the complaint was laid, when the contract had been made in another jurisdiction, and where the relationship between the parties could be construed as one of partnership rather than service.[77] When there was disagreement between the parties as to the terms of a verbal agreement, the magistrates frequently looked for evidence of custom. Thus one construction worker's claim that the amount held back from his wages for board was owing him was upheld on his testimony that he never undertook out of town work without board supplied by the employer. The employer in question had in fact supplied board on another job some years previously, although, as the complainant admitted, nothing had been said about board in agreeing to the recent job. A tradesman hired to do lathing was held justified in refusing to do other construction work on the house. A woman who left her job in a textile factory immediately upon receiving two weeks' notice was held to have forfeited the wages held back by her employer. There was a shop rule posted in the factory covering the situation and her own evidence hardly aided her claim: 'such notices may have been posted up but I do not know the purport of them. ... There was half of my first pay kept back ... don't know why it was kept only it was the custom of the shop.'[78]

Customary notions that domestic service was a monthly employment and farm labour seasonal seem to explain the outcomes of several cases in which workers were charged with leaving their employment before its term without the employer's permission. A servant's claim that he or she had given proper notice but had been asked by the employer to remain a few days until a replacement could be found usually resulted in conviction when the servant got tired of waiting and left. But when, upon agreeing to work for another month, a servant became ill, his claim for wages was dismissed, 'on account of the Plaintiff not appearing at his work on Monday morning and not stating to his employer why he was not there.'[79]

The Galt magistracy frequently ordered defaulting servants to return to work, thus in effect awarding specific performance. A girl who left her service after a dispute over the peeling of potatoes, in the course of which her employer, as the latter testified, 'gave her a little push,' was given a month to pay a $1 fine and $2.35 costs, with the alternative of two days in jail, and was told to work out her month's notice or repay the balance of wages advanced her. The textile factory worker who ignored the 'custom' of the shop was told to serve out her time or forfeit the wages. A boy who was hired to work on a farm for six months and took his commitment literally, so that he served from 22 April to 22 October, and not to the end of the calendar month, was ordered to return to work and make up the nine days or spend twenty days in jail. A man who grew impatient with his employer's lethargic search for a replacement was offered the alternatives of returning to work for three days, forfeiting a week's wages ($7), paying a $7 fine, or spending ten days in jail. A woman in the same situation was given the further alternative of finding a replacement herself. A boy who left his place in the third year of a four-year term because he was being paid less than his fellows was ordered to serve out the year: the alternatives were a $20 fine or a month in jail. In another case the option of a fine was not made available: the servant was to return to work or spend fifteen days in jail.[80]

Employees who left their work before its term were not the only ones who found themselves brought before the justices: insubordinate or disobedient workers would occasionally be brought up to be disciplined. One boy was charged with 'behaving improperly, wasting or loosing [*sic*] his said Master's time, preventing the other boys from proceeding with their work, by scuffling with them, slapping and kicking them.' His master agreed to take him back, 'upon his promising to be a better boy, and attending to his work' and he was released upon payment of $2.85 in costs, probably more than a week's wages. The same parties appeared again three months later, but the new complaint was withdrawn when the boy promised 'to behave himself in a proper manner for the future and perform the lawful commands of his Master.' Another boy's case was dismissed on a similar promise, after his master pointed out that 'if accused would only keep his tongue quiet he would not be interfered with by the other boys.' Not only children were brought up for insubordination. A factory worker who had been four years in his place walked out of the shop one morning after being told to work more quickly.

He was brought before the Justice that afternoon and, upon his agreeing to return to work, let off with $3.50 costs. His daily pay was sixty cents.[81]

In fact the costs of an action, if assessed on the servant, were frequently punitive. In the case just referred to, they included fees for the information, warrant, copy, attendance, and hearing. Costs could be even higher if there were witness fees and mileage to be paid. A grocery clerk making about $30 a month was fined $15 (or twenty days) and $6 costs for leaving his situation. A workman whose action for unpaid wages was dismissed when his employer testified that he had been fired for incompetence was assessed costs of $4.75: his wage had been $1.50 per day. A servant girl hired, she said, for $5 monthly lost her suit for wages: her employer testified that they had agreed that 'when her time was up would give her the money if she was worth it,' and she was left to pay $1.85 costs.[82] When a servant who had been given only six days' work on what he alleged was a monthly hiring brought action for a month's wages, his employer was ordered to pay him $2 for the six days, and the plaintiff was assessed costs of $2.35.[83]

The rather solomonic character of some of the judgments handed down by Adam Ker and his colleagues makes the compilation of a 'win-loss' record a rather tricky matter, but the assessment of costs may serve as a rough guide. In twenty-two actions for wages, the plaintiff worker was ordered to pay costs twelve times and the defendant master ten times: a record for evenhandedness that could be matched by only the most experienced of contemporary labour arbitrators. The record of actions against servants tells a different tale. In only two of twenty-three cases were costs assessed against the employer; in the remaining twenty-one the servant came out the loser.[84] The Galt magistrates, for all that they might have strayed upon occasion from the strict letter of the law, faithfully upheld the policy of the Master and Servant Act: to keep recalcitrant workers to their labours for fear of punishment.

The object of this essay has been to describe one aspect of the law of employment in mid-nineteenth-century Ontario. Its principal finding – that the law favoured the employer and dealt harshly with the employee – is hardly surprising. Of more significance, perhaps, is the realization that the law which made breach of contract by the employee a criminal offence, rendering him liable to imprisonment, was not simply an archaic survival. It was that, to be sure: its lineage can be traced directly to the middle ages. But when, in mid-century, it was discarded by the courts (in part, at least, for its very antiquity), the legislature promptly reinvented it, and in so doing gave it the mark of modernity. The persistence of the master and servant legislation after 1847 cannot be put down to the conservatism of the law or the inertia of the law-makers. It must be seen as an act of policy springing from the social conditions of the Ontario of its day, and it must be explained by reference to the economy and society of the middle of the nineteenth century. Whatever may have been the proximate cause for its re-enactment in 1847 (and for that we have as yet insufficient evidence), its roots were in the ambivalence about wage labour that tormented propertied Ontario on the threshold of industrialism.

This study has hardly begun to explore its subject. Much more remains to be done before an adequate outline of nineteenth-century employment law can be pieced together. Numerous substantive areas of the law require investigation: a partial list would include apprenticeship, implied terms of the employment contract, employers' liability for the acts of their servants, liability for industrial accidents, criminal and civil conspiracy in the employment context, and the development of the law relating to trade unions and strikes. But a description of the law based on the statutes and the law reports will hardly be sufficient: what is really required is a social history of the law of employment. Perhaps the best place to begin is with the reconstruction of the experience of being brought to law, and the obvious locus for this is the magistrate's court. Finally, it is clear that the social history of the law of employment is but one aspect of the larger social history of employment itself in Ontario's transition to industrialism. We know so little about this topic as yet that every claim must be tentative. This is at once a source of much frustration and a compelling incentive to scholarship.

NOTES

An earlier version of this essay was presented to the 'Class and Culture' conference, McGill University, 8 March 1980.
I would like to thank The Osgoode Society for financial support and Fred Ernst for research assistance. For convenience, throughout this essay I refer to Ontario rather than to Upper Canada and Canada West.

1 Specific performance of the employment contract was available as an equitable remedy in England until the early nineteenth century. Even after the rule against specific performance had been adopted, it would appear that a similar effect might be obtained by seeking an injunction restraining an employee from working for a competitor. No Ontario cases have yet been located in which such an injunction was awarded during the period considered in this essay. It is worth noting in this connection that the 1867

revision of the English Master and Servant Act enabled magistrates to order specific performance against employees. For a general discussion of specific performance in the English context, see M.R. Freedland *The Contract of Employment* (London 1976) 272–8.

2 10 and 11 Vic. (1847), c. 23. Analogous law and legislation was in existence regulating the relations of masters and apprentices: the differences are sufficiently significant, however, that the latter is not treated here.

3 *Debates of the Legislative Assembly of United Canada* ed. Elizabeth Nish (Montreal 1970–) VI 670 (hereafter *Debates of United Canada*)

4 Copied in Guelph and Galt *Advertiser* 5 Nov. 1847; emphasis in original

5 The principal exception seems to have been the law relating to the necessity of a seal in employment contracts entered into by corporations. Compare, for example, the decision of the Chief Justice Robinson in *Raines* v *The Credit Harbour Company* (1844), 1 *Upper Canada Queen's Bench Reports* (hereafter UCQB) 174, with that of Chief Justice Harrison in *Hughes* v *The Canada Permanent Loan and Savings Society* (1876), 39 UCQB 221.

6 For a contemporary layman's guide see J. Whitley *Canadian Domestic Lawyer* (Stratford, Ont. 1864) 300–4. The discussion that follows deals only with the enforcement of the employment contract; other matters of law proceeding from the employment relationship, such as the master's liability for the acts of his servant, or liability in industrial accidents, are not treated here.

7 *Sprague and Wife* v *Nickerson* (1844), 1 UCQB 284

8 *Jacob Perlet* v *Margaret Perlet* (1857), 15 UCQB 165

9 *Redmond* v *Redmond* (1868), 27 UCQB 220 per Hagarty J

10 *Henricks* v *Henricks* (1868), 27 UCQB 447

11 *Ferris* v *Fox* (1854), 11 UCQB 612

12 *Robinson* v *Shistel* (1873), 23 *Upper Canada Common Pleas Reports* (hereafter UCCP) 114

13 (1878), 28 UCCP 603

14 *McGuffin* v *Cayley* (1846), 2 UCQB 308

15 *Rettinger* v *MacDougall* (1860), 9 UCCP 485

16 *Dick* v *Heron* (1858), 8 UCCP 67. Chief Justice Robinson decried the tendency of juries to strike compromises in favour of plaintiffs who sued for back wages. He rebutted the argument that such outcomes might be 'consistent with justice and ought therefore not to be disturbed,' by noting that such a consideration 'would encourage juries to commit a breach of duty, by finding verdicts contrary to law, and would enable them to set aside the contracts of mankind.' *Blake* v *Shaw* (1853), 10 UCQB 180, and compare *The Bank of British North America* v *Simpson* (1874), 24 UCCP 354, where a jury's verdict that was apparently motivated by the equities of the situation was overturned as contrary to law.

17 *Blake* v *Shaw*, above note 16

18 *Patterson* v *Scott* (1876), 38 UCQB 642 per Harrison CJ

19 *Raines* v *The Credit Harbour Company*, above note 5

20 *Hunter* v *Foote* (1862), 12 UCCP 175

21 *Roche* v *Walsh* (1877), 27 UCCP 555 per Wilson J; see also *The Bank of British North America* v *Simpson*, and *Watson* v *Miller, Ritchey and Davis* (1864), 23 UCQB 217.

22 Compare *O'Neill et al.* v *Leight* (1846), 2 UCQB 204.

23 The legal historian of Ontario has available for investigation a wide range of sources on case law besides the reported appellate cases. These include Quarter Sessions and Assize minute-books, judges' notebooks and, perhaps the richest though least consulted source, newspaper accounts of legal proceedings.

24 The Statute of Labourers, 23 Edw. III (1349) and 25 Edw. III (1350); compare W.S. Holdsworth *History of English Law* II (London 1966) 459–66.

25 The Statute of Artificers (sometimes called the Statute of Apprentices), 5 Eliz. (1562), c. 4; for a list of the later statutes see S. Webb and B. Webb *The History of Trade Unionism* (London 1920; facsimile ed., Clifton NJ 1973) 250n. See also Philip Selznick, *Law, Society, and Industrial Justice* (New Brunswick, NJ 1980) 122–30.

26 Quebec Act, 14 Geo. III (1774), c. 83; An Act for the Further Introduction of English Criminal Law into Upper Canada, 40 Geo. III (1800), c. 1; An Act Introducing the English Civil Law into Upper Canada, 32 Geo. III, c. 1 (UC)

27 Public Archives of Canada Record Group (hereafter RG) 5.A1 *Upper Canada Sundries*, O'Hara to Harrison 1 Nov. 1839 and enclosures (hereafter *Sundries*)

28 W.C. Keele *The Provincial Justice* (Toronto 1843). Keele (1835) 408–9 considered 20 Geo. II, c. 19; 31 Geo. II, c. 11; 6 Geo. III, c. 25; and 32 Geo. III, c. 56 to be in force in Ontario.

29 Consider the case for the prosecution: 'The plaintiff's case was within the mischief of the statute. That he contracted with Wetherley as an husbandman to labour upon the land, one particular class of labourers pointed out by the statute, persons whose regular employment in their occupations was essential to the well-being of society. That the being employed with oxen should make no difference, that being the usual mode of employment in this country.' *Whelan* v *Stevens* (1827), *Taylor's* 439

30 *Mitchell* v *Defries* (1846), 2 UCQB 430

31 *Fish* v *Doyle* (1831), *Draper* 328

32 *Dillingham* v *Wilson* (1841), 6 UCQB (Old Series) 85. Sherwood had sat on the *Fish* case and concurred in Robinson's decision.

33 Keele *Provincial Justice* (1843) 24n

34 *Shea* v *Choat* (1846), 2 UCQB 211

35 S.R. Clarke *The Magistrates' Manual* (Toronto 1878) 329

36 Nish, ed. *Debates of United Canada* v 955: 'Mr. Hall suggested that the bill should refer to Upper Canada also.'

37 Ibid. vi 669–70 reports the debate.

38 The reference to women, following from the *Globe*'s assumption that the Master and Servant Act was directed at domestic servants, was also inspired by the newspaper's violent opposition to J.H. Cameron's bill for the reform of marriage laws, then before the legislature. (Toronto *Globe* 14 July 1847)

39 For Prince, see R.A. Douglas 'John Prince' in *Dictionary of Canadian Biography* ix (Toronto 1976) 643, and *John Prince 1796–1870: A Collection of Documents*, ed. with an introduction by R.A. Douglas (Toronto 1980).

40 18 Vic. (1855), c. 136

41 Anna Brownell Jameson *Winter Studies and Summer Rambles in Canada* (London 1838; Toronto 1965) 71; H.H. Langton, ed. *A Gentlewoman in Upper Canada: The Journals of Anne Langton* (Toronto 1964) 43, 103; Catharine Parr Traill *The Canadian Settlers' Guide* (Toronto 1855; Toronto 1969) 2–3; Susanna Moodie *Roughing It in the Bush* (London 1852; Toronto 1962) 140–1

42 *Sundries* James Radcliffe to Lieutenant Governor (Colborne) 13 July 1829

43 Bytown *Gazette* 6 Oct. 1836

44 For a brief account of Wakefield's career and thought, including his debt to Gourlay, see Craufurd D.W. Goodwin *Canadian Economic Thought* (London 1961) 20–30. Gary Teeple 'Land, Labour, and Capital in Pre-Confederation Canada' in his *Capitalism and the National Question in Canada* (Toronto 1972) reviews Wakefieldian policy and finds it misguided since Ontario's problem was not so much the attraction of unpropertied labor as its retention, given high rates of migration to the United States. Teeple concludes that the object of the policy, pricing land out of the reach of new immigrants to force them into the labour pool, had long before been achieved in practice by the concentration of land ownership in the hands of non-settling speculators.

45 Quoted in Leo A. Johnson 'Land Policy, Population Growth and Social Structure in the Home District, 1793–1851' in J.K. Johnson, ed. *Historical Essays on Upper Canada* (Toronto 1975) 49; emphasis in original

46 *Sundries* 'An Observer' to E. McMahon (nd, but judging from internal evidence, probably of the rebellion or immediate post-rebellion period)

47 M.S. Cross 'The Shiners' War: Social Violence in the Ottawa Valley in the 1830s' *Canadian Historical Review* LIV (1973) 1–26; Bytown *Packet* 30 Oct. 1847

48 Toronto *Globe* Mar. 1848

49 Ruth Bleasdale 'Class Conflict on the Canals of Upper Canada in the 1840's' *Labour/Le Travailleur* VII (Spring 1981) 9–39

50 8 Vic. (1845), c. 6; 14 and 15 Vic. (1851), c. 76
51 See, for example, Kenneth Duncan 'Irish Famine Immigration and the Social Structure of Canada West' in W.E. Mann, ed. *Canada: A Sociological Profile* (Toronto 1968) 1–15; Harry Clare Pentland 'The Development of a Capitalistic Labour Market in Canada' *Canadian Journal of Economics and Political Science* xxv (1959) 450–61; and J.M.S. Careless *The Union of the Canadas* (Toronto 1967) 113–14.
52 Judge James Robert Gowan *The Canadian Constables' Assistant* (Barrie, Ont. 1852) 3; emphasis in original
53 Hamilton *Spectator* 29 Sept. 1847
54 Susan Houston 'Politics, Schools, and Social Change in Upper Canada' and 'Victorian Origins of Juvenile Delinquency: A Canadian Experience' both in M.B. Katz and P.H. Mattingly, eds *Education and Social Change: Themes from Ontario's Past* (New York 1975); Alison Prentice *The School Promoters: Education and Social Class in Mid-Nineteenth Century Upper Canada* (Toronto 1977)
55 18 Vic. (1855), c. 136. It is tempting to speculate, on analogy with the case of *Whelan* v *Stevens* discussed above, that artisanal workers had been considered exempt from the Master and Servant Act because they brought property in the form of their tools or their skills to the job. For a discussion of the artisan's property in his skill, see David Montgomery 'Workers' Control of Machine Production in the Nineteenth Century' in his *Workers' Control in America: Studies in the History of Work, Technology and Labor Struggles* (Cambridge, Eng. 1979).
56 *Upper Canada Law Journal* (hereafter UCLJ) v (1859) 225; compare John McNab *The Magistrates' Manual* (Toronto 1865) 573n: 'It was lately decided in the sessions of York and Peel, that proceedings could not be taken before a Justice to recover the amount agreed to be paid for a day's work with a threshing-machine, because the owner of the machine did not belong to any trade, calling, or craft, and could not be considered a servant or labourer. (*Wood* v *Peterman*, ses. 1864.)'
57 Richard Dempsey *Magistrate's Hand-Book* (Toronto 1860) 19n
58 McNab *Manual* 573n
59 Copied in Guelph and Galt *Advertiser* 5 Nov. 1847
60 *Consolidated Statutes of Upper Canada* 1859, c. 75
61 UCLJ VIII (1862) 278. In *Regina* v *Walker* (1861) 21 UCQB 34, a servant's evidence had been received without objection and he was later prosecuted for perjury.
62 29 Vic. (1865), c. 33
63 *Ranney qui tam* v *Jones* (1862), 21 UCQB 370; *Helps and Eno* (1863), 9 UCLJ 302
64 UCLJ VIII (1862) 279; UCLJ X (1864) 111

65 UCLJ VIII (1862) 27
66 *Perrin* v *Neil* (1863), 9 UCLJ 218; *Cummins* v *Moore* (1875), 37 UCQB 130; *Regina* v *Milne et al.* (1875), 25 UCCP 94. In addition, the courts ruled that schoolteachers were not servants for the purposes of the Master and Servant Act: *In re Joice and Anglin* (1857), 19 UCQB 197.
67 40 Vic. (1877), c. 35 (Canada); *Revised Statutes of Ontario* (hereafter RSO) 1877, c. 133
68 G. Kealey *Toronto Workers Respond to Industrial Capitalism 1867–92* (Toronto 1980) 148–53; D. Simon 'Master and Servant' in J. Saville, ed. *Democracy and the Labour Movement* (London 1954). The explanation of repeal is addressed further in the sequel to this essay.
69 43 Vic. (1880), c. 8
70 RSO 1914, c. 144; RSO 1927, c. 177; RSO 1937, c. 197; RSO 1950, c. 224; RSO 1960, c. 230; RSO 1970, c. 263
71 In this Parliament followed an earlier Ontario act, applying specifically to railway companies, and imposing special penalties on employees in breach of contract, including the breach of company regulations. Where person or property were put at risk by the breach, the penalty could be a fine of up to $100, five years' imprisonment, or both: otherwise, the penalty would be the loss of a month's pay. Informers would receive half the amount of the penalty for their trouble. In addition to the penalty imposed by a JP, the railway company could assess the loss of an additional month's pay itself. (An Act for the punishment of the Officers and servants of Railway Companies, 19 Vic. [1856], c. 136)
72 See, for example, Guelph and Galt *Advertiser* 14 Dec. 1848.
73 Picton Magistrate John Rose's conviction book (1851–3) recorded a total of 78 cases of which two were complaints by masters under the Master and Servant Act (Public Archives of Ontario (hereafter PAO), Miscellaneous Series 1851/9). The legal papers of Peel County Magistrate Oliver Hammond contain a copy of a conviction in the master and servant case of *Grunians* v *Lee*, 17 July 1868; Hammond probably kept this document because his decision was appealed to Quarter Sessions. The bulk of Hammond's legal papers relate to transactions in land. (PAO Mss Hammond Papers, Series III)
74 PAO RG 22 series 7, v. 23, 23 Nov. 1849
75 PAO RG 22 series 13, vv. 1–5
76 Ibid. *May* v *Bydon* 20 Sept. 1870
77 Ibid. *Black* v *Eagel* 11 Apr. 1866; *Martin* v *Smith* 7 July 1868; *Leader* v *Haller and Pabst* 28 Oct. 1869; *Kay* v *Burrows* 29 Dec. 1871; *Dudley* v *Cadieux* 22 May 1877; *Battye* v *Taylor* 9 Apr. 1873

78 Ibid. *Holland* v *Ferguson* 5 Jan. 1870; *Cromwell* v *Levomie* 29 Nov. 1871; *Bunston* v *Thompson* 18 Jan. 1872

79 Ibid. *Caldwell* v *Dennis* 20 June 1871; *Murdock* v *Ramsay* 28 Oct. 1872; *McBean* v *McCormac* 10 Oct. 1874; *Flatt* v *Warnock* 11 Mar. 1874

80 Ibid. *Heath* v *Whistler* 31 Dec. 1870; *McBean* v *Shambough* 24 Oct. 1872; *Murdock* v *Ramsay* 28 Oct. 1872; *McBean* v *McCormac* 10 Oct. 1874; *Messrs. Jaffray Bros.* v *Kinsman* 19 Nov. 1872; *Brydon* v *Montgomery* 10 February 1873

81 Ibid. *Allan* v *Grant* 10 Jan. 1867; *Allan* v *Grant* 6 Apr. 1867; *Bittman* v *Laffray* 13 Sept. 1871; *Gourlay* v [?] 6 July 1877

82 Ibid. *Fisher* v *Ashbaugh* 21 May 1868; *Beale* v *Tottier* 5 Feb. 1870; *Morris* v *Scott* 16 Aug. 1871

83 Ibid. *Murdoch* v *Stoddard* 17 Feb. 1877; and see the peculiar case of *O'Hanly* v *McPherson* 24 Mar. 1877, in which Stoddard apparently was employed under an alias: the magistrates found they had no jurisdiction.

84 A few cases in which costs were not recorded are excluded here.

6

Shifting Patterns in Nineteenth-Century Canadian Custody Law

CONSTANCE B. BACKHOUSE

The nineteenth century witnessed a marked transformation in Canadian law concerning the custody of children. During this century the courts and legislatures began to retreat from the well-established traditional system of pure patriarchy by restricting paternal rights and granting more responsibility to the mother. During the first part of the century children were viewed as a species of paternal property, and the legal system treated a father's rights to custody as absolute. By the end of the century, although paternal and maternal rights were by no means equal, courts were increasingly granting mothers custody of their children. Courts awarded custody to mothers in cases where the father had serious defects of character which caused him to engage in behaviour considered socially intolerable. In general, mothers were awarded custody only when they were living under the protection of some other male, usually their fathers or brothers, and only if they had not disqualified themselves by an adulterous relationship or some other conduct that the Canadian courts considered unseemly.

The displacement of the pure patriarchal system of custody occurred at a time of changing perceptions about maternal responsibilities and rights which reflected new conceptions of the role of women and children. Industrialization altered the traditional economic functioning of the family, splitting most work off from the home and moving it into centralized areas of production. Women alone in the home became more responsible for holding the family together and instilling moral virtues into the children. Childhood itself began to receive increasing emphasis as a distinctive stage in life, and notions of the need for nurturing of children inside the family unit became prominent. By the late nineteenth century the processes associated with urbanization and industrialization created a recognition that the vast majority of children must eventually leave the family unit to strike out on their own, economically as well as socially. The emerging capitalist society increasingly was perceived as ruthless, while the big city was viewed as a threat to a wide range of traditional values. In these circumstances, the concept of the home as a 'haven in a heartless world' took firm hold.[1] Given the individualistic and competitive working environment, society began to be more concerned that to release children into the world without adequate nurture and education was dangerous not only to the children themselves but, perhaps more important, to the new middle class community then emerging with such force and apparent self-assurance.

Various developments in the nineteenth century ensured that mothers occupied an increasingly central position in the nurturing of children. Industrialization left mothers and young children alone in the home, no longer tied to the necessary duties of cottage production. Faced with this domestic void, women came to occupy their time and energy by elevating motherhood to the status of a profession.[2] The domestic void theory, however, does not completely explain this transformation in parental status. To a great extent this shift arose from an early form of the recognition of women's rights and children's needs. Questions remain about which of these formed the dominant element. To date much of the scholarly analysis and popular discussion surrounding these changes has focused on women's rights. In reality, however, it seems likely that it was the newly emerging concept of childhood and adolescence that improved women's custody rights. The basic and dominant impulse seemed to be not justice to women but the need to recognize and protect children and to prepare them for their forthcoming role in industrial society.

These several trends resulted in an increase in the power of the state over custody. Once the father was no longer automatically entitled to custody, it became necessary for the first time to examine closely whether he was fit for such responsibility. In making such decisions the welfare of the child came into prominence. As parental power was redistributed, parental rights were necessarily diminished. The state began to intervene as the ultimate decision-maker on the question of custody. Examination of parental responsibility and the welfare of the child at the end of the nineteenth century and throughout the twentieth century led to more state encroachment on parental rights.

The following analysis focuses mainly upon reported court decisions, even though there are obvious difficulties in attempting to derive a picture of Canadian custody jurisprudence from reported cases.[3] The danger of class bias exists, since those who pursued their custody battles to courts must have had an above average amount of disposable income. The lack of historical research in this area means that it is not now possible to look behind these reported decisions to the types of disputes which were settled informally or along traditional lines of patriarchal dominance. Relying upon reported decisions also presents the additional problem that before 1850 very few decisions were reported or published.[4] The first reported decision on custody in all of English Canada appeared in 1846.[5] Nevertheless reported decisions are important in that they reflect the attitudes of litigating counsel and the judiciary about the proper disposition of custody. Insofar as lower courts were bound by these decisions and practising lawyers advised their clients in light of these precedents, the reported cases must have had a great impact on the changing law of custody. The cases which went through several levels of appeal represented controversial situations in which judges differed in their approach; they serve as a helpful guide to the types of intellectual arguments that were made about custody, even if their usefulness as a reflection of the social reality of the time may be limited.

This essay does not attempt a detailed analysis of nineteenth-century custody law in Quebec. The influence of the Quebec Civil Code, the Roman Catholic Church, and French-Canadian culture were such as to differentiate this area from the English-Canadian situation. Although the custody law of nineteenth-century French Canada deserves a separate study, some preliminary comments can be made. The Quebec Civil Code of 1866 determined that marriage could only be dissolved by the natural death of one of the parties.[6] 'Separation from bed and board' could be obtained by court order under certain circumstances.[7] When applications for such separation were made, the Code provided that the *provisional* care of the children was to remain with the father, unless the court ordered otherwise for the greater advantage of the children.[8] Section 214 set out the criteria for custody upon the ultimate decision to grant separation: 'The children are entrusted to the party who has obtained the separation, unless the court, after having, if it think proper, consulted a family council, orders, for the greater advantage of the children, that all or some of them be entrusted to the care of the other party, or of a third person.'[9] Although the provisional custody rule assumed patriarchal superiority, there was clear authority for a court to order temporary custody to someone other than the father. Section 214 even set forth a preliminary rule that custody was awarded to the party who obtained the separation, presumably the wronged party. If women were successful applicants for separation in equal numbers with men, it would appear that unless a court ordered otherwise, 'for the greater advantage of the children,' mothers would be equally entitled to custody. In other words, there was no barrier on the face of the Code to maternal custody. This feature of the legislation, as well as the focus on the advantage of the child, was progressive for mid-nineteenth-century Canada.[10] Further research will be necessary to determine whether the situation in practice corresponded to the potential of the legislation.

THE DOMINANCE OF PATRIARCHY

In tracing the development of nineteenth-century English-Canadian custody law, one must look first to the period from the turn of the century to 1839, which reflected a stage of patriarchal supremacy. The father's legal authority over his legitimate children was dominant and superior to the mother's. Blackstone stated that the father was the guardian of his child by nature and that he possessed such power over the child as was sufficient to keep him in order and obedience.[11] Distinguishing the mother's position from the father's, Blackstone stated that a mother as such was entitled to 'no power but only reverence and respect.'[12] The right of the father to supreme control over his legitimate children was based on a hierarchic conception of society; throughout these early periods 'guardianship and paternal powers were regarded rather as profitable rights than as duties.'[13]

Even during the pure patriarchal stage, however, courts of equity intervened in a limited manner in a few cases where paternal power was recognized as excessive. William MacPherson, author of a major English treatise which was often referred to by Canadian attorneys and courts, commented on such intervention:

> parental authority ... was founded in nature, and the care which it was presumed the father would take for the education of the child; but if he would not provide for its support, he abandoned his right to the custody of the child ... or if he would educate it in a manner forbidden by the laws of his state, the public right of the community to superintend the education of its members, and to disallow what for its own security and welfare, it should see good to disallow, went beyond the right and authority of the father.[14]

Courts of equity were cautious in exercising their jurisdiction, and the predominant judicial approach of the time was to treat the father's rights to custody as virtually absolute.

Since there are no reported cases on custody in Canada during this early period, reference must be had to English cases. One can assume that since Canadian courts tended to follow English precedents in other areas, Canadian decisions reflected the jurisprudence of English family law. One of the best cases to illustrate the absoluteness of paternal rights was the English case of *R.* v *De Manneville* in 1804.[15] Mrs De Manneville alleged that not long afer her marriage she had separated from her husband on account of ill treatment. She had kept their child, whom she was nursing. The father found means by force and stratagem to get into the house where she was staying. He carried the child away almost naked in an open carriage in inclement weather. But in the absence of proof of the father's failure to nurture the child, the court determined that he was entitled by law to custody. 'The father of a child is entitled to the custody of it, though an infant at the breast of its mother.'[16]

Pressure mounted to reduce the extent of a father's legal power over his children. Concern over the need to provide mothers with limited rights of access and custody of very young children in special cases culminated in the passage of English legislation in 1839. The celebrated case of Mrs Norton provided the impetus behind the legislation. Caroline Sheridan Norton was a distinguished literary woman, acclaimed as one of the beauties of the day. Married to George Norton, an English barrister, she bore him three sons. He subjected her to physical violence, and she ultimately left him. Norton refused Caroline access to her children and launched a civil suit for damages for alienation of his wife's affections against Lord Melbourne, the Prime Minister and one of Caroline's closest friends. This claim was ultimately rejected by the courts. At this point Caroline undertook a campaign to have the custody laws revised to ensure mothers greater rights of access. Caroline selected Thomas Noon Talfourd, a young Whig barrister, as the person most likely to introduce such legislation into Parliament. Talfourd had been a junior defence counsel on the Lord Melbourne-Norton case and had also acted as counsel for fathers in two custody cases, which made him aware of the injustice of the custody laws.[17]

Talfourd introduced a bill to amend the custody law in the House of Commons in 1837. Speaking in defence of the bill, he stated that the legislation would allow judges to deal with 'husbands who denied to their innocent wives the last happiness which a woman so circumscribed could enjoy – the sight of her child.'[18] Talfourd made this argument for maternal custody because he had identified affection as a bond between parent and child. Those who spoke against the bill also accepted the principle of the unique strength of maternal devotion but argued that granting custody rights to mothers would encourage the breakdown of the marriage. The reasoning was that an overwhelming desire to be with the children would force mothers to remain within a marriage.[19] The newspapers of the day attacked the bill and criticized Talfourd and Mrs Norton for their role in the legislative campaign. Although the bill was defeated in 1838, Talfourd reintroduced it in 1839. Mrs Norton prepared a pamphlet for distribution to members of Parliament, drew up petitions, and campaigned endlessly with her friends and influential acquaintances.

As a result of this pressure, an Act to Amend the Law Relating to Custody of Infants, subsequently known as Lord Talfourd's Act, was finally passed in 1839.[20] The legislation granted mothers the right to appeal to a court for custody of very young children. Judges in equity were given the discretionary authority to issue an order awarding mothers access to their infant children. If the child was under seven years of age, the judge was also given the discretion to award custody to the mother. Adulterous mothers were not entitled to the benefit of the act. Lord Talfourd's Act became the foundation of all English and Canadian legislation on custody.

CANADIAN REACTION TO LORD TALFOURD'S ACT 1839–55

Until the enactment of counterpart legislation in Upper Canada in 1855, Canadian courts struggled with the lack of legislation similar to Lord Talfourd's Act. The first two reported Canadian custody decisions of the century occurred in this period. In *The Queen* v *James Baxter*, a case heard in Toronto in 1846, the child in question was a six-month-old girl in the possession of the mother, who had left her husband's home to seek sanctuary at her father's residence.[21] The evidence indicated that the husband was accused of intemperance resulting in brutal conduct against both his wife and infant daughter. The question at issue was not the custody of the infant but an application for *habeas corpus* brought by the father to request that the court order the infant to be delivered to him. The arguments by both counsel reflected conceptions of legal principles as well as attitudes concerning the proper role of mothering in the care of infants. J. Hillyard Cameron, counsel for the wife, was careful to stress that the child was 'of such a tender age that its mother is its proper guardian.' He argued that it was 'in the discretion of the court to determine with whom the custody of the child should be' on an application for *habeas corpus*, 'there being no rigid or inflexible rule of law on the subject.'[22] Counsel for the husband replied that 'as regards the child ... the father is her legal guardian, and however tender her years may be, and however necessary her mother's care may be to her, the law does not recognize any such reasons for depriving the father of her custody.' The husband's counsel also argued that 'all the authorities that can be cited on the subject of custody of infants recognize the father's right, and under no circumstances will the court interfere, unless there has been ill-usage of the child.'[23]

The court's decision was remarkable, given the unmistakeably clear common law position of primary paternal rights. Chief Justice John Beverley Robinson noted that the 'modern statute' passed in England in 1839 was not in force in this country. However, he was clearly influenced by some of the arguments made by the wife's counsel. He noted that the child was 'an infant of very tender age: not more than seven months old, requiring the tender care of a mother, and whose health if not its life might be endangered by depriving it of that care and of the natural food which the mother supplies to it.'[24] Robinson attempted to balance the attributes of the parties, noting that the father was allegedly intemperate and violent. The mother's habits and character were not impeached, and she was living under her father's roof. The judge clearly wished to see the mother retain possession of the infant. He managed to rationalize his decision to deny the husband's request for possession by distinguishing between a custody award and a denial of a *habeas corpus* application: '[The father] no doubt [is] the person entitled by law to the custody of the child. We are not called upon to deprive him of that right by taking the child from him and giving it to the mother. But what we are asked to do is to force the child from the mother, and place it in the custody of the father. ... We decline ... to take that course.'[25]

The progressive nature of this decision is perhaps surprising in view of Chief Justice Robinson's background and reputation. A leading member of the Family Compact, Robinson was a staunch conservative who detested democracy. The *Upper Canada Law Journal* noted in his obituary that he viewed 'ancient and venerable institutions,' 'respect for rank and family,' 'the power of wealth,' and 'the control of numerous landlords over a grateful tenantry' as part of the essential fabric of a stable society.[26] Essentially distrustful of American experience, Robinson was a firm proponent of British immigration, political institutions, and the maintenance of British constitutional ties with the colonies. This traditionalist cast would seem to suggest a patriarchal view of custody rights rather than a more modern sensitivity to the needs of mothers and children. However, the decision may be explained in part by reference to Robinson's very anglophile position. He had received much of his legal training in England (1815–17) and was present in England conferring on the Durham *Report* when Lord Talfourd's Act was passed.[27] This perhaps explains his familiarity with the English legislation. It is likely, then, that Robinson perceived his decision in *Baxter* as following British example rather than as deliberately progressive or reformist.

Another reported Canadian decision in the first half of the nineteenth century, *In re R.* v *Armstrong*, was heard in Ontario in 1850 and was a less startling decision in view of the time.[28] At issue was an illegitimate daughter living with the putative father. The mother obtained a writ of *habeas corpus* to bring the child before the court and argued for its return to her. She made allegations about the father's destructive character and claimed that he had deprived her of the child through violence and force or fraud. The father alleged that the mother had agreed to relinquish custody of the child to him for the price of ten sovereigns and that he provided for the child's comfortable sustenance. Justice Archibald McLean refused the mother's application. An illegitimate child was *filius nullius* (son of nobody) and could therefore have no legal or natural guardian, 'unless the mother can be so considered from the fact of her having given it birth, and its continuing in her charge and custody.' However, since the mother had chosen to part with her child and to make an arrangement for support with the alleged father, the court would not interfere to assist in breaking up such an arrangement, 'more especially if it appears, as in this case, to be one obviously for the advantage, not only of the child, but of all parties concerned.'[29] The judge viewed the mother's role and corresponding right to custody as minimal. As in *Baxter*, the court observed that the present case was not an application for custody. McLean stated that he was only called upon to relieve the child from illegal or improper custody and he declined to make that order.

In 1855 the legislature of the United Canadas passed legislation for Upper Canada strikingly similar to Lord Talfourd's Act.[30] It gave the court discretion to make an order for access or custody to a mother of infant children in cases where the judge 'saw fit.' The order could not be made in favour of a mother guilty of adultery. However, there were two distinctly different features. The upper age limit for maternal custody was set at twelve years in Upper Canada, whereas seven years was the limit in

England. The courts in Upper Canada were also empowered to order payments for maintenance, a power that did not appear in the English statute. Thus this legislation appeared to duplicate aspects of the English law but took the matter of maternal custody rights further in two significant areas. It is difficult to determine why the Canadian legislation exceeded its English model. There were no recorded debates on the legislation, and the Toronto newspapers of the time carried no discussion. The preamble to the act, where one would hope to find some hint as to the thinking and motivation of the legislators, is of little use. It reads as follows: 'Whereas it is desirable that the law relating to the custody of infant children shall be so amended as to enable the Judge of the Superior Courts of Law or Equity in Upper Canada to give the custody of such children to their mothers, in certain cases.'

One can hypothesize that Canadian legislators, in view of the time-lag between enactment of these statutes, were able to respond more forcefully to changing perceptions of mothering and the role of childhood. When Lord Talfourd's Act was passed, the concept of awarding mothers custody of young infant children was novel, and the age limit of seven was considered sufficient. By 1855 Canadian legislators may have recognized the validity of newer notions pertaining to the lengthening of the childhood stage and the age of twelve may have seemed more realistic. The provision for maintenance payments in addition to custody indicates the legislature's sensitivity to the financial needs of women who were not self-sufficient. For these women, without monetary support from their husbands, custody rights without support would have been relatively meaningless. That this feature should appear in Canada before it did in England indicates that the principle of patriarchal authority was less firmly embedded in fast-developing Upper Canadian society than in the United Kingdom.

TWO OPPOSING VIEWS: JUDICIAL INTERPRETATION OF CUSTODY LEGISLATION 1855–86

Judicial interpretation of the 1855 Upper Canadian statute quickly divided into two camps. An identical split between conservative and progressive approaches had occurred in England over the application of Lord Talfourd's Act.[31] The conservative analysis held that the act had left the legal right of the father intact. Since courts of equity previously had jurisdiction to award custody to mothers within narrow limits, it was held that there should be no change of principles now that the jurisdiction was legislative. For many of the judges who took this approach, this analysis was a thinly veiled attempt to cloak hostility to the legislation. The progressive position contended that the legislature had intended to create a right in the mother, to which the court should give effect in all cases of separation between husband and wife, where she had not been guilty of adultery. The judges associated with this interpretation appear to have been more affected by changing societal attitudes towards childbearing, nurturing, and the role of maternal affection. Although the progressive interpretation was advanced clearly and strongly in a number of cases, the conservative position soon became dominant.

Following closely on the heels of the 1855 legislation, the case of *The Queen* v *Smith & Corbett* illustrated a progressive position in favour of expanding the mother's rights to custody.[32] In 1856 Margaret Corbett and her brother, James Smith, of Toronto responded to a writ of *habeas corpus* before the court, seeking to keep control of Margaret Corbett's infant son. They testified that Margaret had been forced to leave her husband because of his great violence caused by intoxication from 'strong drink.' Corbett stated that she had been subjected to repeated ill treatment, and at one point her husband had thrown her out of the house with her sixteen-month-old infant in her arms. She had taken refuge with her brother, in whose home she now resided. Chief Justice Robinson, speaking in chambers, delivered a short judgment discharging the mother and child and leaving her to decide whether to return with her child to her husband, as she thought proper.[33] While there was no reference to the 1855 legislation in the decision, it would seem that Robinson was again responding positively to the English-influenced legislation extending mothers' rights to custody.

The series of decisions involving the custody of the children of Dr and Mrs William Allen provide the best illustration of competing judicial viewpoints. When the dispute began in 1869, Dr Allen, who was a physician and the mayor of Cornwall, Ontario, had evicted his wife, angered that she had voluntarily given testimony against him at a recent trial.[34] The Allens had three children under the age of twelve: a son aged six years and two daughters aged eight and three years. The older daughter was in the mother's custody with Dr Allen's consent. The dispute was over the custody of the other two children, who were with their father. In 1869 the mother successfully brought an *ex parte* application before Justice Morrison of the court of Queen's Bench for custody of these children under the provisions of the 1855 legislation. Dr Allen failed in an application to rescind the *ex parte* order in front of Morrison, sitting in chambers.[35]

The points raised by each side in argument were illustrative of some of the new attitudes concerning 'mothering' and child nurturing. The mother's counsel argued that Dr Allen, if for no other reason than that he was mayor of Cornwall and so more or less occupied with public duties, was quite incompetent and unfit to take proper and necessary care of the children. It was alleged that the infant daughter was delicate and sickly and that her health was greatly endangered without maternal devotion. Mrs Allen's counsel concluded that 'the children were all tenderly attached to her: that while so deprived of them and under fear of losing the one [child] with her she was compelled to endure the utmost distress of mind and misery.'[36] Dr Allen's counsel asserted that she had voluntarily appeared as a witness in a lawsuit and had given perjured testimony against her husband. Mrs Allen was intemperate, verbally abusive, and neglectful of her motherly responsibilities. Dr Allen's counsel further argued that 'the children were in good health, and not suffering from want of care: that he had ample time to take care of them: that while his wife was living with him the care of the children devolved upon him to a great extent, as their mother was almost always absent ... and that he had engaged a lady of mature age, competent to take charge of the children and his household matters.[37]

Morrison was not convinced by Dr Allen's evidence. He concluded that Mrs Allen had 'been subjected to great cruelty, unhappiness, and misery; and it is almost incredible that she could have lived for any time under the same roof with Dr. Allen, and it is only explicable upon the ground which she herself swears to, and which is corroborated by the members of her family and others, that so strong were her affection and attachment for her children that rather than be separated from them, and be deprived of their society, she suffered, and patiently bore the cruel treatment and misery ...'[38] The judge based his reasoning directly upon the new legislation, pointing out that at common law the father was entitled to the custody of his children. 'Were it not for the eighth and the following sections of the Con. Stat. of U.C., chap. 74, I would not have entertained Mrs Allen's application.' He continued that 'the object and intention of our Legislature was ... to leave the Court or Judge untrammelled by any previous principle or practice of law or equity.'[39] He concluded that it was necessary for the interest and welfare of these children that they be placed under the care and custody of their mother.

After Dr Allen refused to obey the order to hand over the children, Morrison made a finding of contempt against him.[40] At this point Allen appealed from the orders of custody and contempt.[41] His counsel argued that the father was entitled to custody even after the passing of the statute, unless 'a very strong case' was made 'to justify an interference with his rights.'[42] Counsel continued that in this case there was not sufficient reason to remove the children from their father. The majority of the court of Queen's Bench, with Morrison in dissent, overruled the original award of custody to Mrs Allen. Justice Adam Wilson recounted at some length the common law rules regarding custody, noting that 'at common law there is no authority to remove children from their father's custody for any cause whatever.'[43] Although he made note of the passage of the new legislation, Wilson seemed swayed primarily by the traditional common law position. In his view the new legislation had been of little effect: 'The general policy of the law with reference to father and child was not altered by recent legislation ... The statute controls the paternal rights; but if his marital duty and the interests of his child can be secured consistently with his retaining the custody of his children, his common law rights will not be interfered with.'[44] Chief Justice William B. Richards, while he did not delve into the implications of the 1855 statute, agreed with Wilson's conclusion. Recognizing the seriousness of depriving a father of custody of his children and expressing a judicial hesitation to exercise that power, he concluded that the original award of custody to the mother could not be sustained, considering the material upon which it was granted.[45]

Morrison dissented vigorously. Reiterating his earlier opinion, he stated that the statute conferred upon the judge absolute jurisdiction as to the custody of infants, leaving them untrammelled by any previous principle of law or equity. He argued that the Upper Canadian statute was more comprehensive than the imperial statute from which it was drawn, both in its preamble and in giving judges the authority to award maintenance. The decision in each case should be left wholly to the discretion of the judge. 'In the case of a father living separate from his wife,' Morrison stated, 'his rights are only conditional as against the mother, I may say only concurrent.'[46] The mother should be awarded custody if it would be for the general benefit and interests of the infant, if she were living apart because of her husbands' compulsion, and if her purity of life was unimpeached. Furthermore, Morrison heartily approved of the new legislation:

> Happily, in the interests of humanity, our Legislature has broken in upon the Common Law principles which deprived the wife of nearly every right, and among others the right to look after her infant children, 'adopting' (as Mr. Macpherson in his treatise on Infants, c. 16, remarks) 'the opinion that those rights

fell short of what natural feeling and public policy demanded,' principles which sprang from a state of society quite different from that of the present day, and under cover of which much injustice and heart-rending cruelty was perpetrated.[47]

In view of the progressive stance taken by Morrison in this case, it is of some interest to outline his career. Born in Ireland in 1816, Joseph Curran Morrison emigrated to Canada sometime in the 1820s. His mother died while he was still young and his father remarried. Upon his father's death in 1834, Joseph became involved in a dispute with his stepmother over the division of the estate. As a result the children from the first marriage all left their stepmother, and Joseph at age eighteen became the head of a household consisting of four younger brothers and sisters. This early family disruption may in part account for his later sensitivity to the problems facing families involved in custody disputes. Called to the bar in 1839, Morrison had a prominent political and legal career, sitting as a member of parliament in the Reform interest during the Baldwin-LaFontaine administration, the Hincks administration, and serving as Solicitor General during the Cartier-Macdonald 'coalition' administration. As a moderate reformer in the 1840s and 1850s Morrison espoused many progressive goals, including the establishment of a public school system and extension of the franchise. Appointed a puisne judge of the Common Pleas in 1862 and to the Queen's Bench in 1863, Morrison developed a reputation as a judge based on his understanding of human nature. An obituary in the *Canada Law Journal* expressed doubts whether the 'reasons for his judgments were always sound,' but paid tribute to Morrison, concluding that he was 'singularly correct in the result.'[48]

In summary, the *Allen* cases illustrate the two diverse interpretations of the 1855 legislation. The progressive position, as adopted by Morrison, was that the legislation created a right in the mother to which the court should give effect in all cases of separation where the wife was not guilty of criminal or immoral conduct. According to this view the legislation created a positive right of access and custody in the mother, and the interest of the children was the only consideration which could be allowed to interfere with the mother's right. The opposite and more conservative approach, adopted by the majority, was that the new legislation did not interfere with the common law right of the father to sole custody of infant children, at least not so far as to have destroyed that right. Instead the legislation had introduced new elements and considerations under which that right was to be exercised.

In re Leigh, heard in Toronto in 1871, the same year as the final decision in *Allen,* provided another interpretation of the effect of the 1855 Ontario statute.[49] Justice John U. Gwynne's view was much closer to the majority opinion in *Allen* than to Morrison's dissent. '[A] judge, in the exercise of the discretion conferred by the Act, is bound to recognize the common law right of the father, and should not assume to impair or interfere with that right, so long as the father fails not in the due discharge of his marital duties.'[50] In this case the mother sought custody of her four-year-old daughter, alleging repeated acts of verbal and physical cruelty attributable to fits of insanity on the part of her husband. The husband denied these charges. Gwynne concluded that he should not disturb the father's right to custody. He told the mother that she had failed to satisfy him that she had any excuse for leaving her husband's home or her duties as a wife: 'I cannot do otherwise than discharge the application, without incurring the danger of giving rise to a belief in ignorant minds that the duties of the married state are less obligatory upon the wife than upon the husband.'[51]

In another Ontario decision, *In re Carswell* (1875), Gwynne again had an opportunity to consider the interpretation of the 1855 statute.[52] The children in question were a six-year-old girl and four-year-old boy. The wife alleged that due to domestic quarrels caused by the improper conduct and personal cruelty of her husband, she had been forced to leave the marital home with her children. She claimed that her husband was not fit to superintend the religious training of the children because of his dangerous and fanatical religious views. He subscribed to the religious sect called the 'new Jerusalem Church' or 'Swedenborgians' and was in the habit of urging this faith 'in season and out of season with the impressiveness and ardour of all recent converts.'[53] Gwynne nevertheless ordered the custody of the infant children to the father. He discussed common law principles at length with specific concentration on the supremacy of paternal rights. His preoccupation with the common law indicated a basic antipathy to the 1855 statute. Gwynne concluded, as he had done in *In re Leigh,* by advising the couple to forget their past differences and to come together to live in accordance with the vows they had taken as man and wife. Perhaps hoping that this decision would promote marital harmony, he gave the father custody of the children.

The case of *In re Kinney* (1875) dealt with the custody of a seven-year-old girl, the daughter of parents domiciled in the United States.[54] The parents lived apart from each other and were engaged in a divorce action on the grounds of adultery and extreme cruelty. The father placed the child in the custody of a Mr Henry who was living in the township of Clinton, Huron county, Ontario. The husband next launched a prosecution against the person whom he alleged had had criminal intercourse with his wife. Mrs Kinney alleged that her husband had offered to settle all their differences if she would sign a paper releasing all her rights to the child. He told her this was necessary to get the child back from Canada and that he would destroy the document when they were all living together once more. Reluctantly she signed, and he then attempted to use the document as evidence in the proceedings. Mrs Kinney applied to an Ontario court to obtain the child on the ground that by the law of the state of Michigan, their domicile, she was entitled to custody. Justice Adam Wilson determined that he must make his judgment conform to the law of Michigan, subject to the general principles of Ontario law. The applicable Michigan law was that the mother was *prima facie* (on the face of it) entitled to the custody of infant children within the age of twelve years when she was living separate from her husband, subject to the right of the court to interfere with and remove the child from her custody for cause.[55] In Wilson's opinion, the fact that allegations of adultery had been made against the mother and that she had renounced her rights to custody by giving her child up to her husband's care, constituted 'cause' to defeat the mother's application. He also made an interesting comparison between the Michigan and Ontario laws: 'If I had decided the case according to our own law affecting our own local cases, by which the father is entitled to the custody of his children, and is not to be deprived of them unless a very strong case is established against him, I should not have had the least difficulty in discharging the application.'[56] However, Wilson also made an interesting side comment about the nature of maternal care. He expressed a hope that the mother would not be denied access completely: 'There is a law of nature which no other law is able to repress, and which it would be unreasonable, perhaps almost cruel to enforce in its full rigour even if it should be proved that an unpardonable fault has been committed by her.'[57]

THE JUDICIARY AND THE LEGISLATURE: DIFFERING RESPONSES TO CUSTODY ISSUES

With several notable exceptions, it seems clear that as compared with the legislature the Ontario judiciary took a cautious stance on the issue of expanding mother's rights to custody. It is difficult to provide any definite explanation why this situation developed. That Canadian courts were reluctant to innovate and slow to respond to changing societal needs has been noted in other areas of law.[58] It has been suggested that this conservatism may have been based on Canadian reliance on English precedents which retarded the development of a creative judiciary.[59] While this may account for some of the conservatism in custody law, the likelier explanation is that most of the judiciary were unsympathetic to the notion of increased rights for mothers to the custody of their children. The majority of the reported decisions during this period illustrate a desire to preserve patriarchal control and a reluctance to undermine the father's authority in the family.

The response of the Ontario courts can be contrasted with that of American courts during a similar time span. Jamil S. Zainaldin, who has written the seminal work on nineteenth-century American custody law, has divided developments in the nineteenth century into three stages.[60] In the first third American courts 'exhibited high regard for the welfare of the child in the resolution of custody contests, and a disposition to view the family more as a copartnership than a corporate entity defined by patriarchy.'[61] Courts used their judicial discretion and increasingly declined to enforce the father's common law right to custody. They based their decisions on a sensitivity to the changing notions of childhood and family.[62] Robert H. Bremner has suggested that this 'modern' trend, well in advance of the English and Canadian situation, may in part be explained by the democratic nature of American society: 'the hierarchical family, reaching to its apex in the father, was undermined and finally leveled by the force of democratic social principles.'[63]

Zainaldin views the 1830s as a conservative decade for custody law, despite the fact that it was the great decade of so-called 'Jacksonian democracy.' The courts curtailed the use of their own discretionary authority and reinforced the presumption of patriarchy.[64] Only a clear-cut case of unfitness would permit an intrusion upon the father's common law rights.[65] Zainaldin asserts that the American courts during this decade were significantly influenced by English cases. Attorneys for fathers referred regularly in their arguments to English decisions from the first decade of the nineteenth century.[66] In the third phase, which began in the 1840s and continued throughout the century, state courts began to rediscover their earlier, more liberal precedents. This was due in some part to initiatives by state legislatures, which began to formalize the earlier liberal rulings of the state courts: 'New York, Massachusetts, Georgia and Mississippi amended laws governing divorce and judicial separation to provide for the exercise of judicial discretion in custody matters. The lawmakers equalized the maternal and paternal rights of guardianship, in the absence of misconduct, and instructed the court to attend only to the welfare of the child.'[67]

American courts seem to have responded to changing notions of childhood and motherhood at an earlier point than contemporary Canadian courts. The first third of the century witnessed more court intervention on behalf of the mother than was seen in English Canada at a comparable period. The 1830s, when American courts seemed drawn to English precedent, may mirror the Canadian situation of the time to a greater extent than either before or after. By the 1840s and 1850s American courts again seem to have outpaced their Canadian counterparts in the equalizing of maternal and paternal rights. The legislation enacted by a number of states seems much more progressive than any comparable Canadian or English legislation. As well it is highly significant that the primary impetus in this direction came from the courts, with only occasional statutory assistance from the legislatures. This contrasts with the Canadian situation where the judges in the main seem to have been opposed to increased custody rights for women and even reacted unsympathetically when the legislature did take a leading role in developing a more liberal approach to the subject.

Why did the Ontario legislature initiate legislation improving the status of mothers with respect to custody rights? It appears that the lawmakers, far more than the judiciary, were responding to changing societal notions of parenting and maternal rights. The elected politicians were more responsive to societal change than appointed judges; and the Canadian judiciary as well may have been less willing to respond to change than many of their American counterparts who were, after all, elected. Furthermore, as more Canadians moved to towns and cities, and as the demands of an emerging industrialized society were felt, the changing nature of family life was increasingly recognized. Sex role differentiation was accentuated as men left the home to take wage labour jobs, leaving women behind with the responsibility of raising young children.[68] Motherhood began to take on an almost sacred quality during the later nineteenth century. According to Ann Douglas, the cult of domesticity arose in part to take the place of the void left when economic production moved out of the home: 'Praise of motherhood could bolster and promote the middle-class woman's biological function as tantamount, if not superior, to her lost economic productivity.'[69]

These economic changes had as dramatic an impact upon children as on women. The modern notion of childhood as a distinct stage of development was a concept that did not exist in pre-industrial society.[70] Instead children were distinguished from adults primarily by their dependence: 'As soon as the child could live without the constant solicitude of his mother, his nanny, or his cradle-rocker, he belonged to adult society. On the other hand, the infant still requiring this attention ... was treated by grown-ups with "indifference." Too fragile as yet to take part in the life of adults, the infant simply "did not count".'[71] The prevailing notion of family relations was that of authority. The wife was to obey the husband and the child was to be subservient to the parents. The parent served as a patron, supplying the economic and status needs of the child. During the course of the nineteenth century, however, a new understanding of the role of family and childhood took hold.[72] The rise of commercial capitalism isolated the family and created an historically new sphere of personal life. Eli Zaretsky has claimed that the family now became the major space in society in which the individual could be valued 'for itself.'[73] Correspondingly, 'childhood was assigned a separate identity and exalted as the time of life untainted by the roughness of material necessity.'[74] Christopher Lasch has written of the startling changes in attitudes towards children: 'No longer seen simply as a little adult, the child comes to be regarded as a person with distinct attributes – impressionability, vulnerability, innocence – which required a warm, protected and prolonged period of nurture.'[75] Economic conditions permitted the lengthening and elevation of childhood at exactly the time when women were relegated to the role of wife and mother.

These changing perceptions provide the background of attitude and *mentalité* which help explain why Ontario legislators sought to amend the traditional law of custody. The politicians of the 1870s recognized that the legal positon of women must be brought more into line with their growing responsibilities in the home. During this decade legislatures in England and Ontario enacted new statutes expanding mothers' rights to custody. It might be inferred that this activity was a legislative response to the narrowly conservative interpretation that the courts had given to earlier legislation. In 1873 the British Parliament extended the seven-year-cut-off mark for Lord Talfourd's Act to sixteen years.[76] This legislation also legalized separation agreements which gave custody to the mother, provided that it was also for the benefit of the infant. In 1878 English legislation gave the courts the authority to award custody and maintenance for infants under the age of ten years to non-adulterous mothers who had been assaulted by their husbands.[77] Ontario legislation passed in 1877 provided that mothers could be appointed as guardians to minors upon the death of the father.[78]

By the 1880s there was some indication of a shift in judicial decision-making on custody issues. Although elements of this change in judicial thinking had emerged in earlier cases, by the 1880s more members of the judiciary were recognizing and articulating new attitudes towards parenting. The Ontario case of *Re Ferguson* in 1881 illustrated a departure from the notion of quasi-property paternal rights over children.[79] Upon the death of his wife, the father had left a three-year-old son with his grandmother, who was living with her brother-in-law. The father later sought an order for custody which the court refused, noting the comfortable circumstances of the grandmother and the care and affection with which she regarded the infant. The father had suffered a severe attack of paralysis which had affected both his physical and mental capacities. He was also without means of support. The court noted that the father's infirmities 'disable him from discharging those duties and kindly offices which the law regards as the foundation whereon rests the parent's right to claim the custody of his offspring.'[80] The court concluded that while the father was in this state, it should consider what was best for the interest of the child and treat as suspended any superior claim which the father might otherwise have to recover possession of the infant.[81] The focus on the infant's best interests represented a new direction. The rights of parents were recognized as resting upon the discharge of duties and kindly offices towards the child. While this case had unusual features due to the father's illness, a new way of thinking about the question of custody nevertheless appeared to be emerging. It is perhaps difficult to suggest that the court's treatment of this disabled father illustrated a new trend towards paternal rights to custody. However, it is often in the unusual cases that judges first begin to articulate new concepts which later took root in a more general sense.

Another Ontario decision in 1882, *In re Murdoch*, further illustrated changing judicial perceptions about parenting.[82] The case concerned the custody of a five-year-old girl who was in the possession of her mother. The parents had separated, and the mother had moved to her own father's home, taking the child with her. On a writ of *habeas corpus* the father contested the question of custody. Justice Featherston Osler, quoting from a number of English decisions, first gave consideration to the application of the 1855 Ontario legislation:

> Where it is for the interest of a child to be with its mother, it is hard towards the child that the mother should not have her, whatever may be the cause of the difficulty between the parents; but if the father's conduct towards his wife and children is shewn to have been open to no imputation, if the wife has left him from mere caprice and wilfulness, and the Court is satisfied of that, the father's common law right to the custody of his child seems to be recognized since the Act as before.[83]

The wife argued that she had left her husband because of his unfounded charge of adultery against her. Although Osler noted that there were well-founded suspicions concerning the husband's infidelity, a clear double standard was operating in relation to custody decisions. The judge stated that if the wife was shown to have been guilty, not even of actual unfaithfulness but even of any grave indiscretion, he would be compelled to hold that she was unfit for the custody of the child, 'more especially so when that child is a female.'[84] Osler concluded that the wife was not guilty of adultery, however, and found that while that charge remained unretracted she was justified in living apart from her husband. Revealing much of the new attitudes towards mothering and parental responsibilities, he awarded custody to the mother:

> I am satisfied it will be more for the interests of the child, a little girl four or five years old, to remain in the custody of the mother than in that of a father, however affectionate and kind, whose business engagements and frequent absences from the home render it impossible for him to afford the constant care and attention which a child of such tender years demands.[85]

In re Coram, while not a custody dispute between a father and mother, illustrated some of the conflicting tensions between the notion of a quasi-property paternal right over children and the newly emerging concept of 'the interests of the child.' This was a New Brunswick case heard in 1886, in which a father, being in poor circumstances, had left his seven-year-old daughter with her uncle and aunt.[86] The understanding was that she should be considered as their child and that they should support and educate her. She remained with her uncle and aunt until she was nearly fifteen years old, when her father attempted to regain custody. Apparently the child's mother was in poor health, and her father's main interest in wanting her home was to provide assistance with the housekeeping. The child seemingly was better off with her aunt and uncle, who maintained a much more comfortable home. She was greatly attached to her uncle and aunt and expressed a desire to remain with them.

The majority of the New Brunswick court decided that the girl's father was entitled to custody, starting with the presumption that the father had an absolute right to custody until the children reached sixteen, unless it appeared that 'their safety or welfare would be endangered by being in his custody.[87] The young girl had obtained a very comfortable position with her uncle and aunt, and the court noted that it would be a hardship to take her away from her luxurious surroundings to the humbler house of her parents. However, this was not 'according to the recent cases ... any reason for depriving her father of his legal right.'[88] The court stated that while it should also consider what was most beneficial for the child, 'it is not enough to justify the interference with a parent's rights, that it would not merely be better for the child, but that it would be essential to its safety or welfare that it should not be given into the custody of its parent.'[89] The majority added that the girl should be taught a wholesome lesson in the duty of children to their parents and be required to go to the assistance of her mother who was in ill health.[90] The dissenting judges expressed the opposite position: 'it will not be for the interest of the child that the father should exercise his right of custody in this case ... which will force her into a different position in life from that which education and the habits she has acquired has led her to believe that she would occupy.'[91] The dissent argued that the power of the parent over the child was a qualified one, only given to enable them to discharge correlative duties. The principal issue was the welfare of the child.[92]

EQUALIZING TRENDS AND THE INTERESTS OF THE CHILD FROM 1886 TO THE END OF THE NINETEENTH CENTURY

These judicial decisions indicate that by the 1880s Canadian judges were beginning to appreciate the need for greater custody rights for mothers. The recognition was late in coming, and in the minds of the legislators at least, the judges were still too cautious in their approach. The years 1886 and 1887 marked the legislative high-water mark for custody issues in both England and Canada. The English Guardianship of Infants Act enacted in 1886 expanded the right of a mother to be appointed guardian upon her husband's death and to appoint others as guardian.[93] The most important provision of the new legislation, however, related to disputes concerning custody and access between living parents. In an attempt to put the position of mothers and fathers on a more equal footing, the legislation provided that the court could make 'such order as it may think fit regarding the custody of such infant and the right of access thereto of either parent, having regard to the welfare of the infant, and to the conduct of the parents, and to the wishes as well of the mother as of the father.' The period during which a mother could seek custody was extended from sixteen to twenty-one years of age.

The Ontario legislature soon followed this lead and in 1887 enacted An Act respecting the Guardianship of Minors.[94] The speed with which Ontario moved to duplicate the English legislation indicated a reduced time-lag compared with the earlier enactments. The explanation for this may be that Canadian social development was beginning to catch up with that in England, and the legislators perceived the need for such legislation more quickly. The Ontario legislation reproduced the provisions of the English statute relating to the appointment of guardians and adopted a new test for custody and access in terms virtually identical to the English statute. Prior to the passage of these acts, the situation in both England and Ontario had been that a judge was authorized to make orders concerning custody and access, awarding such to the mother 'as he shall see fit.' The new test required judges to consider 'the welfare of the infant,' 'the conduct of the parents,' and 'the wishes as well of the mother as of the father.' Given the wording of the last phrase, it appears that the legislatures felt that the courts had been giving too much regard to the wishes of the father. More certainly, the focus on the interests of the child was a truly significant new direction. It reflected a change in attitude from a sense of children as representing a form of property to an explicit examination of the duties and responsibilities of parents. It also reflected changing notions about childhood.

The Ontario legislation, introduced by the Honourable A.S. Hardy, does not seem to have been the subject of recorded debate in the legislature. A brief summary of the act was contained in the Toronto *Globe*'s 'Assembly Notes,' but it was not discussed in the newspaper editorials of the time, nor in the debates of the House as reported in the press.[95] Given the lack of public interest this reflects, one can only speculate as to why the legislature enacted this statute. The passage of this legislation came at a time when women's rights were a topic of great discussion in the legislature and elsewhere. Issues such as married women's property rights and the franchise were seen as extremely controversial, whereas custody legislation seems to have been an issue upon which there was some consensus. In fact, the *Canada Law Journal* simply described the new Ontario legislation as follows: 'This Act, which appears to be based on a recent English Statute, very properly gives the mother a voice in the custody of her children ...'[96] The *Law Journal* regretted that the legislation was not retroactive: 'why this particular class of children [those on behalf of whom custody application had been made before the passage of the Act] should be deprived of the benefit of the Act is not very easy to divine.'[97]

This consensus doubtless was based in large measure on the economic and social changes Ontario was undergoing. As those who spoke and wrote about women's proper sphere in the nineteenth century increasingly idealized motherhood and domesticity, it came to be seen as not only natural but essential to grant women greater authority over children and household matters. Changing perceptions about children's needs naturally necessitated a far greater emphasis on the mode of their upbringing. Some Canadians began to argue strongly that societal welfare was intricately linked with the health of the family unit, and middle class social reformers began to suggest new notions about how character was formed. Environment and example came to be viewed as critical in the development of upstanding citizens. J.J. Kelso, a Toronto *World* reporter and one of the leaders of the child-saving movement in Toronto, argued that modern society was experiencing an increase in criminality, much of it due 'to the neglect of child-training in the homes of vice and drunkenness.' To remedy this, Kelso urged that the standards of home life must be raised.[98] The Reverend Albert Carman, a general superintendent of the Methodist Church, reflected similar views from a somewhat different perspective. Children who were properly reared, he explained, would 'come forth holy, earnest, well-informed Christian men and women; multitudes better equipped for the great struggle than their fathers; better furnished in a godly understanding and instructed mind.'[99]

As Canadians became more convinced of the significance of environmental influences on children, mothers were taught that how they reared their youngsters at home controlled what sorts of citizens they would become. They were cautioned to take great care that the physical, spiritual, and educational setting was well suited to this nurturing. The future of society as a whole was deemed to be at stake.[100] Neil Sutherland has summed up this concern:

> To ensure that their offspring would live their adult lives in a satisfactory social environment, they had to interest themselves in how all the young in their society were brought up. Thus these concerned Canadians did not view the family as a sentimental end in itself, but as a means; it was the social agency that had the prime responsibility for ensuring that the whole of the next generation represented the best that Canadian society could produce.[101]

In this spirit large numbers of 'inspirational' tracts were published to urge women on to even greater endeavours as mothers. In 1890 the Reverend B.F. Austin, a leading Methodist minister, published his *Woman: Her Character, Culture and Calling*. Widely circulated in Canada and the United States, Austin's tract contained a strong affirmation of female domesticity. Describing women's role in nation-building, the publication stated: 'What is to be the physical character of the nation? ... Whether we shall be a strong, pure, intellectual people depends most of all upon our women, and their just apprehension of all the possibilities attaching to the holy office of motherhood.'[102] Growing recognition of motherhood, coupled with the need to 'mould' children, were the prime factors motivating legislatures to insist that judges give more consideration to maternal custody rights.

Although politicians took the initiative in Canada, the judiciary finally began to respond to these changing ideas. Increasingly courts showed themselves more willing to award custody to mothers. *Re Dickson Infants* was the first case to consider the newly enacted Ontario legislation of 1887.[103] In 1888 the father brought a writ of *habeas corpus* to compel the delivery of his two infant children, aged three and five, from his wife. The court found it an easy matter to refuse to award custody to the father under the new legislation. The judge concluded that the father was a man of drunken habits, that he had on more than one occasion beaten his wife, that she was justified in leaving him on account of his ill treatment, and that his habits rendered him unfit to have charge of the children. The mother meanwhile appeared to be a moral and sober woman who was living with her own mother and was capable of maintaining the children in a proper manner. Applying the new legislative test, 'the welfare of the infant, the conduct of the parents, and the wishes as well of the mother as of the father,' the court awarded custody to the mother, basing its opinion upon the 'enlarged' and 'simplified' powers granted to the courts under the 1887 statute.[104]

One of the most significant custody decisions of the century involved a dispute between David Smart, a barrister and solicitor who resided in Port Hope, and Emilie Ardelia Smart, his wife, over their three children, two girls and one boy, all under the age of twelve. In a series of decisions issued between 1886 and 1892 the question of custody was reviewed by a succession of courts and appealed through the Ontario Court of Appeal to the Privy Council in England.[105] The parties married in 1874 and had three children born before 1880. Until 1883 the family resided in Port Hope, where David Smart engaged in the practice of law. Due to her husband's habitual drunkenness, Emilie Smart left home in 1883 with her children. Being independently wealthy, she moved to Toronto, supporting herself and her children. In 1884, upon the signing of a written agreement, the Smarts agreed to resume living together. David promised to stop drinking and Emilie agreed to pay his debts of $8000 and to maintain the entire household and family in Toronto out of her own funds. The agreement further provided that should David Smart return to his intemperate habits, Emilie would be at liberty to live apart from him and would get exclusive custody of the children under the obligation to maintain them. In 1885 David again began to drink. Emilie immediately instituted a suit to obtain custody according to the agreement, which led to a second agreement, signed 23 November 1885, wherein Emilie covenanted to maintain and educate the children at her own expense with provisions for their religious upbringing, their residence in Toronto, and for her husband's access to them.

In Ontario, agreements by a father to part with the custody of his children remained illegal at common law, since the province, unlike England, had not passed legislation legalizing such separation agreements. As a result in June 1886 David Smart applied for the custody of his three children. He charged his wife with unchaste, depraved, and abnormal habits but failed to furnish specific evidence. He did lead evidence from the testimony of Emilie's midwife that his wife had contracted 'base habits.' At trial, Justice Thomas Ferguson determined that David Smart's allegations had no foundation in fact. Due to his cruelty, the judge reasoned that he had made it impossible for his wife to live with him. Custody was awarded to Emilie Smart. The Ontario Court of Appeal accepted the trial findings, though the judges had some difficulty concluding that David Smart's drunken habits were by themselves a justification for depriving him of his children. Given his additional false accusations, they affirmed the judgment of the first court. Justice George W. Burton dissented, stating that Emilie Smart was not justified in leaving her husband on account of his drunkenness, and that the accusations did not serve to alter the father's right to custody.

The Judicial Committee of Privy Council affirmed the decision of the majority of the Court of Appeal. While the Law Lords noted that the facts were such that they would likely have granted custody to the mother, even if the case had occurred earlier in the century, the decision clearly reflected changing societal views. The Judicial Committee stated:

> For many years the tendency of legislative action and of judicial decision, as well as of general opinion, has been to give to married women a higher status both as regards property and person, and in family questions, to bring the marital duty of the husband and the welfare of the children into greater prominence, in both respects diminishing the powers accorded to the husband and the father.[106]

The Judicial Committee explicitly recognized that these social changes were altering judicial decision-making. They remarked that no one could state in other than elastic terms the grounds on which the Judicial Committee should think fit to interfere: 'There must be a sufficient amount of peril to the welfare of the children. But that sufficient amount can hardly be fixed for one age by the standards of another.' Focusing on David Smart's intemperance, the Judicial Committee concluded: 'Drunkenness, for instance, is looked upon as a much graver social offence now than was the case two or three generations ago, and its effects upon the welfare of a family must be judged accordingly.' A custody judgment must in its essence be a discretionary one, 'guided by views on social and domestic matters absolutely incapable of being brought under legal rules and definitions.' Nevertheless the Judicial Committee pointed to changing social perceptions: 'The course of legislation distinctly shews a growing sense that the power formerly accorded by law to fathers of families was excessive, and that the welfare of the children required that it should be cut down.'[107]

The *Smart* case was clearly a high point in judicial recognition of changing societal expectations. The Judicial Committee of the Privy Council as the legal tribunal of last resort articulated its conscious perceptions of the new social mores and views and pointed out that judicial decisions must reflect societal trends. The court acknowledged the diminishing power of the father, but it is not completely clear whether the main driving force for this change was an increase in women's rights or a more modern view of the needs of children. The Judicial Committee did refer to the trend towards giving married women higher status, but the focus of the discussion seemed to highlight the welfare of the children.

During the last decade of the nineteenth century there was another flurry of legislative change. Three other Canadian provinces followed Ontario's lead and enacted legislation to equalize maternal and paternal rights to some degree. New Brunswick enacted The Supreme Court in Equity Act in 1890, which gave the court discretion to award custody to a mother of infants up the age of sixteen years.[108] The test to be used was different from the 1886 English and 1887 Ontario tests. The court was specifically directed that in custody or access applications, 'it shall be the duty of the Court to take into consideration the interests of such infant ... in deciding between the claims of the parents of such infant ...' There was no adultery 'rider' attached to this legislation, as was the case with the counterpart English legislation, Lord Talfourd's Act of 1839. Separation agreements regarding custody were not made specifically enforceable, as in the 1873 English legislation. There was no explicit authority to award maintenance against the father.

In 1893 the Nova Scotia legislature passed An Act respecting the

Custody of Infants.[109] This statute, more closely than its New Brunswick counterpart, duplicated the English legislation. Courts were authorized to award custody to mothers of infants up to the age of majority. The test was 'the welfare of the infants, the conduct *or circumstances* of the parents, and the wishes of the mother as well as of the father.' The additional factor of 'the circumstances of the parents' was a novel feature, not seen elsewhere in Canada or England at this time. Mothers were given some authority with respect to the appointment of guardians and the responsibility of acting as a guardian, and maintenance orders were authorized. Finally, separation agreements concerning custody matters were made enforceable provided they operated for the benefit of the infant involved.

British Columbia was the fourth Canadian province to pass custody legislation in the nineteenth century. In 1897 the legislature passed An Act to Consolidate and Amend the Law relating to the Custody and Care of Infants.[110] This legislation was considerably less far-reaching than the enactments in Ontario, New Brunswick, or Nova Scotia. The position of the father with respect to guardianship was supreme. The statute authorized the father of unmarried children under twenty-one, by deed executed in his lifetime or by his last will and testament, in such manner and from time to time as he should think fit, to dispose of the custody of his children. There was no mention of a mother's right in this regard. The act basically re-enacted Lord Talfourd's Act, bringing British Columbia to the position of English law of 1839. The upper age limit for maternal custody was only seven years, and the test used by the court to determine whether to grant access or custody to the mother was the broad discretionary one of 1839 rather than the more explicitly equal balancing test between the mother and father enacted in the 1886 English legislation. In addition, the act provided that no order for custody or access should be made on behalf of a mother who had been proven guilty of adultery.

This flurry of provincial legislation may have represented a pattern of colonial imitation of the mother country. In part, however, these provinces may also have been reacting to the enactment of custody legislation in other Canadian provinces. Despite this imitative character, each of the statutes exhibited distinctions and new features which may have reflected different social and cultural situations prevalent in the several provinces at this time.[111] The enactment of these statutes can also be viewed as a more generalized response to the developing cult of motherhood, childhood, and domesticity. Such thinking was actively advanced by the newly emerging voluntary women's organizations of the time. In 1893 many such groups organized together to form the National Council of Women of Canada. The major goal was the support of women as home-makers. The Council's founders believed that the family was being weakened by industrialization and urbanization. The father had been removed from the home into the corrupt business world. Dominated by materialistic values and male management, the industrial world was contaminating family life. Lady Aberdeen, the wife of the Governor General and one of the founders of the Council, saw women in this critical situation as divinely appointed guardians of the family, an institution which in its nurturing of the virtues of kindness, love, duty, respect, and honour was essential to human development.[112] The Toronto *Globe* described the Council's mission as follows: 'Working with God's laws of the family,' women were 'the centre through which all healthy influence should spread.'[113] The link between the cult of motherhood and increasing rights of mothers to child custody had become obvious to these women's associations as well as to the legislators who enacted these statutes on custody.

Custody legislation in Canada presented a rather diverse picture by the end of the century, and judicial decisions in various provinces during the 1890s reflected this diversity. In *Re Foulds*, a Manitoba case heard in 1893, the court awarded custody to the father based largely on the strong paternal rights found at common law.[114] *In the Matter of Ethel Davis*, an 1894 Ontario decision, awarded custody to the mother in circumstances where a Manitoba court would likely have granted custody to the father.[115] Similarly, the court in *Re Young* (1898), operating within the framework of the progressive Ontario legislation, awarded custody to the mother.[116] Two New Brunswick cases seem to stand out as anomalies: *In re Annie E. Hatfield* (1895) and *In re Armstrong* (1895).[117] In both cases custody was awarded to the father, with the court either ignoring the effect of the New Brunswick Equity Act, or refusing to change its decision, based on common law reasoning, due to the weakness of the legislation. Paternal rights still seemed to be paramount in this province, at least as articulated by these decisions.

The power of the judiciary clearly stands out as an overriding theme in the history of Canadian custody law. It is not clear to what extent the judges based their decisions directly upon the relevant legislation or whether they simply awarded custody in the manner they saw fit, regardless of legislative dictates. Some courts seemed willing to take cognizance of changing societal attitudes about maternal rights and the needs of children, despite the absence of statutory direction. Other judges disregarded legislation, maintaining that the common law position was virtually unchanged.

Nevertheless some changes in Canadian custody law seem clear insofar as they can be traced through the legislative enactments and reported decisions. While the pattern was not a straight-line progression, and there are anomalous decisions and statutes sprinkled throughout, custody awards underwent an obvious transformation in the nineteenth century. From a position of complete and unquestioned supremacy, paternal rights were restricted and concern for maternal rights correspondingly began to intervene.

A great many questions still remain unanswered. How frequent were divorces and separations in this time period? How common was it to be involved in a custody dispute? Under which circumstances did litigation of this type arise? What was the outcome of custody cases below the level of reported decisions? When there was no legal hearing, how were custody arrangements handled? Who normally kept custody of children in actual practice? How frequently did parties simply desert their spouses, leaving them with the children? Did the spouse who obtained custody through the legal process or otherwise keep that custody or were children often farmed out to relatives? What use was made of institutions to care for such children? When fathers received custody, did they often resort to domestic servants or housekeepers to care for such children? What of fathers who obtained custody but lacked the economic ability to hire help?

One additional social theme emerged before the end of the nineteenth century, that of the state's right to custody. Domesticity and a heightening of women's role in the home challenged the authority of the father inside the family. Inherent in the redistribution of paternal power and in the new concept of responsibilities parents owed to children was a diminishing of parental rights in general. Once questions about custody shifted from a quasi-property analysis to consideration of parental nurturing ability, the welfare of the infant became the new test. Custody disputes now required state intervention. As the state took on this responsibility, judges began to query whether in the interests of the child, it might have to be removed from both parents' custody. State custody emerged as a new issue and one which gained increasingly in importance as the nineteenth century yielded to the twentieth.

Legislative enactments and judicial decisions awarding custody to a state or a charitable institution instead of to the parent did not in fact emerge with any strength in Canada until after the turn of the century. However, hints of things to come did appear before that time. In 1891 the British Parliament passed An Act to amend the Law relating to the Custody of Children, which authorized courts to refuse custody to a parent who had 'abandoned or deserted' a child.[118] Courts were also given the power, in the case of children who had been brought up by another person or by an institution, to order a person who was applying for custody to repay such person or institution for the costs of bringing up the child. This legislation began a trend, which was to be evidenced in Canada in the early twentieth century, towards protecting the rights of institutions and foundling homes over the rights of parents. Statutes passed in New Brunswick, Ontario, and Nova Scotia refused custody to parents who abandoned their children and awarded custody of these infants to charitable institutions.[119] Most of the judicial interpretation of these Canadian statutes involved racial minority parents and children. Of the six reported decisions on this issue in the latter part of the nineteenth century, four involved either Chinese or native Indian parents and children.[120]

These decisions evidence the growing authority of the state, extending to deprive 'unfit' parents of custody of their children. R.E. Kingsford, a barrister and solicitor in Toronto and author in 1896 of *Blackstone's Commentaries Adapted to Ontario*, wrote glowingly of the benefits of this new legal development: 'This new branch of jurisprudence is only in its initiatory stages, but already the results are satisfactory. Unworthy parents may be deprived of their children and foster homes may be sought out and children may be sent there by order of a police magistrate ... Children's aid societies in a municipality, when formed, are given extensive powers of interference. Great hopes are entertained that this long-felt want is at last in the way of being supplied.'[121] In part this new focus on the welfare of the child was a direct result of equalizing trends of mothers' and fathers' rights to custody. As maternal rights increased, paternal claims correspondingly diminished. A balancing was required to determine which parent deserved custody. As this balancing occurred, focus was necessarily directed to the welfare of the infant. The obvious extension of this reasoning was to award custody to the state or a charitable institution when the interests of the child so required. It may have been easier for courts to begin to intrude on parental rights when racial and class factors were operating. In any event this was a trend which would grow in the twentieth century.

NOTES

I would like to acknowledge my indebtedness to Professor Morton Horwitz of Harvard Law School, who taught me legal history and supervised the research for this essay.

1 Christopher Lasch *Haven in a Heartless World: The Family Besieged* (New York 1977)
2 See Barbara Ehrenreich and Deirdre English *For Her Own Good* (Garden City, NY 1978).
3 In an effort to ensure that all reported cases for the nineteenth century were found, the author examined the index of each volume of every published series of Canadian law reports, which begin in 1824.
4 Decisions of the Upper Canada courts were first collected and published in 1824. Various reporters were appointed from 1824 onwards, although for many years no fees were paid and work was discontinued and disrupted according to the fortunes of the reporters and the society in which they lived. (William R. Riddell *The Legal Profession in Upper Canada in its Early Periods* (Toronto 1916) 108
5 *The Queen* v *James Baxter* (1846), 2 *Upper Canada Queen's Bench Reports* (hereafter UCQB) 370
6 Quebec Civil Code of 1866, Title Fifth, Marriage, Chapter Seventh, s. 185. It was possible to have the marriage annulled for such reasons as forced consent, or lack of proper formalities. Furthermore, marriage could be dissolved in Parliament through a private bill, but few Quebec Catholics utilized this procedure.
7 The grounds were that: (1) a husband could request separation on the ground of his wife's adultery; (2) a wife could request separation on the ground of her husband's adultery, 'if he kept his concubine in their common habitation'; (3) husband and wife could request separation on the ground of outrage, ill usage, or grievous insult committed by one towards the other; and (4) a wife could request separation for her husband's refusal to furnish her with the necessaries of life, according to his rank, means, and condition. (Quebec Civil Code of 1866, Title Sixth, Of Separation from Bed and Board, Chapter First, s. 186–90)
8 By 'provisional' it would appear the Code was implying temporary interim custody until the action for separation was completed. (Ibid. Chapter Third, s. 200)
9 Ibid. Chapter Fourth, s. 214
10 Despite the progressive custody provisions, there were portions of the Code which supported a more typical patriarchal status. Article 243 of the Civil Code dealt with parental authority, which was expressly granted to the father alone: 'He [the child] remains subject to their authority until his majority or his emancipation, but the father alone exercises this authority during marriage.' Even if custody had been awarded to the mother, the father's existing parental authority remained intact.

11 William Blackstone *Commentaries on the Laws of England* (London 1765–9; facsimile ed. Chicago 1979) I 441, 449
12 Ibid. 441
13 Elsie Edith Bowerman *Law of Child Protection* (London 1933) 3–4
14 William MacPherson *Treatise on the Law Relating to Infants* (London 1842) 142
15 *R.* v *De Mannville* (1804), 5 *East* 221; 102 *English Reports* 1054 (King's Bench)
16 Ibid. headnote
17 Jane Grey Perkins *The Life of Mrs Norton* (London 1909)
18 *Hansard Parliamentary Debates* 3rd Series v. 43 (1838) 164
19 Ibid. 782, 787
20 2 & 3 Vict. (1839) c. 54
21 See above note 5 at 370–1.
22 Ibid. 373
23 Ibid. 374
24 Ibid. 376–7
25 Ibid.
26 Robert E. Saunders 'Chief Justice John Beverley Robinson' *Dictionary of Canadian Biography* IX (Toronto 1976) 678 (hereafter DCB)
27 Ibid. 668–78
28 (1850), 1 *Practice Reports* (hereafter PR) 6
29 Ibid. 9. The report of the case gives no indication of where the father lived.
30 An Act Respecting the Appointment of Guardians and the Custody of Infants, 18 Vict. (1855) c. 126 (Can.)
31 See MacPherson *Treatise on Infants* 165–7 for an outline of the English division of opinion.
32 *Upper Canada Law Journal* (1856–7) 185
33 Ibid.
34 This trial appears to have been the result of a lawsuit between Dr Allen (as plaintiff) and Mrs Allen's father (as defendant). Mrs Allen had testified that her husband committed a 'certain gross offence,' a charge which Dr Allen asserted amounted to perjury. The term *ex parte* means that the hearing occurred in the physical absence of the husband.
35 *In re Allen* (1869), 5 PR 443
36 Ibid. 444
37 Ibid. 445
38 Ibid. 450
39 Ibid. 452
40 *In re Allen* (1869), 5 PR 453
41 *In re Allen* (1871), 31 UCQB 458
42 Ibid. 473

43 Ibid. 486
44 Ibid. 499–500
45 Ibid. 521
46 Ibid. 517
47 Ibid.
48 *Canada Law Journal* XXI (1885) 425–6; 'Joseph Curran Morrison' DCB XI (Toronto forthcoming 1981)
49 (1871), 5 PR 402
50 Ibid. 411
51 Ibid. 417
52 (1875), 6 PR 240
53 Ibid. 242
54 (1875), 6 PR 245
55 The Michigan legislation, passed in 1873, provided as follows:

> Sec. 1. That in case of the separation of the husband and wife having minor children, the mother of said children shall be entitled to the care and custody of all such children under the age of 12 years, and the father of such children shall be entitled to the care and custody of all such children of the age of 12 years or over; Provided that any probate court or any court of competent jurisdiction may, on petition and hearing thereof, make and enforce such order or orders as it may deem just and proper as to the care and custody of such minor children, excepting in cases where an order or decree may have been made by any court in chancery, regarding such children: And provided further, That nothing in this act shall prevent any court of competent jurisdiction from making and enforcing any such order or orders as it may deem just and proper as to the care and custody of such minor children in the same manner and with like effect as it could if this act had not been passed.

An Act to establish the right to the care and custody of minor children in case of the separation of husband and wife, being the father and mother of said children, *Michigan Public Acts*, 1873, no. 192, effective 31 July; 37 *Michigan Compiled Laws Annotated*, 1967, s. 732.541

56 *In re Kinney* above note 54 at 248
57 Ibid.
58 See Jennifer Nedelsky 'Judicial Conservatism in an Age of Innovation: Comparative Perspectives on Canadian Nuisance Law 1880–1930' in this volume.
59 Ibid.
60 Jamil S. Zainaldin 'The Emergence of a Modern American Family Law: Child Custody, Adoption, and the Courts 1796–1851' *Northwestern University Law Review* LXXIII (1979) 1038–89

61 Ibid. 1059–60
62 Ibid. 1052
63 Robert H. Bremner, ed. *Children and Youth in America: A Documentary History Vol. I 1600–1865* (Cambridge, MA 1970) 343–4
64 Zainaldin 'Modern American Family Law' 1060
65 Ibid. 1062–3
66 Ibid. 1063
67 Ibid. 1070
68 Ramsay Cook and Wendy Mitchinson, eds *The Proper Sphere: Woman's Place in Canadian Society* (Toronto 1976) 5
69 Ann Douglas *The Feminization of American Culture* (New York 1977) 74
70 Neil Sutherland *Children in English-Canadian Society: Framing the Twentieth-Century Consensus* (Toronto 1976) 4–11
71 Philippe Ariès *Centuries of Childhood: A Social History of Family Life* (New York 1962) 9, 128
72 Lawrence Stone, in *The Family, Sex and Marriage in England 1500–1800* (London 1977), states that the evolution of family relations was not a continuous linear development from pure patriarchy to a growing recognition of the rights of mothers and children:

> In England an era of reinforced patriarchy and discipline lasted from about 1530 to about 1670, with the high point in the 1650s. This in turn gave way to an era of growing individualism and permissiveness which was dominant in the upper middle and upper classes from about 1670 to about 1790. The next stage in the evolution of the family was marked by a strong revival of moral reform, paternal authority and sexual repression, which was gathering strength among the middle classes from about 1770. (ibid. 666)

Following this stage of repression, which was at its peak, according to Stone, from 1800 to the late 1860s, the tide turned slowly again and patriarchal authority was eroded (ibid. 680)

73 Eli Zaretsky *Capitalism, the Family and Personal Life* (New York 1976) 31
74 Ibid. 52
75 Lasch *Haven in a Heartless World* 5
76 An Act to amend the Law as to the Custody of Infants, 36 Vict. (1873), c. 12 (UK)
77 An Act to amend the Matrimonial Causes Act, 41 Vict. (1878), c. 19 (UK)
78 Amendments to the Law, *Statutes of Ontario*, 40 Vict. (1877), c. 8, s. 31
79 (1881), 8 PR 556
80 Ibid. 559
81 Ibid.
82 (1882), 9 PR 132

83 Ibid. 133
84 Ibid. 137
85 Ibid. 141
86 (1886), 25 *New Brunswick Reports* (hereafter NBR) 404. No legislation with respect to custody had been passed in New Brunswick at this time.
87 Ibid. 409
88 Ibid. 411
89 Ibid.
90 Ibid. 415
91 Ibid. 415–16
92 Ibid. 417
93 An Act to amend the Law relating to the Guardianship and Custody of Infants, 1886, 49 and 50 Vict., c. 27 (UK). The enactment of this legislation may have been prompted by the celebrated case of *Agar-Ellis* v *Lascelles* (1883), 24 *Chancery Division* 317 (Court of Appeal) in which the court expressed sympathy towards the mother but felt compelled to award to the father.
94 50 Vict., c. 21
95 Toronto *Globe*, Assembly Notes, 1 Apr. 1887
96 *Canada Law Journal* XXIII (1887) 228
97 Ibid.
98 Sutherland *Children in English-Canadian Society* 17; Ontario *Sessional Papers* 1895 no. 29
99 Sutherland *Children in English-Canadian Society* 17; 'The Sabbath-School as a Centre' *Canadian Methodist Magazine* XXV (1887) 44–5
100 See Carl Berger *The Sense of Power: Studies in the Ideas of Canadian Imperialism, 1867–1914* (Toronto 1977) for discussion of the strong imperialist dimension underlying the changing mood towards family and social problems.
101 Sutherland *Children in English-Canadian Society* 20
102 Mrs Dr Parker 'Woman in Nation-Building' in the Reverend B.F. Austin *Woman: Her Character, Culture and Calling* (Brantford, Ont. 1890) 462–6
103 (1888), 12 PR 659
104 Ibid. 661
105 *Re Smart Infants* (1886), 11 PR 482; *Re Smart Infants* (1887), 12 PR 312; *Re Smart Infants* (1888), 12 PR 438; *Re Smart Infants* (1888), 12 PR 635; *Smart* v *Smart*, [1892] *Appeal Cases* (hereafter AC) 425
106 *Smart* v *Smart*, [1892] AC 425 at 432
107 Ibid. 432, 435
108 53 Vict., c. 4
109 56 Vict., c. 11
110 *Revised Statutes of British Columbia* 1897, Vol. 1, c. 96

111 Further research comparing such matters as provincial rates of industrialization would be necessary to attempt to explain the backward nature of the British Columbia custody legislation. Whatever the reasons for this conservative statute, the situation did not escape the notice of women's lobby organizations at the turn of the century. British Columbia women's rights activists pointed out that in other jurisdictions mothers had been placed on an equal footing with fathers, both as to guardianship and responsibility for custody, and they demanded similar justice for mothers in British Columbia. (*Daughters, Wives and Mothers in British Columbia* [Vancouver 1913] ch. 10, 11 32–6) Similar sentiments were also responsible for the demands made by the Woman's Christian Temperance Union of British Columbia in 1912: 'Whereas we believe that the present laws of this province are unjust to the wives and mothers in the control of children and as they relate to property, therefore, *Resolved,* that we urge upon the government the importance of amending the present laws, that fathers and mothers may be made joint owners of their children, and husbands and wives of their property.' (Woman's Christian Temperance Union *Report* [British Columbia 1912] 79–82)

112 Susan Trofimenkoff and Alison Prentice, eds *The Neglected Majority: Essays in Canadian Women's History* (Toronto 1977) 101

113 Toronto *Globe* 2 Apr. 1896 as quoted in ibid. note 114.

114 (1893), 9 *Manitoba Law Reports* 23. Manitoba had enacted no custody legislation equalizing the balance between mothers and fathers.

115 (1894), 25 *Ontario Reports* (hereafter OR) 579

116 (1898), 29 OR 665

117 *In re Annie E. Hatfield* (1895), 1 *New Brunswick Equity Reports* (hereafter NBER) 142; *In re Armstrong* (1895), 1 NBER 208

118 54 Vict., c. 3

119 Since this problem did not heavily influence Canadian provinces until after the turn of the century, the development and application of this type of legislation is not explored in depth in this essay. It should be noted, however, that several statutes of this kind were passed in Canada during the nineteenth century: Minors and Apprentices Act 1889, *Consolidated Statutes of New Brunswick* 1903, c. 83; An Act for the Prevention of Cruelty to and Better Protection for Children 1893, *Statutes of Ontario,* c. 45; An Act to regulate the Immigration into Ontario of Certain Classes of Children 1897, *Statutes of Ontario,* c. 53; The Prevention and Punishment of Wrongs to Children, *Revised Statutes of Nova Scotia,* 5th Series, c. 95.

120 *Re Mahoney Children* (1892), 24 *Nova Scotia Reports* 86; *In re Granger and the Children's Aid Society of Kingston* (1897), 28 OR 555; *In re Ah Gway, ex parte Chin*

Su (1893), 2 *British Columbia Reports* (hereafter BCR) 343; *In re Quai Shing* (1897), 6 BCR 87; *In re Soy King* (1900), 7 BCR 291; *Regina* v *Redner* (1898), 6 BCR 73

121 R.E. Kingsford *Commentaries on the Law of Ontario Being Blackstone's Commentaries on the Laws of England, Adapted to the Province of Ontario* (Toronto 1896) 380

7

The Origins of the Canadian Criminal Code

GRAHAM PARKER

Canada's criminal code became law in 1892. With the exception of the Indian Penal code, this was the first national 'code' of criminal law to be enacted in the British Empire. To question the word code is not an exercise in semantic pedantry. Indeed, calling the Canadian legislation a code was something of an afterthought suggested by Judge James Gowan, who strongly influenced the conversion of the criminal law of Canada to statutory form. Whether this constitutes 'codification' is a matter of debate.

While codification was frequently discussed in the nineteenth-century English-speaking world, it had no one accepted meaning. Although all its proponents professed to be influenced by the philosophic radicalism of Jeremy Bentham, there appear to have been three distinct elements in the movement. At one level codification was an exercise in legal housekeeping through the consolidation of several centuries of statute and case law. Another aspect was law reform.[1] At a more sophisticated level there were attempts to systematize the law while reforming it, first by Thomas Babington Macaulay and later by James Fitzjames Stephen and his Canadian disciples. Some 'codes' were introduced in the United States, but the Benthamite-Austinian concept of a code which would supplant the common law and provide a totally new approach, a fundamental rethinking of the law, was never more than an ideal. Although the various aspects of codification had a great impact throughout the English-speaking world, the common law resisted eradication. The result in Canada, as elsewhere, was an uneasy truce.

The judges and commentators of the seventeenth and eighteenth centuries were convinced that the law was certain, immutable, and unambiguous, and that its interpretation should be left to the judiciary to articulate. The most famous spokesman for this view was Sir William Blackstone, whose influential *Commentaries on English Law* endeavoured to set out the basic principles of the law as culled from the decisions of the judges.[2] However, Blackstone gave very little thought to the criminal law, believing that both crimes and punishments 'were ascertained and notorious; nothing is left to arbitrary discretion.'[3]

Jeremy Bentham disagreed profoundly with this Blackstonian analysis. To Bentham, for whom criminal law and penal reform in general were a life-long passion, nothing was more uncertain than the common law, a 'fathomless and boundless chaos made up of fictions, tautology and inconsistency.'[4] He advocated legislation to clear up the legal accretions of the centuries, which Blackstone had glorified and purportedly 'systemized.'

Another critic of Blackstone who gave serious consideration to codification was John Austin, a professor of jurisprudence at the University of London.[5] Austin suggested that a code should be the work of many hands, but one person could make a start by preparing a digest. Austin devoted considerable attention to the classification of private law concepts but admitted he had great problems in adapting his scheme to the purposes of the criminal law. Yet it was in the area of criminal law that most of the early efforts were made. This is remarkable considering that there was no single, easily distinguishable philosophy or framework for prospective codifiers to draw on. Bentham's notorious pleasure-pain calculus was more applicable to penal discipline and prison design than to drafting fundamental principles of substantive law. The less dogmatic Austin was more sympathetic to an historical approach to the task of codification and was prepared to recognize legal experience and the lessons of comparative law: still, Austin's scheme never progressed beyond a very sketchy framework.

European models had different roots. The Prussian and French codes were products of the Enlightenment and revolution and were seen as necessary measures for national unity or the absorption of local customs. These factors were less relevant in England, a unitary state with a peculiar legal system, divorced from Roman law influences and therefore dominated by its own idiosyncratic priesthood, the English bench and bar.

Beginning in 1830 a series of commissions were appointed to report on the state of the English criminal law.[6] An 1837 report was unequivocally critical of an unwritten system which, however flexible and adaptable, could not be intelligible to the mass of the population and therefore could have little deterrent effect.[7] The Commissioners pressed for a digest of the criminal law, as well as procedural and substantive reforms which would rationalize and simplify the legal process. Though their suggestions were less revolutionary than commonsensical, they were generally ignored. Parliament repealed hundreds of statutes, various consolidation acts were passed, and several specific reforms were achieved, but no truly systematic revision of the criminal law ever came to fruition.

The closest approximation to a proper trial for codification was Macaulay's remarkable proposal of an Indian Penal code in 1835. After many revisions, this code was enacted in 1858 and went into effect in 1862. Macaulay's aims were explicitly Benthamite; he sought to draft a code based on two great principles, that 'of suppressing crime with the smallest possible infliction of suffering, and that of ascertaining truth at the smallest possible cost of time and money.'[8] Macaulay believed a code should cover all contingencies – what was not in the code would not be law. Vague technical terms such as manslaughter should be avoided. Every criminal act was to be separately defined, and illustrations would explain the laws, which were to be firmly based in principle. Macaulay's code had an elegance and flair seldom found in legal drafting. Unfortunately, James Fitzjames Stephen lacked Macaulay's ability in this regard, and the Canadian Criminal Code of 1892, which was to a great extent based on Stephen's work, suffered as a result.

Some English lawyers made light of the clarity of the Indian code, suggesting that it was necessary to keep things simple for the native population and magistrates of limited abilities. Stephen did not agree.[9] He deplored the clumsy English consolidation statutes. He castigated those who adhered to technical rules at the expense of individual hardship. Overdefinition he felt should be avoided, because such language resulted in a 'still greater refinement in quibbling,' though this might mean that not every contingency would be covered.[10]

A conservative in politics and a Benthamite in his adherence to codification, Stephen was unable to prepare a code which embraced major principles. His adherence to Hobbes often overshadowed his admiration for Macaulay's clarity and vision. He saw crime as a sin which should be punished; this seems to have resulted in carelessness in definitions; the essence of sin is that it is universally recognizable. In addition, there was enough of the common lawyer in Stephen that he made ample provision for the exercise of a judge's instinct and discretion. Stephen was a middle-of-the-road codifier. He saw his Draft Code as a distillation of the 'accumulated experience' of seven centuries of English law and the common law as of 'immense moral importance.'[11]

In Canada, folklore would have it that Sir John A. Macdonald thought a federal criminal law would help unify the country. That Macdonald simply wanted uniformity in the criminal law is closer to the truth. Sir John looked on the central government's criminal jurisdiction as a 'necessity,' believing that one of the defects of the US Constitution was the legislative powers of the states in this sphere. However, Macdonald did not have immediate plans for a federal code and was prepared to move slowly.

Nevertheless the idea of codification preceded Confederation, as did the need. By 1867 there were numerous differences between the criminal laws of the founding provinces. In Upper Canada William Lyon Mackenzie hoped to emulate the American experiments at codification in order to rid the Canadian system of unnecessary delays and complexities. As early as 1840 a commission was appointed to inquire into the statute law of Upper Canada. In 1858 another commission advised a 'complete, classified consolidation,' which led to the Consolidated Statutes of 1859.[12]

In 1870 the Colonial Office prepared a lengthy memorandum, *Some Considerations Preliminary to the Preparation of a Penal Code for the Crown Colonies.*[13] The writer advised colonial administrators to use the work of Macaulay and Edward Livingston, an American codifier whose work does not seem to have had any specific attraction for Canadian reformers. The English writer saw no great need to use the bulk of English case law, which was not as useful in criminal law as in civil cases. In explanation, the memorandum declared that case law was no longer necessary at criminal trials to restrain 'corrupt or arbitrary judges.' Whereas a code would arouse much controversy in England, it was contended that in the colonies the legislatures were unlikely to raise much opposition, and in any event the crown 'has absolute power of legislation in the last resort.' Finally, the writer urged that in the preparation of 'theoretic or innovating legislation' preference should be given to reports of commissions and parliamentary committees which had already examined the problems of criminal law revision. While there is no evidence that this document was distributed in this country, Canadian reformers certainly employed this last device.

Some commentators have suggested that English legislators and lawyers had a 'colonial' attitude towards codification – it might not be good enough for England but it would do for Australia or Canada. This is something of a distortion. The English common law was so complicated and encrusted with precedent and historical anomalies that it was difficult to reduce it to a cohesive set of principles. Admittedly there was some Blackstonian smugness among the English lawyers, but the colonies were clearly a better proving ground for codification. Their legal systems were still unformed and ripe for experimentation. Furthermore the colonies produced an aura of enthusiasm for new ideas and the men to put them into effect. India had the extraordinary trio of Macaulay, Sir Henry Maine, and Stephen. Canada had James Gowan, the political force behind the code; Justice Henry Elzéar Taschereau, who had already prepared a detailed commentary on Canadian criminal law and whose own offer to draft a code for Canada was not accepted; and George Burbidge, a judge and former Deputy Minister of Justice and an admirer of Stephen's *Digest of the Criminal Law*. Along with Robert Sedgewick, the Deputy Minister of Justice, these men were the greatest influences on the 1892 Code. They were good legal technocrats and fair draftsmen but they could hardly be called law reformers or radical codifiers.

THE CLIMATE OF CODE REFORM IN CANADA 1850–90

The legal profession in Canada probably gathered most of its information about codification from the legal periodicals established in the mid-nineteenth century. The Canadian literature shows that codification was considered a newsworthy idea. However, the articles and editorials have little theoretical content. One is left with the impression that no one was very sure what was meant by a code or even whether such a reform was desirable.

The *Canada Law Journal* was founded by Gowan in 1855. Although he was never officially its editor, he was the major contributor. Like its sister publications, the *Journal* contained little original material, drawing heavily on reprints of English and American articles. Given Gowan's own perspective, it is not surprising to find the first volume agreeing with *The Times* of London that codification was a good thing but asking 'how are we to codify so as to exclude a conflict upon the construction of almost every word in the code?'[14] The editors never made an attempt to define codification.

In 1857 an editorial noted the difficulties experienced in trying to pass the English consolidation acts and conjectured that the champions of codification were trying to prevent the success of a rival scheme.[15] At this stage Gowan was not so much an advocate of codes as of consolidation of existing statutes. The following year the *Canada Law Journal* again supported consolidation, reasoning that codification would not simplify the law and would rob it of flexibility. Codes, it was argued, were not the perfection of wisdom and were subject to ambiguity.[16] A year later the same opinion was expressed; and also language was viewed as an imperfect instrument. The editors believed that codification meant the passage of immutable laws which could not be amended. They preferred consolidation because it was codification 'stripped of the ridiculous.'[17] A slightly different view was expressed in an 1860 editorial and in an article reprinted from the English *Solicitors' Journal*, which discussed codification in the United States. The English author had argued that the Anglo-Saxon race took the English law wherever it went, and codification would be a mistake because it would 'entirely obviate this dependence on the mother country.' A colony which adopted a code 'would no longer draw its current of law from the fountainhead but would, for the future, depend on its own resources for the maintenance and advancement of its laws.'[18]

The *Canada Law Journal* did not discuss codification again for a decade. The topic resurfaced in 1874 with news that the Lord Chancellor was proposing codification of the criminal law. The task was not regarded as an easy one.[19] In an 1875 reprint of the *Report of the Commission for the Consolidation and Revision of the Statutes affecting the Province of Ontario* (1875), the editors decided that codification was almost impossible. By contrast, consolidation had the virtues of simplicity and uniformity and 'would form a rung in the long ladder to that legal millennium, the Age of the English Code.'[20]

The influence of American law and legal institutions on Canadian law is rather hard to assess. Governments paid almost exclusive attention to British developments. Yet the contents of the legal journals gave a very different impression. In *Legal News*, published in Montreal, American cases were referred to as frequently as English ones. Articles from American periodicals were regularly reprinted, probably because academic law was more advanced in the United States.

The editors of *Legal News* noted in 1878 the passage of a criminal code in Virginia. In the same year there was praise for the American Bar Association and its plan for a code, which was described as one of the 'most noteworthy events in the history of jurisprudence.' *Legal News* enthused over the plan to 'assimilate and unify' the commercial and criminal laws of the several states as a 'consummation devoutly to be wished by every lover of his country, for not only will it facilitate intercourse and harmony among the people, but it will also be one of the strongest bonds of union among the several states.'[21]

British influences were not ignored by Canadian legal periodicals. There was a report on the 22nd Annual Congress of the British Social Science Association, particularly a paper on 'Jurisprudence and the Amendment of the Law.'[22] There was also a reference to Attorney General Holker's Bill (based on the Draft Code), and special attention was paid to the extension of the summary jurisdiction of magistrates.[23] In 1879 *Legal News* reprinted a long article from the *American Law Review* on the impending success of the long-awaited reform of a criminal code for England.[24] Reference was made to the complexity of the law found in 18,000 statutes and 100,000 cases, Tennyson being quoted to prove the point:

> The lawless science of our law
> That codeless myriad of precedent
> That wilderness of single instances.[25]

Macaulay's code for India was also mentioned. There was praise for the 'extraordinary brevity and clearness' with which Stephen had condensed the criminal law in his *Digest*, but, somewhat inconsistently, the article criticized the English Draft Code (1879) because the general principles were inadequately described. On balance, however, the Draft Code was 'skilful' and a 'great reform.' In 1882 *Legal News* reprinted an article by Stephen arguing for codification, which he defined as 'giving literary form to large bodies of law.' Stephen was pessimistic about bringing codification to fruition because it was a task the 'British Parliament is quite incompetent to perform itself, and most unlikely to entrust to anyone else.'[26]

Another legal periodical, *Canadian Law Times* (founded in 1881), also reviewed the merits of codification. In 1881 there was discussion of the amalgamation of the English and French systems of legal procedure.[27] Two years later there was mention of the codification movement in New York state. The common law was admittedly confused and inaccessible, but the author argued that codes would not necessarily lead to simplification of the law and that brevity and popularization of the law could lead to 'interpretive disputes.'[28]

The 1884 *Canadian Law Times* reviewed the Report of the Commissioners responsible for the consolidation of Ontario statutes.[29] In commenting on the English Draft Criminal Code, the editors made the telling comment: 'The whole Code might with advantage be adopted. It is a matter of no little importance to (the practising bar) that the law of England should be identical with our own – where circumstances permit – for we have the advantage of the English decisions upon it to guide us.'[30] A draft Bill to codify the law respecting indictable offences, which was based chiefly on the English Draft Code, had also been printed with the Report and the editors recommended its adoption.[31]

Quebec journals also discussed the question of codification. Judge Louis Loranger in 1879 referred to the humane influence of English criminal law but suggested that there should be equal accessibility for both peoples and that the French found it difficult to know the English law, particularly criminal law. He believed codification should be easily attained because the common law was not as entrenched in Canada as in England. Four years later B.A. de Montigny, the Recorder of Montreal, explained the criminal law to French Canadians. Until recently, French-Canadian lawyers had had little contact with the criminal law because a Queen's Bench judge had ruled that indictments could not be made in the French language.[32]

Between 1886 and 1889 there were further articles, mostly reprints from American periodicals, debating the virtues and shortcomings of the code proposals of David Dudley Field in the United States.[33] The *Canadian Law Times* noted that one of the most 'popular subjects of experiment for legislative theorists' had been the criminal law. An 1887 editorial discussing this dispute said that 'without denying that many beneficial results must certainly flow from codification where codification is practicable, we do not think that those most desirable ends, certainty, cheapness, convenience and universal knowledge of the law, will ever be attained by simply codifying...'[34] The *Canada Law Journal* warned against unreal expectations about codification because 'the habits, modes of thought, practices and traditions of a people ... are deeply rooted and incapable of legislative extirpation.'[35] The most that could be hoped for was reduction of the law on a particular subject to a single statute with a minimum of judicial interpretation. In 1890 reference was made to Sir John Thompson being at work on a Code bill. The *Journal* thought this could 'possibly be desirable, but we trust the authorities in Ottawa do not intend to follow our Provincial legislators in the annual game of tinkering and amending the statutes.'[36] *Legal News* made the same point two years later, citing 'the amendments made without reasonable grounds' which had had an unsettling effect on the Quebec Civil Code.

In 1892, the year in which the Canadian Criminal Code was passed, the *Canada Law Journal* observed that codification had been the dream of the Macdonald government though carried to fruition by Thompson. It would not have been possible without the revision and amendments put into place by Macdonald in 1869. While Thompson deserved credit for a 'great and important measure of criminal law reform,' the *Journal* believed that the 'science of penal law is, in Canada, almost in its infancy, very few of our legal minds having donated much attention to it.'[37] *Legal News*, however, briefly reviewed the Code definitions of murder and found them 'comprehensive and exhausting.'[38]

THE CANADIAN CODIFIERS

If one person could be chosen as pre-eminent in Canadian codification, it would be Judge James Gowan. He was responsible for much consolidation of Ontario statutes and did considerable drafting for the Mowat government. A reading of the *Canada Law Journal* might suggest that he did not have a clear idea of a code, but this did not make him very different from many other common law practitioners. Among Gowan's many correspondents in England was Charles Greaves, the editor of the great consolidation of criminal law statutes in the middle of the nineteenth century.[39] In no sense could this be called a meeting of minds of two great theorists on codification. Gowan, like Greaves, simply worked assiduously on creating some system out of the great bulk of criminal legislation. Surprisingly, there is no mention in any of the Gowan correspondence of J.F. Stephen or the English Draft Code.

Gowan was an influential back-room Tory and a confidant of Sir John A. He had been an important figure in papering over some of the more urgent problems of the Pacific Scandal for which, in part, he was eventually rewarded with a knighthood and a Senate seat. Gowan liked to give the impression that Macdonald found it difficult to make a political decision without his advice. In his letters he claimed that he had been telling Macdonald since 1867 that a criminal code would be a very worthy aim of the Tory government. However, there is no evidence that Macdonald took much notice of such sage advice.

Gowan was wont to think that he was the father of the Canadian Criminal Code of 1892. Although this is an exaggeration, there are indications that he made important contributions. Some letters from the Department of Justice later acknowledged his help. Although he was quite elderly and unable to be in Ottawa at the time of the drafting and debates, Gowan apparently managed to have some impact on affairs by writing often from his home in Barrie. In a long memorandum on the Code he wanted to change the name of the legislation from 'Criminal Law of Canada' to 'Criminal Code.' His somewhat superficial approach to codification can be seen in his comment that the numbering of the parts was 'certainly the most scientific' way of presenting the document. There are further insights into his views on the idea of a code, and his political acumen, when he said that 'this Bill is not the introduction of a new law – the application of no new principle. It is a faithful rendering of existing principles and existing laws.'

Gowan for some time was concerned that the Code was not complete in terms of principles and rules. He decided on reflection, however, that Thompson would be best advised to follow the ill-fated English Code bill of 1880. Obviously he was strongly influenced by that abortive legislation. Since Canadian decisions were not 'out of harmony' with the law described in the 1880 measure, it should be closely followed: 'If then the learning and experience of those from whence proceed this English Bill and their special training do not afford a sufficient guarantee of accurateness, I am unable to se what can.' By passing 'this great measure' Canada was leading in the 'field of science,' and the Code would be a 'glorious triumph.'[40]

Gowan made three comments, in his memorandum, on substantive law, about insanity, compulsion, and carnal knowledge, but they were of no great moment. He was, nevertheless, possessed of a keen political sense. He wrote to Thompson in May 1892 admitting that the Code could be made more perfect, but the 'great and important point is to get your measure through Parliament *in some form or another*.' The Act, when passed, could be polished and completed. He advised Thompson to 'accept little amendments as long as it does not affect the *general* structure' rather than hamper the bill 'through antagonism.' He added: 'sober second thought comes and if necessary, excrescences could be removed next session. The *great* object is a Criminal Code for Canada and now.' Gowan had received letters which said that a Code would be a great advantage in order to have the criminal law easily understood by judges and magistrates, free of all obscurities. He did not imagine that there would be many serious students of the Code measure, because otherwise the book he had taken from the Parliamentary Library would have been requested by others. The volume was a collection of the hostile criticism, mostly by judges, of the English Draft Code. Gowan commented that 'the book before me would have been a *rich find* for the enemy in attacking your bill – you could answer the fire with effect but it would take time and the missiles for the time would be dangerous in the extreme – such helped to *kill* the English Bill.'[41]

In the same month Gowan wrote to congratulate Sedgewick and

Burbidge on their enthusiasm for the Code. 'For more than twenty years I have had codification "on the brain" and there are few in Canada who have tried harder than I have to master it in all its bearings.' Gowan considered that Thompson had been courageous in undertaking the 'great and intimidating responsibility' of such a large measure when a similar venture had failed in England. He also sent some suggestions for amendment, relating to abortion, libel, corroboration, and spousal immunity. Sedgewick was appreciative and wrote several times thanking the old judge for his encouragement and lobbying.

However extensive, Gowan's influence was nonetheless indirect, and the actual origins of the idea to codify the criminal law of Canada remain difficult to determine. There is no evidence that any Canadian politician or civil servant led a delegation to London to consult with Stephen, any other British advocate of codification, or draftsmen. Sir John Thompson visited London in 1888, but there is no written record of consultations with anyone who would have influenced the Canadian Government to embark on codification. Although the godfather of the measure was Stephen, he was in failing health by 1891, when the Canadian Criminal Code Bill was first presented, and his contribution was purely through his writings.

The titular father and political force behind the Code was Thompson, the energetic Minister of Justice. Thompson, who was eventually fourth Prime Minister of Canada, was a man of great legal talent. A founder of Dalhousie Law School, where he taught part-time for some years, he was a judge of the Supreme Court of Nova Scotia until persuaded by Macdonald to seek a federal seat. The actual work of preparing the Code for the House was undertaken by two Maritimers who were successive Deputy Ministers of Justice. George Burbidge, a disciple of Stephen, became an early judge of the Exchequer Court. He was succeeded as Deputy Minister by Robert Sedgewick, another great influence on Dalhousie Law School, who eventually became a judge of the Supreme Court of Canada. The draftsman of the Code, who did the mechanical work under the supervision of Burbidge and Sedgewick, was C.H. Masters, a lawyer and reporter in the Supreme Court of Canada. At that time there was a law clerk attached to both the House of Commons and the Senate, but his task was merely to tinker with legislation already drafted and to assist the legislative committees. Most drafting was done by the Department of Justice, although in those days the Department was not heavily burdened with matters of legislative policy and drafting. A survey of the legislation of the period shows that the statutes were either makeshift, pragmatic laws to solve an immediate problem or, more frequently, were lifted from English statutes with few changes in deference to Canadian conditions.

The bête noire of the Criminal Code was Henry Elzéar Taschereau, judge of the Supreme Court of Canada and a severe critic of the Code after it became law in 1892. Taschereau was the author of an annotated collection of statutes on criminal law, first published in 1874.[42] This was no doubt a handy collection for the busy practitioner, but it is somewhat flattering by today's standards to call it an annotation, let alone scholarship. The editor quoted very freely from the great authorities such as Sir Edward Coke and Sir Matthew Hale. Most of the cases cited were English. Taschereau's work was typical of a period when English authorities and decisions were held in awe. When Canadian precedents were cited, it was done with almost no explanation. There was no attempt in his work to prepare an exposition of the criminal law of Canada or elsewhere. Taschereau had written to Thompson in 1889 offering to draw up a Code. He thought that the task could be done in six months without too much interruption in his judicial duties, so long as he had additional clerical help. This offer was not taken up for reasons that we can only surmise. Perhaps Chief Justice Samuel Henry Strong did not want one of his judges preoccupied with drafting. Perhaps someone in government felt that a judge of the highest court should have no part in drafting legislation he would eventually be asked to interpret.

After Taschereau's offer was rejected, Thompson evidently turned to Burbidge, who that year had published a book entitled *A Digest of the Criminal Law of Canada (Crimes and Punishment) Founded by Permission on Sir James Fitzjames Stephen's Digest of the Criminal Law*.[43] At least two-thirds of the effort was taken verbatim from Stephen's work. With the exception of some definitional and reception provisions, the parts which supplemented Stephen were purely descriptive of offences. There was no attempt whatever to set out underlying principles, and most of the rules in the early part of Burbidge's *Digest* were taken directly from Stephen. In his very short foreword Burbidge made no general statement about codification. The only item of interest was the acknowledgment of the assistance of C.H. Masters. Burbidge initially refused Thompson's offer to draft a Code. On second thought he wrote to the Minister of Justice apologizing for his 'selfish' behaviour and offering his services. He had refused, he said, because he was afraid that the Code would interfere with the sale of his *Digest*.

The 1892 Criminal Code was drafted by Burbidge and Sedgewick in their spare time in the space of a year. Perhaps because they gave very little thought to principles and drew many of the rules they propounded from elsewhere, a bill was ready for Parliament in 1891. The preparation of the Code nevertheless shows remarkable expedition by Burbidge, Sedgewick, Masters, and G.B.L. Fraser, a senior official in the Department of Justice. Fraser, an industrious civil servant who wrote acute opinions for the Department of Justice for more than two decades, acted as a trouble-shooter.

Thompson, Sedgewick, and Burbidge planned a careful campaign for the introduction of the Code. In October 1890 Sedgewick wrote to J.A. McCord, Assistant Law Clerk to the House of Commons, announcing that the government intended to introduce a bill codifying criminal law and procedure. The Deputy Minister also told McCord 'confidentially that Mr. Justice Burbidge and myself propose to give two months to the work and to employ a professional gentleman to assist us.' By July 1891 two thousand copies of the Code had been printed and distributed to superior court judges, provincial attorneys general, lawyers of high standing, and the 'most prominent' magistrates. By May of the following year supplies of the Code were exhausted.

The 1891 draft was seen as a trial balloon. Thompson only intended to achieve a second reading that year. Sedgewick explained the underlying policy to Thomas Carswell, City Solicitor of Toronto: 'It is thought advisable that it will be for the public benefit not to pass a Code in the same session as it is introduced. Its introduction and publication will call public attention to it and in the interim between one Session and another all persons interested in the Criminal Law will be able to make and will doubtless make many verbal suggestions by way of amendment.'[44] In May 1892 Sedgewick asked the Queen's Printer for 20,000 English copies of the Code and 2800 in a French version. After some bickering about money, $6000 was found for printing and distribution. On 4 July the first copies were delivered to the Department of Justice. This time every member of the judiciary, whether on the Supreme Court of Canada or a county JP, received a copy. Possibly due to this very wide circulation, the correspondence of the Department of Justice does not contain many requests for copies of the Code. Most such letters are from mid-1891, when the circulation of the document was much more restricted.

The most enlightening evidence on the history of the Code is found in the internal documents of the Department of Justice. Almost all anonymous, they were probably written by Gowan, Sedgewick, and Fraser. Some are memoranda written only for the Department. Others are background papers for Thompson's speeches. One or two are detailed criticisms of the 1891 and 1892 bills. Once again there was little discussion of codification as such (except for the contributions of Gowan) and almost none about policy or general principles. There are specific criticisms of particular provisions and extended analyses of procedural matters. There are also frequent references to English sources but only very general mention of American ones.

One anonymous memorandum (probably written by Gowan) praised the wisdom of following 'in the main' the English Draft Code and commented that, when passed, Canada would have 'the most complete measure of its kind existing in any country in the world.' The parts of the English Bill of 1880 had been 'selected and worked in with admirable judgment.' The writer accepted those legislative transplants 'without hesitation as the written law and substantially representing the principles of the existing English law and ours which they cover; those principles have been obtained by a process of induction from numerous cases.' One wonders why he found it necessary to make this observation, but law reformers are always a little afraid of the innate conservatism of the bench and bar. The writer tried to reassure Thompson that 'no one will hesitate to accept these provisions' and that the Bill for the new Code was an improvement because it minimized the use of wordy language and frequently used Canada's own statutes, only changing the wording 'to bring out sharply and clearly their true meaning.' There was little evidence of novelty for novelty's sake, he said, and in the few instances where the law was altered, the changes were 'based on the highest authority.'[45]

After some obvious hesitation, the writer was content with the exclusion of the terms 'malice' and 'maliciously' from Part XVII, which defined homicide. The retention of such technical terms often 'occasions a failure of justice.' He added: 'Every lawyer knows the legal import of the terms differs from its acceptation in ordinary conversation – that it is not as in ordinary speech, only an expression of hatred and ill-will; to the individual such terms are eminently well calculated ... to overcloud and bewilder an ordinary man.' The preamble to Livingston's Louisiana Code was quoted: 'Whereas it is of primary importance in every well-regulated State, that the Code of Criminal law should be founded on one principle, viz. – the prevention of crime, that all offences should be clearly and explicitly defined, in language generally understood; that punishments should be proportioned to offences.'[46] The influence of the Enlightenment penal philosopher Cesare Beccaria was obvious, though

Beccaria would have been less happy with the Canadian observer's comment that he had 'always thought that the largest discretion should be given to the courts in assessing punishments on conviction. There are shades of guilt, degrees of turpitude ... and I can best estimate the right punishment.'

Another document, probably written by Gowan in 1891, is the best available source for the intellectual history of the Code.[47] Stephen's strong criticism of the English common law was quoted, but the writer defended the Canadian Code's retention of the common law by saying that courts were the 'best subordinate legislature in the world' and should be given some discretion. Although Canada had the advantage of the prior examples of the Livingston and New York criminal codes, the reader was reassured that this did not mean that Canada was adopting American law, for these codes themselves had incorporated the principles of English law. The language of the common law was improved upon and, adopting the words of Stephen, the writer asserted that the language of a code must be clear, 'large,' and divested of 'obsolete and technical' terms. In other words, Canada was engaging in moderate codification, expressing the common law in neat statutory language to be interpreted by common law judges.

Honour was given in this document to Sir John A. for the consolidation acts, which were the first step on the way to codification, although it was conceded that they were hastily drawn, and it had been politically expedient to retain the language of the provincial statutes.[48] Nevertheless, it was 'some preparation toward a scientific code' and had 'harrowed the field' for a Code. The English Draft Code had failed, it was argued, largely because of the heavy schedule of the British Parliament, and because of the controversies the matter had generated. The Minister of Justice's Code Bill had more promising prospects, because 'there is an absolute necessity for such a measure having regard to our Confederated condition.' Furthermore, this 'young and growing country' had a better chance, in Stephen's words, of 'disengaging the pure metal from the rich but rough ore.' The writer believed that 'science will reign supreme' if the details were discussed in a 'proper and liberal spirit.' The result would not be a mere consolidation but the law 're-cast and reconstructed.' The Code Bill did not contain mere definitions of crimes but also defined the 'general elements.' After describing the Code as a 'great national undertaking' and a document of 'scientific completeness,' ensuring that Canadian jurisprudence would be in the 'forefront of progress,' the writer assured his readers that it was 'not a Code in the sense of being perfectly original, but

... a comprehensive, condensed and complete presentation of the whole body of criminal law now in force in this Dominion.' In some ways it was an improvement on the law of the mother country, but only when it 'seemed necessary to adapt it to modern times and the exigencies of a new country, as well as the habits and transactions of the Canadian people.'

The files of the Department of Justice also listed the sources of the Code Bill – the English Bill of 1880, Stephen's *Digest*, Burbidge's *Digest*, and Canadian statutory criminal law as consolidated in 1869.[49] There are references to English Attorney General Sir John Holker's second reading speech on introducing the English Draft Code as a Bill,[50] and to nine articles in American and English periodical literature which described the New York Civil Code and the Italian and Indian Codes.

This same document further noted the items which the Department probably viewed as the most innovative. The distinctions between principals and accessories and between felony and misdemeanour were abolished. The use of 'malice' as a legal term of art was discontinued. The law of murder and infanticide was changed, and provocation was statutorily defined.[51] The law of theft was expanded to include much more than simple common law larceny. Writs of error were abolished and replaced by appeal courts which could order new trials. Pleading was simplified. Justices of the Peace were granted wider powers. The scheme of punishments was made more uniform, and attempts were made to 'make the punishment fit the crime.' None of these changes was original to Canada.[52] They could all be found in the writings of Stephen, the English Draft Code, or in earlier legislation. Thus, the 1892 Code was not a document of radical law reform. Given the resources of the Department of Justice, the Code admittedly showed remarkable industry but it could hardly be called a feat of imagination and intellectual ingenuity.

RESPONSE TO THE DRAFT CODE

The idea of consultations with the judiciary, the legal profession, and concerned citizens is not an invention of modern law reform commissions. The English Home Office made frequent use of this device in the last half of the nineteenth century, seeking the views of police chiefs, magistrates and, in particular, high court judges on any important changes in the law.[53] The Canadian Department of Justice followed this example in obtaining the reactions of the legal community to the Code Bill. The archives of the Department of Justice in Ottawa contain hundreds of letters written in response to the Department's request. However, with the exception of some euphoric but rather vapid letters (as opposed to his useful memoranda) from Judge Gowan about his long love affair with codification, there was no response, positive or negative, to the idea of codification per se. This is not surprising because the periodical literature indicates that in general lawyers equated codification with statutory consolidation. Gowan's previous efforts, Burbidge in his *Digest,* and Sedgewick in his correspondence did not go beyond consolidation.

Discussion of legal principles and policy are missing from the correspondence and the Code Bill. The common lawyers who drafted the Code had no love for Yankee ideas of democracy, civil liberties, or bills of rights. In addition to believing that such general principles were dangerously republican, the drafters no doubt also believed that formulation of the principle of legality or the rule of law (which includes, for instance, the presumption of innocence) were either unnecessary, because they were too obvious to require reiteration, or undesirable, because they would impede the discretion of the trial judge. Moreover, a peculiarly Canadian legal culture hardly existed. Legal education was rudimentary, consisting of office apprenticeships, rote learning, excessive formalism, and slavish adherence to precedent, mostly English. The few Canadian treatises which existed were severely practical. The legal periodical literature was not rich in ideas, and any reflective material was usually reprinted from England or the United States. The profession, in short, was suffering from 'cultural cringe,' an attitude which could not but inhibit originality and intellectual force in the process of codification.

There is some indication that the citizens of the Canadian Dominion felt that a Criminal Code would have a unifying and stabilizing influence on the country. This evidence, however, is rather sparse. The Department of Justice received very few letters praising the prospect of codification. Some post-1893 presentments of grand juries thanked the presiding judge for explaining the new Code to them and expressed the hope that the new uniform criminal law would have a beneficial effect on the country as a whole, and, in particular, would lead to a decrease in crime, make the prosecution of the law more efficacious and, of course, make the law itself more certain. Clearly the Canadian public took some pride in its new Code; the new dominion it was believed would be perceived as innovative and progressive, even though the Code itself was largely imported and its content was devoid of an overriding philosophy.

One would not expect letters to Sir John Thompson from the general public to be concerned with the theoretical niceties of the criminal law. But if the Department of Justice anticipated correspondence from the legal profession discussing fundamental reforms, it must have been sorely disappointed. The criminal bar had never been blessed with the intellectual giants of the profession, and few lawyers took much theoretical interest in crime. There were several letters from judges but the lawyers were remarkably silent, except for some crown attorneys and a few lobbyists. Very few asked questions about general policy. A letter from an Ontario lawyer did ask whether the drafters were contemplating degrees of murder, which was an important question given the fact that the only punishment provided for murder was the mandatory death penalty. The enquiry received a very terse negative reply from Sedgewick.

A few lawyers wrote with specific complaints. A London, Ontario, practitioner wanted it made easier to prosecute corporations which, he claimed, escaped liability due to procedural loopholes. He was concerned, in particular, about a pollution case. The Crown Attorney of Guelph cited a recent case where a local man had faked a robbery; the Crown wanted it made possible to charge the miscreant with public mischief. A third lawyer sought the help of the Department of Justice in strengthening the law relating to blackmail and suggested the adoption of the laws of New York State.

With a few exceptions letters from the judiciary did not discuss matters of principle or the idea of codification. Two Ontario High Court judges wrote letters about the law of bigamy, but it was narrow legal talk. The most informed and intelligent letter from a legally-trained person was from Judge Matthew Baillie Begbie of British Columbia, who wrote on a variety of subjects, many of which concerned substantive law. He discussed the issue of consent in carnal knowledge cases, increasing the punishment for incest, more stringent laws about receiving stolen goods, opposition to the abolition of the distinction between felony and misdemeanour, and bigamy, and entered strong objections to the increased power of JPs.

L.W.A. Genest, a Clerk of the Peace of Trois Rivières, was concerned about procedural defects and photography of nudes, which he thought to be 'scandalous, lewd, immoral and indecent.' In February and May 1892 Genest prepared very detailed critiques of the Code Bill, asking for better definitions and clearer classification. He wanted the drafters to include a definition of manslaughter, made detailed criticism of the law of larceny, and also had many procedural quibbles.

The simplification of procedure received strong support from G.H. Grierson of Ottawa who described himself as an 'old magistrate.' He had suggestions for the use of short forms. Grierson complained that the present forms were 'all based on antiquated models' and 'verbose to an astonishing degree when we consider the multitude of words required to accomplish a possibly trifling result, such as the levy of a small fine, and in tautology they approach the absurd ... giving the whole system ... a semi-sanctimonious character in no way necessary to the furtherance of the ends of justice.'

One item which attracted disproportionate attention was the appropriate jurisdiction of magistrates and Justices of the Peace. Many correspondents did not approve of the relatively wide jurisdiction given to the lay judiciary to hear criminal offences summarily by consent of the accused under the Speedy Trials Act.[54] Judge Begbie deplored the low quality of magistrates, a view shared by Edward Hodgson of Charlottetown, who wrote to Thompson as early as 1889 complaining of a 'dangerous power in the hands of the most ignorant and illiterate magistracy in Canada.' Another correspondent commented that 'the Country Justice is not usually a very highly educated or experienced man, and generally he feels competent to try, and wants to try, every case which comes before him, and is susceptible to influence which does not appear in that evidence.' In 1889 William White, a lawyer in Pembroke, wrote to his brother Peter, who was an MP, describing the 'absurd anomaly' of having magistrates with no legal training trying criminal cases in which the 'liberty of the subject is made dependent upon their whims and prejudices.' White did not doubt that they were well-intentioned but he added: 'If Mr. Mowat will persist in appointing men like these ... whose training for the position has been behind a counter selling newspapers and notions like Mitchell (who, by the way, still carries on his business) in a backwoods sawmill like Doran or a farmer like MacNaughton or in a jeweler's shop like Thompson, then the Dominion Government should take away from them powers that should only be exercised by a person of the highest legal training.'

James Masson, an MP, wrote to Sedgewick in May 1892 complaining of too much power residing in JPs under the Code Bill. He said: 'In the hands of an ignorant and prejudiced class, such as nine-tenths of our Justices of the Peace are, they would legalize oppression and tyranny.' On the other hand, a JP from Charlottetown wrote complaining of the fees paid to his brethren. He thought there should be 'some reasonable recognition of the service of a class of men who have done more perhaps to preserve the peace and promote the prosperity of the people than any class in the community.' The JP had to provide his own courtroom, fire, light, and stationery, yet the fees paid were 'a pittance that would disgust any ordinary laborer.' The JP had played a most important role in the administration of justice in England, but the system did not travel very well, in this individual's estimation, because the gratuitous public service of the English squire JP could not be duplicated in Prince Edward Island, where the Justices were farmers and businessmen and there were 'few men of independent position willing for the sake of position to work for the honor of the thing.' These pleas went unheeded, and the provisions of the Speedy Trials Act were incorporated in the new Code.

Only three issues elicited more than one or two replies – lotteries, sexual morals, and the powers of Justices of the Peace. The most popular subject was lotteries. Correspondents were deeply concerned that lottery tickets from the United States, particularly Louisiana, were corrupting the morals of Canadians. There was similar moral indignation about the subterfuge of art unions, particularly in Quebec, which ran lotteries, allegedly as a method of subsidizing artists.

D.A. Watt was one of the few who discussed the policy of criminal law while raising a basic issue. A staunch Presbyterian, Watt was the driving force behind the Society for the Protection of Women and Young Girls, which campaigned against lax sexual morals. He was responsible for the most fundamental changes to the first draft of the Code Bill. As a result of his efforts, Canada's Criminal Code of 1892 had and retains the most comprehensive system of offences for protecting young women and girls from sexual predators.[55] In addition to printing two pamphlets, which were distributed to all MPs and Senators, Watt and his colleagues in the Society wrote to Thompson and the Department of Justice nineteen times between 1889 and 1892.[56] These were not form letters written by superficial lobbyists. Watt wrote long dissertations on the social evils of Montreal, the need to protect poor young girls from seduction and abduction (as the law had always done for their 'more fortunate sisters' who were heiresses), the operation of brothels, the seduction of female immigrants on trains, and procuration of the underaged for lives of prostitution. He quoted freely from the publications of the Massachusetts Society for the Prevention of Cruelty to Children and UK royal commissions and also drafted bills for inclusion in the Code.

Watt was a skilled propagandist who deserved his success, although he was sometimes given to extreme demands, such as his desire to raise the age of consent to twenty-one years. He exposed the shocking injustices imposed on children sent to prison for two to five years merely for being vagrants and pointed out that many of these unfortunate youths were females in need of protection, not punishment. Yet even here the ideas were secondhand. Watt had been strongly influenced by W.T. Stead's similar campaign in England, which had resulted in the passage of the Criminal Law Amendment Act of 1885, raising the age of sexual consent from twelve to fourteen years.[57]

Another lobbyist was John King, QC, of Berlin (now Kitchener), the son-in-law of William Lyon Mackenzie and father of a future prime minister.[58] King wrote many letters and drafted sections for inclusion in the Code but was less successful than Watt. Acting on behalf of newspaper owners, he wanted to make it more difficult for his clients to be sued for libel. King's transparent attempts at lobbying received courteous but unco-operative responses from the Department of Justice.

Most of the other suggestions in the files of the Department of Justice were the efforts of citizens with private axes to grind or whose suggestions were already well covered by the Code. A catalogue of these complaints and 'reformist' ideas furnishes some gauge of public opinion and citizens' concerns, even if they are not statistically significant. Illegal obstetrical practices were condemned; the letter writer was somewhat coy in describing this particular practice, but one gathers that he was talking about sterilization. Concern about obscenity took a form not likely to come to the mind of the modern reader. The writers wanted the depiction of prizefights to be banned, along with magazine advertisements peddling intimate items of female attire. The censors were also convinced that sexual congress between white men and Indian women should be treated as criminal. Another deplored the behaviour of Mormons living in open bigamous marriages. The temperance lobby was worried about the trade in liquor with the Indians, although Americans were suspected to be the major culprits. Americans were in fact looked upon as a source of moral pollution on many fronts. A grand jury recommended that there should be more stringent laws about concealed weapons, particularly when carried by foreigners. A citizen suggested that the vagrancy laws should be extended to catch professional criminals infiltrating the country from such places as Buffalo. An incensed correspondent from western Ontario wrote to Sedgewick asking that it be made an offence to live in adultery; there was such a flagrant episode in his neighbourhood, but he assured the Department that the couple were Americans and that Canadians were above such depravity. This writer may have been too optimistic a nationalist, because a writer from Manitoba complained about farmers who eloped, deserting their wives and making them public charges. He urged that adultery should be made a crime, as it was in some Maritime provinces. The drafters gave this serious consideration but finally decided against including it in the Code.[59] There were suggestions that parents who neglected their children should be fined. Similarly, children should be legally obliged to support their parents. Finally, a recommendation was made that parents should contribute to the upkeep of children in reformatories. Most of these ideas had already emerged in English and United States legislation.[60]

The files also contain a long and intriguing correspondence between the Department of Justice and a Mr Martin of Chatham, who was worried about the unethical practices of newspapers and merchants using circulation boosters and advertising gimmicks such as 'Prize Rebuses.' Martin was so persistent that he was finally invited to draft a section to make criminal such misleading advertising and sharp commercial practice. There were also letters on jury unanimity, the legality of air guns, stealing from graves, cock fighting, the proscription of cigarette smoking among children, deploring corporal punishment in schools, fraudulent bankruptcies, and bicycle thieves. A few peculiarly Canadian concerns were also aired. Ice holes should be properly fenced. One writer with experience in the Yukon said that it should be an offence to neglect to rescue someone who would otherwise freeze to death. Farmers complained that sharp operators were defrauding them of their hay, promising future payment which never arrived.

Some special interest groups made requests for amendment of the law. A railway company pointed out that tramps were a great problem for its operation because they loitered in stations and broke seals on freight cars. A municipal politician wanted to end corruption in elections. Another criticized situations which allowed conflicts of interest to arise so that, for instance, no alderman should be an architect, although the letter writer probably meant the contrary to apply. At least two labour unions wrote to the Department. There was a long letter from the Legislation Committee of the Toronto Trades and Labour Council, which was very concerned about the restraint of trade laws and hoped that Thompson would protect the interests of the working man. A piece of draft legislation was enclosed, but the union received a standard polite reply.

The squirearchy also expressed its views, seeking more stringent poaching laws, although this did not receive a sympathetic hearing from the drafters. One Ontario gentleman-farmer was irate that there was such a differentiation between larceny of a dog, attracting a fine and up to two months' jail, and stealing a pig, which could result in a prison term of fourteen years. This was a ridiculous situation because many dogs were worth much more than pigs. A Mr Jones of Brantford had similar complaints, specifically about the difficulty of making a rural JP believe that a dog was worth more than $5. Furthermore, 'we may value our cow but we love our dog.'

THE CODE IN PARLIAMENT

The parliamentary debate on the Code was a mild affair. The House of Commons contained many lawyers but very few who knew much about the criminal law. Thompson made his speech on second reading on 12 April 1892, and the Bill passed within two months with committee hearings in the interim.[61] Thompson adopted the thoughts of Stephen in describing the bill as a 'reduction of the existing law to an orderly written system' freed from technicalities and obscurities. The rest of his speech followed very closely the memoranda of the Department of Justice already discussed. For tactical reasons he concentrated on an item not in the Code. The 1891 Bill had proposed the abolition of the grand jury, but this item of doubtful constitutionality was abandoned in the second Bill. Thompson nevertheless spoke on the subject at some length. The opposition fell into the trap, making 'impassioned defences of an institution that the government had just announced it did not propose to touch.'[62]

The rest of the House debate was a desultory discussion of technical detail with no serious criticism or comment. Only three Opposition members spoke, Wilfrid Laurier, David Mills, a future Minister of Justice, and Louis Davies. Laurier pointed out that there were many innovations in the Bill but none which would 'startle the country or take the people by surprise.'[63] He was a little concerned about omission of the term 'malice' and wondered what would take its place.[64]

Most of the detailed work was done in Joint Committee. Even at that stage there was no concerted effort to discuss general principle, ie, the underlying theory of the general part of a code which would be the intellectual foundation for the more specialized parts of the enactment. The simple explanation for this uncritical approach was that the general principles were not explicit. The lawyers on the Committee were content with the sections of the Code which depended on the common law to fill in the gaps left by the Code. The fact that these provisions were necessary shows the half-hearted character of the attempt at comprehensive codification; the absence of any challenge to those sections indicates how shallow was the knowledge and concern about the concept of a code.

Questions asked about the Code in Committee were rather haphazard.[65] Long discussions were held about a few matters, including the insanity defence. Other provisions (or lack of them) passed unnoticed, such as the lack of a section on intoxication. Many members restricted their contribution to raising or lowering punishments. The Committee was carefully managed, and the members were deterred from critical comment by the fact that Thompson was well briefed and had the constant support of Sedgewick, who, in turn, was briefed by Fraser. At this stage Liberal MP Sir Richard Cartwright objected to the Bill because it was based on the English Draft Code, which had never become law. Cartwright, who tended to be an anglophobe, seems to have felt that if it was not good enough for England then it was not good enough for Canada. Thompson defended the English effort and assured him that the Draft Code had failed only because of the political situation then existing in Britain. Cartwright also objected to the broad police powers conferred by the Bill, enlarging the right to search and arrest. He admitted that these might be necessary in England, but Canada did not yet have a 'regular criminal class.'[66]

The Committee spent much time on sedition, riots, perjury, and libel – topics more likely to interest politicans than the dry, technical concepts of malice, constructive murder, and *animus furandi* (intent to steal). Other comments were more social than legal. One member thought indecent acts were sins not crimes, and that the actors should be flogged not imprisoned. Another said that there were problems in defining obscenity, since it was so subjective. In discussing the prohibition of card-playing on trains, a member objected to the passage of laws which would not be observed (or enforced for that matter). Much of the Committee's time was spent on the procedural parts of the Code, and there were long discussions about the incompetence of the police and the lower judiciary.

Only one section of the Code discussed in Joint Committee directly raised the issue of codification. In talking about the libel section, which one member thought was too harsh on journalists, Thompson explained that the provision was 'an exact rendering of the present law, and I am sure that the honourable gentleman will realise that it will not be less subject to proper administration in practice than the common law is now, notwithstanding that it is embodied in a statute. All these provisions of a statute which merely state the common law are interpreted as making no new law, but as mere statements of the existing law, and are interpreted precisely as if they formed part of the decision of the courts.'[67] In response to Thompson's remarks Laurier reiterated the argument that converting common law into statutory form would rob the law of elasticity.

Time was a greater obstacle than opposition speakers. Although the architects of legislation had a two-year plan for its passage, there were voices asking for further delay. J.L. Archambault, the Montreal Crown Prosecutor wrote to Thompson in April 1892 on behalf of that city's bar. The lawyers wanted more time to consider the merits of the legislation 'in view of the importance of this general law applicable to the different provinces.' Archambault did not personally agree with the idea of postponement but nevertheless asked for a special committee of the House or a commission to examine the Bill more thoroughly. The Senate for its part almost scuttled the Code because of the lateness of the session. Senator Samuel Prowse wrote to Thompson in May 1892 after the Bill passed the House that some Senators were complaining that the Bill was being railroaded through the Senate. However, nothing came of this, since the passage through the Senate was well stage-managed. Richard Scott, the only Senator openly opposed to the idea of codification, did not attend the committee hearings. Of the few dozen amendments made by the Senate nearly all were to correct typographical errors.

THE AFTERMATH OF ENACTMENT

The last hurdle was Justice Taschereau, who made very stringent and detailed criticisms after the Code had passed both the Commons and the Senate but before it came into force. In so doing he emulated the behaviour of the English Chief Justice, Lord Cockburn, whose criticisms of Stephen's English Draft Code and Code Bill were important factors in killing that measure. The rejection of Taschereau's offer to draft a code has already been mentioned. Two other episodes may throw some light on his behaviour. In 1889 Thompson wrote to Taschereau regretfully informing him that it was contrary to current Departmental policy to order four hundred copies of Taschereau's book on criminal law. In August 1891, after the first version of the Code Bill had been introduced and, presumably after Parliament had recessed for the summer, Taschereau wrote to Thompson about the Bill. Although the letter is lost, the Minister of Justice replied that before the letter had been received, 'the Bill had passed all its stages except the Third Reading and I had understood that before its introduction it had received the approval of the judges.'

On 20 January 1893 Taschereau published *Criminal Code of 1892: Letter by Judge Taschereau to the Attorney General of Canada with Comments and Suggestions.*[68] A week later he wrote a private letter to Thompson:

It is not necessary for me, I hope, to assure you personally that it is not for the pleasure of faultfinding or of indulging into [sic] criticisms that I have addressed you in the matter. I thought that the special attention I have paid to that branch of the law might be of some usefulness, however so small, to the public interest, on the occasion of the codification. I only regret that I have not been able to present my views in some shape or other, before the House of Commons when the measure was under consideration.

Despite Taschereau's procrastination, poor timing, or bad manners, it must be said that some of the criticisms in his published remarks had substantial merit, though his best comments were cribbed from Cockburn's attack on Stephen's Bill, and the greater part of the open letter is mere nitpicking criticism.

Taschereau spent all but three pages of the six-page open letter and twenty-three-page appendix on technical matters, but his dissection of the Code's 'intrinsic defects' was very accurate. He said the Code was 'replete of contradictory clauses, of redundant enactments, of clumsy, needlessly minute and irrational, or repugnant provisions, obviously leading ... to incongruities and anomalies ... cumbrous, yet not complete; the classification is unsystematic, and the whole without attempt at symmetry.' The pruning knife was not used by the drafter to lop off dead branches. The 'weeding was left undone.' Taschereau said he had once believed in codification but now was not so sure. Perhaps consolidation was sufficient. If codification were advisable, however, then it must be complete. The code should not need to be supplemented by statutes or common law. These comments were all borrowed from Cockburn (with due acknowledgment). Taschereau believed that Sedgewick and his colleagues had 'forgotten that a codifier must not rashly cast down without also building up.' He quoted Austin, who said that a codifier must keep before him a 'map of the law as a whole, enabling him to subordinate the less general under the more general ... and to analyse and translate the general into the particulars that it contains.'

The judge's most damaging criticism was of the General Part of the Code. He deplored the lacunae which had been left in not defining *mens rea* (guilty intent) and defences such as intoxication. In these comments he was on safe ground, and Sedgewick and other members of the Department of Justice made no reply. Taschereau was quite right in saying that the drafters of the 1892 Code had relied too heavily on Stephen. Yet Taschereau himself seemed to have the same failing. The judge had many suggestions on the sections which described specific offences yet he offered no positive recommendations for drafting a General Part either in his letter to Thompson or in his subsequent annotation of the Criminal Code.[69]

Sedgewick defended his Code in a long memorandum of February 1893 to Thompson. That the perfect code should contain all the law on a subject 'within the four corners of the volume' was a view that 'may be right in theory' but impossible in practice. The 1892 Code was more complete than the English Draft Code. The Deputy Minister was incensed at Taschereau's suggestion that Thompson had 'smuggled' changes through Parliament. Sedgewick reminded his Minister 'how careful we were, as well before the Joint Committee as in the House to point out any change made by the Bill, either in the common or statute law.' Parliament had been apprised of Cockburn's criticisms and had still passed the Code.

In the memorandum a somewhat defensive Sedgewick told his Minister that of 'the 120 sections to which the Judge draws attention, we have discovered 11 sections only which suggest amendment and only two or three are *necessary* although, on the whole, we think them all *desirable.*' After reviewing Taschereau's suggestions, Sedgewick added: 'You can state positively that the foregoing are the only amendments which his long criticism would seem in any way necessarily to call for, and you may, therefore, point out the absurdity of his suggestion that Parliament should temporarily withdraw the Code or postpone the date of its coming into force.'

In one of Sedgewick's few comments on the lack of general principles, he appears as a true disciple of the Stephen who could not forget his common law heritage. Sedgewick seemed to believe with Blackstone that the common law was a 'brooding omnipresence in the sky.' In the most intemperate words of his reply, the Deputy Minister tried to refute Taschereau by saying:

> The principles and rules of the common law in all ordinary cases have been stated and in favour of the life and liberty of the subject. There has been secured to him as there ought to have been secured to him, the benefit of any defence opened to him at common law, even although this should be of such an unusual character, as not hitherto to have been the subject of any decision. It is not every mind that has such a sublime confidence and conceit in its own powers as to feel safe in declaring that a statement of rules of excuse or justification is so complete as to justify the exclusion of the common law.[70]

For Sedgewick, one of the principal objects of the Code was placing existing law in 'short and attainable compass.' The drafters did not look upon themselves as law reformers.

Someone in the Department (probably Fraser) had prepared a brief from which Sedgewick wrote his reply to Taschereau. Two comments reinforced the Stephenesque quality of the drafter's philosophy on alleged codification. Taschereau had deplored the fact that the law was not all found in a 'complete' code. The writer commented: 'I suppose it is not thought that we can free ourselves from case law. It would not be desirable, and if it were possible to get rid of all the case law of the past, it would tomorrow commence again to grow and to assert itself.' The writer also addressed himself to the question of preserving the common law despite the existence of a Code. He reassured Sedgewick that the wiser course had been followed because it would provide greater elasticity. There would be 'less danger in the early days of its administration of offenders escaping punishment, and it will adjust itself the better to changing circumstances and modes of life.'

Taschereau may not have found the Fraser-Sedgewick response convincing, but his objections did not attract the support which would have been necessary to stall the enactment at this stage. On 1 July 1893 the Criminal Code of Canada was proclaimed in force. Over eighty years later in 1976, the Law Reform Commission of Canada published a study paper entitled *Towards a Codification of Canadian Criminal Law*.[71] This excellent document re-examined all the familiar arguments for and against codification and concluded that Canada must work towards a 'genuine code.' It must be intelligible to the ordinary citizen, not just to the expert lawyer. The Commission believed that the courts 'have abdicated their creative role,' in that they have 'failed to consider the totality of Canadian criminal law and then to seek solutions within that framework.' A true code should state 'the aims and purposes and essential principles of criminal law, as well as the concepts governing criminal justice.' Let the Commission have the last word, since these comments contain thoughts which were vaguely framed by Bentham, slightly more carefully enunciated by Austin, but ignored or not understood by Stephen, Sedgewick, and Burbidge.

NOTES

1 See generally Leon Radzinowicz *A History of English Criminal Law and its Administration from 1750* 4 vols to date (London 1949-) I

2 William Blackstone *Commentaries on the Laws of England* (London 10th ed. 1787)

3 Ibid. IV 3

4 Jeremy Bentham *A Comment on the Commentaries: A Criticism of William Blackstone's Commentaries on the Laws of England* ed. C.W. Everett (Oxford 1928) 153

5 John Austin *Lectures on Jurisprudence* (London 1861)
6 The best reference to these reports is found in W.R. Cornish et al., *Crime and Law in Nineteenth Century Britain* (Dublin 1978) 66–71.
7 *Report from the Royal Commission on Criminal Law* (London 1834) 117
8 John Clive *Macaulay: The Shaping of the Historian* (London 1973) 436 and generally ch. 14.
9 J.F. Stephen *A History of the Criminal Law of England* III (London 1883) 302–4
10 Ibid. 306
11 J.F. Stephen *A Digest of the Criminal Law (Crimes and Punishments)* (London 1877)
12 See M. Banks's essay in this volume.
13 Printed document 'for the use of the Colonial Office 20 May 1870' found in Public Record Office, England. CO 885 HP 00062
14 *Upper Canada Law Journal* I (1855) 197 (hereafter UCLJ). This journal later became CLJ
15 UCLJ III (1857) 175
16 UCLJ IV (1858) 125
17 UCLJ V (1859) 73
18 UCLJ VI (1860) 220, 223
19 CLJ X (1874) 269
20 CLJ XI (1875) 7. See also CLJ XII 33
21 *Legal News* I (1878) 431 (hereafter LN)
22 Ibid. 505
23 LN II (1879) 13, 19, 27
24 Ibid.
25 Ibid. 20
26 LN V (1882) 209, 219, 225, 230
27 *Canadian Law Times* I (1881) 230 (hereafter CLT). See also André Morel 'La Réception du droit criminel anglais au Québec (1760–1892)' *Thémis* XIII (1978) 449–541
28 CLT III (1883) 139
29 *Report of the Commission for the Consolidation and Revision of the Statutes affecting the Province of Ontario* (Toronto 1875)
30 CLT IV (1884) 432
31 The *Manitoba Law Journal* published some excerpts from Bentham's writings because of recent interest in the topic. The editors commented that the criminal law would be largely codified in the next session. (*Manitoba Law Journal* I [1884] 153, 167)
32 *La Thémis* I (1879) 269, V (1883) 21–57
33 For an appraisal of Field's work see Alison Reppy, ed. *Dudley David Field: Centenary Essays* (New York 1949) and especially essays by Pound and Reppy

at 3 and 17 respectively. Field's criminal code became law in 1881 but his civil code was rejected in 1886.

34 CLT VI (1886) 97–100, 244, 437; VII (1887) 219; VIII (1888) 252; IX (1889) 261; X (1890) 191

35 CLJ XXII (1886) 133

36 CLJ XXVI (1890) 577

37 CLJ XXVIII (1892) 450–1

38 LN XV (1892) 222–3

39 Charles Greaves *The Criminal Law Consolidation and Amendment Acts of the 24 and 25 Victoria with notes and observations and forms for summary proceedings* (London 1861)

40 Most of the correspondence and memoranda concerning the origins of the Criminal Code of Canada were found in the records of the Department of Justice in Ottawa. They have not been transferred to the Public Archives, nor have they been classified. There are some hundreds of letters from Canadians who wished to comment on the Code Bill. In addition there are about 200 pages of typewritten and holograph memoranda which were prepared for or by the Department. Without exception, these memoranda are anonymous. I am most grateful to the Deputy Minister of Justice, M. Roger Tassé, for permission to use these materials.

41 Ibid.

42 H.E. Taschereau *The Criminal Law Consolidation and Amendment Acts of 1869, 32–33 Victoria for the Dominion of Canada* (Montreal 1874–5)

43 Toronto 1891

44 See note 40 above.

45 See note 40 above.

46 Edward Livingston *A System of Penal Law for the United States of America Consisting of A Code of Crimes and Punishments* (Washington 1828)

47 This memorandum appears to be by Gowan because it is written in the style of his enthusiastic political prose. In addition, it makes specific mention of codification and Gowan was one of the few who tried to discuss that question, although his arguments show more vigour than precision.

48 See note 42 above.

49 See note 11 above and text at note 43 above.

50 Parl. Deb. 3rd Series vol. 245 col. 315 (UK). The most accessible discussion is found in J.C. Martin *The Criminal Code of Canada* (Toronto 1955) 1–3

51 The effect of the *Tolson* decision on the law of bigamy was also incorporated (*Regina* v *Tolson* [1889] 16 *Cox's Criminal Cases* 629)

52 The Canadian content, which can hardly be said to have included jurisprudential concepts, related to basic definitions, the application of English law in Canada, the consequences of felony, prize fights, inciting Indians to riotous

acts, explosives and weapons, public meetings, the sale of liquor, the corruption of public officials, escape of prisoners, seduction of women passengers on ships, the prostitution of Indian women, gambling in stocks, pure foods, recklessly setting fire to forests, counterfeit money, trade marks, loitering near ships, leaving unguarded ice-holes, stealing from the mails, larceny of trees, stealing from Indian graves, using false tickets on railways, members of the NWMP fraudulently obtaining pensions, and several other sections on fraud.

53 The Public Record Office in England has numerous files which concern reform of the criminal law. In the period form 1840 to 1900, there are frequent contributions to the process by Her Majesty's High Court Judges. The PRO classification is HO 45

54 42 Vict. c. 44; RSC 1886 c. 175

55 The Criminal Code 1892 55–6 Vict. c. 29 Parts XIII and XIV. Criminal Code 1953–4 c. 51; RSC 1970 PARTS IV and V

56 For example, D.A. Watt *Moral Legislation: Prepared for the Information of the Senate* (Montreal 1890). This was published in several forms between 1887 and 1893

57 48 and 49 Vict. c. 69 (Imp.)

58 King (1843–1916) was a lawyer and lecturer at Osgoode Hall Law School, a former newspaper editor, and author of *A Decade in the History of Newspaper Libel* (Woodstock 1892) and *The Law of Defamation* (Toronto 1907). See Henry J. Morgan *The Canadian Men and Women of the Time* (Toronto 1912, 2nd ed.)

59 Given the fact that there were several letters condemning adulterous behaviour and urging criminal penalties, it is a little surprising that the Department of Justice decided to exclude it from the Code. There is only 'official' comment in one of the several anonymous memoranda. The memorandum writer who seems to speak with some authority simply comments that Sedgewick and Burbidge were wise to exclude adultery from the list of criminal offences.

60 Such law reform is discussed in Graham Parker 'The Century of the Child' *Can. Bar Rev.* XLV (1967) 741–63

61 *House of Commons Debates* 1892 I 1312

62 Robert C. Macleod 'The Shaping of Canadian Criminal Law 1892 to 1902' Canadian Historical Association *Historical Papers London 1978* 66

63 *House of Commons Debates* 1892 I 1316

64 In response to Laurier, Thompson simply replied: 'I propose to substitute a new definition of the crime of murder, and new definitions of those crimes in which the word "malice" was previously used.' Ibid. 1317

65 Ibid. II 2701 *et seq.*

66 Ibid. 2783

67 Ibid. 2812. Thompson was being quite prophetic. Canadian judges (even French Canadians who had experience with a code system) have never used the Code as a code. They have always treated it as a piece of the common law in written form and have, until recently, shown no hesitation in using English decisions as good authority in Canada.

68 Ottawa 1893. The CLJ XXIX (1893) 94–5 was very critical of Taschereau's letter to Thompson. The judge had had ample opportunity to make his views known in 1891 and, in any event, he should express himself 'unostentatiously.' The CLJ also added: 'it was a duty, and should have been a pleasure, for any one occupying the position of a judge, enjoying the confidence of the public, and receiving public money, so far as he conveniently could, the matter having come to his attention and being on a branch of the law of which he has special knowledge, to aid in making any legislation affecting it as complete as possible.'

69 H.E. Taschereau *The Criminal Code of Canada as Amended in 1893 with Commentaries, Annotations, Precedents of Indictments* (Toronto 1893, reprinted 1980). In that work he quoted at great length from the reports of the Commissioners which introduced the English Draft Code.

70 See note 40 above.

71 (Ottawa 1976)

8

Judicial Conservatism in an Age of Innovation: Comparative Perspectives on Canadian Nuisance Law 1880–1930

JENNIFER NEDELSKY

THE MEANING OF CONSERVATISM

Lawyers and scholars, critics and admirers, seem to agree that Canadian courts are conservative. The meaning of this claim is, however, not at all clear. 'Conservative' may be a literal description of the courts' behaviour, or it may be a claim about the reasons for the judges' behaviour. These meanings need to be distinguished and tested in order to understand the extent and significance of judicial conservatism. Taken as a description, conservatism refers to a tendency literally to conserve or maintain existing law by strictly, even mechanistically, applying established rules. The conservative judge is unwilling to modify rules and thus little interested in policy arguments about the effect of his decision or the social function of a rule. The possible reasons for such an approach are various: judicial approval of existing rules or their effects; insensitivity to new problems; lack of creativity; or intellectual timidity, an unwillingness to take on the common law's difficult task of balancing continuity and change. But a different order of explanation is also possible, what might be called principled conservatism. Judges may apply rules strictly because they believe in the principle that changing the law is the province of the legislature, not the judge.

This principle is often associated with formalist jurisprudence, which conceives of judicial decision-making as the determinate, sometimes scientific, application of rules and principles contained in precedent. The importance of formalism should not be underestimated because of the apparent paradox on which it rests: common law is judge made law, but judges do not and should not make law. The Blackstonian resolution to the paradox is that judges do not make law, they merely 'find' it. Once found, the immutable principles of the common law need only be faithfully applied. Modern formalism accepts the existence of underlying principles and binding rules of law, but recognizes that these rules are created through the long-term process of judicial decision-making. Once settled, however, these rules can and should determine the outcome of cases. The task of the judge is, accordingly, to apply these rules impartially, not to change them in the name of policy or the public good. The principles of consistency and of democracy require that changes be made only by the legislature.[1]

The political dimension of formalist doctrine is not incidental. Robert Stevens associates the late nineteenth-century rise of formalism in England with utilitarian attacks on judicial discretion and policy-making.[2] The mantle of formalism, the claim that judges simply applied precedent, insulated the judiciary from attack and corresponded to the democratic argument that law-making should be done by responsible representatives. Morton Horwitz argues that in the United States the rise of legal formalism after the civil war served to disguise 'both the recent origins and the foundations in policy and group self interest of all newly established legal doctrines.'[3] Moreover, the political significance of claims for a limited judicial role is not limited to any particular school of jurisprudence or its historical origins. Any such claims play an important part in the legitimating function law can serve.[4] If judges merely apply the law objectively, they may truly claim to be apolitical. The assertion that courts make neither law nor policy is the basis for their image as neutral arbiters. This image is in turn the basis for the claim that behind the force of law lies the force of justice, not the power of interests or the will of individuals. The role the courts have played and the way legal rhetoric portrays this role are thus important for understanding the function of law in sustaining the structure of power in any political system.

In the United States formalist jurisprudence is no longer taken very seriously.[5] Dominant in the late nineteenth century, it was challenged early on by Oliver Wendell Holmes and thoroughly undermined by the Realists in the 1920s and 1930s.[6] In England, however, formalism remained an important doctrine, reaching its peak in the 1950s.[7] Canada has followed, and perhaps exceeded, the English model. Amid growing diversity and confusion, one still finds judges asserting that it is not their role to make or modify the law.[8] Some law school courses and texts still present law as doctrinal development virtually devoid of political or economic context or significance.[9] Such presentation of course fosters the formalist image of the political neutrality of law and the courts. And in Canada the endurance of formalist jurisprudence is accompanied by a judicial reputation for caution and a reluctance to innovate or to articulate policy. The Canadian judiciary may thus be conservative both in the literal descriptive sense and in the sense of principled conservatism underlying judicial behaviour.[10]

While there are broad reasons of both theory and politics for courts maintaining a limited role, the specific explanation for the conservatism of Canadian courts has usually been historical and institutional, focusing on the Canadian reliance on English decisions imposed by the structure of the legal system. Until 1949 the Judicial Committee of the Privy Council in England, not the Supreme Court of Canada, was the highest court of appeal. English judicial decisions were considered binding, and the Supreme Court was often bypassed as an unnecessary step in the appeal process. This is said to have undermined the prestige of the Supreme Court and retarded the development of a distinctively Canadian law and legal philosophy.[11] Moreover, if Canadian judges merely followed English precedent, they gained little experience in making the ongoing modifications intrinsic to the common law and engaged few opportunities to attain the stature of a Mansfield, Denning, Holmes, or Cardozo.

This essay challenges the above explanation and tests the image of the Canadian courts as conservative and as passive followers of English precedent. By focusing on the era in which Canada experienced its major surge of industrialization, one can try to determine whether the courts maintained a conservative stance even when the demand for judicial innovation must have been especially pressing. By looking closely at one particular area of law, nuisance law, one can determine the extent and nature of such conservatism as did exist and the reasons for it.

LAW AND INDUSTRIALIZATION

Students of both English and American law have found the response of the courts to the demands of industrialization a particularly useful way of studying the forces which affect the development of the law and the role it plays in society. The common law at the beginning of the nineteenth century was ill suited to the rapid and inexpensive development of industrial capitalism. The pre-industrial doctrines of property law, nuisance, and riparian rights permitted small, and comparatively unproductive, landholders to enjoin or exact damages from industries interfering with traditional rights. Common law actions could thus have impeded or vastly increased the cost of development. American courts did not, however, permit this to happen. Morton Horwitz shows that in the first half of the nineteenth century the courts radically changed the substance of common law in order to facilitate and, in effect, to subsidize development. American judges clearly acknowledged what he calls an instrumental conception of the law. They modified the law explicitly in order to meet the requirements of industrialization. Horwitz argues that the judges consciously wrought a transformation of American law which fostered economic development and concentrated wealth and power in the hands of the few.[12]

Similarly, Joel Brenner's study of nuisance law and the industrial revolution in England points to the emergence of an instrumental transformation of the law.[13] Starting with the question of why nuisance law did *not* hamper industrialization, Brenner shows that during a 'crucial period in the 1850s and 1860s' the courts accepted 'reasonable care' defences appropriate to negligence, but alien to traditional nuisance. He also demonstrates that nuisance law was applied differently to factories than to individuals and that this 'dual standard had been long operating before it was effectively ratified by the House of Lords in *St. Helen's Smelting Co.* v *Tipping* in 1865.'[14] In *St. Helen's* the Lords drew novel distinctions which permitted 'a balance between comfort and health on the one hand and economic interests on the other.' The Lords had explicitly modified the application of nuisance law to industry in order to facilitate development: 'where great works have been created and carried on, and are the means of developing the national wealth, you must not stand on extreme rights and allow a person to say, "I will bring an action against you for this and that, and so on." Business could not go on if it were so.'[15]

If both English and American judges modified the law to facilitate industrial development, were Canadian judges also willing to make concessions to the economic demands of burgeoning industry and the new social reality of crowded industrial towns? By the late nineteenth century, industrialization and urbanization were changing the shape of Canadian society:[16] between 1880 and 1920 the population doubled from 3,689,257 to 8,788,483; 74.35 per cent of the population were classified as rural by the census of Canada in 1881; by 1921 the percentage had decreased to 50.48. Capital investment in manufactures increased from $165,302,632 in 1880 to $2,923,667,011 in 1920 and the gross value of all manufactured products from $469,847,886 in 1880 to $3,706,544,997 in 1920.[17] Manufacturing, once diffused, was concentrating in industrial towns. Factories increasingly replaced small workshops, and steam-powered engines brought noise as well as productivity.[18] As the nuisances of industrialization increased, so did the costs of eliminating them. Manufacturing establishments, for example, were becoming sufficiently large and important to local economies that ordering them to take their nuisances elsewhere would have had serious consequences.[19]

Industrialization brought problems and promises which were common to the United States, England, and Canada. The hope for prosperity and progress through industry was as compelling in Canada as elsewhere. Encouraging manufacturing was a national priority and official government policy.[20] The question, then, is whether Canadian judges let traditional common law impede this policy or joined their British and American brethren in modifying the law to facilitate development.

To answer this question we need to focus on the period in which the courts first had to cope with the challenges of industrialization in a serious and sustained way. The dates 1880–1930, while not otherwise a neat periodization, encompass the initial surge of industrialization and the continued high rate of industrial development through the 1920s. Cases from this period should thus allow us to see the extent of judicial accommodation to early industrialization.

A study of this period cannot, of course, tell us whether there was a significantly different judicial approach to nuisance law in the period prior to 1880, when the conflicting claims were relatively less common or important. However, my findings and Professor Risk's work suggest that this was not the case.[21] Also beyond the scope of this study is the question of whether the courts began to modify nuisance law when Canada's industrialization and urbanization were more developed. This essay shows only that changes did not come in the early period of industrialization, the era in which English and American courts judged modifications to be necessary for the development of industry.

In one important way the challenges facing Canadian judges did not parallel those in England and the United States. Canadian industrialization came comparatively late. By the time most issues of industrialization arose in Canada, English and American courts had already grappled with major problems and provided guidelines and precedents. One could argue therefore that the same kind of judicial creativity was not required in Canada. Yet at least in the case of nuisance, the English modifications of the law did not always offer clear solutions to Canadian courts. The way Canadian judges fashioned their approach to the conflicts of industrialization from the judicial experience of others and their own principles and predilections is the ultimate subject of this essay.

NUISANCE LAW

Nuisance law is particularly revealing because it deals with pressing clashes between traditional rights and the demands of industrialization. Nuisance law protects an occupier's right to enjoy his property free from unreasonable interferences.[22] Nuisance suits could, for example, prevent a neighbour from destroying one's comfort and enjoyment with disgusting smells, acrid smoke, corrosive fumes, or loud and continuous noise. But with the advent of industrialization, the smoke, smell, and noise of industry so encroached upon town dwellers that the very meaning of one's right to reasonable enjoyment came into question.

Traditional nuisance law asked only whether the plaintiff's rights were unreasonably interfered with, not how carefully conducted or economically important the defendant's activities were. Strict application of this law should have entitled aggrieved neighbours of smelters or foundries to an injunction. Yet industry and its nuisances flourished, and courts in England and the United States saw to it that nuisance law was not a significant impediment.[23] The judicial techniques for accomplishing this gave nuisance law a flexibility and uncertainty which makes it especially useful for studying the Canadian application of these approaches.

The English cases which formed the basis of most Canadian arguments and decisions abound with conflicting opinions, open-ended terms, and essentially subjective judgments. The judges themselves described the rules of nuisance law as 'elastic,' meaning that they had no fixed content but took their practical meaning from each judge's assessment of the circumstances of the case.[24] This left considerable leeway for the Canadian judiciary to develop a distinctive law of nuisance, while faithfully citing English precedents. In fact, Canadian courts did deal with the nuisances of industrialization in a way different from that of the English or the Americans.

Nuisance cases from 1880 to 1930 show that the Canadian courts were considerably less willing to abridge the common law rights of occupiers in response to the pressures of industrialization than their American counterparts or their English mentors.[25] Canadian judges were by and large unwilling to accommodate the law of nuisance to the 'onward spirit of the age' either by explicitly balancing the public good of industry and utilities against individual injuries, or by using the variety of techniques available for defeating claims, such as statutory authority, public nuisance, or local standard of comfort.[26] The courts were also generally unwilling to deny traditional remedies in order to foster development or minimize its costs.

One might argue that nuisance law is not a good gauge of the conservatism of the Canadian courts because in both the United States and England the law of nuisance appeared to maintain 'the pristine purity of a pre-industrial mentality' long after other areas of the law showed substantial innovation and accommodation.[27] But by the time of Canadian industrialization, even the appearance of purity was virtually gone from English precedent.[28] More important, the cases show that what was mere appearance in the United States and England had considerable reality in Canada. Not only did the formal statements of nuisance law remain 'pristine,' but the Canadian courts took little advantage of either English 'elasticity' or American techniques to deny claims or limit remedies.

Canadian nuisance cases did nevertheless generally centre on these rules and techniques, some of which are particularly revealing of the Canadian courts' response to industrialization: 'the character of the neighborhood,' 'local standards of comfort,' and 'reasonable use'; public nuisance; and the question of remedies. The cases involving these issues best show the extent to which the Canadian courts were willing to accommodate the law to the new problems of industrialization and the shape that accommodation took. Specifically, one can see the extent to which the courts were willing to uphold traditional common law rights of occupiers in the face of conflicting demands of industry, on whom the law placed the burden of the costs of development, and the extent to which, tacitly or explicitly, the judiciary took social and economic factors into account in their decisions.

CLASS, PROGRESS, AND THE CHARACTER OF THE NEIGHBOURHOOD

One of the chief elements of the 'elasticity' of English nuisance law was the concept of the character of the neighbourhood. The leading English cases set forth the proposition that the question of what constitutes a nuisance must always be considered in the context of the neighbourhood in which it occurs.[29] As courts in England and Canada were fond of repeating, what would be a nuisance in Belgrave or Grosvenor Squares (posh residential neighbourhoods) might not be in Bermondsey or Smithfield market (areas of lower class housing and tanneries and butcher-shops, respectively). The local standard of comfort varied according to the class of person living there and the kind of annoyances it was presumed they had become accustomed to or could reasonably be expected to tolerate. Cozens-Hardy's judgment in the much-cited case of *Rushmer and Polsue* v *Alfieri* (1906) made it clear that the issue was class rather than long-standing neighbourhood practices. 'The lower standard of comfort existing say in Whitechapel would equally exist in one of the numerous districts which have sprung up in late years on the outskirts of the City, which are occupied by persons of the same class as those who occupy the older houses in Whitechapel.'[30] *Hole* v *Barlow* (1858) was one of the few cases which challenged the class implications of the neighbourhood concept. Plaintiff's counsel argued that 'the enjoyment of pure and undefiled air is the common law right of every subject of her Majesty, whether he resides in a hovel or a mansion.'[31] Needless to say, this view of the rights of Englishmen did not prevail.

St. Helen's Smelting Co. v *Tipping* (1865) made the character of the neighbourhood particularly important by establishing two categories which were accepted in both England and Canada from that time forward: nuisances which affected physical property itself and those involving the enjoyment of property. When the interference complained of was 'merely' with the latter category (which is primarily what nuisance law protects), the character of the neighbourhood was said to be crucial in determining whether the court would provide a remedy. This qualification of occupiers' rights was necessary, the court bluntly said, for 'where great works have been created and carried on, and are the means of developing the national wealth, you must not stand on extreme rights and allow a person to say, "I will bring an action against you for this and that, and so on." Business could not go on if that were so.'[32]

While the thrust of these cases was clear, there was very little clarity in the tests to determine the character of the neighbourhood. This uncertainty was increasingly emphasized in the later leading cases of *Rushmer and Polsue* v *Alfieri* (1906) and *Colls* v *Home and Colonial Stores* (1904): all the surrounding circumstances must be taken into consideration; the test was an 'elastic' one; the question of nuisance or no nuisance was one of degree, and in the last analysis it was always a matter of fact.[33] All of which really meant that it depended on the attitude of the court.

The Canadian nuisance decisions regularly cited at least one of these leading cases and recognized all of the principles outlined above, but the

Canadian emphasis was selective. First, there was rarely the explicit statement of concern with the progress of industry and of great works found in English decisions. Canadian courts chose rather to suggest a timeless quality to the importance of neighbourhood. They incorporated quotes which emphasized the different standards between town and country, suggesting that there had always been different standards of comfort rather than the idea that the progress of the nineteenth or twentieth centuries required such distinctions. This emphasis of course disguised the novelty of the English use of 'neighbourhood.' Canadian judges did not, however, completely ignore the central issue of manufacturing: 'all the circumstances of the property must be taken into consideration, amongst them the notorious fact that manufactures cannot be carried on without noise and vibration and that one in a manufacturing district cannot expect to have the same freedom from annoyance of that kind which he would have a right to in a residential quarter.'[34] But even in this unusually explicit statement of 1911, there was no emphasis on the importance of industrial development. The identification of industrialization with progress and prosperity was widespread, but it was not reflected in judicial opinions. If the judiciary shared this perspective and accepted its legal relevance, they chose to implement it unobtrusively.

Canadian judges were also less explicit about the class implications of the 'local standard of comfort,' although they quoted English judgments in which these were clear. The most explicit comment was in a leading Supreme Court of Canada judgment, in which Chief Justice Samuel Henry Strong offered the following extreme, and hence rather useless, comparison:

> It would be of course absurd to say that one who established a manufactory in the use of which great quantities of smoke are emitted, next door to a precisely similar manufactory ... whose works also emit smoke, commits a nuisance as regards the latter, though if he established his factory immediately adjoining a mansion in a residential quarter of a large city he would beyond question be liable for damages for wrongful use of his property.[35]

As we shall see, judges sometimes displayed a particular sympathy for well-to-do plaintiffs, when the encroachment of industry interfered with the enjoyment of their substantial homes. One also finds occasional concern for the lower classes as the prime victims of the annoyances of development: 'That Hillingdale Ave. [where street railway tracks and car barns had been built] is a street of comparatively humble homes is no justification' for the failure to apply for a permit from the legislature.[36] In general, however, the class dimension of both the problems and the legal concepts remained implicit.

Canadian courts adopted the categories of *St. Helen's* but did not take advantage of the limitation on liability they provided. Judges did not focus on the requirement of material injury to property and did not stress the difficulty of proving that mere interference with enjoyment by an industry amounted to an actionable injury. Plaintiffs' complaints were almost never dismissed as 'trifling inconveniences,' as the *St. Helen's* approach would have allowed.[37]

What the Canadian courts wholeheartedly adopted was the later emphasis on the 'elasticity' of nuisance law. As long as some acknowledgment of local standards was made, judges had extraordinary latitude in deciding whether as a 'matter of fact' a nuisance existed.[38] This did not involve an issue of judge versus jury, since almost all nuisance cases in this period were tried without a jury. Wherever the remedy sought was an equitable one, the rules of civil procedure excluded a jury. In all other cases a jury trial was at the discretion of the judge, although counsel could request and oppose it. The emphasis on fact did mean that appellate judges were very reluctant to overturn a trial judge's decision.

LOCAL STANDARDS OF COMFORT AND REASONABLE USE

The courts' use of 'local standards of comfort' should be examined along with the companion concept of 'reasonable use.' The latter issue is whether the defendant should be able to claim as a defence that his use of the land is in and of itself, ie, aside from its effects on the plaintiff, reasonable. *Bamford* v *Turnely* (1862) is almost always cited as the authority on this question.[39] But as usual in nuisance cases, it offered no clear simple standard. The clearest statement of the Bamford 'rule' was by Justice Edward V. Williams:

> whenever, taking all the circumstances into consideration, including the nature and extent of the plaintiff's enjoyment before the acts complained of, the annoyance is sufficiently great to amount to a nuisance according to the ordinary rule of law, an action will lie whatever the locality may be: then surely the jury cannot properly be asked, whether the causing of the annoyance was a reasonable use of the land.[40]

This issue sometimes appeared together with arguments that the defendant carried out his operations in the best possible manner, implying the courts should import a negligence standard into nuisance law.[41]

An examination of the Canadian cases in which these issues were raised shows more specifically how the courts used legal categories and issues in dealing with the competing rights of property. A numerical breakdown of the key cases furnishes an initial overview of the courts' response. Of sixteen cases where local standards or character of the neighbourhood was an issue (usually raised by the defence, since only four of the cases arise in purely residential neighbourhoods), relief was denied in only one case. Twelve injunctions were sought, seven were allowed, with only two cases in which the character of the neighbourhood was the basis for the denial. Canadian courts rarely used the notion of variations in the standard of comfort as a means of limiting liability. The effectiveness of the defence of 'reasonable use' was not as clear-cut. Of eleven cases where it was raised, it was accepted in four, three to deny relief and one as the grounds for awarding damages in lieu of an injunction.

The few Canadian reference texts of the period also provide an indication of the state of the law. The most striking thing about the presentation of the principles of character of neighbourhood and reasonable use in both the *Canadian Encyclopedic Digest* and in the Canadian notes to Underhill's *The Law of Torts* was the lack of any clear position.[42] The main offering of the *CED* was the following statement: 'An arbitrary standard cannot be set up which is applicable to all localities ... though the local standard may be higher in some districts than in others, yet the question in each case ultimately reduces itself to the fact of nuisance or no nuisance having regard to all the surrounding circumstances.' This statement was taken from the judgment in *Oakley* v *Webb* (1919), which quoted the rule stated by Justice William E. Middleton in *Appleby* v *Erie Tobacco Co.* (1910) and adopted in *Beamish* v *Glenn* (1916).[43] *Oakley* and *Beamish* were also cited for 'reasonableness of place' in Underhill. The approaches of these three cases were so different that they could not possibly stand for any single proposition, except one, like that quoted, that is so vague as to be virtually meaningless.

Oakley v *Webb* appears to have been an anomalous case; it was the only one of the sixteen in which relief was denied. Yet it is a standard citation in indexes, texts, and abridgements and is an interesting example of the way character of neighbourhood or local standard could be used. The plaintiff appealed a judgment dismissing an action to restrain the defendant from carrying on his business as stone cutter and sawyer so as to interfere with the plaintiff's health and comfort. The alleged interference arose from hammers and chisels, air compressors, and a six-blade gang saw next door to the plaintiff's house in Toronto. The issue, Justice Frank E. Hodgins said, was whether the defendant's exercise of his legal right to carry on his business was an unlawful invasion of appellant's competing right to enjoy life in reasonable comfort. The judge described the neighbourhood in some detail, noting in the immediate vicinity of the plaintiff's house a grocery store, lumber yard, sanitary excavator and housemover with a manure pit, and Canadian Pacific Railway tracks. Hodgins noted that the railway right of way, including the plaintiff's property, was excluded when the surrounding area was zoned as residential. But the most important consideration was the effect of life in such a neighbourhood on the inhabitants: 'the indifference of all those who live near by to the discomforts caused by the operation of freight and passenger trains is significant of the dulling effects of constant familiarity with the clatter and smuts regularly distributed by those agencies.' The respondent's witnesses, the judge said, afforded examples of those who 'like all the local residents in respect to railway noises, have become insensible to the noise produced by the sawing and chipping, from being accustomed to it or from not listening for it,' although the appellant's witness described the noise as excruciating. Here indeed was a 'local standard of comfort,' which the trial judge was prepared to impose on the plaintiff and his daughter, who claimed to be 'affected in health' through the effect of the continual noise on her nerves.[44] Hodgins said that the rule quoted above from the *CED* was the 'proper test,' though citing the *Rushmer* case he added that 'the uncertainty of the test makes the question of nuisance or no nuisance a question of fact.' But the test he actually seemed to apply contradicted the judgment in that case: that is, the statement in *Gaunt* v *Fynny* (1870), that nuisances by noise 'to offend against the law, must be done in a manner which, beyond fair controversy, ought to be regarded as excessive and unreasonable.'[45] After considering these authorities, Hodgins concluded:

> while I think there is evidence from which the learned trial judge might have arrived at a different result, I am not sufficiently certain that he came to a wrong conclusion ... [to reverse]. He had to consider not only the evidence as to the noise but also the character of the neighbourhood, the *reasonable use* of the respondent's property and the weight of the testimony offered.[46]

By contrast, *Appleby* v *Erie Tobacco* (1910),[47] which *Oakley* purported to follow, stands for the proposition that the reasonableness of defendant's use is no defence to a nuisance. Appleby, a Windsor merchant, complained of smells from the defendant's tobacco factory, which the plaintiff's witnesses described as sickening, offensive, and nauseating.[48] Justice Middleton canvassed the leading English cases from *Walter* v *Selfe* (1851) to *Rushmer and Polsue* (1907), quoting the latter at length. The key statements quoted formed the basis of many Canadian cases:[49]

> A resident in a noisy neighbourhood must put up with a certain amount of noise. The standard of comfort differs according to the situation of the property and the class of people who inhabit it ... But whatever the standard ... the addition of a fresh noise caused by defendant's works may be so substantial as to cause a legal nuisance ... and it would be *no answer* to say that the steam hammer [newly introduced] is of the *most modern approved pattern and is reasonably worked.*[50]

Middleton concluded that this case 'puts an end to the controversy upon the question whether the reasonableness of defendants' use of their own premises affects the plaintiff's rights.'[51] He ordered an injunction to be stayed for six months to allow the defendants to abate or remove that part of the business causing the odour.

Beamish v *Glenn* (1916), the third case usually cited with respect to neighbourhood and reasonable use, adopted the test from *Appleby*, but took yet a different approach.[52] While gathering the usual quotations about differing local standards, Chief Justice William Meredith did not intend to use the concept to defeat the plaintiff's claim. One can almost discern an anti-industrial attitude in his protective concern for beleaguered town dwellers. The defendant had set up a blacksmith shop on a Toronto block where resident owners used covenants to try to maintain the residential character of their street in an area that was 'to some extent a factory location.' The covenants had been omitted when the defendant purchased the land, and he had succeeded over the protest of his neighbours in obtaining a city permit to build and operate a blacksmith shop. The judge noted with sympathy the efforts of the plaintiff and his neighbours to maintain the 'repose and comfort incident to a home in a residential locality' and remarked that the defendant 'forced himself and his forge onto this block' against the opposition of the plaintiff and others. In awarding an injunction and damages, Meredith concluded that the city's regulatory powers could not deprive a man of his property or other rights and that carrying on a lawful trade in an ordinary, reasonable, and careful manner was no defence to nuisance. In keeping with Blackstone's rule, defendant had to take his trade elsewhere.

Character of neighbourhood and local standard of comfort are both concepts that could allow courts the flexibility to deny claims for nuisance in industrializing towns while faithfully reciting the principles of traditional nuisance law. But Canadian courts rarely used the concepts in this way. With respect to the concept of reasonable use on the other hand, the courts seem to have taken advantage of conflicting lines of opinion among early English cases. *Gaunt* v *Fynny* (1870) was employed to support the defence of reasonable use in an Ottawa case in 1904,[53] and the defence that a private stable was reasonably and properly kept was accepted in a Nova Scotia case in 1906.[54]

The endurance of the reasonable use defence is particularly surprising, since in 1896 the majority of the Supreme Court of Canada took a very clear stand on the issue in *Drysdale* v *Dugas*.[55] The plaintiff in that case complained of noise and smells from a commercial stable in a residential area. Chief Justice Strong canvassed the English cases on local standards and the leading English stable cases.[56] He concluded that in the latter the argument that stables were absolutely necessary and that 'the maintenance of one was a reasonable use by a man of his own property, was repelled as no answer to the action.'[57] This was only a slight distortion of the decision, which dealt with a private stable and made remarks about hypothetically necessary trades. Strong also determined that the contention that 'extreme care and caution' in carrying on a business was a justification that had been shown to be 'utterly without foundation' in *Bamford* v *Turnley* (1862).[58] This was also a slight exaggeration, but whatever his grounds the Chief Justice's refusal to import a negligence standard was clear. Although he accepted defence arguments that the stable business was a necessity in a large city like Montreal and that the stable was constructed on the most approved and scientific plan, he found an actionable nuisance. Justice John Gwynne's dissent on this is worth noting: the majority's judgment was 'substantially equivalent to a judgment that it is illegal to maintain a public stable for horses anywhere within the limits of the city of Montreal, for it is impossible that any stable could be more perfect.' The results of such a strict application of nuisance law in an urban setting were, he suggested, impractical and unacceptable.

Although neither *Drysdale* nor the English precedent *Rushmer* (1906) was followed uniformly, the Canadian courts did not adopt a policy of using reasonable use as a means of limiting liability for industry.[59] Two of the cases where the defence was accepted involved not industry but private music lessons and a private stable.[60] In *Appleby* (1910) and *Beamish* (1916) the defence was clearly rejected. Finally, the fact that the latest of the leading Canadian cases, *Oakley* (1919), allowed the reasonable use claim, tells us little. A briefly mentioned fact in that case may have had more to do with the court's decision than any general policy on industrial liability. The plaintiff had lived in the house for six months, while the respondent's noisy operations were 'in full swing,' before executing his option to buy the house. While 'coming to the nuisance' is no bar to the action in a technical sense, judges were not likely to be sympathetic to plaintiffs suspected of using a court action to extort a high settlement. The reasonable use defence could be used to prevent a plaintiff from succeeding.

In sum, the doctrine of reasonable use was not settled. When the facts of the case suggested that a plaintiff's claim was unreasonable, judges were prepared to accept the reasonable use defence. But there was no consistent pattern or trend towards using it to limit the liability of developing industry.

PUBLIC NUISANCE AND THE PUBLIC GOOD

The Supreme Court of Canada case of *Canada Paper* v *Brown* (1922) raised several of the most important defences to nuisance and offers a useful perspective on the Canadian approach to the problems of industrialization.[61] It also provides insight into the related problem of appropriate remedies. Brown brought an action to restrain Canada Paper from emitting 'nauseous and offensive odours and fumes in Windsor Mills, Quebec.' The first defence was one used effectively in the United States: the confusion between public and private nuisance.[62] The argument was that if a company inflicted foul smells, smoke, or fumes not only on the plaintiff but on all his neighbours as well, the interference was by virtue of its extent not a private but a public nuisance, and hence only the Attorney General could prosecute. As recognized in *Cairns* v *Canada Refining and Smelting Co.* (1913),[63] this was a confusion between interference with rights the plaintiff enjoyed as a member of the public (like the use of highways) and interference with rights enjoyed as an owner or occupier of property. A person might incidentally suffer the latter kind of interference in common with neighbours. In that case the annoyance might be a public nuisance as well, but should not lose its character as a private nuisance. Justice Francis Alexander Anglin's judgment in *Canada Paper* illustrates a common Canadian approach: he accepted the public/private confusion, but was unwilling to deny relief on that basis. He found that the plaintiff suffered an injury 'distinct in character from that common to the inhabitants at large,' which was the requirement for a private action on a public nuisance. But as usual in such cases, Anglin did not explain how the injury was distinct. He merely stated that the plantiff's property rights were inferfered with; the implication was that any such interference was by definition 'distinct,' even if it were clear that the interference was in fact identical to that suffered by his neighbours. Anglin also explicitly recognized one of the major problems with limiting redress to an action by the Attorney General: most of the inhabitants 'are so dependent upon the operation of the defendant's mills for their support that they are quite prepared to submit to some personal annoyance rather than jeopardize their means of livelihood. The inaction of the municipal authorities is no doubt ascribable to similar influences.'[64] This was no doubt a common deterrent to actions for nuisance.

Canada Paper's second main line of defence concerned the importance of the industry. Defence counsel urged the court to consider the uses and character of the neighbourhood and cited *St. Helen's* (which was indeed good authority) for the proposition that 'the courts will not interfere as against a trade on the mere ground of personal discomfort and inconvenience of a private individual.' Finally, counsel concluded that 'the courts will not destroy an industry when compensation ought to be awarded.'[65]

Three judges wrote opinions and the difference in their responses to this line of argument is especially interesting. Justice John Idington, with whom Chief Justice Louis Davies concurred, began by noting that the plaintiff's expensive home was built on property that had been the home of his father and ancestors for a hundred years. It was clear from the start that Idington would accord no special privileges to a trade as against the right to reside in comfort in this ancestral home: 'the appellant *for mere commercial reasons*, disregarding the rights of respondents and all others, saw fit to introduce ... a process in the use of sulphate which produced malodorous fumes which pollute the air.' Idington completely rejected the relevance of the economic importance of the industry. He complained of the mass of 'irrelevant evidence' intended to support 'the remarkable conclusion that because the prosperity of said town or village would be enhanced by the use of the new process therefore the respondent has no rights upon which to rest his rights of property.' The courts would not be party to the undermining of private property rights to 'suit the grasping tendencies of some and incidentally the needs or desires of the majority in any community benefiting thereby.' Courts should not yield to the 'demands and assertions of social right unless and until due compensation made by due process of law.' This, of course, was the province of the legislature. Reasserting his basic premise, Idington concluded that an injunction was the proper remedy and urged that 'we keep in view the essential merits of the remedy in the way of protecting the rights of property and preventing them from being invaded by mere autocratic assertions of what will be conducive to the prosperity of the local community by disregarding such rights.'[66]

Justice Lyman Poore Duff began with the clear assertion that Brown had a right to relief. The substantial question was whether he was entitled to an injunction. Duff was 'far from accepting the contention ... that ... the effect of granting the injunction upon residents of the neighbourhood and indeed upon appellant company are not considerations properly to be taken into account' in deciding whether to grant an injunction.[67] It was a matter of judicial discretion, and the disparity between the advantage to the plaintiff and the disadvantage to the defendant and others might be a sufficient ground for refusing injunctive relief. He then paraphrased the standard English rules for granting damages in lieu of an injunction and explicitly rejected the argument that this was 'equivalent to subjecting the plaintiff to a process of expropriation.'[68] In this case he found that enjoining the sulphate process would not put the company out of business. Since there would be no disproportionate injury, the injunction should be upheld.

Justice Francis Anglin also found that the sulphate process was not essential to the defendant's operations and that this 'is an answer to the objection based on the balance of convenience – if indeed mere balance of convenience would be a sufficient ground under the Civil law of Quebec for refusing to enjoin a process which necessarily entails an unjustifiable invasion of the plaintiff's legal right to the enjoyment of his property.'[69] Damages would not be an adequate remedy and to limit the plaintiff to this method of redress would be to force him to 'submit to partial expropriation of his property ... without statutory authority for such an exercise of eminent domain.'[70] The injunction should stand, but if 'scientific discovery' made the process possible without interference with the plaintiff's rights, the defendant could apply to be relieved of the prohibition.

Both the range and character of these judgments are illustrative of contemporary Canadian judicial attitudes to nuisance. The most forceful of the opinions is Idington's, which upheld the traditional approach, the absolute protection of private property rights regardless of the effect on industrial progress or the local economy. This position was rooted in a clearly articulated philosophy of the importance of individual rights and the role of the courts in protecting them. Idington, however, prevailed on only one of his brethren to concur in his reasons. Duff's more present-minded and accommodating position, by contrast, did not offer an alternative philosophy. He did not argue for the importance of recognizing that industrial development inevitably raised questions of competing rights, or for the need for the law to accommodate to radical changes in society. He did not respond to Idington's remarks about the proper role of the courts vis-à-vis the legislature, nor did he offer a serious counter to the claim that a denial of an injunction amounted to expropriation by the courts. This was characteristic of the Canadian judiciary: hesitant to articulate new policy, but slightly less hesitant to implement it. The judiciary as a whole were not as conservative as their most forceful and articulate spokesman.[71]

REMEDIES

The question of remedies brings out the Canadian approach to the conflicts of industrialization most clearly. In deciding between an injunction and damages and in determining the amount of damages, the courts were forced to confront the problem of allocation of the indirect costs of industrial progress. Judges were more likely to explain the reasons for their decisions in policy terms when exercising the discretion inherent in equitable remedies, such as injunctions.

Here again numbers provide an initial overview. Of the fifty nuisance cases I analysed, relief was denied in eleven.[72] Plaintiffs sought an injunction in thirty-four cases and were successful in twenty. Damages were awarded in seven of fourteen cases where an injunction was denied. Nine of the injunctions, however, were stayed, often with leave to apply for extensions. The reported cases do not indicate whether stays were extended or how often they were extended indefinitely. There were also cases where injunctions were denied, but the plaintiff was given leave to reapply within a set time, in one case if scientific evidence of cause was produced, and in another if the defendants did not live up to their undertaking to abate.

Once substantial interference with a right was proved, the courts were generally willing to grant an injunction.[73] Not surprisingly, judges were particularly ready to restrain offensive activities if it was clear that the defendant was making no effort to minimize the annoyance. The courts had little sympathy with the view that private property rights included the right to use one's property as one wished. Chief Justice William G. Falconbridge commented with disapproval in a 1918 case that the 'defendant had not adopted the simplest device to minimize either form of nuisance [smoke and burning garbage]. He took the defiant stand, by conduct and in the witness box, that he "didn't have to." Sometimes very independent gentlemen of this type find out that they must have some regard for the rights, feelings, and comforts of other people.'[74] The court was prepared to teach him this lesson by means of an injunction with, however, the additional pedagogical device of a twenty-day stay. 'Should the defendant show honest and substantial progress in this direction within the twenty days, he may apply ... to extend the time.'[75]

The courts took a similarly restrictive approach even with major industry. In *Hopkin* v *Hamilton Electric Light and Cataract Power Co.* (1901) the plaintiff lived next door to the defendant's company and complained of the vibrations. The trial court refused to substitute damages for an injunction. 'I see no sound reason for exercising any discretion, even if I have any, in favour of the defendants, for it appears to me that in the present case they have exercised their supposed rights with a degree of disregard for those of other people, which corporations with large special powers are usually prudent enough to make some effort to conceal.'[76] Here too, the injunction was stayed in order that the 'defendants may have time to make such arrangements as will enable them to carry on their works in a manner not creating a nuisance to the plaintiff.'[77] The purpose of the injunction generally seems to have been to put pressure on the company or town to take steps to abate or at least minimize the nuisance. Accordingly, the accepted form of injunction restrained not the enterprise but its operation so as to cause a nuisance.

Turtle v *Toronto* (1924) is an interesting example of different judicial views on the extent to which the courts should use injunctions to perform a kind of supervisory function.[78] The plaintiff in this case bitterly complained of a range of annoyances caused by the street railway, including car barns recently built in front of his house. All three judges in the Ontario Court of Appeal seem to have agreed that a good part of the noise resulted from careless and unnecessary practices. Chief Justice Francis R. Latchford saw that an injunction would ensure that the company would issue proper orders and see to it that they were carried out. Justice Middleton, on the other hand, took the view that the company discharged its duty when it employed competent employees. He opposed an injunction which, if disobeyed through employees' negligence, would place the defendant company in contempt. Justice Cornelius Masten compromised, accepting the defendants' undertaking to stop particularly offensive practices and offering the defendants a declaration of right and leave to apply for an injunction after six months if necessary. The latter two justices made a point of noting that the defendant was performing a public service and that this should be taken into consideration. The result was that the railway was left to change its practices without the incentive of an injunction.

When faced with clear evidence of an interference with plaintiff's comfort and enjoyment of his property, the courts expressed little doubt that property was a basic right they were bound to protect. They rarely found the plaintiff's suffering to be a 'trifling inconvenience' and were generally agreed that being kept awake by noise, sickened by smells, or choked by smoke were not injuries which could be compensated, or even estimated, in money payments. In some cases the courts did not have the option of using an injunction as a means to pressure a company to abate. When abatement was not possible, the choice was between protecting a plaintiff's rights and closing a company down. This situation often forced the courts to recognize that competing interests were at issue and that they had a policy choice to make. Not surprisingly, industries sometimes claimed this to be the case when it was not, hoping to force an award of damages instead of an injunction. But this was by no means always successful. Justice Haughton Lennox's trial judgment in *Taylor* v *Mullen Coal* (1915) is illustrative.[79]

The request for an injunction in *Taylor* elicited an articulation of the conflicting interests rare in English-Canadian decisions: 'The disposition of this action has given me a great deal of anxious thought. I should be careful on the one hand, that industrial enterprise and the company's business is not unnecessarily obstructed, and, on the other, that the reasonable comfort and enjoyment, quiet and happiness, of the plaintiff's home are not unlawfully and wantonly sacrificed or set at naught.'[80] It is worth emphasizing that Lennox did not pose the issue in terms of conflicting rights of *property*, the right to free use versus the right to quiet enjoyment, but rather as individual property rights versus the public importance of industry.

After disposing of the 'public nuisance' defence, Lennox turned to the main issue:

> As to all the nuisances complained of [smoke, dust, and noise] the company has devoted a lot of effort to showing that a remedy or further improvement is impossible. This does not meet the issue; for if actionable wrongs exist, and a remedy is impossible, then an injunction must be granted; and if I believed this I should feel compelled to order an immediate, perpetual injunction restraining defendant company from operating its plant.[81]

But he did not believe abatement was impossible and ordered a stayed injunction instead. He made clear, however, that if the company persisted in claiming that abatement was impossible it would serve only to 'force a very unfortunate alternative. The existing condition is not to be tolerated.'[82]

This firm stance must be seen in the light of Mullen Coal's history. They were subject to a previous injunction, and Lennox offered the following assessment of their attempts at abatement: 'It is impossible to believe that such a method would work out as a practical remedy; and it did not; and it is also impossible to believe that the company expected that it would.' But hope springs eternal, and Lennox not only stayed the injunction for four months; he added that if the company 'acting diligently and in good faith' could not abate or relocate in that time, they could apply for an extension. He was clearly willing to do everything possible to avoid closing the company down – short of directly modifying the plaintiff's rights or remedies to accommodate the needs of industry.

Of course not everyone took this approach. The Ontario Judicature Act (1877) offered an alternative: the court could, if it saw fit, substitute damages for an injunction.[83] Just how freely the courts should use this rule was something on which there was no unified judicial opinion. English and Canadian judges agreed that the English case of *Shelfer* v *London Electric Lighting Co.* (1895) provided a good working rule. *Shelfer* held that damages should be awarded if four conditions were met: the injury to the plaintiff's legal right was small, capable of being estimated in money, could be adequately compensated by a small money payment, and the case was one in which it would be oppressive to the defendant to grant an injunction.[84] The rule was almost ritually repeated in every relevant Canadian case, along with a conclusion as to whether or not the conditions had been met. But there was rarely much detailed discussion of exactly how they were or were not met. For example, there was little agreement on what constituted a 'small' money payment. *Colls* v *Home and Colonial Stores* (1904) was often cited as well, with little comment on the fact that it offered quite different criteria: it questioned whether the amount of damages recovered was a satisfactory test and suggested that if the defendant had acted in good faith, the court ought to incline to damages.[85]

The Canadian courts offered a variety of explanations for substituting damages for injunctions. In 1910 one judge suggested that awarding damages would provide sufficient pressure to encourage defendants to lessen the offending noise or to reach 'such amicable settlement ... in respect to the future as will avoid hampering the very creditable industry the defendants have established.'[86] A 1924 opinion noted that 'defendant company had acted throughout in a reasonable manner and without the slightest desire to injure plaintiff or his property' (citing *Colls*) and found acquiescence, although only delay was really shown. This judge also noted that the steam hammers in question were absolutely necessary for the manufacturing operating and had been installed 'in the most approved manner.'[87] In *Chadwick* v *City of Toronto* (1914) Middleton concluded that, 'in as much as the pumping of water is necessary for municipal purposes, the case, I think, falls under the provision of the Judicature Act empowering me to refrain from granting an injunction and to substitute damages.'[88]

Black v *Canadian Copper Co.* (1917) was one of the few cases in which the court explicitly emphasized the importance of a private industry, as opposed to a public service or utility, a distinction important in Canadian decisions: 'The court ought not to destroy the mining industry – nickel is of great value to the world – even if a few farms are damaged or even destroyed.'[89] In fact, nickel was one of Canada's great hopes for a major industry. The country had a virtual monopoly on the necessary minerals, and nickel was important for armour plate. The much-contested issue was whether the actual processing would be done in Canada or lost, with all its profits and jobs, to the United States.[90] The case in question was one of about a dozen pending against two manufacturers, and abatement was not possible without closing down the operations. These circumstances elicited an unusual willingness to weigh the public good against the protection of individual rights: 'there are circumstances in which it is impossible for the individual so to assert his individual rights as to inflict a substantial injury on the whole community ... once close the mines, and the mining community would be at an end, and farming would not long continue.' But Middleton was spared actually having to deny an injunction on these grounds, although it is fairly clear that he would have: 'The consideration of this situation induced the plaintiffs' counsel to abandon the claims for injunctions.'[91]

By 1928 Middleton's views seem to have changed somewhat. Faced with an entirely different situation, a local dairy which could easily eliminate the noise in question, he joined Justices Masten and Riddell in a careful examination of the application of the Ontario Judicature Act, and the English Lord Cairn's Act, which authorized substituting damages for an injunction. This case, *Duchman* v *Oakland Dairy*, became the leading authority on the issue.[92] Riddell stated that Canadian courts were more liberal in applying Lord Cairn's Act. Masten said that this 'accorded with my own recollection and experience. However on further investigation and consideration, neither on authority in our own cases nor on principle can I find a basis for such a modification of the English rule ... prima facie and in the absence of special circumstances of a sufficiently strong character an injunction should be granted.'[93] Middleton's comments were the most illuminating. There was a period of time in England and Canada, he said, 'in which the courts had no settled policy as to the application of the Act in question. Each judge did that which was right in his own eyes without recognizing any guiding principle, but as the law came to be settled, the principle crystallized in the *Shelfer* case gradually emerged.' It was now a binding authority which should be 'unhesitatingly followed.'[94]

It seems likely that Middleton was right about an earlier unsettled period, but it was probably not the same in England and Canada. Canada's take-off period of industrialization did not begin until the 1880s (some argue 1900) well after England's, and the crystallization in *Shelfer* took place in 1895, late in England's industrial development.[95] The Canadian judiciary faced most of the hard problems posed in *Black* after the *Shelfer* rule was available. The fact that in 1928 both Masten's and Riddell's own experience led them to believe that Canadian courts had been freer to use the Canadian version of Lord Cairn's Act suggests that the 'unsettled' period may well have been in the first decade of the twentieth century, the peak period of Canada's industrialization.

But 'unsettled' remains the operative word. The cases do not suggest that the Canadian courts ever systematically refused injunctions to protect industry. Statements like Middleton's in *Black* v *Canadian Copper Co.* (1917) were rare.[96] It is more common to find remarks to the opposite effect that 'to grant damages in lieu of an injunction is to compel parties against their will to sell their rights at a price fixed by the courts, and such a course should be taken with hesitation' or that denial of an injunction 'would compel petitioner and other sufferers to resort to a multiplicity of suits and interminable litigation without reaching the suppression of the grievance or furnishing adequate compensation.'[97]

Even in considering interim injunctions, the courts were not willing to give automatic weight to the public benefits from industry. In *Francklyn* v *Peoples Heat and Light Co.* (1899) the defendants had built their gas and coke works next to the plaintiff's substantial home in one of the loveliest spots in Halifax, the Northwest Arm.[98] The plaintiff sought to restrain the emission of noxious and unwholesome gases and vapours. The defendant's main argument was that as against a trade the court should not 'summarily interfere, by way of injunction, before trial, on the mere grounds of personal discomfort and inconvenience ... The injury, to justify an interim injunction, must be an injury to property.' Justice J. Norman Ritchie rejected these arguments. He was sure that there was no case in which an interim injunction had been denied when defendants had not even denied the plaintiff's allegation. The balance of convenience was only to be considered when the right of law or fact of violation was doubtful. He found a clear case of irreparable injury, for 'what damage will compensate the plaintiff having been deprived of the comfortable enjoyment of his home?'[99]

Justice Charles Townshend accepted the trial judge's view that none of the defendant's arguments or cases showed that 'a proprietor could be expelled from the occupation and enjoyment of his property for the accommodation of another' except by express direction of the legislature. He did, however, find that the defendants could operate without causing a nuisance and would stay the injunction if they offered security for compensation. Justices Wallace Graham and Nicholas Meagher agreed, but the latter noted that 'I do not wish to be understood as entirely concurring in the view expressed in the opinions just read as to the position taken by the defendants' counsel.'[100] Here again the 'non-accommodationist' position was most strongly stated, with the contrary view being only hinted at. The court in this case granted only a stayed injunction with leave to apply for an extension, but Ritchie's view that if an injury to a legal right was proved, the balance of convenience was irrelevant, seems to have been the generally accepted one.

In concluding the discussion of remedies, some brief comments on the assessment of damages are appropriate, since this issue clearly shows the ways in which the courts allocated the costs of industrialization. One of the unsettled areas of the law was whether a plaintiff who proved injury was entitled to compensation for permanent depreciation in the value of his property. The question arose both when a plaintiff sought damages and when the court decided to substitute damages for an injunction. One of the techniques which emerged was the refusal to recognize an obviously permanent establishment, such as a power plant, as 'permanent in law.' Some courts took a common sense approach, saw that the nuisance of a power plant was in effect a permanent interference with a plaintiff's rights, and awarded permanent damages. Others argued that they could presume neither the permanence of the structure nor the continuance of the particular nuisance, and hence awarded damages only up to the time of assessment.[101] This often meant excluding any consideration of loss to property values, leaving only (often minimal) damages for personal discomfort.

The most interesting and innovative technique involved an apparent confusion of law and equity. The rules of civil procedure as of 1887 in Ontario and 1900 in Nova Scotia stated that where there was a continuing nuisance, damages were to be assessed from the time of assessment. This was copied from an English rule whose purpose was not to cut off the extent of damages but to ensure that the plaintiff could recover for injuries between the commencement of the action and its resolution. The rationale for both the rule and the need for the rule was said to be that each act of a continuing nuisance gave rise to a fresh cause of action. Thus the rule assumed the plaintiff's right to bring a new action for injuries subsequent to the decision, but provided that the plaintiff need not bring separate actions for injuries occurring while waiting for the decision. What is interesting about this rule was that Canadian courts applied it in cases where the plaintiff was seeking not the *legal* remedy of damages, for which the rule was intended, but an injunction, which is an *equitable* remedy to which legal rules should not apply. This unintended application became possible when the courts invoked the Judicature Act to award damages in lieu of an injunction. There are clear statements in the cases and texts that when damages are substituted for an injunction they were to be 'for once and all' and hence to cover permanent loss to property value. Yet there are cases in which law and equity were mixed to drastically reduce the awards: the courts cited *Shelfer* rules as grounds for substituting damages and then instead of granting permanent damages announced that the rules of civil procedure limited damages to the time of assessment.[102] This often meant that a plaintiff could recover only minimal damages for personal inconvenience, even if the market value of the property had been destroyed. There is also a Supreme Court case (originating in Quebec) which seems to make the peculiar claim that in an action for damages the court cannot award damages for once and all without the consent of both parties, because the court has no means of preventing a plaintiff from bringing another action for later damages.[103] These cases, techniques, and arguments deserve a closer examination. Assessment of damages was one area in which the Canadian courts developed means for limiting the costs they would impose on developing industries and public utilities – without, however, any explicit comment on what they were doing, and without having to modify the substance of nuisance law.

CONCLUSION

What can one conclude about the role of the judiciary in Canada's chief period of early industrialization and what does it tell us about judicial conservatism? First of all, the Canadian courts were conservative in the sense that they followed traditional nuisance law and were generally unwilling to modify substantive rules or rights in order to accommodate the demands of industry. But this was conservatism in a special sense: Canadian courts had to exercise their ingenuity in order to circumvent the innovations English courts had made. Canadian courts conserved traditional nuisance law by avoiding rather than following English precedents. English law gave them the flexibility to ease the burdens on industry, but the Canadian courts rejected this course when it involved a substantial modification of traditional rights. The Canadian response to *St. Helen's*, probably the single most important case in English nuisance law at the time, was to modify its application so that in practice it did not serve to limit liability. The courts would not accept the general proposition that industry should be treated differently from individuals, and the cases show that plaintiffs were frequently successful against industry, at least to the point of getting a stayed injunction. Canadian conservatism in this sense appears to be the result of principle, not passivity.

This principled approach is thus something different from 'formalism,' as it is usually understood.[104] The essence of formalism is an emphasis on the deductive or scientific nature of judicial decision-making. Opinions in Canadian nuisance cases emphasized neither. The emphasis on fact, on 'all the circumstances of the case,' made nuisance law particularly ill suited to claims for scientifically deduced decisions. Canadian judges did not argue that precedent determined outcomes with perfect certainty and predictability. This is of course not surprising since Canadian courts were not in fact following the English practices in the cases they cited. The Canadian approach is thus properly called conservative and not formalistic. The judiciary seem to have been acting on a principled conviction that their job was to protect traditional rights, and they carried out this conviction in the face of contrary precedent.

This judicial conservatism also does not present the same problems as formalistic styles of reasoning. When judges insist that precedent dictates the outcome of the case, leaving them no choice consistent with their limited role, one has reason to be suspicious. But Canadian judges rarely made such professions. Instead they quietly protected traditional rights, only occasionally arguing that it was their role to do so rather than to balance those rights against non-legal factors such as economics. Canadian judicial conservatism may have been influenced by formalist jurisprudence, but calling the Canadian approach formalism would obscure the distinctive departure from precedent which characterized Canadian nuisance law.

Canadian courts were also conservative in their approach to those modifications they did adopt or devise: the modifications appeared without policy statements offering a rationale in either legal or social terms. The cases, for example, where 'reasonable use' was accepted as a defence provided no indication that a policy choice had been made between conflicting lines of opinions. The clever device of superimposing a legal rule on an equitable remedy was never discussed, but simply used. Injunctions did call forth more policy statements than other issues. But even the most explicit statements in *Black* v *Canadian Copper Co.* (1917) were not accompanied by any discussion of the proper role of the courts in responding to the changing demands of society.[105] There was altogether very little discussion of the nature of the problems and conflicts with which industrialization confronted the courts. The only really serious articulation of these problems was provided by those who took the strict view that the courts' role was to protect individual rights, not to weigh benefits and assess the needs of modern industry and economy. These views were not fully representative, but their unchallenged force must have had some impact on the development of the law. And indeed, later cases suggest that the strict approach prevailed.

Canadian courts were not willing to modify the substance of nuisance law or to deny remedies. Either would have affected basic rights and amounted to their own judicial law-making, or an endorsement of England's. The accommodation to the progress of industrialization they were willing to make was to limit damages. (I have not, however, found a case in this period, although there is one in 1937, where the court was persuaded to deny an injunction on grounds of the cost, as opposed to the impossibility, of abatement.) To assess the societal significance of this approach to nuisance law, one would need to know its actual impact on industry.[106] How often were businesses actually closed down, how often were they forced to invest in pollution control devices, and were the associated costs serious impediments to the development of industry? On the other side, one would like to know how often the damages awarded really provided adequate compensation and how often they were so minimal as to impose no real burden on industry. It may be that substantive modification of nuisance law was unnecessary because Canadian courts achieved the desired protection or subsidy of industry through the more subtle transformation of remedies. If Canadian courts systematically awarded damages which did not impose substantial costs on industry, then the substantive purity of nuisance law would be far less important.[107] But it seems unlikely that there would be a complete disjuncture between their approach to remedies and to substantive law, given the stand they took on injunctions. Unfortunately, some of the information necessary to determine this issue may be virtually irretrievable, because the assessment of damages was often given over to a special master. The actual amounts are therefore not contained in the printed reports. An assessment of the economic impact of damage judgments and injunctions would, in any case, require a different kind of study than the present one.

A related question for further study is whether the Canadian courts applied the same strict rules to very large and important industries. There does seem to be some indication of a greater hesitancy to grant an injunction against major industries,[108] but stayed injunctions seem fairly common.[109] The primary purpose of injunctions against industry seems to have been to pressure the company to abate (in only five of the cases is it clear that the result of the injunction would be to force a business to close or move), and the courts were just as willing to apply this pressure to large industries as to small. The exception was *Black* v *Canadian Copper Co.* (1917) where the court was faced with the prospect of shutting down one of Canada's most important and promising industries.[110] In this case even Canadian justice was not blind to economic realities. Only further study of cases and their background can tell us whether the Canadian courts consistently made exceptions where the importance of the industry was universally accepted, or whether *Black* was an anomaly, perhaps attributable to wartime.

Despite the limits of present information, one can conclude that the Canadian courts were less willing than their English or American counterparts to accommodate nuisance law to the demands of industry and hence more willing to make industry bear the costs of the damage it wrought. Why was the Canadian approach so different? There are two possible approaches to this question. One focuses not on the specific content and effect of the decisions, but on their general conservative position. The second looks at judicial attitudes towards industrialization itself. In the former, the question is why Canadian judges, regardless of their views on industrialization, insisted on adhering to traditional nuisance law. One answer is that a long history of following another country's judicial developments did not lead to an independent and creative judiciary. This 'colonial' experience could account for their being, in general, more conservative than the courts they purported to follow. But this does not account for the fact that on important issues judges chose not to adopt the innovations laid out for them in English cases. Defence counsel argued the English position, but Canadian courts rejected it in favour of a more 'pristine,' 'preindustrial' view of nuisance.

Another answer is the argument that the judiciary themselves set forth about the proper role of the courts with respect to the legislature. Considerable weight should be attached to this view. When the courts granted an injunction saying that limiting the remedy to damages amounted to expropriation without 'due process of law,' they gave a purely procedural meaning to that phrase. They generally betrayed no hostility to the idea of expropriation to benefit industry, so long as it was properly done by the legislature and provided for adequate compensation. The deference to the legislature and the insistence on the strict division between judicial and legislative roles may have been influenced by the formalist jurisprudence which was dominant in both England and the United States in the late nineteenth century. This jurisprudence developed in countries where the gains of industrialization were being consolidated and where the earlier modifications in the law were being formalized. Canada, however, was in the early stages of industrial development and was thus arguably being influenced by jurisprudence suited to a very different stage of development. Such influence might explain why Canadian judges remained conservative during the peak of Canadian industrialization, while during comparable periods in England and the United States their brethren actively modified that law to facilitate industrial development. Formalist influence might, for example, explain the reluctance of the more present-minded Canadian judges to articulate their positions – positions which their English and American counterparts had stated much earlier and were now replacing (or obscuring) with professions of formalism. But the influence of formalism cannot account for the Canadian refusal to adopt the modifications provided by English precedent. Coming late to industrialization, Canadian law could have had both modifications and formalism, but judges rejected this option in favour of a consistent conservative approach.

Whatever the origins of Canadian deference to the legislature, it is arguable that this is indeed the proper approach for the judiciary in an industrializing country with a democratic government. But this raises one of the most interesting issues: the courts' faith in the legislatures, which surfaces at two levels. The first is the question of whether the courts' hard line on nuisance rested on a confidence that if the costs imposed should impede the progress of industrial development, the legislatures would intervene. *Francklyn* v *Peoples Light and Gas* provides an example of how such an interaction between the courts and legislature could work. A permanent injunction against the company went into effect on 20 January 1899. On 14 March a bill amending its act of incorporation was introduced into the Nova Scotia House of Assembly. The bill provided that if the company operated 'according to methods usually employed in the operation,' no adjoining landowner could bring an action for an injunction against the company. Damage suits were limited to a single action for past, present, and prospective damages. The bill, however, was withdrawn when the company's owner agreed to buy Francklyn's estate for 'what was said to be $10,000 above the market price.' But this was not the end of the story. The episode prompted the introduction of a far broader bill prohibiting individuals from bringing suits against manufacturers. 'Hotly debated, the bill passed the House of Assembly, but was emphatically rejected by the Legislative Council.'[111]

A still more dramatic case occurred in 1948, when the legislature directed the courts to take economic impact into account when considering an injunction and then, when this failed, specifically exempted the company in question from liability.[112] For a full understanding of the courts' role, it is important to know how frequently the legislatures responded to the courts' strict stance by passing such general or specific acts limiting industrial liability.

The other issue of faith in the legislature was the willingness of courts to hand over matters affecting the rights of private property. Were they completely unconcerned about the dangers of democratic egalitarianism, of giving the legislature a free hand even in the sacred matter of property rights? Canadians do not seem to have shared the long-standing American distrust of democratic legislatures as threats to private property. Perhaps the élite in one form or another so successfully dominated the legislature that there was little fear of the rabble taking over. But in the early 1900s there were splits within the dominant commercial class, between small, local manufacturers and the internationally oriented financiers. In Ontario this split resulted in claims by the latter that the provincial government was threatening private property and attempts by the financier group to seek protection from both the federal government and the courts. Neither would oblige. The federal government would not exercise its power of disallowance and a challenge through the courts was dismissed with Justice Riddell's remark that 'The prohibition "Thou shalt not steal" has no legal force upon a sovereign body.'[113] Just why the courts stood so firmly by this view of parliamentary supremacy needs further investigation, but it is clear that they took the view of their limited roles vis-à-vis the legislature very seriously. This view may have been buttressed historically by a general confidence in the legislatures, but the courts' forbearance cannot simply be reduced to a lack of fear for the security of property.

The importance of the judiciary's principled belief in their limited role is indirectly supported by a study of judicial attitudes between 1880 and 1920 as reflected in the *Canadian Law Times,* the major legal journal of the era.[114] The author of this study claims that in the 1880s there was concern about the proliferation of legislation, its poor quality, and the need for lawyers to be involved in its drafting. But what is particularly interesting is that all the articles cited which directly suggest that the legislature was overstepping its bounds and that the courts should play a greater role are reprinted *American* articles.[115] The apparent absence of Canadian statements of this position gives added weight to the corresponding silence in nuisance cases: I found no instance of Canadian judges of the period saying that the courts were best suited to adapting the law to the new demands of modern times.

Finally, a brief comment is in order on the attitude of the judiciary towards industrial development and the changes it involved. The judiciary's commitment may have been not only to their limited role, but the substance of the rules they upheld. They may have believed that traditional property rights were somehow basic or that industry should bear the costs of the harm it inflicted. Judges may have refused to modify the law to accommodate industry because they had little sympathy with this development or with the industrialists who were making a profit while inflicting their noises, smells, and smoke on all around them. Certain comments in the judgments quoted above suggest such antipathies, such as the hostility to manufacturers' 'grasping tendencies.' The judgments almost never include commendations of industrial enterprise as the road to progress and prosperity, but then those judges most inclined to accommodate the law to the demands of industry were least likely to offer an explicit articulation of their views. A general lack of sympathy might account for the willingness of courts to circumvent the policies of British precedent which favoured industry. Or perhaps a better formulation is that a lack of enthusiasm for industrialization may have buttressed a principled judicial conservatism. But to develop this will require more research on the divisions among the Canadian élite over the issue of industrialization, and more information on the background of the judiciary in order to place them in this context.[116]

In sum, then, the Canadian courts seem to have been comparatively conservative even during the chief period of early industrialization. They displayed a consistent adherence to the principle that the role of the judiciary was to protect established rights by applying existing law, not to create new law. Their conservatism cannot be directly attributed to English precedent, though it may be attributable in part to their English heritage, both as a colony and as a parliamentary democracy. But the response of the Canadian courts cannot be understood only in terms of theoretical understandings of their proper roles, however deeply held. The full explanation must also take into account their actual relation to and attitude towards the legislatures, and the position of the judiciary in the Canadian social structure.

NOTES

A Killam postdoctoral fellowship at the Faculty of Law, Dalhousie University, supported the research for this essay and the legal training which preceded it.

1 Robert Stevens provides examples of modern English statements of this view, for example Lord Simonds in 1961: 'The law is developed by the application of old principles to new circumstances. Therein lies its genius. Its reform by the abrogation of these principles is the task not of the courts of law but of Parliament ... I would cast no doubt upon the doctrine of *stare decisis,* without which the law is at hazard.' (Stevens *Law and Politics: The House of Lords as a Judicial Body, 1800–1976* [Chapel Hill 1978] 344)

2 Ibid. ch. 3

3 Morton J. Horwitz *The Transformation of American Law 1780–1860* (Cambridge, MA 1977) 254

4 For a discussion of this function see Mark V. Tushnet 'Perspectives on the Development of American Law: A Critical Review of Friedman's "A History of American Law"' *Wisconsin Law Review* 1977, 81–109.

5 Robert Gordon notes that: 'The first-year law school curriculum to this day consists of an enthusiastic Oedipal slaying of our grandfathers – the authors of *formalism* in private law and *Lochnerism* in Constitutional law.' 'Lawyers and Legal Thought in the Age of Enterprise: Notes toward an *Ideological* Approach' forthcoming in *The Professions in the Modern West,* ed. Gerald Geison. See also the dismissive tone of the discussion in Walter F. Murphy and C. Herman Pritchett *Courts, Judges and Politics* (New York 1974) 5–12. The third edition (1979) seems to have a somewhat milder tone. Note that formalism is not simply a claim that judges should not make law, but that it is possible to make judicial decisions without making law or policy. It is this underlying model of law which is the subject of attack.

6 Oliver Wendell Holmes, jr *The Common Law: Skepticism, Reform, and the Judicial Process* (Boston 1881). See generally Wilfred E. Rumble, jr *American Legal*

Realism (Ithaca, NY 1968); Edwin W. Patterson *Jurisprudence: Men and Ideas of the Law* (New York 1953).

7 Stevens *Law and Politics*

8 Consider, for example, the responses of Alberta judges to questions about their perceptions of their role and of *stare decisis*: 'The doctrines of precedent and *stare decisis* are essential to the administration of law ... [If] some precedent or *stare decisis* philosophy [is not in tune with new social realities, it is the legislature, not the courts, which has the burden of adapting the law to the new realities.]' Confused or ambivalent statements were more common: 'A judge who adopts an activist role respecting social questions becomes a protagonist, and loses his capacity as an arbiter. A judge, however, can adapt law to new social realities as a proper judicial function. The courts must take cognizance of changes in conditions in applying rules'; or 'A judge should stay out of the political and social arena for the reason that he doesn't have the facility to canvass public opinion nor to properly assess it ... However, he should not be in an ivory tower impervious to social change.' Gerald Gall concludes that 'some judges hold the view that they must slavishly adhere to the doctrines of precedent and *stare decisis.* Although the number of judges who subscribe to that view without qualification is small, it does represent a certain hard core within the Canadian judiciary.' (Gall *The Canadian Legal System* [Toronto 1977] 142, 199, 200)

9 I base this comment on observations of classes at the Faculty of Law, Dalhousie University, on the lithographed texts used there, and on the nationally-used text *Canadian Tort Law* by C.A. Wright and A.M. Linden (7th ed. Toronto 1980). This text, for example, gives only passing reference to the connection between the rise of negligence and the industrial revolution. Such policy issues as are raised are relegated to lists of questions which, in my experience, students and faculty ignored as irrelevant to the doctrinal issues at hand.

10 In practice, if not in theory, the Canadian courts may thus be more conservative than their English models. Compare, for example, Canadian and English decisions in tort and contract for thoughtful, imaginative argument and articulation of policy. One of my former colleagues at Dalhousie explained that their text on contracts continued to reproduce large numbers of English cases, despite student requests for Canadian cases, because the former provided superior articulation of law and policy. Canadian cases, by comparison, tended to be composed of strings of quotations from precedents with little analysis. I think a comparison of important common law innovations in the two countries over the last thirty years will also bear out the claim of Canadian conservatism. Apparently formalist jurisprudence in England did not stifle judicial innovation.

Canadian judicial conservatism may, however, be changing. Consider the comment by an Alberta judge: 'The role of *stare decisis* will probably be relaxed here as the legislature tends to lag behind social change. The House of Lords declaration in 1966 that it is not binding on itself will be a contributing factor. Also, this latitude will be particularly applicable to certain fields of law, those with social overtones such as pornography.' (Gall *Canadian Legal System* 199)

11 Frank MacKinnon 'The Establishment of the Supreme Court of Canada' *Canadian Historical Review* XXVII (1946) 258; Michael Bader and Edward Burstein 'The Supreme Court of Canada 1892–1902: A Study of the Men and the Times' *Osgoode Hall Law Journal* VIII (1970) 503

12 Horwitz *Transformation of American Law* particularly chs 1, 2, and 8

13 Joel Franklin Brenner 'Legal Policy and Social Costs: Some Economic Functions of English Law, 1790–1870' (unpublished PH D dissertation, University of London 1972) and 'Nuisance Law and the Industrial Revolution' *Journal of Legal Studies* III (1974) 403–33

14 Ibid. 413. Brenner also argues that 'nuisance law was hardly applied at all to quasi public enterprises such as railroads; and that there was no systematic prosecution of public nuisances.' These are two aspects of Canadian nuisance law which invite further study.

15 Ibid. 415

16 There is no consensus on the exact timing and pace of Canada's industrial development. Some disagreement exists about when Canada's economy could appropriately be described as industrial, about variations in development by region and by industry, and about when the most important surges of development took place. For the broader questions this essay raises, it is important to have a clearer sense of Canada's pattern and pace of industrialization compared with that of the United States and England. But for the problems of industrialization relevant to nuisance law, it is reasonably clear that the dramatic growth of industrialization in Canada began around 1880 and continued through the 1920s. On the timing of industrial development see Gregory S. Kealey *Toronto Workers Respond to Industrial Capitalism 1867–1892* (Toronto 1980). Kealey argues that from the perspective of labour history, industrialization began in Toronto in the 1850s. But his figures also show that there was a dramatic increase in the size and number of industries between 1880 and 1890. For other discussion of Canada's industrial development see G.W. Bertram 'Economic Growth in Canadian Industry, 1870–1915' and K.A.H. Buckley 'Capital Formation in Canada, 1896–1930' in *Approaches to Canadian Economic History* W.T. Easterbrook and M.H. Watkins eds (Toronto 1967); H.T. Naylor *History of Canadian Business: 1867–1914*

(Toronto 1975); Stanley B. Ryerson *Unequal Union: Confederation and the Roots of Conflict in the Canadas 1815–1873* (Toronto 1967). James M. Gilmour *Spatial Evolution of Manufacturing: Southern Ontario 1851–1891* (Toronto 1972).

17 *Census of Canada 1921* (Ottawa 1924) I 3; ibid. 1931 (Ottawa 1936) I 55; *The Manufacturing Industries of Canada*, Dominion Bureau of Statistics (1942) 7, quoted in James Forbes 'Reaction and Change: A Study of the Ontario Bar' *University of Toronto Faculty Law Review* XXXII (1974) 51

18 Gilmour *Spatial Evolution* 192. Kealey also cites other economic geographers on this point (*Toronto Workers* 25–9, 33)

19 This would have been the response of traditional nuisance law. According to Blackstone a nuisance may be enjoined even if it arises from a lawful act, 'for it is encumbent upon [the perpetrator] to find some other place to do that act, where it will be less offensive.' (William Blackstone *Commentaries on the Laws of England* [London 1765–9; facsimile ed. Chicago 1979] III 217–18)

20 Kealey *Toronto Workers* ch. 1; J.M.S. Careless *Canada: A Story of Challenge* (Toronto 1963) chs 15, 16

21 See above note 16. Perhaps the most fruitful area to explore for differences between the two periods would be damages, since that seems to be where the courts found the greatest scope for accommodation to industry.

22 Nuisance is an occupier's remedy. To bring a suit in nuisance, one need not own the property affected, but only have a legal right to occupy it.

23 Brenner 'Nuisance Law'; Horwitz *Transformation of American Law*

24 The leading case in which this term is used is *Colls* v *Home and Colonial Stores* [1904] *Appeal Cases* (hereafter AC) 179; 73 *Law Journal Chancery Division* (hereafter LJCh) 484.

25 Nuisance cases in this period were identified using all the sources listed below as well as references within the cases. The predominance of Ontario cases reflects the fact that almost all of the sources were compiled in that province. The *Canadian Encyclopedic Digest* was explicitly said to be for Ontario, but like the other sources, it included cases from other provinces. The same non-Ontario cases frequently appeared in different sources, perhaps suggesting a consensus on their importance, or perhaps a certain circularity of reference among sources. The non-Ontario cases may have been the only Canadian decisions on a particular point.

There is a uniform common law in Canada to the extent that decisions of the Supreme Court of Canada (and, earlier, English high courts) are binding on all of the provinces. Thus a Nova Scotia civil case affirmed by the Supreme Court is binding on the other provinces, and a decision from a respected Appeal court would carry weight elsewhere.

The nature of the sources and the fact that I have included Supreme

Court decisions account for my only partially justified use of the word *Canadian* instead of Ontario. While the cases are primarily from Ontario, they are taken from the basic sources available in Canada at the time. *The All Canada Digest* covering every reported Canadian case from 1910 to 1934 (Toronto 1935); *Canadian Encyclopedic Digest,* Ontario Edition (Toronto 1926–33) vols 3 (damages) 6 (injunction) 8 (nuisance) (hereafter CED); *Canadian Law Times* 1881–1922 (Toronto) selected vols; *The Consolidated Rules of Practice and Procedure* (of Ontario) (Toronto 1884 and 1897); *Digest of Canadian Case Law* 1890–1900, 1900–11, 1911–14 (Toronto); *Index of Canadian Cases Judicially Noticed* 1823–1910, 1910–29, 1929–36 (Toronto); *Nova Scotia Digest of Reports* 1888–1903 (Toronto 1903).

26 The words cited are from *Lexington and Ohio Railroad* v *Applegate* 8 *Dana* (KY 1839), which Horwitz mentions as an exceptional early American case (*Transformation of American Law* 74–5)

27 Ibid. 74

28 The major *substantive* change, the admisson of a standard of care-reasonable use defence, had come and gone by the 1880s (Brenner, 'Nuisance Law') – although we will see that there was some confusion over this defence in Canada. The point in the text is that in the last decades of the nineteenth century the English courts were using techniques to avoid the rigours of nuisance law so as to substantially change its effect, without changing the substance of the law itself.

29 *Bamford* v *Turnley* (1862), 31 *Law Journal Reports, New Series, Queens Bench* (hereafter LJQB) 286; *St. Helen's Smelting Co.* v *Tipping* (1865), 11 *House of Lords Cases* (hereafter HLC) 642; *Sturges* v *Bridgman* (1879) 11 *English Law Reports, Chancery Division* (hereafter ChD) 852. Brenner argues that 'the dearth of reported nuisance actions against factories suggests that this dual standard had been long operating before it was effectively ratified by the House of Lords in *St. Helen's Smelting Co.* v *Tipping* in 1865. This is arguably the most important nuisance case of the era ('Nuisance Law' 413). The other leading cases, those consistently cited as authority in late nineteenth-early twentieth-century English and Canadian decisions, may also have ratified or crystallized practices long in effect. This may be the reason that the leading cases came relatively late in England's industrial development.

30 (1906), 1 ChD 234, [1907] AC at 251. He was arguing that prescription was not the issue. Prescriptive rights are rights acquired by uninterrupted exercise for a certain period of time. Thus a squatter's right to land was legally established after twenty years of occupation, and an interference with another's property rights, such as a nuisance or the use of a short cut across the property, could develop into a prescriptive right if exercised continuously for twenty years.

31 (1858), 4 *English Common Bench Reports, New Series* (hereafter CBNS) 333, 140; 1 *English Reports* (hereafter ER) 1113. *Hole* v *Barlow* introduced reasonable use as a defence.

32 *St. Helen's Smelting Co.* v *Tipping* (1865), 11 HLC 642 at 643. The character of the neighbourhood was not relevant when the damage was to the property itself, but the requirements were strict here too: 'material injury,' 'sensible injury to the value of the property,' thus virtually requiring physical damage.

33 [1907] AC 128; [1904] AC 179

34 *Lyon* v *Borland* (1911), 3 *Ontario Weekly Notes* (hereafter OWN) 204 at 207 referring to *St. Helen's* for the principles involved. A new trial was ordered in this case because the trial judge had explicitly said that it 'does not make any difference whether it is a manufacturing district or not.'

35 *Drysdale* v *Dugas* (1895), 26 *Supreme Court Reports* (hereafter SCR) 20 at 23. This case originated in Quebec, where courts were much more direct in their approach to the class dimension of the neighbourhood concept (here, of course, a civil law concept), as indeed they seem to be in policy questions generally. In *Carpentier* v *La Ville de Maisonneuve* the Chief Justice's quoted remarks were described as a comment on the fact that 'the same act might be a nuisance when committed in the vicinity of properties of a certain class and not a nuisance when committed in the vicinity of properties of a lower class.' The judge then concluded that neighbours must endure inconveniences that 'vary in kind and extent depending on the circumstances of the place and the quality of the population.' (1897) 11 *Quebec Reports, Superior Courts* (hereafter QRCS) 242 at 248.

36 *Turtle* v *Toronto* (1924), 56 *Ontario Law Reports* (hereafter OLR) 252 at 265

37 (1865), 11 HLC 642 at 643, per Justice Mellor. I should note that I do not entirely agree with Brenner's reading of *St. Helen's*. I do not think the court actually said that had there been no property damage, the plaintiff would have lost because the (obviously substantial) interference with his comfort was merely a 'trifling inconvenience.' But the thrust of what I take to be *obiter* remarks was certainly clear.

38 (1911), 3 OWN 204. The trial judge in *Lyon* v *Borland* was rare in his claim that neighbourhood was irrelevant.

39 (1862) 31 LJQB 286. This case overruled *Hole* v *Barlow* (1858), 4 CBNS 333, which allowed reasonable use as a defence.

40 Ibid. 291–2

41 In negligence cases the issue is whether or not the defendant has violated his duty to carry out his activities with the degree of care required by law. Thus if a bale of hay falls off the defendant's truck, the issue is whether he was adequately careful in securing the hay. If he was, he is not liable for

the accident, even if someone is hurt. In traditional nuisance law, on the other hand, the care with which, say, a pig sty is operated is not the issue. The issue is whether or not the effect of the pig sty is to create such a smell as to constitute an actionable injury. It is thus irrelevant for the defendant to argue that he operates his pig sty in the best, most careful manner possible. If a negligence standard is imported into nuisance law, the defendant has an additional defence available.

42 8 CED; Underhill *The Law of Torts* 4th Canadian Edition, by Herbert Smith (London 1922)

43 (1919), 38 OLR 151; (1910), 22 OLR 533; (1916), 36 OLR 10

44 The defendant seems not to have claimed that either father or daughter was abnormally sensitive. This would have been a defence since nuisance protects only the right to reasonable enjoyment according to the standard of the ordinary man. Fastidious tastes are not protected.

45 8 *Law Reports, Chancery Appeal Cases* (hereafter LRCh App) 8, quoted in *Oakley* 38

46 Ibid. my emphasis

47 (1910), 22 OLR 533

48 Ibid. 535. The defendant did manage to find one witness, 'an enthusiastic lover of the weed' as the judge described him, who found the smell 'just splendid.'

49 (1851), 4 *De Gex and Smale's English Chancery Reports*, (hereafter DeG and S) 315; [1906] 1 ChD 234; [1907] AC 121

50 Quoted in *Appleby* (1910), 22 *Dominion Law Reports* (hereafter DLR)

51 Ibid. Middleton also noted that *Gaunt* v *Fynny* (1870) relied on in *Oakley* (1919), had effectively been overruled. In 1889 *Reinhardt* v *Mentasti* (42 ChD 685) held that *Gaunt* v *Fynny* should be interpreted in light of the general rules of law, hence not as support for the view that reasonableness of use is a defence in nuisance. *Rushmer* (1907) also predated *Oakley*.

52 (1916), 36 OLR 10

53 *Pope* v *Peate* (1904), 27 OLR 207

54 *Crowell* v *Archbold* (1906), 1 *Eastern Law Reports* 169 (hereafter ELR)

55 (1896), 26 SCR 20

56 *Ball* v *Ray* (1873), 8 LRCh App 467; *Broder* v *Saillard* (1876) 2 ChD 692

57 (1896), 26 SCR 20

58 Ibid.; (1862), 31 LJQB 286

59 (1896), 26 SCR 20; [1907] AC 121

60 *Pope* v *Peate* (1904), 27 OLR 207; *Crowell* v *Archbold* (1906), 1 ELR 169

61 (1922), 63 SCR 243. This case, like *Drysdale*, originated in Quebec and thus the issues are those of the civil law. But, rightly or wrongly, the judges assert

that both the law of nuisance and the rules pertaining to injunctions are virtually identical to those of the common law. Both cases are regularly cited in common law reference sources.

62 Horwitz *Transformation of American Law* 77–8

63 (1913), 5 OWN 423

64 63 SCR 243 at 256

65 (1865), 11 HLC 642; (1922), 63 SCR 243 at 245

66 63 SCR 243 at 246 my emphasis, 248, 249

67 Ibid. 252

68 From *Shelfer* v *London Electric Lighting Co.* (1895), 1 *English Law Reports, Chancery Appeals* (hereafter Ch) 287. See text at note 84 for a discussion of these rules.

69 *Canada Paper* (1922), 63 SCR 243 at 256 my emphasis

70 Ibid. 258

71 It may be significant that Duff, who supported balancing, and Anglin, who avoided taking a position, were twenty-five years younger than Idington. Davies, who concurred with Idington, was only five years younger.

72 These are the non-western cases, in which nuisance was the central issue, which the sources described in note 25 turned up. They do not include public nuisance cases nor cases in which statutory authority was the primary issue.

73 This appears to be the case for both trial and appellate courts.

74 *Stevenson* v *Colvin* (1918), 13 OWN 426

75 Ibid. 478

76 (1901), 2 OLR 240. The Court of Appeal affirmed this decision in 4 OLR 258.

77 (1901), 2 OLR 240 at 247–8

78 (1924), 56 OLR 252

79 (1915), 7 OWN 764, affirmed 21 DLR 841. The case was tried at Sandwich. It is not clear whether Mullen Coal was located in or near Sandwich.

80 Ibid. 764

81 Ibid. 766

82 Ibid.

83 *Revised Statutes of Ontario* 1877, c. 40, s. 40 which was taken from Lord Cairn's Act, 21 and 22 Vict. (1858) c. 27, s. 2, 2 (6) (UK).

84 (1895), 1 Ch 287

85 [1905] AC 179

86 *O'Keefe* v *Pope* (1910), 44 *New Brunswick Reports* 443

87 *Nestor* v *Hayes Wheel Co.* (1924), 26 OWN 129. Both acquiescence in the nuisance and delay in bringing suit may be bars to the equitable remedy of an injunction.

There is a certain irony to this decision considering that the leading case of *Rushmer* v *Polsue* used steam hammers as their example in saying that it was no defence to argue that equipment is 'of the most modern approved pattern and is reasonably worked.' [1907] AC 121

88 (1914), 32 OLR 111 at 113. This is really a case involving statutory authority.

89 (1917), 12 OWN 243 at 244. Mond Nickle Co. was also being sued.

90 For the history of the nickel industry see H.V. Nelles *The Politics of Development: Forests, Mines, and Hydro-Electric Power in Ontario, 1849–1941* (Toronto 1974).

91 (1917), 12 OWN 243 at 244

92 (1928), 63 OLR 111

93 Ibid. 119

94 (1895), 1 Ch. 287; (1928), 63 OLR 111 at 119.

95 One may question whether *Shelfer* actually crystallized the rule, given the very different approach in *Colls* ([1904], AC 179), but the Shelfer rules are standard in the English texts.

96 (1917), 12 OWN 243

97 *McKenzie* v *Kayler* (1905), 1 *Western Law Reporter* 290; *Adami* v *Montreal* (1904), 25 QRCS 1. This Quebec case is frequently cited in common law cases and texts.

98 (1899), 32 *Nova Scotia Reports* 44. The choice of location is slightly less surprising when one realizes that it was the site of an abandoned penitentiary.

99 Ibid. 56, citing *Salvin* v *North Brancepeth Coal Co.* 9 LRCh App 785, and 58.

100 Ibid. 66

101 *Montreal Street Railway Co.* v *Boudreau* (1905), 36 SCR 329; *Carpentier* v *La Ville de Maisonneuve* (1897), 11 QRCS 242 citing *Drysdale* v *Dugas* (1895), 26 SCR 20. All these cases originated in Quebec, but there is nothing in the judgments to indicate that this issue was peculiar to civil law. The cases are cited in common law reference sources.

102 See, for example, *Nestor* v *Hayes Wheel Co.* [1924] OWN 129.

103 *Montreal Street Railway Co.* v *Boudreau* (1905), 36 SCR 329

104 For discussions of formalism, see Stevens *Law and Politics;* Horwitz *Transformation of American Law*; Walter F. Pratt 'Rhetorical Styles on the Fuller Court' and Charles C. Goetsch 'The Future of Legal Formalism' in *The American Journal of Legal History* XXIV (1980) 189 and 221; Duncan Kennedy 'Legal Formality' *Journal of Legal Studies* II (1973) 351. For a critique of the usefulness of the formalism-instrumentalism dichotomy, see L.S. Paine 'Instrumentalism v. Formalism: Dissolving the Dichotomy' *Wisconsin Law Review* 1978 997.

105 (1917), 12 OWN 243

106 For this, one of the best approaches would be local studies which could examine in detail the economic and social significance of the industry being sued. As in the *Francklyn* case, the history of the industry and its owners, the social position of the plaintiff, and the economic viability of the industry may all be factors, as well as importance to the local economy. None of this information is usually available from the case reports.

107 Even if damages were consistently low it is still significant that Canadian courts refused to take the overtly instrumental path of their English and American brethren.

Interestingly, there is some evidence that the Americans are now turning to what seems to have been the Canadian approach: purity of substantive law and flexibility with remedies. American nuisance law incorporated a negligence standard and permitted the evaluation of the importance as well as the reasonableness of the defendant's conduct. This evaluation could then be balanced against the plaintiff's injury in determining whether the defendant's conduct constituted a nuisance. The balancing was thus made part of substantive nuisance law. Recent notes in the *Restatement of the Law* 2nd *Torts* suggest that this balancing should be removed from substantive nuisance law and retained in the determination of the appropriate remedy, particularly in the choice between damages and injunction. Richard B. Stuart and James E. Krier *Environmental Law and Policy* (Indianapolis 1978).

108 *Atchison* v *Stratford Gas Co.* (1922), 22 OWN 147; *Young* v *Fort Francis Pulp and Paper Co.* (1919), 17 OWN 6

109 *Canada Paper* v *Brown* (1922), 63 SCR 243; *Cairns* v *Canadian Refining and Smelting Co.* (1913), 5 OWN 423; *Gagnon* v *Dominion Stamping* (1914), 7 OWN 530

110 (1917) 12 OWN 243.

111 I owe this history of *Francklyn* v *Peoples Heat and Light* to an unpublished paper by Kyle Joliffe 'A Story of Gilded Age Entrepreneurs in Halifax' (1980). He cites *Debates and Proceedings of the House of Assembly* (Nova Scotia) 1899, 106, 188–9, 185–91, 204–6, 217–18.

112 *McKie et al.* v *The KVP Co. Ltd.* (1948), 3 DLR 201

113 Quoted in Christopher Armstrong and H.V. Nelles 'Private Property in Peril: Ontario Businessmen and the Federal System, 1898–1911' in Glenn Porter and Robert D. Cuff, eds *Enterprise and National Development* (Toronto 1973).

114 Newman 'Reaction and Change' 51

115 These reprintings may suggest that the lawyers and legal scholars of the time were not content with the limited role of the courts. During early industrialization in the United States, by contrast, lawyers and judges (and,

Horwitz argues, the commercial élite) worked together to achieve a broader scope for judicial power by placing the responsibility for modifications of the law with the judges. The success of this effort was probably fostered by the early *judicialization* of protections of individual rights implicit in the American power of judicial review.

116 Tom Naylor has made a controversial argument about splits in the Canadian élite over industrialization. See 'The Rise and Fall of the Third Commercial Empire of the St Lawrence' in Gary Teeple, ed. *Capitalism and the National Question in Canada* (Toronto 1972) and *The History of Canadian Business* 2 vols (Toronto 1976). Among his important critics are L.R. MacDonald 'Merchants against Industry: An Idea and Its Origins' CHR LVI (1975) 263 and Stanley Ryerson 'Who's Looking After Business: A Review' *This Magazine* 10, 5, and 6 (1976) 41.

9

Quebec's Legal Elite Looks at Women's Rights: The Dorion Commission 1929–31

JENNIFER STODDART

It was a moment of triumph for Marie Gérin-Lajoie when on 15 November 1929 she rose to address the Commission on the Civil Rights of Women in Montreal's courthouse. Victories had been few and hard-won for this Catholic feminist, leader of the Quebec women's movement and acknowledged expert on their legal rights, and she must have savoured the obvious deference of the Commissioners after so many years of often vituperative public attacks.[1]

Francophone Quebec feared feminism, even the very mild brand which Gérin-Lajoie represented, because it threatened the national image of a religious, orderly people clinging to their traditional ways. The Catholic Church, arbiter of social values in Quebec at the time, brooked no opposition from those who questioned its definition of the family or the role of women. Only a few years before, the Archbishop of Montreal had forced her to resign the leadership of the suffrage movement. Shaken but still determined, Gérin-Lajoie, joined by other English and French feminists, had continued to press for substantial modifications in the status of Quebec's women under the civil law. It had been well over half a century since Quebec had adopted its Civil Code in 1865, and the legal status of women had remained virtually unchanged since then. Indeed, many of the articles of the Code dealing with the status of women had been modelled on the Napoleonic Code of 1804 or even the provisions of the sixteenth-century Coutume de Paris.

The creation of the Dorion Commission on the Civil Rights of Women in

1929 was a small admission to the forces of feminism and modernism in Quebec that the role of women had been modified and that new circumstances had developed over the years. In the wider context of Quebec's evolution, the Dorion Commission was situated at the historical convergence of the contradiction between unparalleled clerical power and the increasing modernization of Quebec society; it symbolized the resulting dilemma of Quebec élites and of the legal system they controlled. Faced with an increasingly industrial and urbanized society in the post-World War I era, existing anxiously within a Canada whose determinedly anglophone character was ever more apparent, subjected to the militant pressure of an ultraconservative Church reorganized under the banner of social catholicism, the francophone bourgeoisie of Quebec in the late 1920s was faced with the task of defining social norms for collective life which, while adapting to twentieth-century North America, must continue to provide an adequate anchor for a distinctive group identity within a highly traditional population.[2]

For any society the translation of norms into the rules of a coherent legal system is an indispensable key to both self-definition and social control for the group actually drawing up the rules. Family organization clearly lies at the centre of the collective experience of any community. Any inquiry into the possible legal restructuring of family relationships implicitly raises the question of patterns of social existence. The Dorion Commission, whose mandate might at first glance appear to limit its significance to the relatively narrow field of the civil rights of married women, was in reality an inquiry into a wide range of cultural values of Quebec society in the 1920s as they were enshrined in the Civil Code. The legal condition of married women in Quebec remained substantially unchanged from 1865 until 1964. But this was not a result of apathy or lack of interest on the part of the legislators or even the public but rather was a conscious and continuing choice by Quebec lawmakers.[3] From time to time changing social and political realities have compelled them to justify that choice. The Dorion Commission was one such moment of decision, and its reports provide many insights into why the traditional legal status for women was maintained almost unchanged in the period before the Quiet Revolution.

Around the Commission swirled various and often conflicting currents of French-Canadian nationalism, feminism, and the ideological force of the Catholic church. The compromise which was eventually achieved in the particular case of the legal status of women says much about the mentality of Quebec élites at that time. The recommendations of the Commission and the reaction of contemporaries to them not only represent a chapter in the history of the civil law in Quebec but also reveal many of the varied forces behind the complex process of law reform.

WOMEN'S RIGHTS IN QUEBEC AT THE BEGINNING OF THE TWENTIETH CENTURY

During the first three decades of the century, Marie Gérin-Lajoie (1867–1945) dominated the struggle for women's rights. The daughter of a former Chief Justice of Quebec, a self-taught jurist whose manual on the civil law was widely used in Quebec schools, Gérin-Lajoie possessed the expertise, the determination, and the prestige to make her the natural leader of the francophone feminists in a very conservative society.[4] Although Gérin-Lajoie as early as 1900 was writing about the need to reform the legal status of women in Quebec, she was not alone.[5] At its formation in 1896 the influential Montreal Local Council of Women had established a legislative committee. This group worked to bring to public attention what it increasingly perceived as the discriminatory position of women in Quebec law. Then in 1907 when Gérin-Lajoie, along with the other women reformers, founded the Fédération Nationale Saint-Jean-Baptiste, legal reform was prominently inscribed on its program. The Fédération, of which Gérin-Lajoie was President from 1913 to 1933, was an umbrella organization whose affiliated membership numbered some 10,000 women. Its goals were inspired by the doctrines of social catholicism and Christian feminism. Because of those links even its most moderate suggestions for the improvement of women's lot in life, whether through the formation of professional associations for women workers or the extension of secondary education for girls, were subjected to close scrutiny by the church. Nonetheless, as early as 1914 Marie Gérin-Lajoie led a delegation of Fédération women to request the establishment of a formal inquiry into the legal status of women in the province. At that time Premier Lomer Gouin had requested that the Fédération submit a plan for proposed changes, but the war provided a pretext for shelving the project.[6]

Feminists in early twentieth-century Quebec had much reason to be indignant about their legal status. The province was the last North American state to concede to the demands of the women's movement that political and civil rights should be the same for both sexes. Fixed in its traditions, Quebec maintained undaunted the almost complete exclusion of women from the exercise of public rights and the severe curtailment of civil capacity for married women.[7]

In general, legal systems in modern times apply equally to men and women in most areas: tort or delictual responsibility and reparation through damages, criminal acts and their sanction, and contractual obligations, to give only a few examples. However, a special status for women has been created and observed in two major areas of the Western legal tradition: public law and family and matrimonial law. Women have first been assigned a special status in terms of their position within the family unit, especially in relation to their husbands.[8] Second, because the domestic area was deemed to be the habitual sphere of feminine activity, customary or statutory law controlled the extent of their participation in the public arena.

The significance of the creation and outcome of the Dorion Commission becomes clear only against the backdrop of the entire framework of women's rights in Quebec – both political and civil.[9] By 1910 complete female enfranchisement, not only at the provincial but also at the municipal and school board levels, had become a goal of the Montreal Local Council of Women and the Fédération Nationale Saint-Jean-Baptiste.[10] Yet in clerically dominated Quebec there were many who resisted this symbolic extension of the feminine role outside the home, and in the post war era a major campaign was mounted against the suffrage movement and feminism in general.[11] The result was that Quebec successfully resisted suffragist demands until 1940.[12]

Generalizations about the legal status of women often confuse political and civil rights and fail to make it clear that in many countries the peculiar regime restricting women's control over their physical persons and their own property applied only to married women. Under Quebec civil law unmarried women or widows always enjoyed the same legal rights and capacities as men in the administration of their property. Although little more than half the province's adult women were married in 1931, not many could have possessed enough property even to be fully aware of the restrictions placed on their control of it.[13] In early twentieth-century Quebec women who were single, widowed, legally separated as to bed and board, or divorced, thus had a civil law status equivalent to that of men for most acts concerning private property. However, as soon as the nature of a legal act resembled that usually exercised by the male head of household alone, such as tutorship or curatorship of minor children or interdicted persons, women were excluded.[14]

The Quebec Act of 1774 had guaranteed the use of civil law in Quebec. However, some English common law was introduced, notably in the areas of public and criminal law. One of the few advantages English law had conferred on the women, as well as the men of the province since 1801, was an unlimited freedom to make a will. Apart from these few privileges, once married the women of Quebec fell under the yoke of the ironclad principle of the legal incapacity of wives. Article 986 of the Civil Code, which was to arouse the ire of countless reformers, then stated that married women, along with minors and interdicted persons, were incapable of contracting, except in cases specified by the law – that is, only with the express authorization of their husbands. For example, they could neither acquire property, receive donations, make contracts, or engage in business on their own, for without marital permission all these acts were null and void. Nevertheless, once duly authorized a wife could perform most legal acts.[15] However, a husband could refuse such authorization. Sometimes he was simply absent when his signature was required. Since a general authorization was insufficient, a desperate wife in such circumstances had to apply to a judge for the necessary permission. Until 1981 the Civil Code obliged a wife to reside at the domicile of the husband's choice. The latter could request a separation of bed and board because of his wife's infidelity. However, a wife could not cite her husband's adultery as grounds for the same proceeding, unless he entertained his 'concubine' under the family roof. Finally, despite the glorification of women as mothers, ultimate authority over children was exercised by the father alone as head of the family.[16]

In early twentiety-century Quebec couples contemplating marriage had two choices. Either they could draw up a marriage contract before a notary or, in the absence of a specific contract, they were subject to the rules of community of property. Community of property until the end of the 1960s was the basic matrimonial regime.[17] The Dorion Commission estimated, without making any scientific calculations, that in 1930 eighty per cent of women were married under community of property. Another source estimates the figure to be fifty-seven per cent.[18] Probably one of the most complex marriage régimes ever devised, community of property was based on the general principle that assets accruing to either member of a couple belonged to them both for the duration of the marriage, except that the administration of this common property devolved exclusively upon the husband. Property was jointly owned, but the wife's legal incapacity meant that she had no independent power or access to the property, which her husband could handle much as he pleased. The spouses each retained their private property during marriage. Immoveable property owned before marriage and immoveables either inherited from ascendants or received as a special personal legacy were designated as personal property. However, in fact the husband as head of the community administered the private property of his wife. Community property comprised all other property acquired during the marriage in any other way. The moveable property each consort possessed on the day of the marriage, which could be in the form of savings bonds or jewellery, for example, became common community property. Finally, the revenues from all personal property held by the consorts belonged to the community, that is, to both jointly. By the twentieth century the most important block of assets entering the community was usually the revenue or salary earned by husband and wife. Most couples, whether living in a rural or urban community, possessed very little upon marriage. Such acquired assets as the family farm, a home, some furniture, and savings were according to familiar cultural roles administered by the husband in consultation with his wife.

Most women, as brides, possessed neither buildings nor land. The practical implication of this regime was that upon marriage all their property, present or future, fell under their husbands' control. The latter could sell or otherwise dispose of such common property without his wife's consent. He had no obligation, unlike trustees, to account for his administration. A practical exception to the wife's incapacity was the legal fiction of a tacit mandate from the husband to incur household expenses. Other code provisions, while seemingly conferring a privilege on wives, expressed the underlying legal attitude that the helpless wife should entrust herself to her husband's 'protection.' For example, a husband who had authorized his wife to perform a legal act became liable for the debts she might thus incur. Any debts she had brought into the marriage had to be liquidated by the community. By contrast this was not the case for the husband, whose previous debts burdened him alone.

Equality in the community – suspended during its existence – came into force at its dissolution, that is upon death or separation of bed and board.[19] All the assets and liabilities which had accrued to the community during the course of the marriage were divided equally. At this point the wife enjoyed another privilege which supposedly compensated for her lack of control during the actual marriage. She could waive her share, if debts outran assets or if she chose rather to benefit as an heir of the deceased. The wife 'common as to property' also enjoyed a right of survivorship in the form of a dower, that is the use and enjoyment (usufruct) of one-half of the immoveables belonging to the husband. However, this right had to be formally registered to be conserved; by the turn of the century few women availed themselves of this added protection probably because they were unaware of its existence. For women married under the community regime, there were only two methods of bypassing a husband's refusal or inability to authorize legal acts by the wife. The first was to apply to a judge for the requisite powers, although he rarely granted permission where a husband had refused; the second was to institute a suit for judicial separation of property.

Couples who chose to have a marriage contract drawn up by a notary were free to specify whatever property arrangements they wished, provided they did not infringe on basic rules such as the husband's position as head of the family or the wife's legal incapacity. In practice, most marriage contracts adopted the regime of separation of property.

Quebec's financial and commercial bourgeoisie, which included a large section of its anglophone population, preferred separation of property, a choice which gave the maximum possible autonomy to each spouse. It was often the solution favoured both by women who possessed property or did business in their own right and by husbands who were active in commerce and finance and who wished to protect their wives' assets from their own potential creditors.[20] The distinctive advantage for a wife was that it allowed her administration of her property and ownership of the revenues it might produce. There the advantage ended, however, for without her husband's permission she could not sell or dispose of her own immoveables or acquire new ones. Financial arrangements between the spouses were set down in a notarized contract drawn up before the marriage. But many commentators have pointed out that the conditions of the contract were often unsuitable to the lifestyle of the couple and little understood by either of the spouses, especially the wife. Usual clauses included provision for shared household expenses, the husband's assumption of the debts of both parties, and a gift of a specified amount to be settled upon the wife at the dissolution of the marriage, usually by the death of her spouse. Although the scope of action allowed to women was clearly greater than in the community regime, it was often accompanied by increased financial insecurity. Separation of property meant that in the absence of a will wives had no special claim on their husband's property. The amounts specified in the marriage contract, which were irrevocable, were more often than not completely unrealistic in view of the needs and assets of the spouses by the time the gifts became payable. This situation could have serious consequences for a widow who had to content herself with the gifts specified in her contract, notwithstanding the present value of her husband's assets.

The controversy surrounding the issue of women's rights in Quebec at the time can best be understood by comparing the situation to the reforms which women had achieved in other Canadian provinces and at the federal level. In the English-speaking provinces of Canada an active group of women reformers, aware of the importance of the legal system in defining civil rights and opportunities, had been instrumental in pushing through a series of legal innovations.[21] Having won the vote at both the provincial and federal levels, English-Canadian feminists in the 1920s attacked the remaining legal barriers to emancipation in the public sphere. The famous 'Persons case' of 1929, wherein the Privy Council decided that the word persons in the British North America Act included women and thus made them eligible for the Senate, helped to keep the issue of women's rights before the public.[22]

Anglophone feminists had also made considerable progress in modifying the common law, which had a dismal record in terms of women's rights. In England, unlike France, the complete disappearance of the legal personality of the married woman in the seventeenth and eighteenth centuries and the elimination of her customary rights had resulted in a situation of almost complete legal dependency.[23] The passage of a series of Married Women's Property acts in England after 1870 revealed not so much enlightenment in attitudes to women, as many anglophones implied, especially in Quebec, but more probably the political hegemony of the commercial bourgeoisie.[24] A nation of shopkeepers was not slow to recognize the advantages of having part of the family assets beyond the reach of creditors or the poor business judgment of a son-in-law. By the end of the nineteenth century the situation of married women in most Canadian common law provinces had been redefined as it had been in England. It would remain substantially the same until the most recent reforms of the mid-1970s in the wake of the *Murdoch* case.[25] Basically the new laws meant that the wife's property was in her exclusive control as the husband's was in his. No intermediate institution was recognized where family assets were pooled, such as the civil law community.

Hindsight and changing social standards have today revealed many of the injustices to both husband and wife of common law provisions for separation of property. Nonetheless, to many women reformers in Quebec in the 1920s the overall position of married women in the common law provinces was by and large enviable. Anglophone women especially rankled under the principle of the overriding marital and paternal authority of husbands over themselves, their property and their children. Although most married couples doubtless achieved an acceptable *modus vivendi*, the everpresent need for authorization by the husband, whether for a child's emergency operation or department store credit arrangements, must have been a special irritation perhaps for the anglophone community in particular and a constant reminder of the more 'progressive' state of affairs across provincial borders.

POLITICS, NATIONALISM, AND WOMEN'S RIGHTS

The virulence of the debate on women's rights in Quebec and the lag in the modernization of their legal status can only be explained by the political evolution of the province as a whole. It is ironic that the Quebec women's movement articulated its demands at the very time that the clerical machine seemed to have almost stamped out liberalism as a respectable ideology. In the 1920s and 1930s the church in Quebec viewed feminism with horror. Montreal's Archbishop Georges Gauthier took personal pains to block feminist endeavours and in 1922 he forced Marie Gérin-Lajoie to resign as leader of the English and French coalition movement for provincial suffrage. As well, Premier Louis-Alexandre Taschereau, who did not hesitate to oppose the church when the state's increased intervention in the social welfare field demanded it, made use of clerical opposition to the liberalization of family law to deny votes to women.[26]

Quebec, the only society in North America with a clear majority of Catholics, was also the territorial base of French Canada. Postwar Quebec was a society in which Abbé Lionel Groulx was sketching out the blueprint for the separatist vision and where the inroads of urbanization and industrialization meant that the problem of maintaining French-Canadian national identity had reached a new level of intensity. The immediate reaction to renewed threats to national existence was the reinforcement of old values. In these circumstances the familiar nineteenth-century trilogy which had carried francophones into Confederation – 'our language, our religion, our laws' – became an incessant litany. One Quebec historian has described the ideological atmosphere of these years as 'characterized by a double fear, compounded by the Depression. First of all there is the national question ... Next, there is anxiety over social changes caused by industrialization and urbanization. The links between nationalism and the search for social order are both close and complex.'[27]

The francophone élite regarded the Civil Code as one of the bulwarks against anglophone cultural pressures. Unfortunately, the creation of the Dorion Commission in 1929 coincided with what the watchdogs of Quebec's legal traditions and traditional morality perceived as being a formidable new threat to the Civil Code and Catholic values – J.S. Woodsworth's successful effort to introduce judicial divorce to Ontario.[28] The fulminations on the evil of divorce and the infringement of provincial rights published by such leaders of public opinion as Henri Bourassa in *Le Devoir* and Léo Pelland in *La Revue du Droit* (one of the major legal periodicals of the time) did not create an auspicious context for the reconsideration of matrimonial legislation. In fact, only weeks before the commissioners were to release their second report in the spring of 1930, a joint pastoral letter on divorce warning against any change in marriage legislation was published by the Quebec episcopacy and subsequently read in all the churches.[29]

The nationalists' vision of the role of women and the family was central to their hopes for the future of French and Catholic Quebec. Such critics were quick to point out that 'emancipated' women, no longer subjected to paternal or marital authority, free to pursue their own goals and control their own incomes, would not be interested in raising the large families necessary for Quebec's future survival. Family life was central to the contemporary French-Canadian self-image. As conditions of life and work for francophone men became less and less distinctive, especially in urban areas, the family and the role of wife and mother appeared increasingly as the last threads holding together the traditional pattern of community life. It should be remembered that Quebec's civil law heritage ensured that matrimonial legislation evolved according to a rhythm totally estranged from surrounding common law jurisdictions. Reformers of the era often forgot that comparisons between common and civil law provisions were almost irrelevant to civilian jurists. Quebec's legal counterparts were France and Belgium and, within this peer group, the Quebec Civil Code appeared neither especially backward nor unusually repressive. These European countries accorded women a legal status very similar to the situation in Quebec.

The anglophone community of Montreal was by 1920 seemingly unanimous in favour of changes in both public and private law which would bring the status of Quebec women in line with that of their sisters in other provinces.[30] Some of English Quebec's most prominent citizens gave their active support to the women's rights movement. Dean Frederick Walton of the McGill Law Faculty was among the orators who welcomed British suffragette Emmeline Pankhurst to Montreal in 1913. The Montreal *Herald* had definitively thrown its weight behind the feminist campaign with its special suffrage issue in 1912. But by the 1920s the anglophone community wearily recognized that if change was to come in

Quebec, it must originate with its francophone citizens.[31] It was too easy for the proponents of the status quo to equate progressive demands with anglophone attacks on French Canadian national values and thus seriously undermine any chance of change.[32] The nationalist model of the historic evolution of English-French relations in the province, which suggests that the anglophone bourgeoisie clearly dominated francophone professional classes, simply does not account for English-speaking Quebec's inability to lobby successfully for modernized matrimonial legislation. Two explanations may be put forward: as long as the issue chiefly concerned women, it was not perceived by either group as being of enough significance to merit threatening the uneasy peace between the cultural groups. It is even more likely that in the pre-Quiet Revolution trade-off of political and economic power, the domain of family legislation had been conceded to the francophone majority. For anglophones to attack this monopoly directly might widen the cracks in the shaky edifice of Confederation.

The continued opposition of many franchophone religious, political, and intellectual leaders to the modernization of women's role in pre-Quiet Revolution Quebec is well known. In the specific case of the Commission on the Civil Rights of Women, three additional factors completed the mise-en-scène. First, there was Premier Taschereau's old world view on women and his avowed personal opposition to female suffrage.[33] Second, although the Chamber of Notaries and the Quebec bar remained officially silent about the wisdom of reforms in the Civil Code, their resistance to the entry of women into their own professional ranks leaves little doubt as to their opinions.[34] Finally, the most likely retrospective assessment of the viewpoint of the majority of Quebec francophone women helps to justify the defenders of the status quo: it was quite probable that most of them were simply indifferent to the whole controversy. In practice, community of property was often less prejudicial to women than any other existing system since it gave them a share in family assets. Most wives, preoccupied with housekeeping and childbearing and possessing little personal property, were probably content to leave business arrangements to their husbands.[35]

The answer to the crucial question of why the Dorion Commission was even set up lies in the tactics of the feminist movement during the 1920s. Following the church's veto on suffragist activity, leadership of the movement passed from Marie Gérin-Lajoie, who remained active in other areas, to a younger generation of women. New leaders, like Thérèse Casgrain and Idola Saint-Jean, did not quail before ecclesiastical disapproval and their energy reinvigorated the feminist forces in the late 1920s. They instituted what became a rite until 1940: the annual trip to the Quebec legislature to see yet another bill on woman suffrage defeated. By 1928 Taschereau and the Liberals recognized that something had to be done to appease the feminists. The government could buy time and forestall the suffrage issue by dusting off the Fédération's suggestion for a major reconsideration of the civil status of women. At the same time it would quiet anglophone criticism of the archaic nature of Quebec laws. And of course then, as now, the government was in no way obliged to implement a Commission's findings.

In a series of articles in 1927 Marie Gérin-Lajoie reiterated her original demands for reconsideration of the Civil Code. In December 1927 Thérèse Casgrain buttonholed the Premier on the steps of the Montreal City Hall and asked when a full-scale commission would be instituted. On 21 January 1928 the Fédération sent a delegation formally requesting Premier Taschereau to set up a commission.[36] A small victory was produced in 1929 when the legislature passed an amendment to the Civil Code allowing all women to be members of family councils. Married women had previously been excluded because of the principle of their incapacity. This reform was one of those most urgently demanded, and indeed it had been difficult to refute the feminist argument that it was a logical extension of the maternal role.[37]

Yet Taschereau's 1929 decision to form a general commission of inquiry was not prompted by concern for the civil status of women. It was, rather, a political tactic. The Premier wrote to his friend Charles-Edouard Dorion: 'You will remember that during the last session the women put forward various requests to us which I then submitted to you ... We gave them almost nothing ... However, I did say to them that after the session the government might agree to having the whole chapter on the community of property examined by legal experts ...'[38] Fifty years later Senator Thérèse Casgrain commented wryly: 'I always had the impression that it was to keep us quiet.'[39]

THE DORION COMMISSION

Taschereau's hand-picked choice of members of the Commission on the Civil Rights of Women naturally fell on those whose opinion he knew and trusted. Charles-Edouard Dorion, the jurist heading up the Commission, was a former dean of the Laval Faculty of Law and judge of the Appeal Court. As the nephew of the eminent politician Sir Antoine-Aimé Dorion, his Liberal antecedents were impeccable. Not only was he an old friend of Taschereau's but he was also a devout Catholic and a respected public authority on the social questions of the day, and one who consistently represented the clerico-nationalist viewpoint. Indeed, the same year the Commission handed down its final report, Judge Dorion wrote a brochure explaining the Catholic interpretation of the role of the state in matrimonial legislation which was published by a Jesuit organization, L'Ecole Sociale Populaire.[40] The secretary of the Commission was another eminent legal authority, the Dean of the Laval Faculty of Law and Chief Magistrate, Ferdinand Roy. Roy had been a member of the Quebec City law firm of Fitzpatrick, Taschereau, Roy, Parent, and Cannon, a training ground for many Liberal politicians and judges of the era, and he had headed the Quebec bar in 1920.[41] Two notaries were also appointed. Joseph Sirois, who was later to give his name to the Federal Commission on Dominion-Provincial Relations, was a distinguished notary, editor of the prestigious *Revue du Notariat,* and president of the Chamber of Notaries until 1930, when he was replaced by the fourth member of the Commission, Victor Morin. The latter was a man of letters, historian, antiquarian, bibliophile, and apologist for French culture.[42] Probably Morin was the most liberal of the four commissioners and the one most sympathetic to feminist demands. On the other hand, Sirois tended to espouse clerical views on social issues.[43]

Women and representatives of the anglophone community were excluded from membership on the Commission. The Quebec historian Robert Rumilly has made the following judgment about the members of the Commission:

> for Judge Dorion, tampering with the Civil Code would be committing a sacrilege; the lawyer Ferdinand Roy believed in masculine superiority; the notary Joseph Sirois felt obliged to take into consideration the well-publicized opinion of Premier Taschereau ... The four jurists were accomplished men and were in close touch with the highest clerical circles. It was a known fact that the Church leaders were hostile to feminism.[44]

The Dorion Commission was given a triple mandate: to judge whether the Civil Code was in fact outdated, to suggest possible modifications of certain of its provisions, and to consider formally the validity of feminist criticisms.[45] The Commission held public hearings in Quebec City and Montreal during the late fall and early winter of 1929–30.[46] Some half-dozen women's groups presented briefs proposing similar reforms.

The primary demand, and the one reform with which the Dorion Commission became irrevocably linked, was the right of married women to their own earnings. Even though not more than ten per cent of wives in Quebec could have earned a salary at that time, most of those who did were clearly in desperate need of it.[47] As several witnesses related, these were often the very women whose husbands took advantage of their legal powers to seize their wives' earnings for their own purposes. Apart from the principle of limited financial independence, feminists were concerned about the situation of women whose husbands refused to support their families and preyed on their wives' salaries.[48]

Modification of a husband's power to dispose of the assets of the community without even consulting his wife was another urgently proposed reform. The Fédération wished to limit this power by introducing a provision modelled on Article 1422 of the Code Napoléon, which stated that a husband could not give away immoveables or a substantial part of moveable property unless it was for the benefit of children of the marriage. Other groups made various suggestions about methods of limiting the husband's power to dissipate the community assets and thus the wife's property either for frivolous purposes or on behalf of a wife's rival in her husband's affections. The well-known lawyer Eugène Lafleur, pleading on behalf of the League for Women's Rights, noted that even the usual controls of a mandator (principal) over his mandatary's (agent's) actions did not apply to married couples.[49]

A third modification proposed by many women's groups would assimilate moveable capital to immoveables and thus exclude it from initial entry into the community. The legal distinction of moveable/immoveable, useful for the protection of family heritages in a feudal regime, was irrelevant to twentieth-century financial realities. It meant, for example, that a wife's bonds, stocks, and bank account were classed as moveables and therefore automatically fell under the husband's absolute power at marriage. Another important demand was that all women, not just unmarried ones, be eligible as tutors and curators to children and interdicted persons.[50]

Some of the more liberal groups daringly called for the complete abolition of the need for marital authorization. Other suggestions included provisions that a wife receive a fixed share of her husband's property on his death, swifter and simpler separation proceedings, full power for legally separated wives over their own property, raising the minimum age for marriage, and requiring the mother's consent as well as the father's.[51] The Association of Notaries and the Association of

French-Canadian Artisans requested that women be allowed to insure their lives in favour of their husbands. Gérin-Lajoie's disapproval of this idea illustrates the ambivalence within the Catholic feminist movement. In seeming contradiction to her previous assertions that more and more wives and mothers were obliged by circumstances to become breadwinners and thus had a right to exclusive control of their salaries, she wrote that such a change would constitute 'an odious speculation on the life of the wife.'[52] The Partnership Declaration Act imposed additional fines on married women who engaged in business without making the necessary declarations as to their marital status. Idola Saint-Jean simply demanded that these statutes be amended so that women were not 'treated more severely than the other merchants.'[53] Finally, both the Local Council of Women and the Canadian Alliance for Women's Votes requested the abolition of the double standard for marital infidelity.[54]

The briefs presented to the Commission were far from revolutionary. They sought no radical change in the hierarchy of power within the family. No one suggested that wives should no longer obey their husbands, nor that mothers and fathers should be equally responsible for the management of family affairs. The sacrosanct position of the *chef de famille* was not threatened. With the exception of a few oblique suggestions that Quebec was the last of the civilized nations, the briefs which have been preserved did not stress the innate 'backwardness' of the local marital legislation. On the contrary, almost all the representations conceded the basically equitable nature of the regime of community of property and the fundamental soundness of civil law attitudes to marriage and the family. Indeed, most of the feminists made a conscious appeal to collective pride in Quebec's legal institutions. Modernization of the Code, it was suggested, would halt the attacks of those who labelled it outmoded and give Quebecers renewed confidence in their traditions. Marie Gérin-Lajoie succinctly stated the real alternatives: either preserve traditions by updating them or watch them fall into disrepute.

Law reform commissions have rarely interested the popular press and the Dorion Commission was no exception. Even the attention of an intellectual journal like *Le Devoir* focused on Henri Bourassa's bête noire – federal divorce legislation. The content of the women's pages of francophone newspapers showed little interest in the Commission's work; they remained dominated by social chronicles, trends in fashions, and culinary hints. Perhaps more than any other single indicator, this situation reveals the indifference of the vast majority of women to the realities of their legal condition. Had it not been for the Montreal *Herald*,

Editorial cartoons published in the Montreal *Herald*, November 1929

the Dorion Commission might have gone largely unnoticed. While feminists were pleading their cause before the Commission, the *Herald* provoked a public debate on the Code. This long-time champion of women's rights decided to publish a twelve-part newspaper campaign on the legal status of women in Quebec. It hired Idola Saint-Jean to be guest editor of a special bilingual two-page feature appearing daily from 18 to 30 November 1929, timed to coincide with the Commission's Montreal hearings. To ensure even wider coverage, the *Herald* condensed these pages into a brochure which was then distributed by various women's groups. The *Herald*'s campaign was caustic, humorous, and slightly condescending. It reflected the impatience of the better-educated, wealthier, and more secular anglophone community at the strictures of a code which they regarded as reflecting the social values of the Napoleonic era.

La Presse responded forcefully to this assault on the national tradition. In a strongly-worded editorial it affirmed that the Civil Code was 'one of the principal foundations upon which our national life rests.'[55] The editor of *La Revue du Droit* seemed outraged by the *Herald*'s portrayal of the Civil Code. He characterized it as a 'caricature in bad taste,' although conceding that some changes were perhaps necessary so long as they did not threaten marital and paternal authority.[56] Significantly, when the association of rural women, the Cercle des Fermières, which was closely controlled by the clergy, chose to comment on the question, it was to chastize both the feminists and the anglophone press for the noisy controversy they had precipitated. The president of the Cercle des Fermières, Rolande-S. Désilets, was of the opinion that the Civil Code protected women quite adequately and that nothing was to be gained by adopting 'Anglo-Saxon customs.' In the name of some 8000 farm women, she condemned the feminists and declared that most French-Canadian wives and mothers were perfectly content with their present situation.[57] An overall survey of the press indeed suggests that most of Quebec society was quite indifferent to the creation and mandate of the Dorion Commission. The real protagonists of family law reform were arrayed on the fringes: the defenders of national traditions on one hand and the forces of feminism, liberalism, and anglicization on the other.

THE COMMISSION'S RECOMMENDATIONS

The Commission handed down three reports over a period of a year. The first summarized its philosophy on family law reform, the second discussed technical solutions, while the third made concrete proposals for legislative amendment.

Written in a language accessible to the lay person, the first and most important report set forth the principles that had guided the Commissioners in their deliberations and which they wished to see mirrored in the legal system. It was, more importantly, the official response to the variety of recent criticisms of the Civil Code.[58] Cloaked in the prestige of the law and the reputation of the four Commissioners, the francophone bourgeoisie here delivered its version of the ideal role of women and the family in Quebec.[59] Even the organization of the first report suggests that the real task of the Commission was to rehabilitate the Civil Code rather than to modify it. It was divided into four parts: a discussion of the nature and function of the law, the characteristics of the Quebec civil law, the status of women under this law, and the essence of the proposed reforms.

The Commission's exposé of its philosophy of law is one of the most interesting aspects of the report, because without sharing its interpretation of the role of the law, one could not wholly subscribe to its views. Laws were first of all the recognition by those who held power of the wishes of those who were governed. After this brief salute in the direction of liberal democratic theory, the Commissioners returned to their habitual conservatism. A body of laws expressed time-honoured national customs and were 'a reflection of the feeling and the aspirations of a people ... the expression of the values of a society.'[60] They existed for one essential object – to impose social order. Laws were justified if they produced not only social justice between individuals but also protected each of the institutions of society, especially the family. Laws did create barriers and impediments to the principle of absolute individual freedom: 'Every law is made of the shreds of individual liberty which each sacrifices for the common good.'[61]

The authors soon reached one of their themes: the necessity of individual sacrifice for the benefit of all. The extent of this 'immolation' of the individual for a greater good was best decided by an omniscient élite. Their operational definition of individual rights provided the basis for subsequent reasoning. It was 'the possibility which the law guarantees to the individual of carrying out his own function in society without harming others.'[62] Since it logically followed that the function (and aptitudes) of women were so different from those of men, equal rights for the sexes were inappropriate. The Commissioners could then assert 'the absurdity of the so-called theory "of equal rights" for all, that is to say, even for those whom fortune and destiny have not placed in the same condition of life.'[63]

The Commissioners wished to deal once and for all with the criticism that the civil law was in some way inherently deficient – a common prejudice among anglophones. They sought to place in international perspective the legal system of what appeared from a Canadian viewpoint to be a socially backward province. The civil law, they asserted, was an admirable intellectual achievement, 'the very soul of our nation.' It had proved a reliable and faithful guide in the past and had functioned 'to protect the people who created it and who, quite rightly, admire it, against any new and dangerous orientation.'[64] Classifying the critics of the civil law into various categories, the Commissioners delivered an answer to each. To the 'systematic denigrators of everything which characterizes the most important ethnic group of this province'[65] and to those who, blinded by the idea of 'progress' at all costs, compared Quebec law unfavourably with that of other countries, the Commissioners warned 'that the grass on the neighbour's side of the fence might, in fact, contain a few weeds.'[66] The legal system could not be held responsible for the evils of the human condition and especially 'certain evils ... of which women have always been the victims.'[67] No laws could ever prevent unhappy marriages.

The Commission concluded that the Quebec Code was not inferior to other systems because it did not have the remedy to all problems. Although this argument was irrefutable, the Commissioners used it to blind themselves to the too frequently tragic real-life consequences of the law, which concrete reforms would have alleviated. Distinguishing the right to be a tutor to a minor as a 'semi-public' duty, they categorically affirmed that 'as far as civil rights are concerned, the law does not take any away from women simply because they are women.'[68] This sophism permitted the conclusion that 'it is only in the state of marriage that less than full civil equality between the sexes is to be found.'[69] With only fifty-six per cent of the women from the province's rural population and fifty-one per cent of those from the urban population married in 1931, this somewhat tendentious argument must have seemed a perfectly accurate statement at the time.[70]

With a certain self-satisfaction the Commissioners also remarked on the fact that no one, including the most radical feminists, had requested the abolition of the duty of obedience to husbands. This, they suggested, was because it was well known that most women approved of the principle which symbolized the hierarchical order at the very basis of Quebec society. Marriage, the Commissioners stated, led to the necessity to conform to peculiar constraints which in any case were set forth by divine law. On the rare occasions when husbands exceeded and abused their authority, women did have some recourse. They could have acts annulled to which they had forcibly consented. They could also apply for judicial authorization to act. The Commissioners evidently believed that both alternatives were realistically accessible to a majority of women.

While conceding in their first report that after a century and a half changes in the law might very well be expected, the Commissioners noted that if the law was static it was, after all, because the function of women remained the same. The most important reasons for maintaining the legal status quo were that 'women themselves have not really evolved. Created to be the companions of men, women are always, and above all else, wives and mothers.'[71]

Having clarified their general point of view, the Commissioners turned to more technical considerations. Of the twenty-three propositions which the Commissioners considered, fifteen were approved as a basis for reform, although not all with the same degree of enthusiasm. Among the features of the existing Code to be retained the Commissioners stressed the inherent virtue of community of property, which should continue to be the foundation of all matrimonial legislation. Marriage should be considered more than a partnership of material interests; it was a Christian institution guided by the head of the household and, as such, corresponded to the social values of most Quebecers.[72] Pointing to the civil status of unmarried women, the Commissioners asserted that the exclusion of women from certain activities did not stem from any inherent inferiority: 'the incapacity of the married woman is only determined by the need to protect the family by establishing a certain order within it.'[73] Linking a changed status for woman within the family to a greater participation in public life, the commissioners queried whether 'it is not at the expense of the family that the nation would profit from the direct collaboration of women metamorphized into public figures.'[74] They warned that they would only recommend such reforms as would leave the family hierarchy and individual roles intact and in conformity with natural law. Divorce was one of the greatest catastrophes which radical legal change might unleash. But the Civil Code could prevent this: 'Experience has shown that marital authority is one of the ties which prevents or delays a definitive separation.'[75]

The first report of the Dorion Commission was the most important of the three. It expressed the real reason behind the formation of the Commission: to deliver an authoritative reply to feminists and critics of the Civil Code. Its arguments were not legal but moral and its purpose was broadly political. It set out the limits of permissible reforms and justified the rejection of more radical propositions.

The second report explained the Commission's recommendations, particularly to the politicians and the legal profession. Yet even this discussion of the various propositions put before the Commission was surprisingly general, considering that the subtleties of some articles of the Code dealing with matrimonial regimes had preoccupied several generations of Quebec jurists. However, relatively few references to these legal controversies appeared in the second report. Its tone resembles a sermon more than a legal text.[76]

The final recommendations of the Dorion Commission reflected the underlying values of its members. Although sensitive to some of the practical inconveniences for women of a too strict application of the principles of incapacity and marital authority, they were concerned that bending before progressive pressure would compromise Quebec's traditional family values. Again and again they took care to explain the reasons motivating their judgments and to place their decisions concerning women in the wider context of Quebec society. For instance, they rejected any suggestion that women should be able to insure their lives in their husbands' favour, stating that the women themselves had not requested it and, in any case, it would be the husbands who would pay the premiums.

Such was the anxiety of the Commissioners that the existing civil law institutions should be protected and respected that one might well question whether any reforms would have been proposed had it not been for the fact that other civil law jurisdictions, notably France, had already enacted them. Such recommendations as the creation of a category of property reserved exclusively to the use of the working wife, the right of women to witness a will, and the limit placed on a husband's right to dispose of community property had previously been adopted into the Code Napoléon. In fact, the only reform in French law which the Commissioners rejected was the double standard for a separation. Abolished in France in 1884, the double standard remained unchanged in Quebec until 1954 because, as the Commissioners reasoned, 'forgiveness comes *naturally* more easily to a woman's heart.'[77] In the highly politicized debate on divorce in the Quebec of the 1920s and 1930s, any breach in the wall of traditional marriage customs could be interpreted as a concession to anti-clericalism.

Premier Taschereau evidently was satisfied with the work of the Commission. In June 1930, four months after the publication of the second report, he asked the Commissioners to draw up the legal amendments necessary to implement the suggested changes. Their third report stated in technical language the reforms proposed in the earlier reports.[78] Taschereau himself cleverly sponsored the Bill de la Réforme du

Code Civil (Bill 52), thus earning a certain grudging gratitude from those women to whom he simultaneously denied the vote.[79] The legislation was signed into law on 11 March 1931 and went into force immediately.[80]

Most of the fundamental changes proposed by the Commissioners were retained. The single most important contribution of the Commission was the addition of a whole new chapter to the Code dealing with the reserved property of the married woman.[81] It derogated from general principles underlying the community in that a married woman now had complete control (administration and alienation) of all the immoveables and moveables acquired with the proceeds of her salary. However, it still meant that the unpaid contribution of the non-salaried wife to the welfare of the household was not translated into any independent control over community assets. While the new law did not really alter the passive role of the wife in the administration of community property, it did give her a veto over her husband's outright gift of an immoveable or an entire bloc of moveable property.[82] Wives separate as to property could now clearly alienate all types of moveable property including stocks and bonds. Moreover, the wife separate as to bed and board could administer and dispose of all of her property without any further need for judicial and marital authorization.[83] Henceforth a wife could apply for separation of property without marital authorization when deserted by her husband or when her material interests and well-being were threatened.[84] Amendments were introduced so that when a couple separated as to bed and board resumed cohabitation, their marital regime did not automatically revert to community of property. New articles inspired by the Code Napoléon spelled out the limits of the modified regime of community of property reduced to acquests. This meant that couples could through their marriage contract exclude all assets and debts acquired previous to marriage from entering into the community of property between them.[85] Unmarried women and widows were now given full capacity to be tutors and curators, as were married women, so long as they were named jointly with their husbands. Henceforth, women could be witnesses to authentic wills.[86]

The principle of the authority of the husband was implicitly maintained and reaffirmed. However, to lessen practical inconvenience, the law was modified so that a judge could provide the requisite authorization to a wife whose husband was temporarily absent.[87] Other exceptions to this principle of the necessity for obtaining the husband's permission, which was now not required for wives separated as to bed and board, for wives married in the regime of separation of property who could alienate their own moveables, or for the control of the proceeds of the salary of a working wife married in community of property, were clearly delineated and marked out as special, optional situations which only confirmed the general rule. Paternal authority, no less important for the maintenance of social order, also remained untouched. Indeed, it would seem that traditional minds by a great stretch of imagination could just envisage the wife's equality with her husband in the management of her own or even joint property. But it was not until 1977 that Quebec would relinquish its patriarchal model of family life and concede joint authority to both parents over the household and the children.[88]

Perhaps the Commission's greatest achievement and the one for which it had been implicitly established was the public rehabilitation of the regime of community of property. The Commissioners succeeded in devising just enough changes to adapt the law to a twentieth-century urban society without sacrificing the underlying moral principles of the unity of husband and wife and the primacy of the head of the household. In 1930 they arrived at a new equilibrium between the weight of traditionalism and the pressure of modernization. The new balance would not subsist for very long. In 1947 the Méthot Commission was formed to answer persisting criticisms on the legal status of women. However, it was not until 1964, with abolition of the incapacity of married women, and 1970, when the partnership of acquests became the standard marriage regime, that a fundamental restructuring of legal relationships within marriage was undertaken.[89]

REACTIONS TO THE NEW LAW

The task of the Commission had been to gather opinions and to produce a consensus on the legal status of women. The strategy followed by the Commission in publishing first a general policy statement, then suggested reforms, and finally draft articles of the Code over a period of a year ensured that further potential controversy on the issue was minimised. Francophone society seemed to be relieved that the most acute problems had been dealt with, leaving untouched the basic principles which governed marriage and family life.

Feminists realized that the new law represented a considerable improvement for most married women. They were also well aware that many of their proposals, whether the abolition of the double standard or of the necessity for marital authorization, had not been accepted. Suggestions dealing with the rights of disinherited widows against their husband's estate were not translated into law. Raising the legal age for marriage could only be done by the federal parliament; it remained at twelve years for women. Wives in the process of obtaining a judicial separation of bed and board were still obliged to remain at their husband's domicile unless the court ordered otherwise. A mother's consent was still not necessary for the marriage of a minor child.

Yet for Marie Gérin-Lajoie the modifications in the Civil Code were a personal reward after twenty-five years of persistent efforts to arouse public opinion to the need for reform. Most of the changes which she had personally lobbied for had been adopted. The Montreal *Gazette* reported that 'when she was asked ... whether she thought the amendments would tend to make for more happiness amongst women, Mrs. Gérin-Lajoie ... declared that they were a step in the right direction.'[90] She was disappointed, however, that the Code still sanctioned the husband's adultery, except in situations of a veritable ménage à trois, and that the Commissioners had refused to alter this position. She observed that 'this amendment would have been so effective in protecting the family. We must assuredly deplore the refusal of a measure which is so significant to Christians. However, Ladies, the future still lies before us.'[91] This was to be the last major achievement of Gérin-Lajoie's career. Two years later she resigned the presidency of the Fédération and retired from public life.

Many of the reformers who had appeared before the Commission remained noticeably silent when the new law was passed. For some, the changes were long overdue. For others, like Idola Saint-Jean and Thérèse Casgrain, the uphill battle for the vote lay ahead. There was still too much to be done before they could declare victory. In her memoirs Senator Thérèse Casgrain concluded that 'the Dorion Report ... did not go very far ... it is easy to notice the scornful and uncompromising attitude of our masculine elite towards women who were readily treated as inferiors, even within the family.' Moreover, she related that several years after the reports were published Judge Roy 'admitted to me that the members of the Commission had not gone far enough in reforming the Civil Code.'[92]

The leaders of public opinon in francophone society, however, clerics and professionals, felt that the changes had gone quite far enough. The ideological unanimity on the role of women held by the Church and probably most of the legal profession was evidenced by the fact that an article expressing this point of view by no less a person than the Dean of the Faculty of Philosophy of the University of Montreal, Father M.-C. Forest, was reprinted in the *Revue du Droit*. As he succinctly stated, much more was at stake than the liberation of women: 'they [the Commissioners] did not have the right, in order to liberate women, to threaten the traditional Christian principles on which the family rests and through which it is preserved among us.'[93] The reaction of the Chamber of Notaries also was inevitably approving, since its President, Victor Morin, had been a member of the Commission.[94] However, the President's endorsement of the changes did not mean that notaries or lawyers revised sexist attitudes concerning the status of women. A glance at Quebec's legal periodicals in the years following the Dorion Commission reveals not only that attitudes had changed little, but that jurists continued to debate the limits of the sphere of action of married women.[95]

Was the average francophone's view of the role of women modified by the new law? Probably not, judging from the example of *Le Devoir*, which offered its readers a long article highlighting the traditionalist speech of a federal cabinet minister who declared that 'the chief duty of Canadian women ... is to give children to our country ...' or again, by a derogatory and satirical feature on a women's delegation which had just travelled to Quebec to witness yet another defeat of a suffrage bill.[96] In this context, Marie Gérin-Lajoie's summary of the Civil Code amendments, which *Le Devoir* did publish, most likely had little impact.

The anglophone community was pleased with the new law. The Montreal *Gazette* congratulated Gérin-Lajoie and Casgrain for their efforts in breaking down 'certain ancient prejudices.' The *Gazette* optimistically thought it heralded a new era for women: 'the emancipating changes that have now been made in the law at least bear witness that insistence on the invariable sacrifice of the individual interests of the wife to the supposed exigencies of family and social interests is weakening and giving way.'[97] *Labour World*, organ of the international and pan-Canadian unions in Quebec, stated that the feminists had demonstrated 'what can be accomplished by persistent agitation in a good cause' and praised their leaders as 'pioneers,' 'heroines,' 'able and devoted,' and 'splendid women.' *Labour World* also looked forward to further victories in the feminist cause: 'In spite of the jutting projections of prejudice on the rocks of reaction, ill will and contempt, they have clambered higher and higher and are almost at the pinnacle of success.'[98]

However, except for those initiated into the complexities of the Civil Code, little had changed in the overall situation of women in the province. To the majority of the province's wives, the changes in the law probably went largely unnoticed. Despite their unquestionable importance, the amendments did little to alter the daily lives of most women.

CONCLUSION

The significance of the Dorion Commission is not only in the modifications it made to the formal legal status of women in the 1930s. The Commission was important because it reaffirmed the traditional ideology expressed by the clerically-dominated élite. It gave the highest civil sanction possible, that of the law, to the church's definition of social relationships.

Although the law may be analysed as an institution, for example through the courts and the judges, or as a self-contained functional system with its own rules and procedure, it may also be considered as an expression of ideology.[99] Law expresses and imposes a particular set of social beliefs and norms which govern relationships in a given society. Its ideological functions are both instrumental and symbolic. In an instrumental sense, the law forcibly imposes the social relationships that its makers define. A rule of law which is obviously unfair according to current opinion, whether in terms of class, ethnic, or sex relationships, will not be respected and will therefore not bring any advantage to the group which enacted it. As an ideology, law also has a very important symbolic function in representing social ideals. It is a system of images which reflects what should be rather than what is.[100] In an urban industrial society, where older historical forms of loyalty and obedience no longer have a claim upon the individual, law has become 'a great reservoir of emotionally important social symbols.'[101]

The jurists of the Dorion Commission were philosophical idealists and in their deliberations they were carrying out one of the basic purposes of law as ideology. They believed that the explanation and basis of the legal order which they administered lay in the spiritual rather than in the material realm. They chose a certain image of Quebec society and held it to be the universal reality. Their constant references to natural law identify the philosophical basis of their legal reasoning as utopian rather than scientific. The tradition of natural law, as refined by Aristotle and St Thomas Aquinas and taught in Quebec's law faculties, provided the francophone bourgeoisie with a rationalization for conservative social and moral relationships. The Commission's categoric statements of principle on subjects ranging from the nature of women to the need for authority within the household, and to the role of the family, reinforced a symbolic order by reference to the ideology of Catholicism. Its task had been to state how things should be, not how they were. Hence the repeated assertion that the real-life situations drawn to their attention were the 'exceptional cases.' But at the same time the Commissioners and the Quebec government realized that belief in a symbolic order could not be sustained when the contradiction with reality became too flagrant. By the 1930s the criticism of progressive forces like the Montreal *Herald* had become too well founded. To undermine the credibility of attacks on the

Civil Code as 'oppressive' and 'backward,' it was necessary to make a few changes such as the one allowing married women to control their own salaries. Thus the crisis passed, and the ideology embodied in the law could continue to legitimate the utopian order which dominant social groups, and above all the Church, continued to hold out as a model for Quebec through the Depression and into the postwar years.

The definition of the status of women in public life and within the family corresponded to Catholic corporatist thought in the 1930s which posited God-given hierarchies at all levels, beginning within the family and paralleled in labour relations, the structure of the Church, and the political sphere. However, the vision of reality thus proposed was being increasingly challenged, not only by Protestant anglophone society, whose social values were less contradictory in an urban and industrial setting, but within francophone society itself by feminism, labour radicalism, and irreligious materialism. To preserve the ideological hegemony of the Church and its allies within sections of the francophone bourgeoisie, it was necessary to arouse popular fears of imaginary forces threatening to engulf Quebec. Premier Maurice Duplessis later brought this technique to perfection. The Dorion Report's constant evocation of feminist forces, which, if unchecked, would bring the ruin of the family and the downfall of the entire social order, was another use of the same tactic.

The symbolic function of the law was at this time in Canadian history probably more important in Quebec than in any of the other provinces. The civil law heritage was an integral part of the traditional nationalism which held sway well past the 1930s. In defending it, the conservative segment of the francophone bourgeoisie and its ally, the Church, reinforced their hegemony over their own society. The 1930s were for Quebec the decade when the affirmation of provincial autonomy became a viable political slogan. Attacks on a legal system which reflected the ideal social order that intellectual and religious leaders were proposing to the majority of Quebecers could easily be presented as attacks on group survival.

The apocalyptic fate of Quebec, if feminists were heeded, must have impressed the popular imagination.[102] In the climate of fear thus aroused, the image of home as haven, woman as eternal, and hierarchical family relationships as both inevitable and moral must have provided a psychological and social compensation for many men and women for whom there was no ready alternative to the present. As a powerful ideological force, law had an important role to play. The Dorion Commission, then, addressed itself not just to a handful of feminists concerned with the legal status of women but to the entire question of the structuring of social, political, and ethnic relationships in Quebec.

As an exercise in law reform, the history of the Dorion Commission suggests that one of the unavowed purposes of such bodies may not really be to modify the status quo substantially but simply to reply to critics by giving the appearance of seriously considering fundamental change. It may in fact be easier to obtain the consensus necessary to retain controversial laws already in force, if a prestigious commission finds new reasons to justify them.

NOTES

The author wishes to thank Dean John Brierley of the Faculty of Law of McGill University and Professor Veronica Strong-Boag of the Department of History, Simon Fraser University, for their helpful comments, and Pauline Léveillé of the Department of History of the Université du Québec à Montréal for typing the manuscript.

Unfortunately the Dorion Commission has left almost no record of its deliberations. There seem to be no personal papers of any of the Commissioners which bear on the subject. Government documents and papers of the premiers of Quebec during the period yield little on the question of women's rights. Sources used for this essay included the very extensive archives of the Fédération Nationale Saint-Jean-Baptiste (at the Archives Nationales du Québec à Montréal), the papers of Marie Gérin-Lajoie at the motherhouse of the Communauté des Sœurs de Notre-Dame-du-Bon-Conseil in Montréal, archives of other women's groups, newspapers, periodicals, and interviews with contemporaries of the Dorion Commissioners.

1 M. Gérin-Lajoie 'Entre-nous, la femme et le code civil. Les yeux qui s'ouvrent' *La Bonne Parole* fév.–mars 1930 3

2 J.C. Robert *Du Canada français au Québec libre: histoire d'un mouvement indépendantiste* (Montréal 1975) 157–209

3 See, for example, M. Caron 'De la physionomie, de l'évolution et de l'avenir du Code civil' in Jacques Boucher and André Morel, eds *Le droit dans la vie familiale: Livre du centenaire du Code civil* I (Montréal 1970) 302. Between 1866 and 1964 there were, apart from the changes resulting from the Dorion Commission, some minor modifications in the legal regime pertaining to married women, notably the Loi Pérodeau, 5 Geo. v (1915) c. 74, which gave married women

(and men) whose spouses had died intestate, the right to inherit along with parents, children, siblings, nephews, and nieces, or alone in the absence of the latter. Previously, surviving consorts could only inherit after all the relatives up to and including twelve successoral degrees had been satisfied. The non-inclusion of spouses in each other's inheritance reflected the preoccupation of the Coutume de Paris with preserving property within the same group of blood relatives. It must be noted, however, that widows married in community of property automatically received one-half the joint possessions of husband and wife. Other important changes were: 1928 modifications allowing married women to become legal tutors to minor children other than their own, the 1923 changes in the Bank Act (*Statutes of Canada* 1923 c. 32, s. 95.3) permitting women to deposit up to $2000 in their own name, and the 1954 amendment to Art. 188 of the Code Civil (hereafter CC), which henceforth eliminated the distinctions between the adultery of the husband and the adultery of the wife.

4 M. Lavigne, Y. Pinard, and J. Stoddart 'La Fédération nationale Saint-Jean-Baptiste et les revendications féministes au début du XXe siècle' *Revue d'histoire de l'Amérique française* XXIX (1975) 353–73 (hereafter RHAF)

5 M. Gérin-Lajoie 'Legal Status of Women in the Province of Quebec' in *Women of Canada: Their Life and Work* (compiled by the National Council of Women of Canada, Ottawa 1901) 99–107

6 Minutes du Bureau de Direction 1906–39 Archives Fédération Nationale Saint-Jean-Baptiste 25 avr. 1914, 21 fév. 1929 (hereafter FNSJB)

7 See L.Loranger *De l'incapacité légale de la femme mariée* (Montréal 1899) 273, and J. Boucher 'L'histoire de la condition juridique et sociale de la femme au Canada français' in Boucher and Morel, eds *Le Droit dans le vie familiale* 155–68.

8 J.E.C. Brierley 'Husband and Wife in the Law of Quebec: A 1970 Conspectus' in D. Mendes da Costa, ed. *Studies in Canadian Family Law* II (Toronto 1972) 795–844; E. Caparros *Les lignes de force de l'évolution des régimes matrimoniaux en droits comparés et québécois* (Montréal 1975); M. Beard *Woman as Force in History* (New York 1946)

9 On the general question of the significance of obtaining legal rights in the feminist movement, see C. Bacci 'Liberation Deferred: The Ideas of the English-Canadian Suffragists, 1877–1919' *Social History/Histoire sociale* (1977) 433–5; W. Chafe *The American Woman: Her Changing Economic, Political and Social Roles, 1920–1970* (New York 1972); E. Flexner *Century of Struggle: The Woman's Rights Movement in the United States* (New York 1974); W. O'Neill *The Woman Movement: Feminism in the United States and England* (London 1969), and *Everyone Was Brave: The Rise and Fall of Feminism in America* (Chicago 1969). For

Quebec, see W. Riddell 'Woman Franchise in Quebec, a Century Ago' in *Proceedings of the Royal Society of Canada*, 3rd series, 1928, section 2, 85–99 and F. Fournier 'Les femmes et la vie politique au Québec' in M. Lavigne and Y. Pinard, eds *Les femmes dans la société québécoise* (Montréal 1977) 169–90.

10 Lavigne, Pinard, and Stoddart 'La Fédération Nationale Saint-Jean-Baptiste et les revendications féministes au début du xxe siècle'

11 See, for example, H. Bourassa *Hommes-femmes ou femmes-hommes, étude à bâtons rompus sur le féminisme* (Montréal 1925); Mgr L.A. Paquet 'Le Féminisme' in M. Jean, ed. *Québécoises du 20e siècle* (Montréal 1974) 47–73; L. Trifirio 'Une intervention à Rome dans la lutte pour le suffrage féminin au Québec' RHAF XXXII 3–18; and S.M. Trofimenkoff 'Henri Bourassa and the Woman Question' in A. Prentice and S.M. Trofimenkoff, eds *The Neglected Majority: Essays in Canadian Women's History* (Toronto 1977) 104–15.

12 J. Stoddart 'The Woman Suffrage Bill in Québec' in M. Stephenson, ed. *Women in Canada* (Toronto 1973) 90–107. Women were not admitted to the Quebec bar until 1942 and then only because of coercive legislation by Premier Godbout (interview with Me E. Monk, 2 Mar. 1979). Jury duty only became compulsory for both sexes in 1971.

13 *Census of Canada 1931* (Ottawa 1935) III 458. In 1927 the Minimum Wage Commission for Women established the minimum living wage for a female worker living in or near Montreal without dependants at $634 per year. The average annual income of Montreal's women workers in 1931 was $567. See M. Lavigne and J. Stoddart 'Analyse du travail féminin à Montréal entre les deux guerres (MA thesis, Université du Québec à Montréal 1974) 110–15.

14 However, the Code did make an exception for widowed mothers or grandmothers wishing to be tutors to their own descendants. Similarly, a wife could be curator to her interdicted husband. Tutors and curators are roughly equivalent to legal guardians. Interdicts are those whose legal powers have been withdrawn by the court such as those suffering from mental illness or chronic alcoholism.

15 One major exception: she could not, according to the then controversial 1301 CC, either bind herself or contract with or for her husband. This supposedly protected the wife's assets from an opportunistic husband. See, for example, H. Gérin-Lajoie 'De l'obligation de la femme avec ou pour son mari: Art. 1301 du Code civil' *Revue du Droit* (décembre 1930) 199–227 and 'Encore l'article 1301 CC' (avril 1931) 455–9 (hereafter R. du D.)

16 Gérin-Lajoie 'Legal Status of Women in the Province of Québec' 99–107

17 A matrimonial regime is a system of rules governing the administration, acquisition, and disposition of the spouses' assets during marriage. In civil law jurisdictions, such as Quebec, spouses often have a choice of several possible

matrimonial regimes. At this time in Quebec a marriage regime once chosen could not be modified after the marriage.

18 R. Comtois *Traité théorique et politique de la communauté de biens* (Montréal 1964) 317–32. Comtois' calculations are based on less than twenty per cent of the notaries who practised in 1932. He presumes that the sample he has obtained is an accurate representation of the entire province and makes no adjustment for the quality of the data.

19 Separation of bed and board is a judicially pronounced marriage separation. It is not to be confused with the marriage regime of separation of property.

20 Gérin-Lajoie 'Legal Status of Women in the Province of Quebec'

21 M. McClelland 'History of Women's Rights in Canada' in *Cultural Tradition and Political History of Women in Canada: Studies for the Royal Commission on the Status of Women*, no. 8. (Ottawa 1971); L.S. Dranoff *Women in Canadian Law* (Toronto 1977)

22 *Edwards* v *A.G. Can.*, [1930] *Appeal Cases* 124

23 A. Morel 'La libération de la femme au Canada: deux itinéraires' *Revue juridique Thémis* v (1970) 399–400

24 J.S. Mill 'The Subjection of Women' in J.S. Mill and H.T. Mill *Essays on Sex Equality* ed. A. Rossi (Chicago 1970) 151–80; A.V. Dicey *Law and Public Opinion in England* 2nd ed. (London 1962) 390–3

25 *Murdoch* v *Murdoch* [1975] *Supreme Court Reports* 423

26 Lavigne, Pinard, and Stoddard 'La Fédération Nationale Saint-Jean-Baptiste'; Trifirio 'Une intervention à Rome'; A. Dupont 'Louis-Alexandre Taschereau et la législation sociale au Québec, 1920–1936' RHAF (déc. 1972) 397

27 Robert *Du Canada français au Québec libre* 171

28 G. McInnis *J.S. Woodsworth* (Toronto 1953) 194–8; K. McNaught *A Prophet in Politics: A Biography of J.S. Woodsworth* (Toronto 1959) 236–41

29 'Le Divorce: Lettre pastorale de S.E. le Cardinal Raymond-Marie Rouleau et des Archevêques – Evêques des provinces ecclésiastiques de Québec, de Montréal et l'Ottawa,' 2 fév. 1930 in *Revue du Notariat* (fév. 1930) 321

30 Y. Pinard 'Les débuts du mouvement des femmes' in Lavigne and Pinard, eds *Les femmes dans la société québécoise* 61–87

31 For a general history of the suffrage movement in Quebec, see C.L. Cleverdon *The Woman Suffrage Movement in Canada* (Toronto 1974) c. 7.

32 See M. Gérin-Lajoie *La communauté légale* II (Montréal 1927) for a description of how anglophone criticism of 'backward' French laws stung national pride.

33 See T. Casgrain *Une femme chez les hommes* (Montréal 1971).

34 The archives of the bar of the province of Quebec reveal no trace of the issue ever having been formally considered. The Chamber of Notaries admitted women only in 1954.

35 In the interwar period evidence from articles appearing in many Quebec newspapers and periodicals suggests that there were as many women mobilized against the vote and legal reform as for it. See, for example, R. Brossard 'La femme devant la loi' *La Revue Moderne* (fév. 1930) 7.

36 Minutes du Bureau de Direction 1906–1939 Archives FNSJB 21 fév. 1929

37 M. Gérin-Lajoie *La femme et la Code civil*, Plaidoirie de Marie Gérin-Lajoie devant le Comité des Bills Publics (Montréal 1929) 5. The family council is a group of at least seven relatives which has the power to choose a tutor (legal guardian) for a minor child. 251–4 CC

38 Taschereau to Dorion 22 avr. 1929 Archives Dorion Commission 1929 no. 735-29 Archives Nationales du Québec (Québec) Ministère de la Justice (my translation here and in most of the following quotations originally published in French)

39 Interview Senator Thérèse Casgrain 27 Feb. 1979

40 P.C. Roy *Les juges de la province de Québec* (Québec 1937) 177. The question of conflicting religious and secular values had become especially controversial following the Privy Council decision that a valid religious marriage was not necessarily a valid legal marriage in *Berthiaume* v *Dastous* (1929), 47 *Banc du Roi* (hereafter BR) 533

41 See P.G. Roy *Les avocats de la région du Québec* (Lévis, Québec 1937).

42 See R. Morin *Victor Morin, bourgeois d'une époque révolue, 1865–1960* (Montréal 1967). Madame Renée Morin has stated that her father favoured woman suffrage and a greater degree of legal autonomy for wives. Interview 27 Feb. 1979

43 According to Antonin Dupont, Joseph Sirois was probably the author of a clerical counter-proposition to the new law on public assistance, which Taschereau introduced in 1921. Dupont 'Louis-Alexandre Taschereau et la législation sociale au Québec, 1920–1936' RHAF (déc. 1972) 426

44 R. Rumilly *Histoire de la province de Québec* XXXI (Montréal 1959) 161

45 Taschereau to Dorion 22 avr. 1929

46 Dorion to Taschereau, 6 août 1931. Dorion also mentions a 'voluminous correspondence' between the commissioners which does not seem to have survived. M. Gérin-Lajoie 'Entre nous – la femme et le Code civil' *La Bonne Parole* fév.–mars 1930 3, also *Le Devoir* 22 nov. 1929, *La Presse* 22 nov. 1929

47 M. Lavigne and J. Stoddart 'Les travailleuses montréalaises entre les deux guerres' *Labour/Le Travailleur* II (1977) 176

48 A recent Quebec case had confirmed the husband's absolute right to his wife's earnings, even when deposited in her own bank account. *Bonin* v *Banque d'Epargne, Dame Rondeau mise-en-cause* (1923), 34 BR 322

49 'Plaidoyer de Me Eugène Lafleur, C.R.' *La Bonne Parole* fév.–mars 1930 11

50 'Plaidoyer de Madame Henri Gérin-Lajoie' ibid. 9
51 Briefs are reproduced in *La Bonne Parole* fév.–mars 1930 9–22.
52 M. Gérin-Lajoie 'La réforme du Code civil' ibid. déc. 1930 4
53 *Statutes of Quebec* (hereafter SQ) 1925, c. 224, art. 18; 'Plaidoyer de Mademoiselle Idola Saint-Jean' *La Bonne Parole* fév.–mars. 1930 21
54 Although other briefs were doubtless mailed to the Commission, and Judge Dorion mentions numerous representations received by the Commissioners, none has survived. The content of any additional propositions for reform, or indeed defences of the status quo, must be surmised from the text of the Commission's Reports.
55 *La Presse* 23 nov. 1929
56 L. Pelland 'Causerie du directeur' R. du D. fév. 1930 330
57 Rolande-S. Desilets 'Nos droits et nos devoirs' *La Bonne Fermière* janvier 1930 3
58 Dorion to Taschereau 26 août 1929 2 Archives Dorion Commission
59 *Premier rapport de la commission des droits civils de la femme* reproduced in R. du N. XXXII (1929–30) 230
60 Ibid. 231
61 Ibid.
62 Ibid. 232
63 Ibid.
64 Ibid. 233
65 Ibid. 234
66 Ibid.
67 Ibid. 235
68 Ibid. 237
69 Ibid. 238
70 *Census of Canada 1931* III 458. Sixty-three per cent of rural women and fifty-five per cent of urban women were married in Ontario. Women here include all females aged 15 years or over.
71 *Premier rapport de la commission* 243. The authors of the Report had weighed and sorted out the diverse proposals for reform and accurately perceived that there was no unanimity on all the reforms among the feminist ranks. Marie Gérin-Lajoie, for example, had not been able to support the suggestions for eliminating the need for the husband's authorization or sharing parental authority between mother and father. These ideas came from those the Commission labelled bourgeois bluestockings, whose viewpoint was manifestly not shared by a majority of the province's women.
72 The Commissioners could not resist discrediting feminist criticism of the law by claiming that some of the feminists were simply resentful man-haters, who modelled their tactics on those of the more radical European and British

feminist movements. At a time when Quebec women could neither practise law, vote, nor sit in the legislature, the Commissioners brushed aside the suggestion that the laws were exclusively masculine.

73 Ibid. 274

74 Ibid.

75 Ibid. 275

76 *Commission des droits civils de la femme, deuxième rapport des commissionnaires,* reproduced in extenso in R. du N. XXXII (1929–30) 310–19, 312–76, XXXIII (1930–31) 48–61, at XXXII 355

77 Ibid. 365 (their italics)

78 For a complete list of the suggested amendments, see the third report reproduced in extenso in R. du D. fév. 1931 337–59.

79 For a resumé of the amendments see: M. Gérin-Lajoie 'La réforme du Code civil' *La Bonne Parole* mars 1931 3 et seq., avr. 1931 6; R. du N. XXXIV (1931–2) 9–10; R. du D. mai 1931 548–50. The new spirit of liberalism did not extend to the suffrage. Nine months later, the legislature rejected yet another bill on woman suffrage. Thaïs Frémont, who was present at the debate, wrote in dismay to her sister Marie Gérin-Lajoie: 'You could not imagine to what degree the session on woman suffrage was low-down, trivial and degrading. So much so that I am convinced that a theatre play with the same crude and vulgar dialogue would not have passed the censors.' (Frémont to Gérin-Lajoie, 25 janv. 1932, Dossier Thaïs Frémont, Archives FNSJB).

80 21 Geo. V, c. 101

81 1425a CC et seq. The exact wording of the articles of the Code which were thus modified is of little interest today, since many of these amendments were substantially altered, if not completely abolished, in the 1960s.

82 1292 CC

83 210 CC now repealed

84 1090 Code Civil Procedure, 1311 CC (both now repealed)

85 1389a and b CC

86 844 CC. An authentic will is one drawn up by a notary.

87 180 CC (now modified)

88 242–245j CC

89 SQ 1964, c. 66; SQ 1969–70, c. 77. Acquests is the term used to designate the property accumulated by either spouse during marriage which, with a few exceptions, is divided between them upon dissolution.

90 Montreal *Gazette* 13 Mar. 1931 14

91 M. Gérin-Lajoie 'La réforme du Code civil' *La Bonne Parole* avr. 1931 7

92 Casgrain *Une femme chez les hommes* 94

93 'Gazette de Thémis' R. du D. avril 1931 503

94 V. Morin 'Le Rapport du Président' R. du N. xxxiv (1931–2) 9

95 See, for example, the chronicle 'Jurisprudence' R. du N. xxxv (1932–3) 244–6.

96 *Le Devoir* 13 mars 1931, 24 mars 1931

97 Montreal *Gazette* 13 Mar. 1931 14

98 *Labour World* 11 Apr. 1931

99 E.P. Thompson *Whigs and Hunters: The Origin of the Black Act* (London 1975) 260 et seq.

100 M. Maille *Une introduction critique au droit* (Paris 1976) 53

101 T.W. Arnold 'Law as Symbolism' in V. Aubert, ed. *Sociology of Law: Selected Readings* (London 1969) 47

102 To the historian, these prophecies become somewhat of a tragic farce when diligent research reveals that these dreaded feminists were, in fact, no more than a half-dozen eminently respectable ladies, of whom the two most dangerous had the seemingly singular disadvantage of being unmarried.

10

An Annotated Bibliography of Statutes and Related Publications: Upper Canada, the Province of Canada, and Ontario 1792–1980

MARGARET A. BANKS

The British statute known in Canadian history as the Constitutional Act, 1791, made provision for the government of two new provinces, Upper and Lower Canada, which were to be created by order-in-council out of the old province of Quebec.[1] Each was to have a legislative council and assembly, with whose advice the King was 'to make Laws for the Peace, Welfare and good Government thereof.'[2] It was the intent of the act that the constitutions of the two new provinces resemble as nearly as possible that of the mother country. Upper Canada, with its predominantly British population, was expected to come closer to the ideal than Lower Canada, although each received the same system of government. Upper Canada's legislative council was to consist of not less than seven 'discreet and proper Persons' appointed for life, though subject to removal for non-attendance and certain other causes.[3] Provision was also made for conferring titles of honour with 'an Hereditary Right of being summoned to the Legislative Council,' but this was never put into effect.[4] The province's assembly was to consist of not less than sixteen members, elected by persons meeting a specified property qualification.[5]

Alphabetical and chronological lists of members of the legislative council and assembly have been compiled.[6] So have lists of ridings represented in each of the thirteen parliaments of Upper Canada.[7] The first members of the legislative council were appointed on 12 July 1792.[8] They were nine in number, two more than the minimum required by the Constitutional Act. However, one of the appointees, William Robertson, was never sworn or attended a meeting.[9] Between the date of the first appointments and 1839, when the last appointment for Upper Canada as a separate colony was made, sixty additional legislative councillors were appointed, but five of them were never sworn or attended a meeting.[10] One of the original members, Richard Duncan, was dropped in 1805 for non-attendance.[11] Of the total number, sixty-nine, twenty died in office and several others ceased to be members before the last parliament of Upper Canada was dissolved.[12] The reasons are not given, but probably the main one was departure from the province. For instance, William Osgoode, one of the original members of the legislative council and its first Speaker, served only until 1794, when he left to become Chief Justice of Lower Canada.[13] The first assembly of Upper Canada (1792–6) had sixteen members, the minimum required by the Constitutional Act.[14] The thirteenth and last (1836–40) had sixty-one.[15]

The lists of members of the legislative council and assembly reveal many names familiar to students of Upper Canadian history. Others are more obscure. A study of the background of members of Upper Canada's thirteen parliaments would be an interesting project in social history. One fact worth mentioning is that many of those appointed to the legislative council were also members of the executive council. For instance, five of the nine men appointed to the legislative council on 12 July 1792 had been appointed to the executive council three days earlier.[16] The effect this situation had on the passage of legislation is an important theme of Upper Canadian history. The will of the majority of the assembly could be thwarted by a hostile legislative council which represented the views of the executive. Government whereby the executive was responsible to the elected or more popular branch of the legislature was still in the future. Today in Ontario the executive plays a major role in the legislative process, but to secure the passage of government bills it must have the confidence of the elected unicameral legislature.

Each parliament of Upper Canada had four or five sessions, except the tenth (1829–30) and the twelfth (1835–6) each of which had two. There was generally one session a year, though occasionally there were two, and sometimes a session began in one calendar year and ended in the next. Sessions were short, usually lasting from four to six weeks, though a few of the sessions of the last three parliaments were longer. The longest was the first session of the thirteenth parliament, which lasted nearly four months.[17] The number of statutes passed each session varied from five in several of the early ones to one hundred and eighteen passed in the long first session of the thirteenth parliament. The average number of statutes passed in the forty-one sessions of the first ten parliaments was sixteen acts a session. For the eleventh to the thirteenth parliaments, with several longer sessions, the average increased to fifty-five.[18]

Procedure in the legislature of Upper Canada was based on that of the British Parliament. To become law a bill had to pass through the same stages: three readings in each house, with the committee stage (a detailed clause by clause study) following second reading; the final step was the signification of royal assent.[19] It was at this last stage that, because of Upper Canada's colonial status, there were important differences in procedure – the signification of royal assent was a more complex matter than in the mother country.

Though not as firmly established at the end of the eighteenth century as it is today, the tradition that the granting of royal assent is a formality which is never refused was already taking root in Britain. Not since 1708, when Queen Anne vetoed a Scottish Militia Bill, had royal assent been withheld from a bill passed by the two Houses of Parliament. It was, however, quite in keeping with British tradition that the Governor, Lieutenant Governor, or person administering the government of Upper Canada should be given power to assent to or withhold assent from any bill passed by both houses of the legislature. He was in addition given a third choice. He might, if he thought fit, reserve a bill for the signification of the Crown's pleasure; in practice this meant for review by the British government. Even if a bill was assented to by the Governor, Lieutenant Governor, or administrator, it could be disallowed within two years of its receipt in England.[20]

So far as I know, there has been no study of reservation of Upper Canadian bills or disallowance of acts passed by the legislature of that province. Many textbooks on Canadian history refer to these provisions in the Constitutional Act, but say nothing about the extent to which the rights of reservation and disallowance were exercised. It is important to understand the difference between the two procedures. In the case of reservation, royal assent was withheld by the Governor or his representative pending the signification of the Crown's pleasure. In this situation the bill did not become law; it remained a bill, not becoming an act or a statute (the two terms are synonymous) unless the Crown, on the advice of the British government, gave royal assent. In the case of disallowance, royal assent had already been given by the Governor or his representative; the bill had become an act and was printed with the statutes for the session in which it was passed. When disallowed, it ceased to be a law of the province.

The Constitutional Act provided that certain types of bills relating to the religious establishment of the province should be laid before both Houses of the British Parliament before receiving royal assent.[21] In his instructions to Lord Dorchester as Governor of Upper Canada, King George III directed him to reserve 'such Bills for the signification of Our Pleasure.'[22] He was further directed to reserve any bill considered to be 'of an extraordinary or unusual nature,' particularly those which might affect the property, credit, or dealings of British subjects not usually resident in the province or laying duties on British or Irish shipping or manufactures. In addition, the Governor was to refuse assent to any bill enacted for a period of less than two years, to divorce bills and those conferring privileges of naturalization on aliens. It was stated that laws of these three types passed in some of the American colonies and plantations had been disallowed.[23]

It is outside the scope of this essay to consider the reasons why specific bills were reserved or acts disallowed. The main object here is to show how bills that were reserved but afterwards received royal assent and acts passed but later disallowed were dealt with in the statute books. This will be considered presently. I have found no precise statement of the number of Upper Canadian acts disallowed but Wicksteed's chronological table of statutes (Item 27 in the bibliography which follows) notes the disallowance of five acts passed while Upper Canada was a separate province.[24] Reservation was much more common than disallowance. It appears that between 1792 and 1840 forty-three bills were reserved and subsequently received royal assent.[25] Whether additional bills were reserved and failed to receive royal assent is not clear. For purposes of this essay the question is unimportant, since such bills, if there were any, would never appear in the statute books.

After the union of Upper and Lower Canada in 1841, each of the former provinces had equal representation in the legislative assembly of the new Province of Canada.[26] In each of the first four of its eight parliaments there were eighty-four members, forty-two from each section; in each of the last four there were one hundred and thirty, sixty-five from each section.[27] According to the Act of Union, the legislative council was to consist of at least twenty members, appointed for life, but having the right to resign; provision was also made for removal for prolonged absence.[28] There was no statutory requirement for equal representation from each section of the province in the legislative council, but no doubt it was politically expedient to have strong representation from both sections. The first appointments on 9 June 1841 were twenty-four in number, four more than the minimum required by the Act of Union; eleven were from Lower Canada and thirteen from Upper Canada.[29] Between 1841 and 1856, when the legislative council became elective, the total number of appointments, including the original twenty-four, was sixty-eight, thirty-six from Lower Canada and thirty-two from Upper Canada.[30] An 1854 act of the United Kingdom Parliament gave the legislature of the Province of Canada power to alter the constitution of the legislative council.[31] By a provincial act of 1856 the legislative council was made elective, though members already appointed for life retained their seats.[32] The new members were to be forty-eight in number, twenty-four from each section of the province, elected for an eight year term. However, the terms were to be staggered, only twelve members being chosen in the first election.[33]

Although responsible government was not granted to the Province of Canada at the outset, there was not the same overlapping of membership between the executive and legislative councils as there had formerly been in the separate provinces. Of the nine men named to the executive council in February and March 1841, only two were appointed to the legislative council.[34] The others were elected to the legislative assembly.[35] Responsible government was gradually established between 1846 and 1849. In accordance with British tradition, it came about by custom rather than legislation.

It is difficult to generalize about the number and length of legislative sessions in the Province of Canada because the variations were greater than they had been in Upper Canada. Moreover, some sessions were divided into two parts with a recess in between. For instance, the first session of the fourth parliament met from 19 August to 10 November 1852 and again from 14 February to 14 June 1853. This, the longest session during the life of the province, was followed by the shortest, lasting from 18 to 22 June 1854. The most usual length of a session was from three to four months.[36]

The provisions for reservation and disallowance in the Act of Union were almost identical with those of the Constitutional Act.[37] The Governor General, Lord Sydenham, received instructions to reserve for the signification of the Queen's pleasure bills passed by the legislature relating to the following matters: hindrance of religious worship; diminution of royal prerogative; introduction of paper currency, and issuance of securities; raising money by lotteries for public or private interest; divorces; grants of land or money to the Governor General; private acts lacking a clause of protection of the throne's rights, where they might be infringed upon; any bill to which royal assent had previously been refused, except by the Queen's special permission; taxes granted to the imperial government for public uses; aliens; and anything which might interfere with trade and the prosperity of the Empire.[38] Statistics on bills passed and on reservation and disallowance are more readily available for the Province of Canada than for Upper Canada. From 1841 to 1865 three thousand two hundred and fifty-two bills were passed, an average of one hundred and forty-three bills a session.[39] During this period seventy-seven bills were reserved.[40] Of these, sixty-two subsequently received royal assent; the remaining fifteen did not.[41] Only two acts assented to by the Governor General were subsequently disallowed.[42] In the last session of the last parliament of the Province of Canada (1866), not included in the above statistics, one hundred and seventy-six acts were passed and one reserved; it subsequently received royal assent.[43]

When the legislative union of Upper and Lower Canada gave way in 1867 to a more comprehensive federal system, the new province of Ontario chose to have a unicameral legislature.[44] Originally it was composed of eighty-two members.[45] Today the number is one hundred and twenty-five.[46] A study of the Ontario government published in 1969 commented on the shortness of legislative sessions: 'Excluding the special short sessions, the Ontario legislature sat for only 44.3 days in each year from 1867 to 1964 ... while there have been fluctuations in the lengths of sessions there has been no consistent tendency for them to become longer.'[47] In the years since this statement was written the situation has changed. Even allowing for recesses within a session, it is clear from glancing at the title pages of the statute books that in recent years sessions have been growing longer. The size of the volumes also indicates an increase in the number of statutes passed.

Provisions for reservation and disallowance of both federal and provincial legislation were included in the British North America Act.[48] For provincial legislation the Governor General in Council might within a limit of one year grant royal assent to a reserved bill or disallow an act.[49] In a report approved by the Governor General in Council in 1868, Sir John A. Macdonald listed four reasons for disallowing an act passed by a provincial legislature. They were 'as being altogether illegal or unconstitutional; as illegal or unconstitutional in part; in cases of concurrent jurisdiction, as clashing with the legislation of the general parliament; and as affecting the interests of the Dominion generally.'[50] Sometimes, however, an act was disallowed for other causes such as by reason of injustice.[51] Between 1868 and 1910 ten Ontario statutes were disallowed.[52] Disallowance of statutes of some other provinces occurred at later dates, but the practice has now fallen into disuse. Only rarely did the Lieutenant Governor of Ontario reserve a bill for consideration by the Governor General in Council.[53]

A statute thought to be *ultra vires* the provincial legislature can still be challenged in the courts. Federal ministers reluctant to recommend disallowance of provincial legislation have regarded this as a better way to deal with the situation. An example of an Ontario statute judicially considered and found *ultra vires* is the Judicature Act, 1924, which was found to encroach on the federal power to appoint judges.[54]

In some ways Ontario's constitution has developed differently from what was envisaged for Upper Canada by the framers of the Constitutional Act. There is the obvious distinction between Upper Canada, a British colony, and Ontario, a Canadian province. The change to a unicameral legislature simplified procedure by dispensing with three readings in an upper house. But in spite of the changes much of the British tradition remains. Members of the staff of the Legislative Library state that Erskine May, the leading authority on parliamentary procedure at Westminster, continues to be frequently used for reference by members of the Ontario legislature.[55]

The annotated bibliography which follows is divided into three sections: I Statutes; II Statutory Indexes, Citators, and Annotation Services; and III Proclamations, Regulations, and Gazettes. Numbering of the individual entries is continuous throughout the bibliography. Some of the items are rare; the fact that they are included indicates that I have seen at least one copy. The indexes presented considerable difficulty; I was unable to find all those listed for Ontario in Sweet & Maxwell's *Legal Bibliography*.[56] To assist the reader in understanding the different types of publications, there is an introduction to each of the three sections.

STATUTES

It is difficult to compile an accurate bibliography of Upper Canadian statutes because the mode of publishing them in the early years appears to have been somewhat haphazard. Until recently the practice in Ontario was to publish statutes passed at a legislative session soon after the close of that session. These volumes were generally known as session laws or sessional statutes. Sometimes if there was a short session its statutes were bound together with those of the session following it. In 1977, Ontario began to issue annual instead of sessional volumes; that is, it publishes together all the statutes which received royal assent in a calendar year. Because acts are often amended or repealed or through passage of time cease to be in effect, consolidations of statutes in force are published from time to time to make the law more readily accessible. The current practice in Ontario is to consolidate statutes at ten-year intervals. These consolidations are called revised statutes. Some time before a new one is due, a statute revision commission is appointed to consolidate and revise the public general statutes of the province. This involves examining and consolidating the previous revision and subsequent volumes of statutes. The sessional and annual volumes contain local and private acts, relating to specific towns, cities, counties, institutions, individuals, and so on, as well as public general acts. Only the last-mentioned are included in the revised statutes.

The omission of acts and sections of acts which have been repealed or have otherwise ceased to be in force, and the incorporation of amending acts into the statutes they have altered, may appear a relatively straightforward task. However, it is sometimes difficult to determine with certainty whether an act is still in force. The commissioners are usually given considerable discretion in deciding what acts to include; some are omitted from the revision, but not expressly repealed by it. To assist lawyers and other users, tables are included in the revised statutes showing the history and disposal of acts in the previous consolidation and in the volumes published in the years between the two consolidations.

It should be noted that the commissioners are given authority both to consolidate and to revise the public general statutes. It is important to understand what is meant by revision. Clearly the commissioners are not to change the law; that is the function of the legislature. The best way to explain the sort of revisions they may make is to quote the appropriate section from the 1979 Ontario act authorizing the preparation of the *Revised Statutes of Ontario, 1980*. It reads as follows:

> In the performance of their duties under this Act, the commissioners may omit any enactment that is not of general application or that is obsolete, may alter the numbering and arrangement of any enactment, may make such alterations in language and punctuation as are requisite to obtain a uniform mode of expression, and may make such amendments as are necessary to bring out more clearly what is deemed to be the intention of the Legislature or to reconcile seemingly inconsistent enactments or to correct clerical, grammatical or typographical errors.[57]

When the work of consolidation and revision is complete, the new revised statutes are brought into force by proclamation. The statutes included in the new revision supersede the corresponding ones in the previous revision and the volumes published between the two revisions.[58] Acts are then cited by their chapter number in the new revision. Thus The Training Schools Act, 1965 was until the proclamation of the 1970 revision cited 1965, c. 132. After its proclamation, the act was cited RSO 1970, c. 467. Note the calendar year citation of the original act. Although there is no firm rule about citing session laws by regnal or calendar year, the latter is now preferred. In Ontario before 1949 the regnal year of the session was included in the upper right hand corner of each left hand page of the sessional volumes. From 1949 on, only the calendar year appears at the top of the pages, though the regnal year continues to be given on the title page. Lawyers now generally cite by calendar year. In historical writing citation by regnal year is still quite common, especially for older statutes.[59]

During the early years of Upper Canada's existence there does not seem to have been a consistent policy regarding the publication of statutes. It is almost certain that for some years the session laws were not separately published but appeared for the first time at the end of a collection of laws passed during earlier sessions. These collections, covering several sessions or parliaments, were issued at irregular intervals. The early ones printed the complete text of statutes in chronological order, with no attempt at consolidation or revision. The first attempt at revision was made in 1818–19, but the product was nothing like today's *Revised Statutes of Ontario*. Changes in the consolidation and revision process can be traced through the various editions listed in this bibliography.

Some of the collections of Upper Canadian statutes cause confusion for the bibliographer because the date of publication on the title-page is misleading. Another problem arises from the practice of printing British statutes relating to Upper Canada at the front of some of the volumes. In published bibliographies the title-page which applies to these British statutes is sometimes listed as though it applied to the whole volume. Confusion also arises from the manner of dealing with reserved bills which later received royal assent.

W. George Eakins, Librarian of the Law Society of Upper Canada from 1891 to 1913, did intensive research relating to the statutes of Upper Canada and the Province of Canada; his bibliography and checklists remain the starting point for any additional work in the field.[60] Eakins attributed the rarity of copies of early session laws to a number of causes. They were small in bulk, issued unbound, and 'probably thought worthy of preservation by few of those who possessed them.'[61] Undoubtedly some copies of early session laws were destroyed in the fires which struck successive legislative buildings.[62] Others may have been lost during moves of the seat of government of the Province of Canada. Whatever the reasons, session laws before 1820 are very rare. According to Eakins, writing in 1908, 'the best collection known is that in the Legislative Library of Ontario at Toronto, which lacks only the year 1800...'[63] This statement is misleading, since Eakins agreed that session laws were not printed for some of the early years. When I examined the Legislative Library's holdings in the summer of 1980, it had for the 1792 to 1804 period only the 1802 [1804] collection which includes the complete text of statutes from 1792 to 1804.

Micromedia Limited in Toronto recently issued a series entitled *Pre-Confederation Statutes on Microfilm.* In the course of reviewing this series, Paul Murphy, Law Librarian at the University of Windsor, noted that for Upper Canadian statutes there is continuous pagination from 1792 to 1804, non-continuous pagination from 1805 to 1817, and for 1818 to 1819, pagination begins at 399 and ends at 485.[64] Having examined the microfilm I can now identify the sources. The first of the three reels of Upper Canadian statutes was filmed from the collection at the Harvard Law School Library. It begins with an index, which is, in fact, the index to the 1818 [1819] revision, but this is not stated. The index is followed by the text of statutes from 1792 to 1819 derived from different sources. As the 1818 [1819] revision prints only acts in force at that time (it appears also to omit some private acts), and its pagination is different from that of the sessional statutes and early reprints, its index is of little use as a guide to the complete text of statutes. The 1802 [1804] reprint is used for the text of 1792 to 1804 statutes.[65] Session laws are on film from 1805 to 1817. Presumably Harvard does not have the session laws for 1818 or 1819 (they are available in the Legislative Library in Toronto), since pages 399 to 485 of the 1818 [1819] revision were used to provide the statutes of those years. This is highly unsatisfactory, since the text of some acts is omitted. The first reel ends with the text of the 1818 [1819] revision. On the second reel are most of the remaining session laws for Upper Canada ending in 1840, filmed from the collection at York University Law Library. The reel begins with two acts dated 1819, which were not printed with the session laws for that year because they were reserved. Later they received royal assent and were printed separately. Missing from the film are the 1820 session laws. The 1819 reserved acts are followed by the 1821 statutes. From the label on the box containing the second reel it appears that 1822 and 1823 are missing, but in fact they are on the film. The third reel, filmed from the collections at Harvard and York, contains the 1831 revision, the 1859 Province of Canada Consolidation relating only to Upper Canada, and an 1876 volume of statutes of the Province of Canada and Dominion of Canada affecting Ontario. Neither the 1859 nor 1876 volumes properly belongs on this film. It would have been more appropriate to end the film with the 1843 publication *The Statutes of Upper Canada to the Time of the Union*, which was not included. The reader will understand better the deficiencies of the Micromedia microfilm of Upper Canadian statutes after studying the individual entries in the bibliography which follows.

On the other hand Micromedia's film (nine reels) of the statutes of the Province of Canada (1841–66) is very valuable. It is rare to find a set of these statutes which includes all the reserved acts that received royal assent. Micromedia used the set at York University Law Library, which contains all these acts. York made a special effort to obtain them and has bound them at the end of the statutes of the session in which they passed both houses of the legislature. This is the best place for them, since they are cited with the acts of that session, numbering being continuous. The practice of numbering reserved acts in the Province of Canada was more consistent than it had been in Upper Canada.

1 *Laws of His Majesty's Province of Upper Canada, in North America; comprising all the Acts of the Honorable the Legislature, of the Province aforesaid enacted at the First, Second, Third and Fourth Sessions 1792, 1793, 1794, and 1795.* 5th session, 1796, bound with 1st–4th. 88 p. to end of 1795, 96 p. to end of 1796, plus 2 page index. Niagara, Gideon Tiffany, King's Printer, 1795–6

When W. George Eakins wrote the first part of his 'Bibliography of Canadian Statute Law,' he thought that this volume, sometimes referred to as *Tiffany's Laws*, was the first publication of the legislation of Upper Canada and the first book printed in the province.[66] Soon afterwards he disproved this assertion by discovering a printed copy of the laws of 1793 with the imprint of Louis Roy, the first printer in the province.[67] In 1921 the Public Archives of Canada published a reprint of a volume of the Statutes of Upper Canada for the years 1792 and 1793. The original in the Sulpician Library in Montreal was said to be 'so far as can be ascertained, the only one of its kind in existence.'[68]

The Louis Roy imprint appears at the beginning of the 1793 session. Presumably, therefore, the 1792 statutes were also printed before they appeared in *Tiffany's Laws*.

There are minor variations in the different printings of the act numbered 32 Geo. III (1792), c. 8. The normal practice was to begin each act with a preamble, the first enacting clause being included at the end of it without starting a new paragraph. It was not numbered but 's. 1' was implied, the next section being numbered '2' or 'II' depending on whether Arabic or Roman numbering was used. In the volume reprinted by the Public Archives, there is a mistake in the numbering of sections in 32 Geo. III (1792), c. 8. There is an enacting clause at the end of the preamble, but the next section is numbered I instead of II. This mistake was also made in *Tiffany's Laws* but is corrected in subsequent reprints, all the sections being renumbered.

Though the 1796 statutes are not noted on the title-page of *Tiffany's Laws*, they are included at the back of the volume, pagination being continuous. Thus the volume contains all the statutes passed by the first legislature of Upper Canada. An index is included at the end.

This volume is rare. The only copy I have seen is in the Ontario Archives and is in very fragile condition.[69]

2 *Statutes of His (Her) Majesty's Province of Upper Canada*, [1792–1840] King's (Queen's) Printer. Newark, York, Toronto, 1792–1840
These are the session laws of Upper Canada. As already explained, such laws were usually printed soon after the close of the session at which they were passed. However, in the early years of Upper Canada it seems that this was not always the case. Statutes for some years were probably not separately printed before being included in collections. For instance, it seems likely that the laws of 1794 and 1795 were first published as part of *Tiffany's Laws* and that those for 1796, added to that volume, were also published there for the first time. Similarly, there is reason to believe that the laws of 1802 and 1803 were published for the first time as part of the 1802 [1804] collection. It seems quite clear that the 1804 laws were originally published as part of this collection.[70]

There was some misnumbering of chapters in the 1816 session laws, and one act was printed twice, first as chapter 4, than as chapter 17. Probably because of this, an index was included at the end of that year with page rather than chapter references. Except for that year, there are no indexes to early session laws. Indexes begin on a regular basis in 1830. However, as noted in other entries there are indexes to various collected statutes.

The publication and numbering of reserved bills which later received royal assent is confusing. Sometimes they were published separately and given the chapter number that would have been assigned had they not been reserved; in other cases they were numbered and bound with statutes passed in a later session. For instance in the 1798 session (39 Geo. III) six bills were passed, but only three (chapters 1–3) were assented to immediately; the remaining three were reserved for the signification of the King's pleasure. Yet the various editions of statutes which contain acts passed in 1798 include seven chapters for that year. What seems to have happened is that a bill passed in 1797 and reserved received royal assent on 29 December 1798 and was printed as c. 4 of the 1798 session. The three 1798 bills which were reserved received royal assent on 1 January 1800 and are printed as c. 5, 6, and 7 of 1798 in the 1802 [1804] edition and given the same numbering in subsequent reprints. Another example of a confusing situation is c. 54 of 1834 (4 Wm IV) which was not included with the session laws for that year. Having been reserved, it received royal assent on 27 October 1835 and was published as c. 36 of the session laws of 1836. However, in the Revised Statutes of 1843, it was numbered as 1834, c. 54.[71]

3 *The Statutes of His Majesty's Province of Upper Canada, 1792–1802* [1804]. York, John Bennett (King's Printer) 1802 [1804], xxvi, 223, xiii p.
The *Upper Canada Gazette* for 15 September 1804 described this newly-published volume as 'the Revised Statutes of Upper Canada, comprising all the acts enacted in the First, Second, and Third Parliaments of the Province – such British statutes also as relate to Upper and Lower Canada are annexed to this work, to which is affixed a copious alphabetical index.'[72] However, it was not a revision or consolidation, but a reprint of the complete text of the statutes. 'Reprint' is not completely accurate either for this was probably the first printing of the statutes of 1802, 1803, and 1804. The date of publication on the main title-page is 1802, but this is clearly incorrect since pagination is continuous, the text 'runs over' at the beginnings and endings of the years, and an 1803 Act of the United Kingdom Parliament is included.[73]

At the end of the volume (before the index) 'Fourth Session, Third

Parliament' was incorrectly printed as 'Fourth Session, Fourth Parliament.'[74] An errata sheet bound in some copies immediately before the index corrects the error. Unfortunately the microfilm copy produced by Micromedia Limited omits this errata sheet. The pages numbered in Roman figures at the beginning of the volume contain imperial statutes relating to Upper Canada. There is a separate title-page for this section which is likely to be mistaken for the title-page to the whole volume. This volume is probably the best source for the complete text of Upper Canadian statutes from 1792 to 1804 inclusive.

4 *The Statutes of His Majesty's Province of Upper Canada, 1792–1812.* [Cameron's Statutes]. York, John Cameron, King's Printer, 1811 [1812], xvii + [1] + 212 + [6] p.
Like the 1802 [1804] edition, this was not a revision, the statutes being reprinted in full. The date of publication is given on the title-page as 1811, but the statutes of 1812 are included. The six unnumbered pages at the end of the volume contain an index. At the front of the volume is a collection of imperial statutes. The title page preceding these acts is easily mistaken for a title-page to the whole volume.[75] The spine of one of the copies of *Cameron's Statutes* in the Toronto Public Library is incorrectly labelled 'Statutes of Upper Canada, 1774–1812.' This results from the Quebec Act 1774 being the first statute printed in the volume. According to Eakins the error of the 1802 [1804] volume as to numbering of certain sessions is repeated, though corrected on an errata sheet.[76] This, however, is incorrect. The mistake in the 1802 [1804] edition related to the fourth session of the third parliament which was incorrectly listed as the fourth session of the fourth parliament. The mistakes in the 1811 [1812] edition, corrected on an errata sheet, resulted from numbering the fifth session of the first parliament as the first session of the second parliament. This led to incorrect numbering of subsequent sessions from page 56 to page 115 inclusive. One of the copies in the Toronto Public Library contains the errata sheet, and changes in the numbering of some of the sessions have been made in pencil. The other copy lacks the errata sheet and corrections have not been made. The only other copy I have seen is in the Ontario Archives. It lacks not only the errata sheet, but also the first sixteen pages of the volume containing imperial statutes.

5 *The Provincial Statutes of Upper Canada revised, corrected and republished by authority.* York, R.C. Horne, 1818 [1819] 486 p.

This was the first revision of the statutes of the Province of Upper Canada.[77] Although the date on the title-page is 1818, the statutes of 1819 are included. Unlike later revisions this one has no preface or introduction explaining why the work was done or who did it. From an entry in the Journals of the Assembly for 2 April 1817 it can be inferred that the volume originated in the recommendation of a conference on the subject of revising the statutes attended by committees of both houses of the legislature. The conference recommended that the Lieutenant Governor 'be authorized to direct proper persons to be employed to revise and superintend the printing and publishing the said Statutes, as well as such British Statutes as apply to this province...'[78] Undoubtedly the revision of 1818 [1819] was the result, but I have not discovered what 'proper persons' carried out the task.

In this revision acts are arranged as they are in the sessional laws, ie, by session and in numerical order of chapters within the session. If acts or sections of acts have expired or been repealed, this was noted in the appropriate place and the expired or repealed act or section was not printed. If amendments have been made, the reader is referred from the original act to the amending one. The text of certain private acts and acts of limited duration are also omitted. (For example, 1819 acts of this nature are listed by title; some marginal notes, but not the text, are given. These acts must have been in force at the time the revision was published.) The mistake in the numbering of sessions in the 1811 [1812] collection was repeated in this revision.

At the front of the volume is a separate title-page which reads: 'A collection of the Acts passed in the Parliament of Great Britain particularly applying to the Province of Upper Canada and of such Ordinances of the Late Province of Quebec as have force of law therein. York, R.C. Horne, 1818.' It is followed by thirty-two numbered pages and two unnumbered ones, containing acts passed in 1774, 1791, and 1803. (Chief items: the Quebec Act, 1774, and the Constitutional Act, 1791.) They are arranged chronologically. The first unnumbered page contains a note concerning the validity of ordinances of the late Province of Quebec. The second unnumbered page is blank.[79]

6 *The Statutes of the Province of Upper Canada; together with such British Statutes, Ordinances of Quebec, and Proclamations as relate to the said Province.* Revised and printed for, and published by Hugh C.

Thomson and James Macfarlane. Revised by James Nickalls, Junior, Esquire, Barrister at Law. Kingston, U.C. Printed by Francis M. Hill, 1831, 692 p.
This revision, a private enterprise, is said to have 'long supplied the place of a revision by authority.'[80] Hugh C. Thomson, member of the house of assembly for the County of Frontenac, and James Macfarlane were both associated with Kingston newspapers, Thomson with the *Upper Canada Herald*, which he had founded, and Macfarlane with the *Kingston Chronicle*.[81] In the one-page advertisement at the front of the 1831 revision they gave 'the universally acknowledged necessity for a revised edition of the Statutes of Upper Canada' as the reason for taking upon themselves 'the risk and responsibility' of publishing the volume. Their aim was 'to give a faithful transcript of the Provincial Laws ... omitting only such statutes and clauses of statutes as subsequent acts of Parliament have repealed, and those that have expired – retaining, however the titles of said acts, and giving, where necessary, a brief summary of their provisions.' As in the 1818 [1819] revision there is no rearrangement or consolidation of the statutes. If amendments have been made, the reader is referred from the original act to the amending one. There is an index at pages 649–87. The mistake in the numbering of the sessions made in the 1811 [1812] reprint and repeated in the 1818 [1819] revision is corrected in this volume. The British statutes in this volume are grouped in two sections, pages 1–27 and 603–48. Thomson and Macfarlane explained in their advertisement that 'British laws affecting Canada' passed before 1791 were at the beginning of the volume and those enacted later at the end. There is a separate index to the British statutes, pages 689–92.

In the advertisement there is a reference to 'the Gentleman who prepared' the index and notes of reference. Presumably this was the lawyer, James Nickalls, jr, whose name appears on the title-page.

Two acts passed by the legislature of Upper Canada were disallowed by the King in Council between the publication of the 1818 [1819] revision and this one. The first was an 1826 act (7 Geo. IV, c. 2). It is printed in the 1831 revision as if it were in force; no reference is made to its disallowance. The second disallowed act was passed in 1828 (9 Geo. IV, c. 20). The 1831 revision gives the title only, followed by this note: 'Reserved for His Majesty's consent, which was not given within the time allowed by law.' This statement is clearly incorrect, since the act was printed with the session laws for 1828.

It should also be noted that the regnal year citation of acts passed in 1820 is given in the 1831 revision as 1 Geo. IV, whereas in the session laws they are cited as 60 Geo. III. The reason for this discrepancy is that although George III died on 29 January 1820 and the 1820 session ran from 21 February to 7 March, news of the King's death did not reach Upper Canada until after the close of the session. By the law of that time the death of a monarch automatically dissolved parliament, but in a distant colony dissolution occurred when the death was proclaimed there. Thus the acts of the 1820 session were valid even though they were passed in the first year of the reign of King George IV.

7 *The Statutes of Upper Canada to the Time of the Union.* Revised and published by authority. Toronto, Robert Stanton, Queen's Printer [1843] 2v. Vol. I Public Acts Vol. II Local and Private Acts

On 25 July 1840 in anticipation of the forthcoming union of Upper and Lower Canada, a commission was appointed to examine and revise the statutes of Upper Canada that were still in force. The result was the publication in 1843 of *The Statutes of Upper Canada to the Time of the Union.* The commissioners were John Beverley Robinson, Chief Justice of Upper Canada; James Buchanan Macaulay, a judge of the Court of Queen's Bench; William Henry Draper, Attorney General for Upper Canada, and John Hillyard Cameron, a young lawyer soon to be reporter to the Court of Queen's Bench, and who was later to play a prominent part in politics both before and after Confederation.[82] The work they produced was basically the same type of revision as the two previous ones except for the fact that local and private acts, though noted in their correct chronological sequence in Volume I, were for the sake of convenience collected in a separate volume and arranged according to subject. However, the report made by the commissioners and printed at the beginning of Volume I is an important document in the history of statutory consolidation and revision. The following are the relevant paragraphs:

> We are not certain that it might not have been intended that, after ascertaining what Acts, and parts of Acts were in force, we should arrange and classify them according to their subject matter, consolidating in one Statute such as relate to the same object, transposing clauses, and parts of clauses, as well as the Statutes themselves, in order to improve the arrangements, suggesting improvements, supplying deficiencies, and carefully revising the language of the whole.

But, besides that some of the Commissioners, who had been appointed, could not have undertaken this task without being relieved, for the time, from their other duties, it would have been a useless labour, unless it were to be followed by a Legislative revision of the whole of this body of Statute Law, and by re-enacting it all, in the order in which it might be proposed to place it, with such further alterations as the Legislature might deem expedient.

This would have required probably one or more extraordinary Sessions of the Legislature; and without the certainty of such subsequent ratification, of course the disturbing the present arrangement of the Statutes would have been an irregular and unauthorised act, which could only have created confusion, by furnishing as it were, by public authority, a compilation of Statute Law, wanting the necessary sanction.

Such a re-casting of the Statute Book, by classifying the whole, according to the various subjects, without regard to the order of time, has been frequently proposed in the Mother Country, but never yet attempted, nor has it, so far as we know, been effected in any of the British Colonies, though it has been in some other Countries.[83]

The commissioners went on to say that this was probably not the right time to attempt such a consolidation and revision because of the many changes that were being made by the legislature of the new Province of Canada. However, they recommended in the closing paragraph of their report that such a process be undertaken later.[84] Their advice was accepted by the Province of Canada's commissions of 1856–9; the consolidations of 1859 became the models for the first six editions of the *Revised Statutes of Ontario*.

The 1843 revision corrected the mistakes made in the 1831 edition relating to disallowed acts. Both 7 Geo. III, c. 2 and 9 Geo. III, c. 20 were noted as having been disallowed. In the former case the reader was directed to 2 Wm IV, c. 1 where the disallowed act was re-enacted in slightly altered form. The commissioners noted that they had printed acts reserved but later assented to with those of the year in which they were passed by the two houses of the legislature; this involved a change in the numbers of chapters of some of the sessions.[85] This was an improvement over the 1831 edition where the two reserved acts of 1819 were printed between 1820 and 1821.

The index to both volumes prepared by John Hillyard Cameron is found at the end of volume I.[86]

Collections and revisions of Upper Canada statutes (except the 1831 revision which was a private enterprise) were prepared and printed by legislative authority. It was not, however, the practice of the time to repeal the earlier versions of the same statutes and officially replace them with the new ones. In spite of this, the 1843 revision was by general use practically substituted for the preceding volumes of statutes.[87]

8 *Statutes of the Province of Canada*. Law Printer to the Queen, Kingston, Montreal, Toronto, Quebec, Ottawa 1841–66
These are the session laws of the Province of Canada. Each volume contains an index to the acts passed at that session. The first ten volumes (1841–51) are entitled *Provincial Statutes of Canada*.[88] The remaining volumes (1852/3–66) are called *Statutes of the Province of Canada*.[89] This division into two groups results merely from a change in printing policy brought about by 14 and 15 Vict. (1851), c. 81. Since the change was in form only, there appears to be no good reason for dividing the session laws of the Province of Canada into two groups and making separate entries for each.

At the front of some of the volumes, recently enacted imperial statutes which apply to the Province of Canada were printed. Occasionally there were other documents; for instance, the text of the Webster-Ashburton Treaty, 1842, was included at the end of the 1843 volume.

From 1841 to 1848 local and private acts, as well as public general statutes, were printed in the sessional volumes. However, an 1849 act (12 Vict., c. 16) provided that 'in order to diminish the great expense of printing and distribution,' only public acts would be printed for general distribution. Local acts were to be printed in small numbers and distributed only to judges and public departments of the legislature and government and to officials in localities specifically affected. Private and personal acts were to be printed at the expense not of the province but of the parties obtaining them. In accordance with the provisions of this act, only the titles of local and private acts passed in 1849 and 1850 were printed in the volumes for those years.[90]

This new policy evidently proved unsatisfactory, because in 1851 an act (14 and 15 Vict., c. 81) declared that it was 'deemed inexpedient that the Private and Local Acts of the Legislature should not be distributed in the same numbers, and to the same extent, as the Public General Acts' and accordingly repealed the relevant sections of the 1849 act. To compensate for the omission of the local and private acts from the 1849 and 1850 volumes, an 'Analytical Index to the Local, Personal, and Private Acts of the Sessions of 1849 and 1850' was included at the end of the 1851 volume. From 1851 to 1866 inclusive, local and private acts were once more published in the sessional volumes.

Except for the volume listed below (entry 9) and the 1859 consolidations which are a different type of publication, there are no collections or reprints of Province of Canada statutes such as there are for Upper Canada. This makes it harder to find reserved bills which later received royal assent. The pamphlets containing the text of these acts were not always bound with the session laws. As a result of this, sets of Province of Canada statutes in many Canadian libraries lack the reserved acts, especially for the early years of the province's existence. As noted earlier, the set at York University Law Library, used by Micromedia in filming the statutes of the Province of Canada, is complete.[91]

9 *The Statutes of Practical Utility in the Civil Administration of Justice, in Upper Canada, from the first act passed in Upper Canada to the Common Law Procedure Acts, 1856; chronologically arranged and showing such as have been actually repealed or otherwise abrogated. With an index. The whole intended as a circuit companion.* Edited by Robert A. Harrison. Toronto, Maclear & Co., 1857 vii, [1] 296 p.[92]
This volume was prepared by a young man who later had a distinguished career as a lawyer, writer, politician, and judge. When Robert A. Harrison died in 1878 at the age of forty-five, he was Chief Justice of Ontario. In the preface to this volume he wrote that he had prepared it at the pressing solicitation of many members of the legal profession. He described the object of the work as 'to furnish in convenient form, all statutes and parts of statutes unrepealed and in force, akin to the Common Law Procedure Acts, 1856 ... The volume is one of "Practical Statutes" by which is meant, such Statutes as especially relate to the practice of the Courts.'[93] The preface also explained that the statutes from 1792 to 1840 inclusive were passed by the legislature of the late Province of Upper Canada and applied exclusively to Upper Canada, whereas statutes passed by the legislature of [the Province of] Canada since 1840 extended to the whole Province of Canada, unless restricted to Upper Canada.[94]

NOTE: Work on consolidating the statutes of the Province of Canada began in 1856, leading to the publications listed in the following entries. Two commissions were appointed, one to prepare a consolidation of statutes applying exclusively to Upper Canada, the other to prepare a similar work relating to Lower Canada. The two commissions were jointly to prepare a consolidation of statutes which applied to both sections of the province. The original members of the commission for Upper Canada were John Hillyard Cameron (who had served on the 1840–3 commission), Joseph C. Morrison, Adam Wilson, Skeffington Connor, Oliver Mowat, and David B. Read.[95] However, there were several changes in membership before the work was completed.[96] The three consolidations, two of which concern us here, were published in 1859. Unlike earlier revisions of Upper Canadian statutes, these were true consolidations – that is, acts were rearranged and renumbered (the arrangement was by subject) and amending acts were incorporated into the acts they amended.[97] The consolidations were limited to public general statutes, local and private acts being omitted. These were the first consolidations to be officially adopted – acts were passed by the legislature providing for their coming into force by proclamation, earlier versions of the acts contained in them being repealed. The consolidation, rearrangement, and renumbering of acts made such a course necessary.

10 *The Public General Statutes which apply exclusively to Upper Canada, as revised in the first instance by the Commissioners appointed for that part of the Province and since revised and brought down to the end of the Session of 22 Victoria (1859) by the Chairman of the Commission.* Toronto, Stewart Derbishire and George Desbarats, Law Printer to the Queen 1859, xxxvi, 1087 p.
This is a draft or preliminary edition of *The Consolidated Statutes for Upper Canada*, 1859. See next entry.

11 *The Consolidated Statutes for Upper Canada.* Proclaimed and published under the authority of the Act 22 Vict. cap. 30, A.D. 1859. Toronto, Stewart Derbishire and George Desbarats, Law Printer to the Queen 1859, vii, 1229 p.
The statutes in this volume applied to Upper Canada only. Acts are grouped by subject under the following thirteen titles: Title 1. Preliminary Provisions; Title 2. Territorial Divisions; Title 3. Executive Government; Title 4. Administration of Justice; Title 5. Professions, etc.; Title 6. Trade and Commerce; Title 7. Municipal Institutions; Title 8. Education; Title 9. Religious and Benevolent Institutions; Title 10. Domestic Relations, Rights and Remedies; Title 11. Real Estate; Title

12. Criminal Law; Title 13. Administration of Justice in Unorganized Tracts. Included in the volume are various schedules of acts which assist in its use. The general index (pp 1133–1228) applies both to this volume and to the companion volume described in the next entry.

12 *The Consolidated Statutes of Canada.* Proclaimed and published under the authority of the Act 22 Vict. cap. 29, A.D. 1859. Toronto, Stewart Derbishire and George Desbarats, Law Printer to the Queen 1859. xl, 1377 p.
The statutes in this volume applied to both sections of the Province of Canada. Acts are grouped by subject under the following eleven titles: Title 1. Constitution and Political Rights, Legislation, etc.; Title 2. Executive Government and Public Officers Generally; Title 3. Public Departments, Revenue and Property; Title 4. Trade and Commerce; Title 5. Trading Companies and Corporations; Title 6. Benevolent Associations, etc.; Title 7. Religious Matters; Title 8. Professions; Title 9. Private Rights and Remedies; Title 10. Municipal Matters; Title 11. Criminal Law. Included in the volume are various schedules of acts which assist in its use. There is an 'Index to the matters contained in this volume.' (pp 1299–1377)

13 *Statutes of the Province of Ontario,* 1867/8– Toronto, Queen's (King's) Printer, 1868–
These are the session laws of the province of Ontario. Up to the end of 1976, numbering was determined by the session in which they were passed. Beginning in 1977, all acts which receive royal assent within a calendar year are numbered consecutively, regardless of whether more than one session is involved. An example of the pre-1977 practice is that acts passed in the 1962–3 session are contained in one volume; the next volume contains the one act passed at a short session in October 1963, together with the 1964 session laws. In this period there was an index for each session; thus if a volume contained acts passed at two sessions, an index was printed at the end of each session. On the other hand, the volume of *Statutes of the Province of Ontario receiving Royal Assent in the year 1977* contains acts passed in the fourth session of the thirtieth legislature (29 March–29 April 1977) and in the first session of the thirty-first legislature (27 June–16 December 1977), numbered consecutively and with an index to the whole volume at the end. For many years (1933–69) it was customary to arrange and number public general statutes in alphabetical order by short title,

followed by local and private acts in the same order. This meant waiting until the close of a session to assign chapter numbers. As sessions lengthened, this involved too long a delay, so public general statutes are now arranged and numbered in the order in which they receive royal assent. With the change to annual volumes in 1977, numbering is continuous throughout the calendar year. Acts are still listed in alphabetical order in the table of contents at the front of the volume, and from 1937 on, the bill numbers by which they were known during their passage through the legislature are also noted in the table. Since 1959, private bills have been numbered in a separate sequence with the prefix 'Pr'; this has not affected their numbering in the statute books. They continue to be published after the public general acts.

In the 1880s when disallowance of provincial legislation was most common, it became customary to list disallowed acts at the back of the sessional volumes. For instance, the 1882 volume lists two 'Acts of the Ontario Legislature disallowed since the Revision of the Statutes.' Similarly, the 1883 volume lists two 'Acts of the Ontario Legislature disallowed since publication of the Statutes of 1882.' Beginning with the session of 1888, a 'Table Showing Revised Statutes amended by Acts [of current session]' is included. It later becomes a 'Table Showing Revised Statutes and Subsequent Acts Amended by…' A Table of this type appears in most of the volumes which follow, though in a few it is omitted; for instance, there is no table in the 1903 or 1904 volumes. The title and arrangement of the table usually change somewhat following a new revision of the statutes.

In the 1936 volume, in addition to the above type of table, there are two others entitled: 'Table of Public Statutes, R.S.O. 1927–1936 which were to be brought into force by Proclamation. A. Table showing which of such Acts or Parts thereof now in force and the respective dates upon which they came into force. B. Table showing which of such Acts or Parts thereof are not proclaimed as of 9th May 1936,' and 'Table of Proclamations, Orders-in-Council and Regulations made from 1st January, 1933 to 9th May, 1936, which are in force and of general effect.' Similar tables appear in the volumes up to and including 1944, except that in the volume covering the second session, 1937, and 1938, there is no Table of Statutes which were brought into force by Proclamation. At the end of the 1945 (both sessions) volume, there is a note: 'In view of the provisions of The Regulations Act, 1944 the practice of publishing a Table of Proclamations, Orders-in-Council and Regulations at the conclusion of the annual volume of the statutes is discontinued.' Subsequent volumes continue to publish the other two tables.

In the 1965 volume the titles of the tables are as follows: 'Table of Public Statutes' and 'Table of Proclamations setting out the Public Acts and parts of Public Acts in the Revised Statutes of Ontario, 1960 and subsequent annual volumes that have been and that are to be brought into force by Proclamation and that have not been repealed or superseded.' The wording and arrangement of these tables had been the same for some time past, but for the first time in 1965 there was a further table, entitled 'Table of Regulations filed under the Regulations Act to the 31st day of August, 1965. Part I Showing the Regulations contained in Revised Regulations of Ontario, 1960 and subsequent Regulations filed to the 31st day of August, 1965, other than those set out in Part II. Part II showing the Regulations contained in Revised Regulations of Ontario, 1960 and subsequent Regulations filed to the 31st day of August, 1965, that have been revoked, are revoking only or have expired.' With minor variations in title, the tables remain the same to the present. They now relate to RSO 1970 and RRO 1970, and the cut-off date for regulations listed in the Table of Regulations is 31 December instead of 31 August.

It should be noted that for 1971 [1st session] there are two volumes of statutes. In Volume I marginal notes refer to RSO 1960 and subsequent sessional volumes. Volume II contains the same public acts, the notes being updated to refer to RSO 1970. Private acts, not being included in the revised statutes, are contained only in Volume I. Thus, for a complete record of statutes passed during the 1st session, 1971, together with references to provisions in RSO 1970 which they amend, both volumes are needed.

A recent development in the history of statute publishing in Ontario is the institution by the government of a program making certain statutes and regulations available in French. The first translations were issued in pamphlet form in 1979. This is a long-term ongoing project.

14 *Imperial Statutes affecting the Province of Ontario; and consisting chiefly of those Statutes which relate to the Constitution of the Province and the Political Rights of its Inhabitants, and such other of the Imperial Acts which have been heretofore printed with the Statutes of the late Province of Canada and of the Dominion, as affect this Province.* Toronto, John Notman, Law Printer to the Queen, 1875, iv, 356, xxvii p.

This collection was prepared by G.H. Watson and G.L.B. Fraser, barristers-at-law, under the direction of a Committee of the Commissioners for the Consolidation and Revision of The Statutes affecting the Province of Ontario (the first consolidation of Ontario Statutes, 1877).[98] Sections of acts which do not relate to or affect Ontario are omitted. Annotations referring the reader to other relevant acts are inserted throughout the volume. At the back of the volume there is a combined subject and act index with numerous 'see' references.

15 *Statutes of the Province of Canada and Dominion of Canada comprising those portions of the Consolidated Statutes of Canada and Upper Canada, and of the Statutes of the Province of Canada still in force in Ontario, and which are supposed to relate to matters not within the jurisdiction of the Provincial Legislature of Ontario, and those Statutes of the Dominion of Canada, which affect Ontario, up to and inclusive of those passed in 1875 [38 Victoria]* Part I. Toronto, John Notman, Law Printer to the Queen, 1876, xvi, 633 p.
Only Part I was published. The project was abandoned when it was found that the federal government had taken preliminary steps to produce a consolidation of statutes that would include the acts of which the Ontario collection would have been composed.[99] At the front of the volume are both a classified table and a chronological table of statutes contained in it.

16 *Practical Statutes, being a collection of Statutes of Practical Utility in force in Ontario with notes on the construction and operation thereof.* By James Bicknell and Arthur James Kappele. Toronto, Goodwin & Co., 1900. xlvii, 925 p.
The purpose of this volume is described in the Preface:

> The editors have taken those Statutes which, in the opinion of the directors of legal education in this province, are of most concern to the practising solicitor, and have attempted to collect the authorities construing them...
>
> In the present work the decisions affecting the Statutes have been compressed into notes in the shortest possible space and arranged in a manner which it is hoped will be found to lighten labor.
>
> There has been no attempt to show the evolution of the law on any particular subject, but it has been sought simply to give the decisions construing the different enactments. The Statutes are published intact, and the editors' work has been confined to the endeavor to state what the Courts have said the Statutes mean and what their effect is as a result of the decisions.

As the above description indicates, this is a collection of statutes with annotations; that is, it gives the text of the statutes and any judicial interpretation of them. There is an index at pages 851–925.

NOTE: To date there have been nine consolidations of the statutes of Ontario. All are called *Revised Statutes*, but in contrast with the revisions of Upper Canadian statutes and the 1859 consolidations of the statutes of the Province of Canada, it is more correct to describe them as consolidations. The extent to which both revision and consolidation are involved has already been explained.[100] The dates of the *Revised Statutes of Ontario* are 1877, 1887, 1897, 1914, 1927, 1937, 1950, 1960, and 1970. RSO 1980 is now in preparation.

In the first six consolidations (up to and including RSO 1937), acts are grouped together by subject. Beginning with RSO 1950, they are arranged and numbered alphabetically by title. Each of the consolidations contains an index as well as schedules. There is not much variation from one edition to another and those included in the 1970 consolidation are listed below as examples. The title of each edition of the *Revised Statutes of Ontario* follows:

17 *The Revised Statutes of Ontario, being a consolidation of the Public General Acts of the Legislature of Ontario, with such of the Public General Acts of the Late Province of Canada as relate to matters within the authority of the Legislature of Ontario.* Toronto, John Notman, Law Printer to the Queen, 1877 2 v. (paged continuously)[101]
In the Law Library at the University of Western Ontario there is a volume entitled *Revised Statutes of Ontario* Part II, published in 1876. Presumably it is a draft of the 1877 revision; it was known that there had been such a draft.[102] However, inquiries made at the Legislative Library several years ago produced no evidence that the draft had ever been published. There is an entry for an 1876 draft in one of the publications of Olga B. Bishop, the distinguished bibliographer. It indicates that the draft was published in three parts and that 'only part 3 which contains chap. 116–162 was located.'[103] This is clearly part of the same publication as the volume in the University of Western Ontario Law Library which contains chapters 47–115. There is also an entry for a different draft apparently consisting of two parts of which only Part I was located. It contains chapters 1–115.[104]

18 *The Revised Statutes of Ontario, 1887, being a consolidation of the*

Revised Statutes of Ontario 1877, with the subsequent Public General Acts of the Legislature of Ontario. Toronto, John Notman, Law Printer to the Queen, 1887, 2 v. (paged continuously)

19 *The Revised Statutes of Ontario, 1897, being a consolidation of the Revised Statutes of Ontario, 1887, with the subsequent Public General Acts of the Legislature of Ontario.* Toronto, L.K. Cameron, Law Printer to the Queen, v. 1 & 2, 1897, Law Printer to the King, v. 3, 1902 (the three volumes are paged continuously)
The third volume of this revision contains "A Consolidation and Revision of certain Imperial Statutes relating to property and civil rights incorporated into the law of Ontario by virtue of Provincial Legislation up to the end of the year 1897, with An Appendix, containing (1) Imperial Constitutional Statutes, (2) Imperial Statutes of General Practical Utility, passed since 15 October 1792, in force in Ontario, *ex proprio vigore,* (3) The Habeas Corpus Act, and (4) A Table of Imperial Statutes in force in Canada *ex proprio vigore,* at the end of the year 1901.' The statutes in the main part of this volume that remain in force in Ontario have been carried forward to subsequent revisions. In this volume they occupied one hundred and one pages; in RSO 1970, thirteen.

20 *The Revised Statutes of Ontario, 1914, being a revision and consolidation of the Revised Statutes of Ontario, 1897, and the subsequent Public General Acts of the Legislature of Ontario.* Toronto, L.K. Cameron, Law Printer to the King, 1914, 3 v. (v. 1, 2 paged continuously)

21 *The Revised Statutes of Ontario, 1927, being a revision and consolidation of the Revised Statutes of Ontario, 1914, and the subsequent Public General Acts of the Legislature of Ontario.* Toronto, King's Printer, 1927, 4 v. (v. 1–3 paged continuously)

22 *The Revised Statutes of Ontario, 1937, being a revision and consolidation of the Revised Statutes of Ontario, 1927, and the subsequent Public General Acts of the Legislature of Ontario.* Toronto, T.E. Bowman, Law Printer to the King, 1937, 4 v. (v. 1–3 paged continuously)

23 *Revised Statutes of Ontario, 1950, being a revision and consolidation of the Public General Acts of the Legislature of Ontario, published under the authority of the Statutes Consolidation Act, 1949.*Toronto, Baptist Johnston, Law Printer to the King, [1950], 5 v. (each volume paged separately)

24 *Revised Statutes of Ontario, 1960, being a revision and consolidation of the Public General Acts of the Legislature of Ontario, published under the authority of the Statutes Revision Act, 1959.* Toronto, Queen's Printer, [1960], 5 v. (each volume paged separately)

25 *Revised Statutes of Ontario, 1970, being a revision and consolidation of the Public General Acts of the Legislature of Ontario, published under the authority of the Statutes Revision Act, 1968–69.* Toronto, Queen's Printer and Publisher, [1971] 6 v. (each volume paged separately)
Appendix A – Certain Imperial Acts and Parts of Acts relating to Property and Civil Rights that were Consolidated in the Revised Statutes of Ontario, 1897, Volume III, pursuant to Chapter 13 of the Statutes of Ontario, 1902, that are not repealed by the Revised Statutes of Ontario, 1970 and are in force in Ontario subject thereto. Vol. 6, p. 1–13.

Appendix B – Certain Imperial Statutes and Statutes of Canada relating to the Constitution and Boundaries of Ontario. Vol. 6, p. 15–109.

Schedule A – Showing Acts contained in the Revised Statutes of Ontario, 1960 and other Acts of the Legislature of Ontario that are repealed in whole or in part from the day upon which the Revised Statutes of Ontario, 1970 take effect, and the extent of such repeal. Vol. 6, p. 111–46.

Schedule B – Showing Acts and Parts of Acts Repealed, Superseded and Consolidated in the Revised Statutes of Ontario, 1970, and showing also what Portions of the Revised Statutes of Ontario, 1960 and Acts of the Legislature passed thereafter are not consolidated. Vol. 6, p. 147–398.

Information on the preparation and adoption of each edition of Revised Statutes is contained in the act authorizing it and in the proclamation bringing it into force. These are reprinted in the Revised Statutes. Beginning with RSO 1914, the Report of the Commissioners on the Revised Statutes is also printed. A note on the history of statute revisions in the Provinces of Upper Canada, Canada, and Ontario is included in each edition of the Revised Statutes.

The tables which show what has happened to acts in the previous revision and subsequent sessional volumes are useful for various purposes. Not only do they show where they can be found in the new consolidation, if still in force, they also indicate whether an act or section of an act is obsolete or has been amended or repealed. If an act was disallowed by the Governor General in Council, this is noted in the appropriate table. Similarly, if an act is found *ultra vires*, a notation to this effect is included. (See note p. 404 for RSO 1980.)

STATUTORY INDEXES, CITATORS, AND ANNOTATION SERVICES

The statutes of this bibliography include numerous references to indexes in volumes of session laws and in collections, revisions, and consolidations of statutes. When statutes were few in number, as in the early years of Upper Canada, indexing was relatively easy. As they increased in number, it became more time-consuming and expensive. Moreover, it was easier to produce an index of acts than a proper subject index, and this is what some statutory indexes became. Ontario's indexes to its sessional statutes have been better than those of some other provinces; though arranged by act they do include cross-references from subject headings to acts. Indexes in revised statutes are generally better than those in sessional volumes.

Nevertheless, there has for a long time been dissatisfaction with statute indexing in Canada. Now with the aid of the computer, the Canadian Law Information Council (CLIC), a non-profit corporation which aims to make legal information more quickly and easily accessible, is working on the production of subject indexes to the statutes of several Canadian provinces, including Ontario. In this province the results will be seen first in RSO 1980.

The second section of this bibliography deals not with indexes in sessional or revised statutes, but with separately published indexes and other finding aids. Some are government publications, but most are commercial ventures which aim or have aimed to provide either better indexing than that contained in session laws and revised statutes, or a service that the government does not supply at all. The list of indexes presented here does not profess to be comprehensive. As noted earlier, I was unable to find some of those listed in Sweet & Maxwell's *Legal Bibliography*.[105] In addition, space considerations have led me to include only publications restricted to indexing the statutes of Upper Canada, the Province of Canada, or Ontario. Several which index federal statutes and those of some provinces including Ontario have been omitted.[106]

The other finding aids listed in Section II of the bibliography are citators and annotation services. These lawyers' tools are for the most part unknown to historians, which is unfortunate, since they can be very useful in historical research. Statute citators show what acts or sections of acts have been amended or repealed generally since the latest revision of the statutes; some of them print the text of amendments. They also indicate whether acts or sections of acts have been judicially considered, that is, interpreted by the courts. Annotation services perform much the same functions, though they tend to concentrate on judicial considerations more than amendments. One such publication, *Ontario Annotation Service*, is especially useful to historians because it gives a brief history of each act included.

26 *Index to the Statutes in Force in Upper Canada, at the end of the Session of 1854–5, including a classification thereof, a Revision of the Public General Acts, and an Index to the Statutes not in Force.* Edited by G.W. Wicksteed. Toronto, Stewart Derbishire and George Desbarats, Queen's Printer, 1856, (viii, 419 p.) Prepared by order of the Legislative Assembly, on motion of J.W. Gamble, Esq. by G.W. Wicksteed, Q.C., Law Clerk of the House[107]

Gustavus William Wicksteed, the editor of this volume, was a Lower Canadian lawyer who had been law clerk of the legislative assembly of Canada since the union of the provinces in 1841. He also served on the Lower Canada Commission (1856–9) on the revision and consolidation of the statutes.[108] Wicksteed's 'Notice' at the front of the volume (pp 1–vii) outlines the purpose of the index and the techniques adopted in compiling it:

> The rule I have adopted in framing the Index is to refer to all the sections of each Public General Act which are in force, under some one title, making that title the most special which would embrace all the provisions; and to cite any of them which come properly under other titles, either by repeating them under such titles, or by reference to that embracing the whole Act, as might seem best; and it will be found very useful to bear this in mind in using the work ... As regards the Local and Private Acts, the references are to the Acts only, and not to their provisions... (p v)

A 'Supplement-First Part' (pp 395–408) gives a 'Classification of titles in the foregoing Index, and of the Acts and Provisions referred to under them.' In this classification there are two main divisions, 'Public General Acts' and 'Local Acts.' Within each division broad subject headings are given, and specific types of legislation are listed under each subject heading.

A 'Supplement-Second Part' (pp 409–19) lists 'Acts which have been in force in Upper Canada, but which are not referred to in the foregoing Index, as being repealed, expired, or effete by the accomplishment of the objects for which they are passed, &c.' The acts are grouped together under subject headings and listed only by regnal year and chapter.

27 *Table of the Provincial Statutes in Force or which have been in force in Upper Canada in their chronological order, shewing which of them, or what parts of any of them, are now in force, and by what subsequent Acts they have been amended, continued, repealed or otherwise affected. With a continuation of the Index to the Statutes in force, &c. to the end of the Session of 1856.* Edited by G.W. Wicksteed. Toronto, Stewart Derbishire and George Desbarats, Queen's Printer, 1856 (iv, 147 p.) Prepared by order of the Legislative Assembly, on motion of J.W. Gamble, Esq. by G.W. Wicksteed, Q.C. Law Clerk of the House[109]
This is a companion volume to the above entry. Its purpose and the manner of compiling it are described in the 'Notice' at the front of the table (pp iii–iv). Useful remarks concerning it are also included in the 'Notice' at the beginning of the index. (p vi)

The table lists all statutes in chronological order and shows by what subsequent acts each has been amended, continued, repealed, or otherwise affected. 'The Table and the Index supplement and check each other,' Wicksteed explained, 'the former affording fuller information as regards the Statutes and parts of Statutes not in force, and the latter as regards those in force.' He went on: 'The object of the Table is not to show what any Act under consideration itself provides, for this appears on the face of the Act which is supposed to be before the reader, but how its provisions are affected by later Acts which are not before him.' ('Notice' to table, p iii)

Included at the back of the volume are the following sections, supplementing material in Wicksteed's Index: 'Additions and Corrections to the Index to the Statutes in force in Upper Canada, Up to the End of the Session of 1856' (pp 125–44); 'Additions to the Titles in Several Classes in the First Part of the Supplement' (pp 145–6); 'Additions to the Second Part of the Supplement – Acts no Longer in Force' (p 147).

Robert A. Harrison, editor of *The Statutes of Practical Utility* (entry 9 above) and a contemporary of Wicksteed, described his table as 'a very useful little volume' and added that his 'ability and accuracy are well known, both in Upper and in Lower Canada.'[110] To historians seeking information about legislation relating to Upper Canada both before its union with Lower Canada and for fifteen years thereafter, Wicksteed's index and table are most helpful finding aids.

28 *An Index to the Statutes of Canada, from 3 & 4 Victoria to 12 & 13 Victoria, inclusive, 1840 to 1850, comprising all the acts passed, in force & repealed, in Upper and Lower Canada, from the Union Act to the close of the last Session*. Edited by Aemilius Irving. Toronto, Henry Rowsell, 1850 (72 p.)
This item may appear to be out of chronological order because it was published before Wicksteed's volumes. It is listed here because the period dealt with begins much later; it does not deal with Upper Canada before the union. The main index is arranged alphabetically by subject with numerous 'see' references. There is also a chronological index. A few imperial acts relating to the Province of Canada are included in the index. A note at the beginning of the chronological index states: 'The statutes in SMALL CAPITALS are Imperial Acts.' There is no note concerning imperial acts at the beginning of the main index, but in fact the names of the same acts are included there. When listed, the words 'Imp. stat.' precede the regnal year and chapter.

29 *A Synoptical Index of the Consolidated Statutes of Canada and Upper Canada, with notices of the later Acts which affect them; including the session of 1864*. By John Webster Hancock. Toronto, W.C. Chewett & Co., 1865. (479 p.)
John Webster Hancock, who compiled this index, was a lawyer in Berlin (now Kitchener) and the author of *A System of Conveyancing*.[111] His index is useful because it was compiled after the 1859 statutory consolidations and relates to them and to later acts which affected them. Like Irving's work and unlike Wicksteed's index and table, it was an unofficial publication.

The index is arranged alphabetically under broad subject headings. Under these are more specific headings also arranged in alphabetical order. Opposite the latter is given the relevant page number in the Consolidated Statutes of Upper Canada or Canada.

NOTE: The following three entries list indexes of early Ontario statutes. All three were private enterprises, presumably undertaken on their compilers' own initiative. Lewis directed his index to 'the legal profession and the public.'[112] Jelfs recommended his particularly for the use of students but thought that it would also be appreciated by the legal profession generally.[113] The index and supplement (1867–1900) compiled by Harris H. Bligh, Librarian of the Supreme Court of Canada, is by far the most useful to historians. See his comments on the historic value of superseded or repealed statutes in entry 32 below.

30 *Lewis' Ontario Statute Index, being an alphabetical Index of the Statutes of the Province of Ontario, down to and inclusive of the year 1884, including the Revised Statutes.* Edited by Edward Norman Lewis. Toronto, Carswell, 1884. (447 p.)
This is an alphabetical subject index with numerous 'see' references.

31 *Jelfs' Index to Statute Law, being a General Index to the Last Revised (1877) and Subsequent Statutes of Ontario, with the Real Property and Common Law Amendments in abbreviated Text-Book Form, alphabetically arranged, and with References to original Acts and Amendments. Also an Appendix containing the Dominion Acts on Bills and Promissory Notes, and some English Statute Law in force in Ontario, commonly referred to, including the 'Settled Estates Act,' 19 and 20 V. c. 120, as amended prior to 1865.* Edited by George Frederick Jelfs. Toronto, Warwick & Sons, 1892 (218 p.)
This is an alphabetical subject index with many 'see' references. Notes digesting the law on the subjects are included in the index.

32 *The Ontario Law Index, embracing all the Legislation of the Province of Ontario, down to and including the year 1895.* Edited by Harris H. Bligh. Toronto, Carswell, 1895. (268 p.) *Supplement 1896–1900* (published 1900) (104 p.)
The arrangement and scope of the Index are well explained in the preface, which reads in part as follows:

> This Index to the Laws of Ontario contains, not only every Chapter, Public and Private, whether repealed or still in force; but every subject upon which the Legislature has passed, continuing the same with its amendments, in an unbroken succession of references from the earliest enactment down to the present day. The Propriety of indexing Statutes which have been superseded or repealed has sometimes been questioned; but inasmuch as such Statutes have at least an historic value, and besides are at all times liable to be sought for and consulted in their relation to subjects still affected by them; I am, as I always have been, most thoroughly convinced that to make an index complete, it should include, not only the present, but the past, as this work has done.

The Index, so far as it relates to general subjects, is arranged in strict alphabetical order, while under the several headings each subject is followed chronologically, giving in every case the Volume (or year), the Chapter, the Section and (when necessary) the Sub-section or Page.

33 *Annotations to the Revised Statutes of Ontario, 1914*. Edited by Fletcher Cameron Snider. Toronto, Carswell, 1914 (cxx, 1236 p.)
Taylor's Annotations (1930) are described as supplementary, though they are to the next revision of the statutes. Relevant cases are cited and briefly digested under section numbers within the chapters.

34 *Annotations to the Revised Statutes of Ontario, 1914, including statutory amendments for the years 1914–1918, inclusive, and various decided cases.* Edited by H.E. Choppin. Toronto, Carswell; London, Sweet & Maxwell, 1919, (xxxviii, 248 p.)
Arrangement is by chapter number in RSO 1914, followed by the same arrangement for annual volumes. This volume originated in notes and memoranda made for the author's own use, and therefore makes no pretense to contain an exhaustive resume of case law. It is a ready reference to statutory amendments.

35 *Annotations to the Revised Statutes of Ontario, 1927 and Annual Statutes.* [including 1930]. Edited by G. Verone Taylor. Toronto, Carswell, 1930 (cxx, 778 p.)
Arrangement is numerically by chapter in RSO 1927. Annual statutes since 1927 are not listed separately. 'Annual statutory amendments since 1927 have been given only where the section is otherwise considered.' Pref. (iii)

This volume is described in the preface as 'supplementary to Snider's Annotations to the Revised Statutes of Ontario' (iii). Relevant cases are cited and briefly digested under section numbers within the chapters.

36 *Ontario Statute Citator*. Toronto, Canada Law Book Limited (current publisher), 1932– ; Editors: 1932–9, H.L. Cartwright; 1939–46, H.L. Cartwright and R.M. Willes Chitty; 1947–50, R.M. Willes Chitty, QC; 1950 loose-leaf service, R.M. Willes Chitty, QC and L.R. MacTavish, QC; 1960 and 1970 loose-leaf service, L.R. MacTavish, QC, Editor-in-Chief
The *Ontario Statute Citator* began publication in 1932, apparently as a

successor to Bruff Garrett's *Index of Cases Relating to the Revised Statutes of Ontario, 1914 and Acts to 1922*. (There is no entry for Garrett's Index, since I have been unable to find a copy.) Originally the citator took the form of annual bound volumes, but it is now a loose-leaf service. To date the *Ontario Statute Citator* consists of the following volumes:

1932–7 – 6 annual volumes
Consolidation (1927–37) 1938, 1 volume
1939–50 – 12 annual volumes (1950 was the last annual bound volume published. The Citator then became a loose-leaf service.)
Annotating Service to RSO 1950 – one loose-leaf volume
RSO 1960 Edition – one loose-leaf volume
RSO 1970 Edition – two loose-leaf volumes (current)

Title varies: 1st Volume – *The Ontario Statute Citator 1932 (Bruff Garrett's Index) An Index of Amendments to the R.S.O. 1927 and all the Cases decided on the R.S.O. 1927, from Jan. 1, 1928 to Aug. 1, 1932, together with an Annotation The Law of Divorce in Ontario and the Cases on the Rules of Practice since the Consolidated Rules came into effect on Jan. 1, 1929, to Aug. 1, 1932.*

In the volumes which follow the title is somewhat simplified, but varies slightly from year to year. From 1942 to 1950 inclusive it is simply *The Ontario Statute Citator*. The loose-leaf service which began in 1950 is entitled *The Ontario Statute Citator: A Complete Annotating Service for R.S.O. 1950*. The RSO 1960 edition has the same title except for the change of date. The current edition is called *Ontario Statute Citator, R.S.O. 1970 Edition*.

The publisher varies, but this is the result of a change in the name of the firm, and later the amalgamation of two firms (Cartwright and Canada Law Book).[114]

Statutes are arranged alphabetically by title. The citation of the original act is given, followed by citations to subsequent amending ones. The text of amendments is given under the appropriate section of the original act.

Recent cases interpreting statutes are digested under the appropriate chapters and sections, and for earlier cases the reader is referred to other sources. For instance, for cases during the years 1930–70, the *Ontario Statute Citator, R.S.O. 1970 Edition*, refers the reader to *Ontario Statute Annotations R.S.O. 1970 Edition*.

37 *Ontario Statute Annotations, R.S.O. 1960 Edition, being a compilation of case annotations to the Revised Statutes covering the period 1930 to 1960.* Toronto, Canada Law Book, 1961 (xci, 660 p.)
Arrangement is by chapter number in RSO 1960 (ie, alphabetically by the title of the statute). A short history of each act is given; cases relating to the act as a whole are then cited and briefly digested. Similar information is then given for cases bearing on specific sections of the act.

38 *Ontario Statute Annotations, R.S.O. 1970 Edition being a compilation of case annotations to the Revised Statutes covering the period 1930 to 1971.* Agincourt, Ontario, Canada Law Book, 1974
Arrangement is by chapter number in RSO 1970 (ie, alphabetically by the title of the statute). A short history of each act is given; cases relating to the act as a whole are then briefly digested. Similar information is then given for cases bearing on specific sections of the act. The following is an excerpt from the preface (p v):

> This second (R.S.O. 1970) edition of the *Ontario Statute Annotations* is a cumulative replacement of the R.S.O. 1960 edition. It contains all the material from that edition that is still relevant to the statutes in R.S.O. 1970 plus all the relevant cases reported between January, 1961 and December, 1971...
>
> Cases that were reported for the first time after December 1971 are not included in the work, but will be found in the current (R.S.O. 1970) edition of the *Ontario Statute Citator*. However, all appeals from cases reported before that date, and therefore within the scope of this edition, are included up to June, 1974, even though they also appear in the *Citator*. There is therefore no need to look in more than one place for any appeals up to June, 1974.

PROCLAMATIONS, REGULATIONS, AND GAZETTES

In addition to statutes, there are various types of executive orders which have the force of law. Many of them are published in *Gazettes*, which is the name given to official government newspapers issued by authority. Some of these executive orders, especially during the colonial period, derived from the royal prerogative; in modern times most are a type of subordinate legislation authorized by statute. Many acts contain provisions authorizing the Governor General in Council, the Lieutenant Governor in Council, a Minister of the Crown, a local authority, or an administrative board to make rules, orders, or regulations on particular subjects. Systematic publication of this subordinate legislation has begun only in relatively recent years. The Regulations Act, 1944, provided for the central filing of regulations and for their publication in the *Ontario Gazette*.[115]

39 *Fourth Report of the Bureau of Archives for the Province of Ontario*, by Alexander Fraser, Provincial Archivist. Toronto, L.K. Cameron, King's Printer, 1907, xxxiv, 476 p.
The documents published in this volume consist of proclamations issued by the Governors and Lieutenant Governors of the Province of Quebec from 1760 to 1791 and by the Lieutenant Governors of Upper Canada from 1792 to 1840. It does not profess to be complete, although in addition to the usual repositories of official documents the *Quebec Gazette*, the British Parliamentary Papers pertaining to Canada, and the early newspapers of Canada were examined with a view to extracting proclamations. The arrangement is chronological. There is a general index at pages 475–6.

40 *Upper Canada Gazette*, 1793–1849? King's (Queen's) Printer
The *Upper Canada Gazette, or American Oracle* began as a weekly newspaper rather than an official Gazette, but it was printed under government auspices by the King's Printer. In addition to news, it included such items as proclamations which usually appear in an official Gazette. From 1793 to 1798 the newspaper was published at Newark (also called Niagara and West Niagara during this period); then it moved to York, which had already replaced Newark as the seat of government. From 1807 to 1817 it was called the *York Gazette* (the press was destroyed in 1813 during the American occupation of York; publication resumed late in 1814). In 1817 the name was changed back to *Upper Canada Gazette*, and for a short time the *York Weekly Post* was issued along with it. At the beginning of 1822 it became *The Upper Canada Gazette, New Series, and Weekly Register*, Vol. I, but to confuse matters further, numbering began over again with the issue of 18 April 1822, which is headed *Upper Canada Gazette*, New Series, Vol. I, No. 1. This title and numbering (which also included the *Weekly Register*) continued to the end of 1825 (Vol. IV). Then appeared another Vol. I, No. 1 of the *Upper Canada Gazette*, New Series, dated 2 February 1826. With the issue of 3 June 1826, 'New Series' was dropped, and, once again, the numbering started with Vol. I, No. 1.[116] From that date until

June 1828 the *United Empire Loyalist* was published along with the *Upper Canada Gazette*; then the two separated and there was no further change in the title of the latter.

The question of the status of the *Upper Canada Gazette* in relation to the government is almost as confusing as its numbering. The historian W.S. Wallace said that it was published 'by authority' from 1828 to 1841, but the matter is not so simple.[117] Individual items, generally proclamations, were sometimes headed 'by authority' as early as 1799. In 1821 'by authority' began to appear as a general heading with certain notices headed 'Not official.' The general heading 'by authority' always appeared after that date. This is misleading, for the government did not recognize the *Upper Canada Gazette* as official after the end of 1841. Robert Stanton, who had been Queen's Printer for Upper Canada and was continuing to publish it, was ordered on 1 July 1843 to cease using the official seal and the title Queen's Printer.[118] In the issue of 6 July 1843 the following notice appeared: 'The Upper Canada Gazette, heretofore furnished by order of the Government to the several public functionaries in Canada West is by Command, to be discontinued from this date. Toronto, 1st July, 1843.' One would think from the wording that the *Upper Canada Gazette* was to be discontinued, but perhaps the command was only to cease furnishing it to public functionaries. Whatever the intent, the *Upper Canada Gazette* continued to be published and the words 'by authority' were not removed.

Even the date when the *Upper Canada Gazette* ceased publication is in doubt. Both W.S. Wallace and Olga B. Bishop give its final date as 1845, but Edith G. Firth, a Toronto librarian who has done intensive research on early Toronto newspapers, lists its last issue as probably 1 October 1849.[119] Certainly issues later than 1845 have been discovered. The latest available for review is dated 9 March 1848, when the paper was still claiming to be issued 'by authority.' This copy, along with other post-1845 issues, is included on a 'trailer reel' microfilmed by the Canadian Library Association; its main reels of the *Upper Canada Gazette* end in 1845.

41 *Canada Gazette* [Province of Canada] 1841–69. Queen's Printer, Toronto

The *Canada Gazette* began publication on 2 October 1841. It appeared weekly and contained 'proclamations of the Governor, appointments to government posts, some statutes, tenders for government work, notices of bankruptcy, and militia information.'[120] It continued to the end of 1869 two and half years after Confederation.[121] The *Canada Gazette* (federal) began publication on 1 July 1867, but there was no overlapping of information between the two. The new publication dealt with federal matters, whereas the continuing one related to Quebec and Ontario, the two provinces which had formerly constituted the Province of Canada. It published proclamations, news of government appointments, and government and parliamentary notices relating only to Quebec, and bankruptcy notices, dissolutions of partnerships, and court notices relating to both Quebec and Ontario. The advent of the *Ontario Gazette* in 1868 and the *Quebec Gazette* in 1869 led the [Province of] *Canada Gazette* to cease publication. There is an index to the *Canada Gazette*, 1841–4 in the 1844 volume. Thereafter an annual index appeared.

42 *Ontario Gazette*, 1868– Toronto, Published by authority, Queen's (King's) Printer (from 1970, Queen's Printer and Publisher)
The *Ontario Gazette* began publication on 7 March 1868. It contains 'official notices, the text of proclamations, appointments, notices re companies (incorporations, dissolutions, changes of name, etc.), and announcements of sales of land for arrears of taxes.'[122] Since the passage of the Regulations Act, 1944 it has also contained the text of regulations. They have double pagination, as part of the *Gazette* and separately. They are generally bound separately.

An index to the *Ontario Gazette* is published every six months. A table of regulations cumulating from the latest revision appears annually.

NOTE: Since the passage of the Regulations Act, 1944, there have been three consolidations of Ontario regulations issued as companion volumes to the *Revised Statutes*.

43 *Consolidated Regulations of Ontario, 1950. A Revision and Consolidation of Regulations published under the authority of the Regulations Consolidation Act, 1949*. Toronto, Baptist Johnston, King's Printer, [1951] 3 v.
Volumes 1 and 2 contain the official consolidation. Acts are arranged in alphabetical order by title, and all regulations made under an act are given a single main number. Volume 3 contains an 'appendix being an unofficial consolidation of Public General Regulations which are not included in the Consolidated Regulations of Ontario, 1950, as contained in Volumes 1 and 2.' The regulations appearing in the

unofficial consolidation are numbered in the same series as those in the official consolidation: eg, the last official entry is 'Regulation 372,' while the first unofficial one is 'Regulation 373.'

44 *Revised Regulations of Ontario, 1960. A Revision and Consolidation of Regulations published under the authority of the Regulations Revision Act, 1959*. Toronto, Frank Fogg, Queen's Printer, 1960, 3 v.
This revision includes regulations in CRO 1950 and regulations filed from 1 January 1951 to 31 December 1960. Acts are arranged alphabetically by title; regulations under them are numbered, beginning with Regulation 1 under the Active Service Moratorium Act, 1943.

45 *Revised Regulations of Ontario, 1970. A Revision and Consolidation of Regulations published under the authority of the Regulations Revision Act, 1968–69*. Toronto, William Kinmond, Queen's Printer and Publisher [1971] 4 v. and supplement (1 v.)
Acts are arranged alphabetically by title; regulations under them are numbered, beginning with Regulation 1 under The Abandoned Orchards Act. The supplement contains all regulations filed under The Regulations Act after 31 December 1970 and before 15 November 1971, the day RRO 1970 came into force.

46 *Carswell's Regulation Service. Ontario Regulations*. Toronto, Carswell [current service]
This is a supplementary service to the latest consolidation of Ontario regulations (RRO 1970 at the time of writing). Pages containing regulations are extracted from the *Ontario Gazette* for insertion in loose-leaf volumes. The pages are later transferred to transfer binders or bound, depending on the policy of the library.

Carswell provides a cumulative index at the end of each month and a final one for the year. The official Table of Regulations (published in the *Ontario Gazette* and at the back of the sessional volumes of the *Statutes of Ontario*) is also included with the service when it becomes available. The official Table cumulates from RRO 1970 to date, whereas the Carswell index cumulates only the regulations for a calendar year.

Statutes and regulations are primary sources of the law. Their potential for usefulness in historical research is often overlooked. Those historians who do use them tend not to be fully aware of the finding aids available to facilitate their use. It is hoped that this bibliographical essay will make these materials better known.

NOTES

Much of the research for this essay was done in 1965–6 as my contribution to a major bibliographical project, as yet unpublished, directed by Professor J.E.C. Brierley, now Dean of Law at McGill University, who has agreed to my revising and updating the material I then prepared for inclusion in this volume. To the many librarians and archivists in Toronto and London, Ontario, who assisted me with my research in 1965–6 and in 1980, I express my sincere thanks. I also wish to thank my research assistant, Curtis Cole, and my secretary, Linda Aitkins.

1 31 Geo. III, c. 31 (GB). The order-in-council dividing the province is printed in Arthur G. Doughty and Duncan A. McArthur, eds *Documents relating to the Constitutional History of Canada, 1791–1818* (Ottawa 1914) 3–5.
2 31 Geo. III (1791), c. 31, s. 2 (GB)
3 Ibid. ss. 3, 5, and 8
4 Ibid. s. 6
5 Ibid. ss. 17 and 20
6 Frederick H. Armstrong *Handbook of Upper Canadian Chronology and Territorial Legislation* (London, Ontario 1967) 30–6, 38–57
7 Ibid. 58–78
8 Ibid. 33
9 Ibid. Armstrong explains that the dates of appointment given in his Chronological List of Members of the Legislative Council are those of commission, if commissions were issued; members were not sworn until later, sometimes several years later.
10 Ibid. 33–6
11 Ibid. 33
12 Ibid. 33–6
13 William Renwick Riddell *The Courts of the Province of Upper Canada or Ontario* (Toronto 1928) 99
14 Armstrong *Handbook of Upper Canadian Chronology* 58
15 Ibid. 75–8
16 Ibid. 13. The alphabetical lists of members of the Executive and Legislative Councils (11–2 and 30–3) indicate which men were members of both bodies.
17 Ibid. 26–7
18 Ibid. 28–9. I have calculated the averages from the statistics on statutes passed.
19 H.C. Thomson *A Manual of Parliamentary Practice* (Kingston 1828). The rules of the Legislative Council and House of Assembly are printed as an appendix, 77–92.

20 Constitutional Act, 31 Geo. III (1791), c. 31, ss. 30–2 (GB)
21 Ibid. s. 42
22 Doughty and McArthur, eds *Documents relating to the Constitutional History of Canada, 1791–1818* 33 at 38. Lord Dorchester had been governor of Quebec and was appointed governor of Upper and Lower Canada. Many of the duties of the governor in relation to Upper Canada were performed by the Lieutenant Governor of that province.
23 Ibid.
24 G.W. Wicksteed *Table of the Provincial Statutes in Force or which have been in Force in Upper Canada* (Toronto 1856) 26, 29, 52, 53, 56. The acts disallowed were 7 Geo. IV (1826), c. 2, 9 Geo. IV (1828), c. 20, 2 Vict. (1839), c. 3 and c. 38 and 3 Vict. (1840), c. 35.
25 *A Legal Bibliography of the British Commonwealth of Nations*, III *Canadian and British American Colonial Law from earliest times to December, 1956* compiled by C.R. Brown, P.A. Maxwell, and L.F. Maxwell (London 1957) 129–31 (hereafter Sweet & Maxwell's *Legal Bibliography*). These pages list the sessions of each parliament of Upper Canada, indicating the number of statutes passed at each. Information on reserved bills which subsequently received royal assent and their location in the statute books is noted in the right hand column and in footnotes. Some of the same information is contained in Armstrong, *Handbook of Upper Canadian Chronology* 28–9, but six of the bills reserved and subsequently assented to are missing from the tables printed there.
26 An Act to re-unite the Provinces of Upper and Lower Canada, and for the Government of Canada (hereafter Act of Union), 3 & 4 Vict. (1840), c. 35, s. 12 (UK). The Union came into effect by proclamation, as provided by s. 1 of the act, on 10 Feb. 1841.
27 J.O. Coté, ed. *Political Appointments and Elections in the Province of Canada from 1841 to 1865* 2nd ed. (Ottawa 1866) 84–106
28 Act of Union, 3 & 4 Vict. (1840), c. 35, ss. 4–7 (UK)
29 Coté, ed. *Political Appointments* 55–6
30 Ibid.
31 17 & 18 Vict. (1854), c. 118 (UK)
32 An Act to change the Constitution of the Legislative Council by rendering the same Elective, 19–20 Vict. (1856), c. 140, ss. 1–2 (Canada)
33 Ibid. s. 8
34 Coté, ed. *Political Appointments* 21, 84–6
35 Ibid. 21, 63–83
36 Ibid. 2
37 3 & 4 Vict. (1840), c. 35, ss. 37–9 (UK)
38 This quotation is from an unpublished essay 'Reserved Statutes of the Pro-

vince of Canada: A Bibliographical Problem' by Judith (Morgan) Dick, written when she was a student at the University of Toronto Library School. She gave her source as 'Instructions to Sydenham, Metcalfe, Mead 1839–1854. [Manuscript located in the Manuscript Division of the Public Archives, designated as RG7, 3748, G18 vol. 5] pp 334–340.' I am grateful to Balfour Halevy, Law Librarian at York University, for drawing my attention to this paper and to Mrs Dick for lending it to me.

39 Coté, ed. *Political Appointments* 15

40 Ibid. In the essay referred to in note 38 above Mrs Dick correctly stated that many more bills were reserved in the early years of the Province of Canada's existence (before the establishment of responsible government) than later.

41 Ibid. 16–17. The names, dates, and, in the case of acts assented to, the chapter numbers are listed on these pages.

42 Ibid. 17

43 N. Omer Coté *Appendix, 1st January 1866 to 30th June 1867 and Index to Political Appointments and Elections in the Province of Canada from 1841 to 1865* (Ottawa 1918) 146. (The pagination of the appendix continues that of the original volume.)

44 The British North America Act, 30 Vict. (1867), c. 3, s. 69 (UK)

45 Ibid. s. 70

46 The Representation Act, 1975 (1st sess.), c. 13, s. 2 (Ont.)

47 F.F. Schindeler *Responsible Government in Ontario* (Toronto 1969) 261–2

48 30 Vict. (1867), c. 3, ss. 55, 56 and 90. Sections 55 and 56 deal with reservation and disallowance of federal legislation. Though not repealed, there has been an understanding since the passage of the Statute of Westminster, 1931 (22 & 23 Geo. V, c. 4) that these powers will not be exercised.

49 30 Vict. (1867), c. 3, s. 90 (UK)

50 W.E. Hodgins *Correspondence, Reports of the Ministers of Justice and Orders in Council upon the Subject of Dominion and Provincial Legislation, 1867–1895* (Ottawa 1896) 62

51 For a study of the question of reasons for disallowance see G.V. LaForest *Disallowance and Reservation of Provincial Legislation* (Ottawa 1955).

52 Ibid. Appendix A 'Table of Disallowed Statutes' 83–101

53 Ibid. Appendix B 'Table of Reserved Bills' 102–15

54 14 Geo. V (1923), c. 30 (Ont.); *A.G. Ont.* v *A.G. Can.* [1925] *Appeal Cases* 750

55 Sir David Lidderdale, ed. *Erskine May's Treatise on the Law, Privileges, Proceedings and Usage of Parliament* 19th ed. (London 1976)

56 Sweet & Maxwell's *Legal Bibliography* III 89

57 The Statutes Revision Act, 1979, c. 109, s. 3 (Ont.)

58 For further information on the preparation and proclamation of revised stat-

utes and their relationship to sessional statutes, see Margaret A. Banks *Using a Law Library: A Guide for Students and Lawyers in the Common Law Provinces of Canada* 3rd ed. (Toronto 1980) 62–73

59 In the United Kingdom the change from regnal to calendar year citation was made at the beginning of 1963. See Acts of Parliament Numbering and Citation Act, 10 & 11 Eliz. II (1962), c. 34 (UK). For further comments on statutory citation see Banks *Using a Law Library* 44, 63.

60 W. George Eakins 'The Bibliography of Canadian Statute Law' *Law Library Journal* I (1908) 61–71; 'Check-List of Laws of Upper Canada, 1792–1818' ibid. 72–8; 'Bibliography of Candian Statute Law, II' ibid. II (1909–10) 65–6; 'Check-List of Laws of Upper Canada, 1819–1840, and of Canada, 1841–1866' ibid. 66–75

61 Ibid. I (1908) 70

62 For dates of the numerous fires, see ibid. 70–1.

63 Ibid. 71

64 Paul T. Murphy, 'Review of *Pre-Confederation Statutes on Microfilm*' *Canadian Association of Law Libraries Newsletter* Vol. 5 No. 2 (New Series) Nov.-Dec. 1979 93 at 94

65 On the title-page of this reprint the date 1802 appears. However, 1803 and 1804 statutes are included and pagination is continuous.

66 *Law Library Journal* I (1908) 64

67 Ibid. II (1909–10) 65

68 *Report of the Public Archives for the Year 1921* (Ottawa 1922) 3. The 1792 and 1793 statutes are printed in Appendix F 377–425.

69 Other locations are listed in *Collections of Official Publications in Canada* (Ottawa 1976) 450.

70 Eakins 'The Bibliography of Canadian Statute Law' *Law Library Journal* I (1908) 68

71 For information on the location of reserved acts, see Sweet & Maxwell's *Legal Bibliography* III 129–31.

72 Quoted by Eakins in *Law Library Journal* I (1908) 68

73 For further details, see ibid.

74 The same mistake is made at the head of pages 207, 209, 211, 213, 215, 217, 219, 221, and 223.

75 See entry 928 in Frances M. Staton and Marie Tremaine *A Bibliography of Canadiana* (Toronto 1934) 214.

76 Eakins 'Check-List of Laws of Upper Canada, 1792–1818' *Law Library Journal* I (1908) 77

77 'Note as to Statute Revisions in the Provinces of Upper Canada, Canada and Ontario' *Revised Statutes of Ontario* (hereafter RSO) 1877 2465

78 Bureau of Archives *Ninth Report* (Toronto 1912) 416

79 Both the Library of Congress Catalog and Sweet & Maxwell's *Legal Bibliography* III 128, list this collection of British statutes as a separate publication. There seems to be no logical reason for doing so.
80 'Note as to Statute Revisions...' RSO 1877 2465
81 In 1828 Thomson had published the *Manual of Parliamentary Practice* referred to above in note 19. He claimed to have compiled it, but in 1978 Bernard J. Sussman of Washington, DC, an authority on Thomas Jefferson's work of the same name, discovered that Thomson had copied from Jefferson's *Manual*, leaving out the American references. For further information on this matter, see Margaret A. Banks 'An Undetected Case of Plagiarism' *Parliamentary Journal* 20 (Apr. 1979) 1–11. The reference to Macfarlane's connection with the *Kingston Chronicle* was found in *Canadian Newspapers on Microfilm Catalogue* (Ottawa loose-leaf service) I, 2 – Ont. 7.
82 For brief biographies of the four commissioners, see W. Stewart Wallace, ed. *The Macmillan Dictionary of Canadian Biography* 4th ed. rev. by W.A. McKay (Toronto 1978) 122–3, 222, 482, and 714.
83 'Report of the Commissioners, Appointed to Revise the Statutes of Upper Canada' in *The Statutes of Upper Canada, to the Time of the Union* (Toronto 1843) 1
84 Ibid. 3
85 Ibid.
86 Ibid.
87 'Note as to Statute Revisons...' RSO 1877 2466
88 These volumes are listed as 'Session Laws (Quartos)' in Sweet & Maxwell's *Legal Bibliography* III 14.
89 They are listed as 'Session Laws (Octavos)' in Sweet & Maxwell's *Legal Bibliography* III 14.
90 However, since government departments received copies of all acts, local and private as well as public, some government library sets of statutes do include the local and private acts for those years. This is true of the volumes in both the Ontario Legislative Library and the Ontario Archives. The set at York University Law Library used by Micromedia in preparing its microfilm copy of the statutes of the province of Canada, also includes these local and private acts.
91 See above page 368
92 The last two pages of the volume are incorrectly numbered 195 and 196.
93 Robert A. Harrison *The Statutes of Practical Utility in the Civil Administration of Justice, in Upper Canada* (Toronto 1857) iii
94 Ibid. iv
95 All played a prominent part in public life. For details see *The Macmillan Dictionary of Canadian Biography*.

96 For details see 'Note as to Statute Revisions in the Provinces of Upper Canada, Canada and Ontario' RSO 1877 2466
97 Ibid. 2466–7
98 This information is taken from a note on an unnumbered page following the title-page of the volume.
99 'Note as to Statute Revisions...' RSO 1877 2467
100 See above page 365
101 Margaret Evans, Professor of History at the University of Guelph, described the preparation of RSO 1877 as one of Oliver Mowat's greatest achievements. See A. Margaret Evans 'Oliver Mowat and Ontario, 1872–1896: A Study in Political Success' (unpublished PH D thesis University of Toronto 1967) 373. This seems to me an overemphasis of its importance. Apart from the fact that it was the first consolidation of the statutes of Ontario, and that it was necessary to determine what pre-Confederation statutes were in force and related to provincial matters, it was a natural development from the 1859 consolidations and followed the same type of subject arrangement. Mowat had served for a time on the commission which prepared CSUC 1859, and no doubt this was partly responsible for his interest in the process. The 1859 consolidations were far more important landmarks in the history of statutory consolidation and revision, for they were the first true consolidations, the first to be limited to public general statutes, and the first to be officially adopted by proclamation, authorized by an act of the legislature.
102 'Note as to Statute Revisions...' RSO 1877 2467
103 Olga B. Bishop *Publications of the Government of Ontario, 1867–1900* (Toronto 1976) 72
104 Ibid.
105 See above page 364
106 For the titles of these indexes see Bishop *Publications of the Government of Ontario, 1867–1900* 74–5
107 Sweet & Maxwell's *Legal Bibliography* III 128 lists this volume as Wicksteed's [Alphabetical] Index to Statutes in Upper Canada at end of 1854–5.
108 'Note as to Statute Revisions ...' RSO 1877 2466. For further details about Wicksteed's long life see *The Macmillan Dictionary of Canadian Biography* 886.
109 Sweet & Maxwell's *Legal Bibliography* III 128 lists this volume as Wicksteed's [Chronological] Table of the Statutes in force in Upper Canada (1792–1856).
110 Harrison *The Statutes of Practical Utility* iv
111 This information is given on the title-page of the index.
112 Edward Norman Lewis *Lewis' Ontario Statute Index* (Toronto 1884) preface
113 George Frederick Jelfs *Jelfs' Index to Statute Law* (Toronto 1892) 5

114 The publishing history is as follows: 1932 volume published by The Ontario Citator, Toronto; 1933 volume published by The Canadian Law List Publishing Company, Toronto; same up to and including 1959; 1950 bound volume published by Cartwright & Sons, Ltd, Toronto; 1950 loose leaf service published by Cartwright & Sons Ltd, Canada Law Book Company Limited, Toronto; 1960 – loose-leaf service published by Canada Law Book Company Limited, Toronto; 1970 – loose-leaf service published by Canada Law Book Limited, Agincourt, Ontario.
115 8 Geo. VI, c. 52 (Ont.)
116 Olga B. Bishop in *Publications of the Government of the Province of Canada, 1841–1867* (Ottawa 1963) 59 gives the beginning date of this series as 10 June 1826. This is incorrect, the issue of 10 June being the second. The series is listed in this bibliography because it continued to be published after the formation of the Province of Canada.
117 W.S. Wallace 'The Periodical Literature of Upper Canada' *Canadian Historical Review* XII (1913) 12 (hereafter CHR)
118 Bishop *Publications of the Government of the Province of Canada* 58
119 Ibid. 59; Wallace 'Periodical Literature' CHR XII (1913) 12; Edith G. Firth *Early Toronto Newspapers, 1793–1867* (Toronto 1961) 5
120 Bishop *Publications of the Government of the Province of Canada* 58
121 Bishop, in *Publications of the Government of the Province of Canada* 58 lists the last issue as v. 28, no. 26, 26 June 1869. However, the Canadian Library Association's microfilm of the *Canada Gazette* includes later issues of volume 28. The last on the film is dated 11 Dec. 1869. This is followed by a note 'Issues missing,' which suggests but does not confirm that it continued to the end of the year.
122 Hazel I. MacTaggart *Publications of the Government of Ontario, 1856– 1971* (Toronto 1975) 311

NOTE: Arthur N. Stone, QC, Senior Legislative Counsel, one of the Commissioners responsible for preparing RSO 1980, has told me that its arrangement and numbering will be the same as those of RSO 1950, 1960, and 1970. Ontario, unlike some Canadian jurisdictions, is not adopting an alphanumeric numbering system, nor will it follow the current practice of most other provinces in issuing both bound and looseleaf editions. RSO 1980, like previous revisions, will be published only in the traditional bound volumes. A new feature of the 1980 revision will be an Index of Private Acts, 1867–1980.

Table of Cases

Index

www.ingramcontent.com/pod-product-compliance
Lightning Source LLC
LaVergne TN
LVHW090759070826
844660LV00022B/1029